My Chinese Home

CHINA
MOTHER OF GARDENS

By

ERNEST H. WILSON, M.A., V.M.H.
Keeper of the Arnold Arboretum of Harvard University

Author of
Plant Hunting, America's Greatest Garden
Aristocrats of the Garden, More
Aristocrats of the Garden, etc.

威理森

SIXTY-ONE ILLUSTRATIONS FROM
PHOTOGRAPHS TAKEN BY THE AUTHOR

1929

Published by Robert W Strugnell
www.fitzroygardens.com

First Published 2017

ISBN 978-0-9954330-6-9

TO
MY ALMA MATER
THE ROYAL BOTANIC GARDENS, KEW
THIS VOLUME IS AFFECTIONATELY
DECIDED

The subject matter of "China – Mother of Gardens" has been drawn from the author's Previous work. "A Naturalist in Western China," originally published in England in 1913 and now long out of print. The material used has been amended and thoroughly revised and new illustrations added for presentation to the American public in the present form.

E.H.W.

PREFACE

HINA is, indeed, the Mother of Gardens, for of the countries to which our gardens are most deeply indebted she holds the foremost place. From the bursting into blossom of the Forsythias and Yulan Magnolias in the early spring to the Peonies and Roses in summer and the Chrysanthemums in the autumn, China's contributions to the floral wealth of gardens is in evidence. To China the flower lover owes the parents of the modern Rose, be they Tea or Hybrid Tea, Rambler or Polyantha; likewise his greenhouse Azaleas and Primroses, and the fruit grower, his Peaches, Oranges, Lemons and Grapefruit. It is safe to say that there is no garden in this country or in Europe that is without its Chinese representatives and these rank among the finest of tree, shrub, herb and vine.

Few countries are of such perennial interest to the world at large as China, and no other country has succeeded in maintaining such a long, unbroken line of history. Whence the Chinese came or when they settled in the land now called China are things which savants dispute, but that they have been there for some four thousand years is generally admitted; they were a cultured people when Europe was sunk in savagery and before America was dreamt of.

Rumors of the wealth of China and of the Indies reached Europe and created a desire to trade with these lands and participate in their wealth. This was the main incentive to the era of navigation inaugurated by Prince Henry the Navigator in 1418, one outcome of which was the discovery of America by Columbus. The Portuguese reached China by sea in 1516 and took back with them to their settlements in India the Sweet Orange, which later was introduced into Portugal. So far as I have been able to discover, this was the first plant taken to Europe, but it was quickly followed by others. After the formation of the English and Dutch East India companies, respectively, in 1600 and 1602, a regular traffic in the more useful and beautiful of the plants cultivated in China was maintained. By this means some of

PREFACE

our most familiar plants reached Europe.

At the end of the eighteenth and early in the nineteenth century professional plant collectors were sent out for the purpose. These visits culminated in those of Robert For-tune from 1843-1861. This most successful collector sent back about 190 species of ornamental plants, many of which, to-day, rank as the most important and most familiar denizens of our gardens. Nearly everything that For-tune collected came from gardens. How well he and others before him exhausted the field is shown by the fact that since Fortune's time scarcely a new plant has been found in Chinese gardens. In 1879 Charles Maries in the interest of Messrs. Veitch ascended the Yangstze River as far as Ichang, where he collected Primula obconica, but finding the Chinese hostile and the country not attractive turned his face toward Shanghai. He stayed off at Kuling and gathered seeds of Loropetalum chinense and its relative, Hamamelis mollis, finest of all the Witch-Hazels. For awhile gardeners labored under the false impression that the floral wealth of China had been exhausted. It was Maries who made the statement, but that it should have been accepted seems almost incredible in the light of present day knowledge.

As early as 1869 Pere Armand David broached the forests of western Szechuan and sent back to the Paris Herbarium specimens of many extraordinary plants. In 1882 Pere J. M. Delavay commenced to collect in western Yunnan and continued to do so until 1895. From 1885 to 1889 A. Henry began to investigate the flora of western Hupeh and from 1890 to 1907 Pere P. Farges collected in in northeastern Szechuan. To the labors of these men must be added that of several Russian travelers. The accumulated results caused the herbariums of Paris, St. Petersburg, and London to bulge with new and marvellously ornamental plants. These collectors were one and all interested in the purely botanical side of the Chinese flora and rarely gathered seeds. In fact, only Peres Delavay and Farges, who sent seeds to M. Maurice de Vilmorin, can claim to have introduced any of the plants they did so much to discover, but the labors of these men revivified interest in Chinese plants and to this revival I owe the opportunity I enjoyed to collect in China.

PREFACE

It was in 1899 that I first set foot in China, to leave it finally in 1911. Until 1905 my collecting work was done in the interests of the well-known English nursery firm of Veitch, now, alas! no longer in existence; from 1906 to 1911 it was on behalf of the Arnold Arboretum of Harvard University. As a result of my plant hunting in China more than a thousand new plants are now established in gardens of America and Europe. The privilege and the opportunity were great and I claim only to have made full use of both.

In my travels in China I was fortunate. The Chinese treated me with kindly courtesy and respect. I was in interior China during the Boxer outbreak and the Russo-Japanese War and visited places before or after anti-foreign riots, but I never experienced any incivility meriting the name. At the commencement of my collecting work I engaged and trained a number of Chinese peasants, who served me faithfully throughout my journeys and I parted with them with feelings of genuine regret. As a prelude to my collecting work I visited at Szemao in extreme southwestern Yunnan, Mr. Augustine Henry, who imparted to me much sound advice which I had sufficient common sense to follow. To the devotion of my Chinese collectors and to this gentleman the favorable results of my work in China are largely due.

In the following pages will be found some account of my eleven years' wanderings and observations in the Flowery Kingdom. I have endeavored to give a general description of the flora and scenery of western China and of the manners and customs of the little known non-Chinese tribes inhabiting the Chino-Thibetan borderland. I saw China through the eyes of a nature lover and botanist interested in all phases of natural history.

That a country settled for thousands of years and densely populated by an agricultural people who have managed to support themselves off the land, should in the twentieth century boast the richest temperate flora in the world, is in itself extraordinary. One marvels what the flora must have been before so much of the land was subjected to agriculture. A visitor to Peking in the north, to Shanghai, or even a voyager up the Yangtze River for a thousand miles cannot imagine that China is so rich in flowers. Naturally it is not to the

PREFACE

cultivated areas that one looks for trees, shrubs and herbs but to the mountainous regions, where the practice of agriculture is difficult or impossible. And, so, the China I traveled over and the China I tell of is not that to which the visitor or resident is familiar. It is not a China of cities teeming with people or of ubiquitous ricefields but one of forests and woodland, wild ravines and mountains, the higher peaks clad with eternal snow.

E. H. W.

Arnold Arboretum,
Harvard University,
February 15, 1929.

CONTENTS

CONTENTS

ILLUSTRATIONS

ILLUSTRATIONS

CHINA
MOTHER OF GARDENS

By

E. H. Wilson

Keeper of the Arnold Arboretum
of Harvard University

CHINA ∽ MOTHER OF GARDENS

CHAPTER I

WESTERN CHINA

ITS MOUNTAIN AND RIVER SYSTEMS

CHINA PROPER is, speaking generally, a nearly square tract of country some 22° of longitude by 20° of latitude. On the north it is bounded by the arid regions of the Mongolian and Gobi deserts and on the west snow-clad mountain ranges separate it from the Thibetan plateau. Its southern part is just within the tropics while the northern part enjoys a very cool winter climate. The climate is essentially continental with a rainfall varying from 30 inches in the north to over 100 inches in the south. The whole country is broken up into steep mountains, fertile valleys, and alluvial plains, and is drained by a network of rivers, two of which, the Yangtsze and Yellow rivers, rank among the largest in the world.

Western China with which this work is concerned is separated from Thibet proper by a series of parallel mountain ranges running almost due north and south and divided by narrow valleys. It is made up largely of razor-edged ridges, following one another in quick succession and separated by narrow valleys, or rather ravines. The higher peaks are well above the snow-line, and for height, savage grandeur, and wondrous scenery are comparable with the Himalayan alps of India. The whole region is practically uncharted and unsurveyed and it is the author's firm conviction that some of the peaks rival in altitude the greatest of the Himalayan giants.

About latitude 33 °N., in the neighborhood of Sungpan Ting, a mighty spur is thrown out from these ranges of perpetual snow and extends, with a slight southerly dip, due east for some 10° of longitude,

1

terminating in low hills near Anluh Hsien in northeastern Hupah. Innumerable lateral spurs are given off by this system, and the country is extremely broken, especially in the parts with which we are dealing. The province of Kweichou is one mass of mountains and the same is true of western Hupeh and southern Szechuan. In these three areas there are subsidiary ranges of considerable altitude, which, dipping in various directions and connected by spurs, form a heterogeneous and complex mountain system. The outstanding feature of the whole region west of 112th parallel of longitude is the entire absence of plain or plateau or anything in the nature of flat, level country with the solitary exception of the area forming the Chengtu plain. Of this we shall speak in due course. East of the 112th parallel the Yangtsze River flows through a flat, alluvial plain in which isolated, or more or less connected, mountain ranges and spurs occur, but with this region we are not concerned.

The most important region comprised within the mountain systems above described and west of the 112th parallel is that termed by Richthofen the Red Basin of Szechuan. This area includes the whole of Szechuan east of the Min River to near the Hupeh boundary. It is a region of vast agricultural wealth with a magnificent river system teeming with large cities, towns, and villages, and sup-porting an enormous population. With the solitary exception of cotton, which is imported from the coast, it is self-contained, with a surplus of produce to spare for export. Salt is produced in unlimited quantities in many districts; coal, iron, and other minerals of economic importance abound. In short, the Red Basin is one of the richest and fairest regions of the Chinese Empire.

The whole of western China lies within the Yangtsze River basin. According to the geographical information at present available, this river has its source almost due north of Calcutta, in latitude about 35 °N., on the southeast edge of the central Asian steppes. Its exact length is unknown, but it is estimated to exceed 3000 miles. From its source for 1000 miles it pursues a tortuous course nearly due south, through wild and partially unknown country. Then suddenly turning eastward it flows right through the heart of China for some 2000 miles,

PEAK OF THE BARRIER RANGE (TA-P AO-SHAN), CIRCA 21,000 FEET HIGH finally reaching the sea immediately to the north of Shanghai.

From its mouth to the city of Ichang, 1000 miles, it is navigable for steamers at all seasons of the year, though in winter obstructions in the nature of shoals and sand-bars are encountered. The greatest difficulty is experienced between Hankow and Ichang, and this section is operated by a small fleet of shallow-draught steamers especially built for the trade. The regular steamers plying between Shanghai and Hankow are also especially designed for the service and are luxuriously fitted. Ocean-going steamers of deep draught can ascend as far as Hankow, except at low-water season. In summer the river overflows and invades much of the low-lying country contiguous to its course, and the chief difficulty in navigation at such times is to keep to the channel. At Ichang the river is 1100 yards from bank to bank, and the average difference between summer and winter levels is about 40 feet; in the gorges, which commence some 5 miles west of Ichang, the river is narrowed to a third of its usual breadth and the summer and winter difference in depth exceeds 100 feet.

Above Ichang the river is obstructed by rapids, rocks, and other impedimenta, and is navigated by specially built native boats that range up to 80 tons displacement. Beyond Pingshan Hsien navigation is only practicable for small native craft in certain short interrupted sections. The river flows for the most part through gorges or between steep mountains, and its course is frequently broken by dangerous rapids and cataracts that produce a seething, foaming swirl in which nothing can live. In the autumn of 1911 an adventurous French naval officer made an extraordinary journey down the upper Yangtsze to Sui Fu in native boats specially built for the purpose. An account of this journey would prove exciting reading.

The most difficult stretch of the middle Yangtsze is that between Ichang and Wan Hsien. This is the region of the world-famous Yangtsze gorges. Five in number, these gorges extend from the immediate west of Ichang to Kuichou Fu, a distance of about 150 miles. Throughout this stretch the river flows between perpendicular walls of rock, is narrowed to a third or less its usual width and becomes in consequence very deep. Soundings taken by the British gunboats in their ascent in 1900 gave 63 ½ fathoms of water in two places, and this when the water at Ichang was rather less than 6 feet above zero mark. The cliffs, composed largely of hard limestone, are 500 to 2000 feet or more high and commonly from 500 to 1000 feet sheer. The scenery is savagely grand and awe-inspiring.

In ascending the Yangtsze from Ichang to Chungking the observant traveller is struck by the insignificant character of the tributary streams. Apparently the only one of importance joins the main stream at Fu Chou on the right bank. This stream, the Kienkiang, rises in western Kweichou and flows through the heart of the province. It is navigable from its mouth to Szenan Fu, and beyond, for especially constructed native boats. Apart from this river there is no tributary of seeming importance until Chungking is reached, yet nearly every town and village of note stands at the junction of some small stream with the Yangtsze. Here and there men will be found hauling small, stout-bottomed boats over the stones at the mouths of these small rivers. That the main stream is joined by many tributary streams, a glance at the map proves. In western Hupeh the country is widely mountainous and the streams are tor-rents, pure and simple. In eastern Szechuan the country is much less wild and the streams of a different character, and why they appear unnavigable is, on the surface, not obvious. The accepted view is that enormous quantities of debris are brought down by these tributaries and de-posited at their mouths. This theory is all very well when applied to mountain torrents, but most of the streams under discussion pursue a comparatively placid course with easy currents for some 50 miles or more before reaching the Yangtsze. Their volume and force of current is in-sufficient in summer floods to carry down the enormous quantities of detritus which choke up their mouths. My personal observations put the responsibility on the main stream itself. During the summer floods the Yangtsze brings down vast quantities of mud and detritus, which it de-posits wherever opportunity offers. Flowing more or less between steep banks, as the Yangtsze does, the mouths of tributary streams afford the most favorable places for the deposition of this debris. The volume of the main stream is enormously greater, and its current so much stronger than that of the tributaries that it simply thrusts them back and silts up their mouths. The small quantity of debris brought down by the tributary streams would also be deposited hereabout owing to the slacking of the flow consequent upon the damming of their debouchure.

At Chungking the Yangtsze is joined on its left bank by the Kialing or so-called Little River. A glance at a map shows that this river is made up of three streams which unite near Ho Chou. The Kialing River and its tributaries drain a fan-shaped area, in extent more than half of the entire Red Basin situated north of the Yangtsze. Their importance is due to their being navigable for small craft to some 40 miles north of Tunghsiang Hsien; the next branch is navigable to Tungchiang Hsien; and the next to the north of Pa Chou. The central (Paoning) river is navigable for fairly large boats to Kuangyuan Hsien, and skiffs laden with medicines and other native products descend to this town from Pikou, in the province of Kansu. The most westerly branch is navigable to Pai-shih-fu, a few miles north of Chungpa, and one of its western tributaries taps the northeast corner of the Chengtu plain.

The Min River rises some 35 miles north of the Sung-pan Ting, near the boundary of northwest Szechuan and the Amdo region in latitude 33°N. and, except at lowest water, is navigable from Kuan Hsien and Chengtu down-ward. The Chengtu branch is artificially formed by canals led across the plain from Kuan Hsien, and unites with the Kuan Hsien stream and its tributaries at Chiangkou. A tributary of the Min, which joins at Hsinhsin Hsien, is navigable in high water for small boats to Kiung Chou, a city situated at the extreme southwest corner of the Chengtu plain.

The Min is really only a tributary of the Tung River, which it joins at Kiating Fu, but since it admits of navigation it is of more practical importance and for this reason the Chinese give it preeminence. The Tung River is only navigable for a few miles above Kiating, though rafts descend from a much higher point west. Its tributary, the Ya, which joins it immediately west of Kiating, is of greater commercial importance and a very considerable raft traffic

TYPICAL VIEW IN NORTHWESTERN HUPEH

ascends and descends this stream from Yachou, which is the centre of the brick-tea industry of western Szechuan.

The Tung River is really one of the longest rivers in Szechuan, having its source in the northeast corner of Thibet, about latitude 33° N. It flows through the western frontier of the tribes country, where it is known as the Tachin Ho (Great Gold River) and ultimately strikes the highway from Chengtu to Lhassa at Wassukou, a hamlet 18 miles east of Tachienlu. From this point to its union with the Min at Kiating it is called the Tung Ho, though around Fulin it goes by the name of Tatu Ho. Owing to its unnavigability, its commercial importance is small, but this does not excuse the geographer's scant appreciation of it in the past, even if it explains the Chinese viewpoint.

Considerably west of Pingshan Hsien the Yangtsze is joined by the Yalung River, an artery almost equal in volume to the main stream. This river rises in the northeastern limits of the Thibetan highlands in the same general country as the Yangtsze, but to the southeast. It flows more or less due south throughout the whole course, but the region it traverses is, if anything, less known than that through which the Yangtsze itself flows. In its upper parts it is called the Niachu, since it flows through the country of the Niarung tribes and its map cognomen, Yalung, is probably a transliteration of the name Niarung.

On its right bank the Yangtsze receives many streams rising in northern Yunnan and Kweichou, but none equal in importance to those uniting on the left bank. However, all are significant factors in the distribution of merchandise in these parts, even though geographically they are of comparatively small moment. The important thing to be remembered in connection with the river system here mentioned is this—the Yangtsze River is the main artery of China in general and western China in particular, but Szechuan owes its agricultural wealth and general prosperity principally to the Kialing and Min rivers with their network of navigable contributory streams and canals. The rivers west of Sui Fu flow through wild, sparsely populated regions and their waters are so much obstructed that practically no boats ply on their waters and even ferries are scarce.

CHAPTER II

WESTERN HUPEH

TOPOGRAPHY AND GEOLOGY

HE country comprising western Hupeh, with which we are concerned, lies west of the 112th parallel of longitude. The city of Ichang, situated on the Yangtsze River just west of this parallel and about 1000 geographical miles from the mouth of the river, is a convenient starting-point for exploring this region. This town is an important treaty port, opened to foreign trade in 1877. The population is roughly estimated at 30,000. There is also a small foreign community consisting of a British Consul, Maritime Custom's staff, a few business men, and missionaries of Roman Catholic and various Protestant denominations. There is very little local trade, but being virtually the head of steam navigation on the river it is a most important transhipping port. Steamers regularly trade between Ichang and Hankow, and the thousands of native craft lined up in tiers attest its importance as an entrepot of trade. In the near future it is destined to be a most important junction on the Hankow-Szechuan Railway. Ichang is well known, and every year foreigners visit it in increasing numbers intent on seeing the famous gorges immediately beyond. Ascending the river by steamer from Hankow the hilly country commences about 40 miles below Ichang. At first low, the hills gradually increase in height, and by the time Ichang is reached one is fairly among the mountains. In the vicinity of the town the hills are pyramidal in outline with prominent cliffs nearby; north, south, and west of the town the country is much cut up, forming an archipelago of peaks 2000 to 4000 feet high, the peaks themselves being offsets from spurs attaining altitudes of from 7000 to 9000 feet above sea-level and situated some days' distance beyond. The pyramidal hills around

CHINA — MOTHER OF GARDENS

Ichang are very interesting and never fail to attract the attention of travellers. They are made up of a substratum of pebbly conglomerate, on which are reared thin, horizontally deposed strata of marine limestone, red shale, and sandstone, over-capped with sandy clays. The strata are piled with great regularity and when erosion is equal on all sides the characteristic pyramidal shape is produced and maintained. This formation is general from the edge of the great plain to Ichang, and occasionally it contains thin beds of coal. It is comparatively of recent age, dating back to permomesozoic times. The dominant fossils it contains are cycads, and the youngest rocks probably belong to the oolitic series. The cliffs and bold peaks to the north, south, and west of Ichang are made up principally of paleozoic limestones, with a little shale and sandstone, the latter of the mesozoic period. The strata are folded in apparent conformity and are without notable metamorphism. In eastern Szechuan these rocks extend beneath the Red Basin. The Yangtsze has forced itself right through them and formed a series of mighty chasms in which the structure of the various formations is beautifully exhibited.

In the neighborhood of Hwangling Miao, 30 miles west of Ichang, and westward for 10 miles to the Tungling Rapid, granitic gneiss is exposed. These are the oldest rocks in this region and the only pre-cambrian formation known in situ in the middle Yangtsze. This section of the river is called the Ta-shih Ho (River of Dregs and Boulders), and well does it deserve this appellation.

The next oldest rocks of importance are those forming the cliffs opposite Nanto, the Niukan gorge, and the eastern half of the Wushan gorge. This is a massive formation, 4000 to 5000 feet thick, in the major part composed of dark gray or liver-colored limestone free from chert and containing both cambrian and ordovician fossils. It is, in fact, a great marine limestone in all its phases. It weathers into wonderful escarpments, often sheer for 1000 to 2000 feet, with slightly projecting summits, and frequently many miles in extent. The cliffs on the right bank of the river opposite Nanto and extending nearly to Hwangling Miao are typical examples. At one of the major low-water rapids known as the Hsintan, distant some 45 miles west of Ichang, a bed of shale is

SUN-YU-TUNG GLEN: CLIFFS OF CARBONIFEROUS LIMESTONE

beautifully exposed. This bed is some 1800 feet thick and composed in the main of olive green argillite with local black shale and quartzite. It is of the middle paleozoic age.

Resting, apparently conformably on this series of shale, is a vast deposit of upper carboniferous limestone 4000 or more feet thick. This is the characteristic formation throughout the Ichang and Mitan gorges; it occurs also throughout the western end of the Wushan gorge and in the Kui Fu or Wind-box gorge beyond. The prevailing rock is dark gray or blackish limestone, full of marine fossils and with wonderful escarpments, but commonly they are boldly rounded with less linear dimensions. This formation is the most general throughout western Hupeh, on both sides of the river, though greater on the north than on the south, where the cambrian-ordovician formation preponderates. Next in succession come the permomesozoic beds of red shale and sandstone, with thin layers of marine limestone and coal, which were described in reference to Ichang. These beds are characteristic of the country west of the Mitan gorge, as far as the entrance to the Wushan gorge, principally on the left bank. Coal occurs in this stretch in many places, more especially near Patung Hsien.

Glacial deposits and signs of glacial action are in evidence in many parts of western Hupeh, though nowhere on a large scale. The most accessible of these is on the Yangtsze itself, opposite Nanto, a hamlet situated at the extreme western end of the Ichang gorge and some 20 miles above Ichang city. At this point can be seen a glacial deposit about 120 feet thick, overlaid by marine limestone of the cambrian-ordovician age. All the evidences of ice action are well disclosed, and the whole deposit is most instructively exhibited. Since the deposition of these various systems great regional disturbances have taken place and the strata have commonly been bent up from a great depth. The summit of the very highest peaks in western Hupeh are usually comprised of silurian (? devonian) shales.

None of the useful or precious minerals occur in quantity in western Hupeh. Coal is scattered through the entire region, but is nowhere found in abundance and the quality is indifferent. Iron ore is worked in places and in one or two localities the quality is good, but usually it is poor. Copper occurs in two districts (Chienshih and Hsingshan) but is not worked to any great extent. Salt, so abundant throughout the Red Basin of Szechuan, does not occur. The sandy clays and marls are used in brick and tile-making, and lime is burnt in several places and used for building purposes. These clays and the limestone belong to the permo-mesozoic beds. The carboniferous limestones are quarried and used for various construction works.

In the gorges the main river is joined by numerous lateral streams, branches of which flow through glens of wondrous beauty. These riverlets in winding their way usually fill nearly the entire bed of the glen and are bounded by walls of cliff from 300 to 1000 feet sheer. Waterfalls are numerous and wherever it is possible vegetation is rampant. The tops of the cliffs are worn into curious and grotesque shapes. Caves abound and in these stalactites and stalagmites occur. Subterranean springs are common and many of the small rivers originate from such sources. They issue forth from some cave, or from the face of a cliff, or may well up through level rock. The Hsingshan River is an example of this mode of origin. The Chinese attach much legendary lore to all these caves and springs and frequently associate fine temples with such spots.

In the vicinity of the Yangtsze the more commanding peaks and crags are crowned by temples, usually belonging to the Taouist cult. Commonly these temples cap seemingly inaccessible points, and one marvels how the material used in erecting them was transported thither. Whenever possible a few trees, usually (Xylosma racemosum pubescens) Wintergreen, Gleditsia, Cypress, Ginkgo, and Pine are planted near the temples and add much to the beauty of the whole scene. Such temples are well built, but, unfortunately, since the interior is usually dark, filthy, and uninviting, a close inspection robs them of most of their charm. From the distance they look most picturesque, the style of architecture being in harmony with the surroundings and one admires very much the taste and culture which called them into existence. The preservation of the good luck of towns, villages, and communities by the warding off of evil influences is a matter of great moment in China, and with this good work the temples are associated.

CHINA — MOTHER OF GARDENS

The pagodas, found all over China, have been erected solely with this end in view. Geomancy enters very largely into Taouism and holds a most important place in Chinese thought, in fact it governs much of their daily life.

Too wild and savage for extensive agricultural development, and with a marked absence of useful mineral deposits, western Hupeh is one of the poorest, most sparsely populated, and least known parts of China. For these same reasons it is of particular interest to the botanist, since the vegetation there has been less molested than is usual in China generally. Even here, it is hardly necessary to say, every available bit of land either is or has been under cultivation, but much of the country is of such a nature as to preclude agricultural development, even under Chinese patience and ingenuity.

Up to 3000 or 4000 feet above the Yangtsze, wherever it is possible, the mountain-slopes, hill-tops, and valleys are cultivated, but the country is made up so much of sheer cliff and crag, and is generally of such a rocky character, that even where cultivation is possible the crop won from the soil is poor and small recompense for the outlay of labor involved in its production. Above 6000 feet the higher slopes and mountains defy even Chinese skill and patience, and it is here that patches of virgin forest and much woodland remain. The higher mountains are rich in various Chinese medicines, and men eke out a livelihood in gathering them. Considerable areas in this higher country were formerly cleared and crops of the Irish potato raised. But the potato disease attacked and devastated the crops, and ruined the peasants, who were forced to migrate to lower and more congenial altitudes. Ruined houses and numerous graves, overgrown with coarse herbs, brambles, and shrubs, tell of former habitation; but to-day, in the higher parts of this region, it is possible to walk from morning until night without seeing an inhabited dwelling or a living person. Wherever the valleys admit of sufficient cultivation to support them, small riverine villages occur. Tiny hamlets, farmhouses, and peasants' huts are frequent up to 4500 feet above sea-level. Above this little agriculture is attempted and the population is exceedingly sparse.

CHAPTER III

METHODS OF TRAVEL

ROADS AND ACCOMMODATION

THE advent of steam navigation on the upper-middle Yangtsze has brought Chungking, the commercial metropolis of western China, three weeks nearer the coast and Occidental civilization. This is a very considerable gain to the would-be traveller in these regions, yet it only postpones for a little time longer the inevitable. Sooner or later the traveller must dispense with the comforts and luxuries of modern methods of travel and adapt himself to those more primitive and de-cidedly less comfortable. In the regions with which we deal there is nothing in the nature of vehicular traffic save only the rude wheel-barrows in use on the Chengtu plain. There are no mule caravans, and scarcely a riding pony is to be found. For overland travel there is the native sedan-chair and one's own legs; for river travel, the native boat. Patience, tact, and abundance of time are necessary, and the would-be traveller lacking any of these essentials should seek lands where less primitive methods obtain. Endowed with the virtues mentioned, and having unlimited time at his disposal, he may travel anywhere and everywhere in China in safety, with considerable pleasure and abundant profit in knowledge. With her industrious toiling millions and her wondrous scenery, China alternately charms and fascinates, irritates and plunges into despair all who sojourn long within her borders. No other country is of such perennial interest to the world at large. Ever-changing yet ever the same, China is the link which connects the twentieth century with the dawn of civilization, epochs before the Christian era. To travel leisurely through this vast country is an education which leaves an indelible impress on all fortunate enough to have had the experience. The

15

CHINA — MOTHER OF GARDENS

Chinese do not see time from the Westerner's viewpoint, and for the traveller in the interior parts of China the first, last, and most important thing of all is to ever bear this in mind.

The majority of travellers still ascend the river above Ichang in native boats, and it will probably be a long time before a regular fleet of steamers plies these dangerous waters and renders the native boat obsolete. The journey from Ichang to Chungking and beyond has been described so often that the subject is threadbare, and I have no intention of describing it over again. Volumes have been written on this subject, and some day perhaps a writer will arise and do full justice to the theme.

I have made the journey up and down many times, and on each occasion have been more and more impressed with the sublime beauty of the gorges. The scenery in these savage chasms is all and more than any writer has described. It must be seen to be fully understood and appreciated. The more often one travels up and down this stretch of the river the deeper grows one's awe and respect for the many rapids, swift currents, and innumerable difficulties which impede navigation.

The native boats are perfectly fitted for the navigation of these difficult waters; they are the outcome of generations of experience, and the balance-rudder and turret-build have been used in these craft long before their adoption by western nations. The men, too, who earn their livelihood in navigating these boats, understand their business thoroughly. Much has been written by hasty travellers on the shortcomings and incompetence of these men that is as unwarrantable as it is undeserved. These Chinese boatmen are careful, absolutely competent, and thorough masters of their craft, and the more one sees of them and their work the more one's admiration grows. Oriental methods are not Occidental methods, but they succeed just the same! When on the boat the Westerner will do well to adapt himself to Eastern methods; any attempt to enforce those of the West generally ends in disaster. Many accidents on the Yangtsze have been caused through the foreigner, ignorant of local conditions, difficulties, and dangers, forcing the captain of the boat to proceed against his better judgment. The traveller is advised when engaging a boat to do so

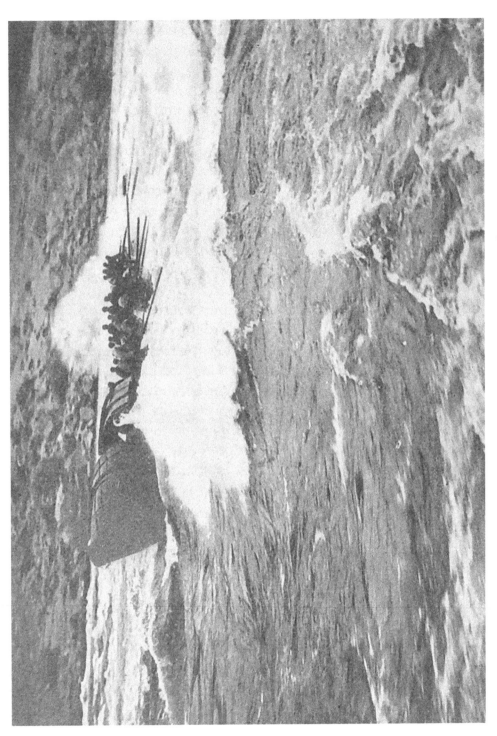

DESCENDING RAPIDS IN THE YANGTSZE GORGES

through a responsible Chinese business house, to have an agreement drawn up setting forth the arrangements desired, and then to leave the boat-master to carry out the engagement in his own way. This is the only way to ensure safety, and on paper no one would attempt to gainsay it, yet in practice this is commonly done, but always to the jeopardy of the transgressor.

Since we shall have much to say on the subject of over-land travel a word or two anent roads seems fitting and desirable. To the uninitiated this subject may seem trivial, but to the experienced it is otherwise. Chinese roads make a lasting impression on all who travel over them, and the vocabulary of the average traveller is not rich enough to thoroughly relieve the mind in this matter. The roads are of two kinds, paved and unpaved. I have yet to meet the traveller whose mind is thoroughly made up as to which of these is worse and the more difficult to negotiate. A clever writer once wrote: "An Imperial highway in China is not one which is kept in order by the Emperor, but rather one which may have to be put in order for the Emperor.'" When any important official takes up duties in a distant part of the empire the local officials put the roads over which he has to travel in some semblance of repair. Such work is always hastily done by labor forced and grudgingly given, and in mountainous districts the first severe rainstorm destroys considerable portions of it.

It is nobody's real business to look after the roads, and nobody does. The land devoted to roadways is commandeered, and in agricultural districts the farmer takes good care to keep these roads down to a minimum width. It usually happens that the roadways get narrower and narrower every year, until the advent of some important official forces the local authorities into having them repaired and restored to their original width.

Throughout the length and breadth of China run imperial highways, few in number, it is true, but of vast importance, since they connect the imperial capital with the capitals of the provinces. These were made for military purposes in early times, when the Emperors were busy conquering the country and extending their territories. They are all of great strategical importance, and were originally paved throughout with blocks of stone. Often, indeed, they were actually blasted and excavated from solid rock. They vary in width according to the configuration of the country and the nature of the traffic they have to carry. In the northern parts overland travel is commonly done by cart, and the roads are adapted to such traffic. In the parts with which we are concerned the country is too rugged for wheels, and the only recognized mode of travelling is by means of sedan-chair. The imperial roads were originally made sufficiently wide to enable two chairs to pass one another freely. Ten to twelve feet is a broad highway in these parts, and it must be conceded that roads of such width amply serve their purpose. Unfortunately this width is rarely maintained for any considerable distance. The grading of these ancient highways was well done, and the whole work speaks volumes for the ability and energy of those old-time engineers. Like much else in China these roads were once magnificent, but to-day they are far from this. In general they are sadly neglected. Floods have destroyed them here and there, often the paving blocks have been stolen for house-building and other purposes, and gaps of unpaved, muddy stretches, almost impassable in rainy weather, occur all too frequently. Sufficient of the original roads remain to stir admiration for the skill and foresight of the engineers, long since dead, who built them, and to set the traveller longing for the halcyon days of old.

In the prosperous parts of China, highways connect all the principal cities, towns, and villages. These are usually 8 to 10 feet wide and, although originally paved throughout, are now in a state of more or less disrepair. Nearly all the towns and villages in western China are situated on the banks of streams for the simple reason that the valleys offered lines of least resistance. Even when the streams are not navigable they afford easier means of access to the interior than the mountains and forest-clad country. In a general way all the older roads in China follow the courses of streams as closely as possible, leaving them only when the nature of the country necessitates the departure, and watersheds intervene.

Bypaths and narrow tracks permeate the country in every direction, even in the most sparsely populated mountainous regions.

CHINA — MOTHER OF GARDENS

Some one has very wisely made out that the exchange of salt was the first commerce engaged in by mankind at large. Salt is, and long has been, a government monopoly in China, consequently the practice of salt-smuggling has gone on from time immemorial, and the majority of the mountain-paths were very probably first struck out by smugglers of salt. Indeed, many important trade-routes in China to-day presumably originated in this way. The province of Szechuan is abundantly rich in salt and also in mountain-paths. From a lengthy study I have come to regard this network of bypaths as a result of salt traffic, and more especially illicit traffic. There are to-day many such paths throughout the Hupeh-Szechuan boundary, used for practically no other traffic than that of salt, and by these paths salt still reaches certain districts in defiance of the law. Very useful, if difficult, the traveller finds these bypaths, for without them it would be impossible to traverse some of the most interesting parts of central and western China.

When travelling overland in China it is not possible to use tents, and one has perforce to make use of such accommodation as the country affords. The Chinese do not under-stand tents, and it is unwise to try innovations in a land where the people are unduly inquisitive. The traveller gets along best when he avoids publicity as much as possible. On all the main roads there are inns of sorts, usually very filthy, and in season abounding in mosquitoes, creeping things, and stinks, the latter, in fact, being always in evidence. On the byways, and more especially in the mountains, accommodation is hard to find and is of the meanest description. However, one is usually tired, and any shelter suffices for a night's halt. In wet weather or when held up through flooded torrents or what not, the absence of proper accommodation is acutely felt. In the wilds of China one hungers for the dak bungalows of India and Kashmir or some similar accommodation.

A traveller in China should have with him an outfit, comprising bed, bedding, victuals, cooking paraphernalia, and insect-powder. It sounds rather formidable on paper, but labor is cheap and a little experience enables one to keep the size of outfit within reasonable limits. The necessary coolies should always be obtained through a respectable agency and an agreement made in writing, stating all necessary details. A head-man, called a Fu-tou, should be given charge of the coolies.

In parts of China where foreigners are well-known it is possible to dispense with the luxury of a sedan-chair, but it must be remembered that a sedan-chair is an out-ward and visible sign of respectability. It is the recognized medium of travel, and, quite apart from its real use, it is a necessity, since its presence insures respect. In the out-of-the-way parts of China, even though it is carried piece-meal, a chair is of greater service and value to the traveler than a passport. According to treaty, all foreigners travelling in China must furnish themselves with a passport, which must be shown on request. This is a matter of considerable importance and should never be omitted.

One thing more is necessary ere the caravan is fully equipped, and that is a good cook. Unless the traveller speaks Chinese he must have a servant able to speak broken English. A good travelling servant is hard to find, but the last thing the average traveller should dream of doing is to engage an interpreter. A good domestic servant is all that is necessary.

CHAPTER IV

THE FLORA OF ICHANG

UR travels began at Ichang and at the outset it may be of interest to give an account of the flora obtaining in the vicinity of that town, which, from the amount of collecting done in its neighborhood, holds a classic place in the annals of botanical exploration work in China. The flora of Ichang and the vicinity up to an altitude of 2000 feet above sea-level is essentially warm temperate in character and includes not a few sub-tropical forms. Nevertheless, we find also a number of cool temperate plants, and what really obtains is a fusion of these three floras with the warm temperate element in the ascendency. The following dozen characteristic plants will serve to illustrate the point: Aleurites fordii, Liquidambar formosana, Ligustrum lucidum, Caesalpinia sepiaria, Toddalia asiatica, Wistaria sinensis, Azalea simsii, Pyracantha crenulata, Primula calciphila, Anemone japonica, Aspidistra punctata, Linum trigynum, and Woodwardia radicans.

The low hills around Ichang are very barren looking, being mostly clad with Spear Grass (Heteropogon contortus), with a few shrubs and herbs relieved here and there by small woods of Pinus massoniana and Cupressus funebris, with occasional groves of Bamboo (Phyllostachys pubescens). However, it is not to the low hills that we look for the floral wealth of Ichang, but to the limestone cliffs of glen and gorge. Here the variety is astonishing, a striking feature being the quantity of well-known flowering shrubs.

The two first shrubs to flower in the early spring are Daphne genkwa and Coriaria sinica. It is a thousand pities that all cannot succeed in growing this Daphne since it is such a lovely plant by far the finest species of the genus. At Ichang it grows everywhere, on the bare exposed hills, among conglomerate rocks and limestone boulders, on graves and among the stones which are piled around the tiny cultivated plats in the gorge, sometimes in partial shade, but more usually fully exposed to the scorching sun. The plants are, on the average, about 2 feet in height, and are but seldom branched. Imagine the annual suckers from a Plum tree, and you have the appearance of these Daphne plants. For two-thirds of their height the stems are so densely clad with flowers that they look like one large thyrse. The color is lilac-purple, often very dark, but a white form is not uncommon. Its outward resemblance to Lilac leads to its being so called by the foreign residents at Ichang.

The Coriaria is not nearly so attractive. Its flowers are polygamous and the plant when in fruit is rather showy. The Chinese consider its foliage and stem poisonous to cattle.

Abundant is Wistaria sinensis, often scaling high trees, but the semi-bush form is the more common. Its flowers are borne in great abundance, and vary much in shade of color, the white form being, however, rather rare.

Another well-known shrub here plentiful is Loropetalum chinense. On the tops of the cliffs, among loose conglomerate and limestone boulders, it forms a well-nigh impenetrable scrub. The bushes are seldom more than 3 feet in height, very much branched, and when in full flower look like patches of snow at a distance. In California, as in Devon and Cornwall, if planted in a rockery, it ought to thrive.

Rose bushes are plentiful everywhere, and in April perhaps afford the greatest show of any one kind of flower. Rosa laevigata and R. microcarpa are more common in fully exposed places. Rosa multiflora, R. helenae and R. banksiae are particularly abundant on the cliffs and crags of the glens and gorges, though by no means confined thereto. The Banksian Rose often wreathes tall trees and a tree thus festooned, the branches laden with flowers, is a sight to be remembered. To walk through a glen in the early morning or after a slight shower, when the air is laden with the soft delicious perfume from myriads of rose blossoms, is truly a walk through an earthly paradise.

In March and April Sophora viciifolia, when covered with

masses of bluish white flowers, is very fine in the glens and gorges. This plant has a very wide distribution. It is common in Yunnan, and in the warm valleys of rivers bordering Thibet. The Ichang plant is much less spiny than that of Yunnan and western Szechuan. Possibly the latter is really the Indian S. moorcroftianum.

Two very common plants on the cliffs in the glens are Eriobotrya japonica (Loquat) and Meratia praecox (Wintersweet). Both flower about Christmas. These are two out of many plants which formerly were erroneously supposed to be natives of Japan.

Among conglomerate boulders Caryopteris incana is frequent but is not nearly so fine as it is farther west. Pyracantha crenulata and Vitex negundo are exceedingly common, and so also is Caesalpinia sepiaria, a thorny shrub, semi-scandent in habit, and very like the better known C. japonica. Its handsome foliage and erect thyrsoid racemes of bright yellow flowers make it a conspicuous object.

The Sapphire-berry (Symplocos paniculata) with its pretty white flowers and blue fruits is abundant. This is a useful and charming shrub and deserves to be better known. Deutzia schneideriana, Lagerstroemia indica, Azalea simsii, Jasminum floridum, Nandina domestica, Ilex cornuta, Viburnum utile, and Buddleia officinalis are all extremely common shrubs. Of other well or lesser known shrubs which are common, I may mention Abelia chinensis, A. parvifolia, Rhus cotinus, Buddleia asiatica, Ilex pedunculata, I. corallina, Deutzia discolor, Desmodium floribundum, Elaeagnus pungens, E. glabra, Spiraea chinensis, Eurya japonica, Hypericum chinense, Hydrangea strigosa, Berchemia lineata, Euonymus alata, Polygala mariesii, Viburnum brachybotryum, V. propinquum, Thea cuspidata, Rubus parvifolius, and many other species. Chaenomeles sinensis with rose-colored and C. cathayensis with white or blush-white flowers are commonly cultivated. Lengthy as is the list, I am not justified in omitting Itea ilicifolia. This Holly-like shrub with long, pendent cylindric racemes of white flowers is one of the handsomest of all the Ichang shrubs. Of fluviatile shrubs the commonest are, Distylium chinense, Salix variegata, Ficus adpressa, Rhamnus utilis, Adina globiflora, Myricaria germanica, and a curious Box (Buxus stenophylla).

YANGTSZE RIVER AT ICHANG IN WINTER

CHINA — MOTHER OF GARDENS

Climbers are very much in evidence, and include such beautiful plants as Lonicera japonica, Trachelospermum jasminoides, Pueraria thunbergiana, Clematis henryi, C. benthamiana, C. armandi, C. uncinata, Vitis flexuosa, Parthenocissus henryana, P. thomsonii and Mucuna sempervirens.

This last is a rather remarkable plant. Two miles above Ichang on the right bank is an enormous specimen, called by foreigners the Big Creeper. It covers several hundred square feet of ground, climbing over several Pine trees and many Bamboos. The base of the main trunk is almost as thick as a man's body; the flowers are fetid, dark chocolate colored and are borne in racemes on the old wood; the legumes are 2 to 2 ½ feet in length, and contain many large black bean-like seeds. It flowers in May. Ichang does not possess a great number of trees but the variety is really astonishing. Paulownia duclouxii and Melia azedarach with their enormous panicles of flowers are very striking in the spring. In the autumn Sapium sebiferum with its wonderful autumnal tints stands alone. In winter the evergreen Ligustrum lucidum and Xylosma racemosum pubescens are very conspicuous. The latter nearly always shelters some wayside shrine. Perhaps the commonest trees are: Gleditsia sinensis, Rhus semialata, Platycarya strobilacea, Quercus serrata, Cedrela sinensis, and Pterocarya stenoptera. Mistletoe occurs on the last-named tree. Other less common trees are Sterculia platanifolia, Populus adenopoda, Crataegus hupehensis, Celtis sinensis, Dalbergia hupeana, Acer oblongum, Cunninghamia lanceolata, Ailanthus glandulosa, Broussonetia papyrifera, Ulmus parvifolia, Hovenia dulcis, Sapindus mukorossi, Salix babylonica and Sophora japonica. Of the latter a curious variety occurs in which the leaves and young shoots are clothed in a dense white velvety indumentum.

As with flowering shrubs, so with herbs, though in a less degree, Ichang is the home of many favorite garden plants. One of the commonest and best known is Primula obconica. This charming herb is everywhere common but more especially in moist, grassy places on the banks of the Yangtsze and in the glens. Occasionally, under very favorable conditions, in height, size of flower, and luxuriance of foliage, it approaches the cultivated form, but more usually it is a small, insignificant weed. Other favorites which are common are:

Corydalis thalictrifolia, Anemone japonica, Sedum sarmentosum, Saxifraga sarmentosa, Iris japonica, Lycoris aurea, L. radiata, Rehmannia angulata, Hemerocallis fulva, and H. flava. Other characteristic herbs are: Adenophora polymorpha, Bletia hyacinthina, Asarum maximum, Ophiorrhiza cantonensis, Viola patrinii, Delphinium chinense, Lysimachia henryi, L. clethroides, Potentilla chinensis, P. discolor, Fragaria indica, Thalictrum minus, Mazus pulchellus, Verbena officinalis, Platycodon grandiflorum, and many Compositae, Leguminosae, and Umbelliferae.

Perhaps Ichang is best known to gardeners generally as the home of the lovely Lilium henryi. This acknowledged favorite occurs on the limestone and conglomerate rocks, but is now by no means plentiful. Lilium brownii and its variety (colchesteri) are fairly common; L. concolor occurs, but is rare.

Ferns are not rich in species but Woodwardia radicans, Osmunda regalis, Pteris longifolia, P. serrulata, Nephrodium molle, Cheilanthes patula, and Gleichenia lineata are abundant. A variety of Adiantum capillus-veneris is very common on stalagmitic limestone in the glens. Pieces of these rocks covered with Ferns are detached and find their way all over China, being popularly known as Ichang Fern-stones.

A hasty reference to the common floating plants of the ponds and ditches around Ichang must bring this account to a close. Euryale ferox with its handsome foliage is common; Nelumbium speciosum is of course cultivated. Other common aquatics are Limnanthemum nymphoides, Jussiaea repens, Salvinia natans, Trapa natans, Azolla filiculoides, Marsilea quadrifolia, Monochoria vaginalis, Eriocalon buergerianum, and several species of Potamogeton and Utricularia. In late autumn, when the Azolla changes to a rich crimson tint, the ponds look very fine. In some rice fields near Ichang, Augustine Henry found a very anomalous plant. It was made the type of a new genus—Trapella sinensis, and doubtfully referred to the natural order Pedalinae.

CHAPTER V

A QUEST OF FLOWERS

A JOURNEY IN NORTH-WESTERN HUPEH

N June 4th, 1910, I left Ichang for Chengtu, via a new route through the wilds of northwest Hupeh. With 600 miles of overland travel ahead the caravan had been fitted up with all the skill at my command, and with enthusiasm to spur us on I felt that the difficulties would not prove insurmountable. Nearly all the men had been associated with me on former journeys of a similar nature.

We took the lesser road by way of San-yu-tung glen for Hsingshan Hsien, in consequence of the main road being congested by coolies engaged in blazing a trail for the Hankow-Szechuan Railway. The caravan consisted of twenty carrying coolies, several men for collecting and general work en route, a chair for the boy, and another for myself. My own start was not propitious. I was riding in my chair and had scarcely cleared the precincts of the foreign settlement when one of the poles snapped. This occasioned an hour's delay, but happening where it did new poles were secured without difficulty. It is never easy to make an early start the first day, and it is always advisable to count on a short stage. It was one o'clock when we reached the mouth of the San-yu-tung glen, 5 miles above Ichang, and overtook the main caravan. The weather was hot, and we only did another 15 li[1] to Sha-lao-che, making 35 li in all. This little hamlet consists of a few scattered houses, and we availed ourselves of the largest, which happened to be a wine-distillery, and the smell of stale brewing was very strong.

The journey up the San-yu-tung glen was very interesting, much of the scenery being rugged and grand. The cliffs of hard limestone are

---

1 Ten li = three English miles.

usually 500 feet or more sheer, and are the home of goral and other animals, and also of many cliff-loving plants. In the crevices and niches a famous Primrose (Primula calciphila) finds its home, but the flowers were past and the flower-stalks all bent towards the cliffs to insure the seeds being deposited in the rock crevices. In February and early March the cliffs present a wonderful picture, being covered with colonies of this Primula, one mass of warm mauve-pink flowers. Wherever the cliffs are not absolutely sheer, vegetation is rampant. Pine trees (Pinus massoniana) fringe the summits and Rosa microcarpa was in full flower, otherwise there was very little blossom to be seen. Most of the shrubs being spring-flowering were in young fruit.

There was considerable delay in starting the next morning. One or two of the coolies gave up, and others had to be found. The road was vile all day, and it took us 10 ½ hours to cover 45 li. For the first 10 li the road continues to ascend the glen, which narrows and presents even finer scenery than that of yesterday. We passed a lovely natural grotto full of stalagmites inside, and with the dripping external rocks one mass of Maidenhair Fern. These rocks are known throughout the lower Yangtsze valley as Ichang Fern-stones, and command a ready sale.

In the glen Parthenocissus henryana is abundant; in the juvenile stage the leaves of this plant have prominent white veins, and are very attractive, but in the adult stage this variegation is lost, and they become quite ordinary in appearance.

The glen soon became impassable, and we climbed the cliffs and ultimately overlooked the country generally. Terraced fields are much in evidence, and every available inch of country is under cultivation. Wheat, barley, and peas, all ripe, were the principal crops, and their yellow culms enlivened the landscape. We saw a small patch or two of the Opium Poppy hidden away under trees and of very poor quality. Pear and Plum trees are commonly cultivated hereabout, Bamboo groves and Cypress trees abound. Here and there we caught an occasional glimpse of the white-tailed paradise fly-catcher (Tchitrea incei). Pheasants were calling, and likewise the English cuckoo.

Around Niu-ping (Cow-flat), which was our destination for the day, much rice is cultivated, and the farmers were busy transplanting the tiny rice-plants. The whole country is finely terraced and is backed by limestone cliffs of cambrian-ordovician age. Near our destination we passed a fine Ginkgo tree showing curious root-like protuberances on the branches. In rocky places by the wayside, and especially in the walls of the terraced fields, Rehmannia angulata abounds. Plants 1½ to 2 feet high carry six to a dozen large, rosy pink, foxglove-like flowers. The local name is Feng-tang hwa (Honey-bee flower).

Cow-flat is a tiny place of about a dozen houses. Our quarters were cramped but comfortable, and the people very nice. There is a road from this hamlet to Nanto, distant 30 li. When I first visited this place in 1901 I was an object of great curiosity from the moment of my arrival to the time of departure. I have been here several times since and am now treated as an old-time acquaintance.

It was quite cool during the night, and a blanket was required. At Ichang the very thought of a blanket was enough to bring forth perspiration! We left about 6 a.m., and after ascending and descending a series of lateral spurs finally reached the small river which enters the Yangtsze at Nanto. After ascending this river for a few miles we commenced a steep ascent. Now by an easy and then by a heavy grade the road winds in and out among the mountains, and we did not reach our halting-place for the night until 6.30 p.m. The last coolie arrived an hour later. The length of the whole journey is supposed to be only 60 li, but we all agreed that it is a good 70 li. Whatever the distance, it is certainly a hard day's travel.

The mountain-sides are very steep, with razor-like ridges. Terraced cultivation is everywhere carried out, rice is cultivated in the bottom-lands and maize on the slopes, with occasional patches of Irish potato. Where it is too steep, or for other reasons unsuitable for cultivation, the mountain-sides are covered with shrubs and trees, chiefly scrub Oak and the common Pine. Small trees of Cornus wilsoniana in full flower were common here and there. Odd trees of C. kousa chinensis also, in full flower, were conspicuous on the outskirts of the woods and copses. This small tree is exceedingly floriferous. In habit it is flat-topped with horizontally spreading branches, and the flowers borne erect, well above the foliage. The mass of white bracts

PRIMULA CALCIPHILA IN SAN-YU-TUNG GLEN

frequently exceeds 5 inches in diameter; with age the bracts become tinged with pink. The fruit is large, red, and edible. This Chinese form will probably prove a better plant under cultivation than the Japanese form with which gardeners are familiar. The plant loves a sunny, well-drained situation. The display of the day, however, was made by the wild Roses. By the side of streams the Rambler Rose (R. multiflora), with both white and pink flowers, was abundant. In the woods higher up a Musk Rose (R. helenae) filled the air with its soft fragrance. Here and there occurred Actinidia chinensis, scaling tall trees and wreathing them with white and buff-yellow fragrant flowers. In the fore-noon I noted Rehmannia angulata, especially common on steep stony places in full sun.

Our halting-place, Lao-mu-chia, is about 3500 feet altitude, and consists of about six houses and a tile-factory. Hereabout much charcoal is burnt for export to Nanto and down river. During the day's journey we met several men laden with bales of Crab-apple (Malus theifera) leaves. These leaves are commonly used as a substitute for tea, and there is a considerable export from these parts to Shasi.

On leaving Lao-mu-chic we immediately commenced the steep ascent of the Hsanlung shan, and a climb of 1000 feet brought us to the summit, where there is a small temple in a ruinous condition. After a precipitous descent of a few hundred feet the road meanders over and among the tops of hills, composed of granitic gneiss, which is rapidly disintegrating, and ultimately descends to the bed of a torrent and joins the main road from Ichang to Hsingshan Hsien.

Near the summit of Hsanlung shan, which is composed of cambrian-ordovician limestones, the Chinese Tulip-tree (Liriodendron chinense) is common in the woods, and so is Viburnum tomentosum with its sprays of snow-white flowers. Styrax hemsleyanum and Amelanchier asiatica sinica, the June-berry, are other trees with white flowers remarkable for their beauty and abundance of blossom. On the more open slopes Symplocos paniculata, Lonicera maackii podocarpa, Diervilla japonica, and Crataegus cuneata made a fine display. Thin woods of Pinus massoniana and Sweet Chestnut (Castanea mollissima) also occur; the Pine trunks are gashed for the ultimate purpose of producing kindling wood. In open places Rubus corchorifolius abounds, and its red, raspberry-like fruits with their delicious vinous flavor were good eating. In the descent Dipteronia sinensis, a small bushy tree with erect trusses of small white flowers, occurs, and Actinidia chinensis is common. The hermaphrodite and male forms of this climber have large white flowers quickly changing to buff-yellow, and the fragrance is very pleasing. A form with purely female flowers is unknown. At the foot of the descent we joined the main road from Ichang to Hsingshan Hsien, and following this route we reached Shui-yueh-tsze, a village of 100 houses, situated in a tiny rice flat, at five o'clock. The people were very inquisitive, and I held an impromptu reception until bedtime.

On joining the main road, we saw evidences of the survey for the Hankow-Szechuan Railway. The proposed route was marked by bamboo poles, and on the rocks with Arabic numerals and initials in Roman letters. The route descends a stream, just before reaching Shui-yueh-tsze, to Liang-ho-kou, and then continues down the Hsingshan River to the Yangtsze, which it connects with at Hsiang-che. Its construction even in this region promises to be a difficult task, and will call for great ability on the part of the engineers. Much tunnelling and blasting will be necessary, yet from Hankow to this point the task is simple com-pared with that which lies beyond. The cost will be enormous even in a land of cheap labor. It is highly improbable that the gentry, who are so violently opposed to the employment of foreign capital in this venture, realize the magnitude of the task and its ultimate cost.

The next day's journey proved interesting but arduous. By an undulating path we reached the top of the ridge, which is known as T'an-shii-ya (Linden-tree pass), from a gigantic Linden which occurs there. This tree (Tilia henryana) is about 80 feet tall and 27 feet in girth, and though hollow appears to be in good health. The young leaves are silvery, and the tree, from its size, is a conspicuous object for miles around.

Descending through a cultivated area we entered a glen which we followed for 20 li: the scenery in the lower end is magnificent. Cliffs of hard limestone rear themselves almost perpendicularly some 2000 feet and more. In the upper part of the glen Pterocarya hupehensis is common along-side the burn. An odd tree or two of the rare Pteroceltis tatarinowii also occurs here. Throughout the glen Lady Banks's Rose (Rosa banksiae) is especially abundant. Bushes 10 to 20 feet high and more through them were one mass of fragrant white flowers. It occurs in thousands and is particularly happy, growing on rocks and over boulders by the side of streams. Caesalpinia sepiaria, with erect thyrsoid panicles of fragrant yellow flowers, is also abundant here-about. Growing on the cliffs, Illicium henryi, with its dull crimson flowers, is also worthy of note. On issuing from the glen we struck a shallow, rock-strewn stream of considerable width, and after ascending it for a short distance made a very precipitous ascent of a couple of thousand feet. Crossing over a ridge and a flat area, a descending road led to Shih-tsao-che, which we reached as night was closing in. This hamlet consists of about a dozen houses scattered through a narrow valley.

During the day I collected specimens of thirty different kinds of woody plants. The striking plants of the afternoon's journey were the Amelanchier and Dipelta floribunda, both masses of flower. Walnut (Juglans regia) and Varnish trees are abundant above 3000 feet; the sides and tops of the mountains are clothed with woods of Oak and Pine, particularly the former. We also saw many fine Willow and Ailanthus trees. Primula obconica, Lysimachia crispidens, and a blue-flowered Salvia are abundant up to 2000 feet. Near the inn a few trees of Catalpa fargesii occur, but were not yet in flower. Hereabout Daphne genkwa is abundant, but it was scarcely in flower at this altitude.

It rained a little in the early morning and showers fell at intervals during the day, nevertheless, the weather was good for travelling, since it was not too hot. Most of the journey was downhill. Soon after starting in the morning we crossed one or two low ridges, intercepted by narrow plateaux, and about noon commenced the descent to Hsing-shan Hsien. The descent is precipitous in parts, but the mountain-sides are mostly under cultivation. About half-way down coal is mined, but the quality appears to be indifferent. Lime is burnt in small quantities

MY CARAVAN

and paper-mills occur near Hsingshan.

Hsingshan, the only district city in these wilds, may claim to be one of the smallest and poorest Hsiens (i.e., cities of the fourth class) in the whole of China. It is situated on the left bank of a stream and contains scarcely a hundred houses, most of which are in a ruinous state. The wall facing the river varies from 4 to 12 feet in height. A road, apparently the main road, runs along the top of this wall. The east gate is closed by sewage; the north gate is so low that one has to bend the head when passing through! The whole town is dull and lifeless, as far as business is concerned, but children are plentiful, as they are everywhere else in China. The town is backed by a steep mountain, up two sides of which a wall is carried: most of the mountain-side enclosed within the wall is given over to terraced fields. The river is broad, with a shingly bottom, and the water clear and limpid. Thick-bottomed boats ply between Hsiang-t'an and Hsiang-che, a village at the head of the Mitan Gorge on the Yangtsze. No one stays in Hsingshan, and we journeyed on to Hsiang-t'an. This name signifies fragrant rapids: the waters may perhaps be sweet, but the village is foul and stinking. We had some little difficulty in securing lodgings, poor as they were, and an objectionable coolie had to be evicted before we could settle down for the night.

Flowers were not common during the day. We passed a magnificent tree of Keteleeria davidiana, 80 feet tall and 16 feet in girth. This tree shelters some graves, and was probably planted long ago. In the descent we passed through orchards of Crataegus hupehensis, all in full flower. This Hawthorn is one of several kinds cultivated in China for their edible fruit. The interesting Torricellia angulata occurs sparingly, and here and there plants of Mucuna sempervirens cover large trees; Catalpa ovata is common on the plateaux and a small-leaved Poplar (Populus simonii) occurs around farmhouses, but is rare.

Hsiang-t'an being in water communication with the Yangtsze boasts quite a considerable trade. Medicines are the principal export. Rifle-stocks, roughly shaped out of Walnut wood, are exported from this neighborhood to Hangyang in increasing quantities annually. They are worth locally 300 cash (about 15 cents) each. The village is situated on the left bank of the river, and possesses an opium likin and a viceroy's bank. Pigs seem more in evidence than human beings, as judged from the four visits I have paid the place in different years. Being only 300 feet above Ichang, Hsiang-t'an enjoys a hot, dry climate.

Leaving Hsiang-t'an we immediately crossed the river by ferry and ascended a narrow valley, which soon becomes a ravine and finally a wild, entrancing gorge. At the head of this gorge we took a small mountain-path which en-tailed a severe climb from the river-bed to the tops of the surrounding mountains. In this ascent a Musk Rose was a wonderful sight, and Loropetalum chinense abundant but out of flower. Once on top of the mountains an undulating path leads to Peh-yang-tsai, where we found lodgings in a new and fairly clean farmhouse.

In the gorge I gathered Rehmannia henryi, a herb less than a foot tall, with large, white, foxglove-like flowers. Hereabout the root-bark of Lady Banks's Rose is collected, and after being dried is pressed into bales for export to Shasi. This bark is used for dyeing and strengthening fish-nets, and it is claimed that it renders the net invisible to fish. In the valley Koelreuteria bipinnata occurs, but is rare; the flora of the ravine generally is similar to that of the San-yu-tung glen.

The mountains are clad with Oak (largely scrub), Pinus massoniana, and Cypress. A few Keteleeria trees occur and also Liquidambar formosana. Populus adenopoda, with its light gray bark, is a very common tree hereabout. Wood Oil trees (Aleurites fordii) were a wonderful sight and most abundant. In the ravine they were in full leaf, and the fruits were swelling, but from 1500 feet to 3000 feet they were leafless and covered with flowers. By the side of streams at low altitudes the Rambler Rose (Rosa multiflora) was a pretty sight with its white and pink blossoms, but the Musk Roses (R. helenae, R. gentiliana, and R. rubus) were the flowers of the day bushes 6 to 20 feet tall and more in diameter, nothing but clusters of white fragrant flowers. Growing on some old graves I found a sulphur-yellow flowered form of Rosa banksiae; this, I think, must have been planted. Rose bushes are a special feature in these parts and numerically the commonest of shrubs. Around our lodgings the Hardy Rubber-tree (Eucommia ulmoides) is cultivated for its bark, which is valued as a tonic medicine.

Peh-yang-tsai is a scattered hamlet, situated in a narrow valley, some 2500 feet altitude. Facing our lodgings is a massive peak called Wan-tiao shan, its face a sheer precipice of hard limestone, the summit and farther slopes apparently well forested. The people of this hamlet, like the country people everywhere in these parts, were extremely obliging, and it was a real pleasure to be amongst them.

Wan-tiao shan looked too tempting to be passed by without investigation, so we spent a day, and a very hard day too, in making its ascent and descent. Leaving our lodgings at 8 a.m., several hours were occupied in rounding the spurs and surmounting the cultivated and scrub-clad land which subtend the mountain proper. At 6000 feet we reached Bamboo scrub, and a path through this led to an area where medicinal Rhubarb was cultivated, and where the drug Tang-shen was extraordinarily abundant. At 6500 feet we entered a wood at the margin of which, and to the left of the road, are extensive plantations of the drug Huang-lien. This interesting plant (Coptis chinensis) is grown under a framework of brushwood reared some 3 to 4 feet above the ground. The drug is used as a tonic and blood-purifier.

As the path winds the trees are at first small, with plenty of Bamboo scrub, but this belt is very narrow and speedily gives place to large trees which extend to within 500 feet of the summit, where Bamboo scrub again becomes troublesome Everywhere above 5000 feet, where the woods are thin and sunlight penetrates freely, Bamboo scrub is found, making travel excessively arduous and, unless a path is cut, impossible. In the dense shade of the forest Bamboo does not thrive.

The forest, though full of splendid timber, is not rich in variety. A Beech (Fagus engleriana) is the commonest tree. This species always has many trunks, and trees from 60 to 70 feet high, with stems from 3 to 6 feet in girth, abound. The interesting Tetracentron sinense is very abundant; trees 60 to 70 feet by 8 to 10 feet girth are plentiful. The leafage of this tree is very thin and characteristic. Large trees of white Birch and of several species of Maple occur scattered through the forest. The smooth-leaved Davidia (D. involucrata Vilmoriniana) occurs

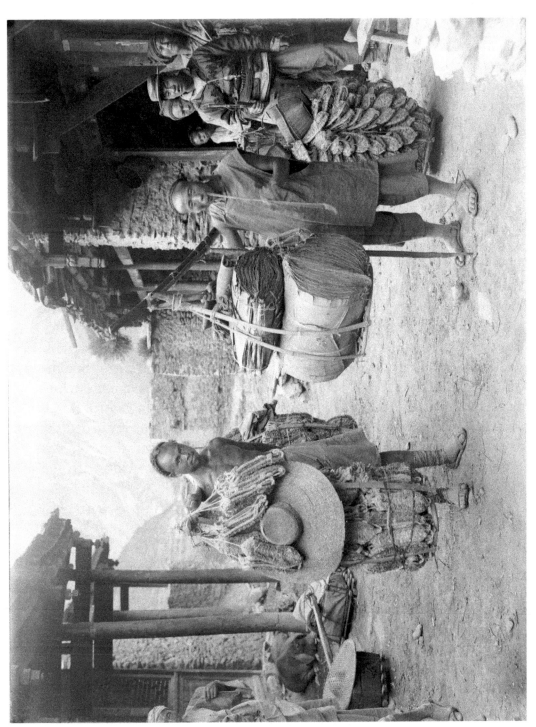

PEDDLERS IN THE MIN VALLEY

sparingly, and good-sized trees of various Cherries, Birdcherries, Mountain Ash, and wild Pear are common. Rambling over the tops of the largest trees is Berchemia giraldiana. Several species of Rhododendron occur; one species (R. sutchuenense) forms a tree 30 feet tall with a trunk 5 feet in girth. Shrubs in variety abound; in the glades Viburnum tomentosum was wreathed in snow-white flowers. In more open places Musk Roses are rampant, and near the summit Rosa omeiensis is abundant.

The summit forms a sloping, undulating flat, about an acre in extent, covered with grass and a few shrubs. On the apex stands a small temple now partly in ruins. A sharp, rocky ridge extends from the summit, linking the mountain up with the ranges to the northward. The face on two sides is a vertical precipice, 2000 feet and more sheer. From the summit, alt. 7850 feet, we got an extensive view of the surrounding country. Nothing but mountains on every side; to the north and northwest these are heaped one beyond another in quick succession and are separated by narrow defiles down which torrents rush and roar. Very difficult looked the country in front of us, but the call of the unknown was strong. We descended by the same devious path, indeed, there is no other, and reached our lodgings as darkness overtook us. Specimens of some forty odd different plants rewarded the day's labor, several of them new and uncommonly interesting. On the extreme summit Boxwood is a common shrub, and growing with it I discovered a new species of Lilac (Syringa julianae).

The following day we continued our journey north-ward. Just beyond Peh-yang-tsai we passed through copses of small Oak (Quercus variabilis), where the Jew's-ear fungus is cultivated. The culture is as follows: Oak sap-lings, about 6 inches thick, are cut down, trimmed of their branches, and cut into staves 8 to 10 feet long. These are allowed to lie on the ground for several months, where they become infested with the mycelium of the fungus. They are then stacked slantingly in scores or thereabout, and the fructifications of the fungus develop. These are ear-shaped and gelatinous and are by the Chinese esteemed a delicacy. I tried them, but did not find them very palatable, and the experiment resulted in a bad stomach-ache!

A QUEST OF FLOWERS

On leaving these plantations the road descends to a ravine along which it meanders for a mile or two. Many shrubs were in flower in the ravine, and I gathered amongst other plants specimens of a new genus, allied to Holbcellia, with fragrant yellow flowers. I subsequently secured seeds of this plant, since named Sargentodoxa cuneata, and succeeded in introducing it into cultivation. At the head of this ravine a steep ascent through woods of Oak and Birch leads to a cultivated area where there are two or three scattered houses and many Tea bushes. Near one house the Chinese Coffee-tree (Gymnocladus chinensis) occurs; the pods of this tree are saponaceous and are esteemed for laundry purposes.

From the Tea plantations the road leads through Pine woods, now by an easy, now by a heavy grade, but always ascending, and we were all glad when our destination (Hsin-tientsze) was reached. Near this place are some fine old woods, rich in a variety of deciduous trees and shrubs. I noted a Horse-chestnut (Aesculus wilsonii), two kinds of Beech, Styrax hemsleyanum, Meliosma veitchiorum, the Davidia, and many different kinds of Maple and Oak—all of them large trees. On the margins of the woods Viburnum ichangense was particularly fine, and many Cherry trees, with both pink and white flowers, common. In moist shady places in the woods a blue Primrose (Primula ovalifolia) carpets the ground for miles. The yellow-flowered Stylophorum japonicum, an Epimedium, and various species of Corydalis are abundant in and near the woods.

The hamlet of Hsin-tientsze, alt. 5600 feet, consists of one rather large house. It is built on a slope a few hundred feet below the summit of the ridge, and from the front of the house a wonderful view of the surrounding country is afforded. Nothing but mountains as far as the eye can range, and not 20 square yards of level ground in sight! Our quarters, though cramped, were, all things considered, fairly comfortable, and as good as could be expected.

The next morning we made an early start in order to cover the 60 li between Hsin-tientsze and Mao-fu-lien. Immediately on leaving we traversed an old wood especially rich in species of Maple. Davidia and Beech are also common, whilst the interesting black-fruited

CHINA — MOTHER OF GARDENS

Cornus chinensis occurs sparingly as a thin tree 40 feet tall. Pinus armandi is present, but Conifers generally are very scarce in this particular locality.

We meandered around the mountain-side, by a tortuous ascending path, until we reached a gap in the ridge and crossing over made a breakneck descent of a couple of thousand feet. A new kind of Poplar, having the young foliage bronzy red, was common on all sides, and in the descent I gathered Primula violodora, Rhododendron augustinii, Acer griseum, and pink-flowered Staphylea holocarpa, the last two both small trees. The most interesting find, how-ever, was a new Hydrangea (H. sargentiana), a shrub 5 to 6 feet tall, with stems densely felted with short bristly hairs and large, dark green leaves with a velvety lustre—. in foliage alone this species is strikingly handsome.

At the foot of the descent we came upon a small woods of Pinus sinensis, a tree averaging 60 feet in height, more or less pyramidal in shape, with bark usually rough and black, but sometimes red in the upper parts. The cones vary considerably in size and are retained on the tree for several years. In the valley near the Pine woods there is considerable cultivation. Walnut trees are common and Cunninghamia abundant.

Leaving this valley, a long but fairly easy ascent led to the top of another ridge, and a precipitous descent brought us to another narrow valley. These ascents and descents were most fatiguing and occurred with exasperating frequency every day, and several times a day at that. Another climb of over 2000 feet and we reached our destination for the day, finding accommodation in an inn which is also a large medicine depot, and is owned by a wealthy man from the province of Kiangsi. This inn is a large, rambling two-storied structure with several outhouses and a large court-yard. There is not sufficient level space to accommodate the whole place, and the front part is supported on posts. It serves as general store for the whole country-side, and in addition is a veritable museum. Dirt in every shape and form draped everything, and the stink from adjacent piggeries was tempered by the odor of various aromatic herbs. The business instinct of the house is strong, as I found to my cost when changing some silver and buying a

HIGHWAY TO TACHIENLU, HERE BLASTED FROM SOLID ROCK

goat. The rites of ancestor-worship were strictly carried out every morning and evening, and everything done to ensure continued and increasing prosperity. The burning of incense and candles and the performance of mystical genuflexions may assist business, but a little more attention to cleanliness and sanitation would make a stronger appeal to the foreigner. At least, such were my conclusions after a thirty-six hours' stay in the place.

It rained a good part of the next day, but as we had decided upon a day's rest it did not inconvenience us. In the forenoon I went out for a few hours to investigate the woods around Mao-fu-lien. Some large trees of Sassafras (Sassafras tzumu) occur here—the largest is nearly 100 feet tall and 12 feet girth. The Chinese Sassafras has no medicinal value, and the wood is used for box-making and fuel only. Oak and a Sweet Chestnut are plentiful and form small woods. The Chestnut (Castanea henryi) is a curious species, with a single ovoid nut inside the spiny fruit; the flowers have a peculiarly unpleasant smell. Around the inn are cultivated many trees of the Hardy Rubber and of Magnolia officinalis. Walnut and Varnish trees are abundant, and behind the house is a fine flat-leaved Spruce (Picea brachytyla). The mountain-tops are clothed with Grass, Brambles, scrub Oak, bushes of the pink-flowered Rhododendron mariesii, and the scarlet R. simsii.

The view from the inn is one of steep ridges and high mountains, separated by deep, narrow chasms as far as the eye can range. It is indeed a fascinating country, but exhausting to travel over.

A fine morning followed yesterday's rain, the country looked refreshed, and the air was laden with fragrance from a myriad flowers on every side. The coolies grumbled loudly over the extortionate charges at the inn, and several hours elapsed before they recovered their cheerfulness. The day's journey commenced in a steady ascent to the top of a ridge followed by the usual precipitous descent. Hereabout Staphylea holocarpa, a small, very floriferous tree, with both white and pink flowers, is very common and most strikingly beautiful. Another interesting plant is Salix fargesii, a dwarf-growing Willow, having large dark green leaves. A small torrent marks the foot of the descent, and from this point on we were occupied for several hours in an exhausting climb to the summit of another ridge, finally crossing over at 7300 feet altitude. In the ascent a Spruce (Picea wilsonii) having short, quadrangular leaves and small cones, was discovered, and many small trees of Hemlock Spruce (Tsuga chinensis) were noted. Near the head of the ridge, on cliffs, Box (Buxus microphylla sinica) is very common, and a rosy red flowered Primrose is abundant in grassy places. A dwarf Bamboo forms dense thickets on the top of the wind-swept ridge.

The descent quickly leads into copses of Birch, and later into fine woods composed of mixed deciduous trees and shrubs and a few Conifers. In these woods we spent a profitable time, collecting in all specimens of some fifty different kinds of woody plants. We saw one or two large trees of Davidia and many of Tetracentron. Cherries in variety are plentiful, and were a wonderful sight nothing but masses of pink and white. Three kinds of Rhododendron were collected, and six in all noted. Maples in variety are very common, but one large tree of Acer griseum, with its cinnamon-red bark, exfoliating like that of the River Birch, was the gem of all. Various Pomaceae and one or two species of Lauraceae make up a fair percentage of the small trees. Viburnums in variety, Honeysuckles, Diervillas, Deutzias, Philadelphus, and Neillia sinensis are everywhere abundant. In rocky, more open places Viburnum rhytidophyllum with its long, thick wrinkled leaves looked particularly happy, and in exposed places a Crab-apple (Malus theifera) a wealth of pink and white flowers, was a sight for the gods. On wet, humus-clad rocks Pleione Henryi luxuriates, and herbs in endless variety crowd every available spot. A fine torrent collects the waters of countless smaller streams, and falls down the narrow ravine, often in a series of waterfalls hundreds of feet high, the noise of the falling water alone breaking the silence of the forest depths.

With some difficulty, owing to the timidity of the people, we obtained lodgings in a peasant's but at Wen-tsao, alt. 6150 feet. This tiny hamlet consists of four small houses, scattered and pitched on the steep mountain-slope. It is surrounded on all sides by precipitous mountains covered with forests. Around the houses small patches have been cleared, and wheat, a little maize, and a few peas and vegetables are cultivated.

CHINA — MOTHER OF GARDENS

The forests of this region are particularly rich, and in order to better appreciate them I propose to interpolate here extracts from my journal of another date:—

"May 30.—Wen-tsao. On a precipitous slope facing our lodgings a score or more Davidia trees occur; they are one mass of white, and are most conspicuous as the shades of night close in. Two large trees of Pterostyrax hispida are growing amongst these Davidias, and are laden with pendulous chains of creamy white flowers."

"May 31.—Go over and investigate the Davidia trees and the forests generally. Crossing a narrow neck, a wood-cutter's circuitous path leads us down to a narrow defile through a fine shady wood. Ascending a precipice with difficulty, we soon reach the Davidia trees. There are over a score of them growing on a steep, rocky declivity; they vary from 35 to 60 feet in height, and the largest is 6 feet in girth. Being in a dense wood they are bare of branches for half their height, but their presence is readily detected by the numerous white bracts which have fallen and lie strewn over the ground. The tree sprouts from below when felled; indeed, it naturally throws up small stems after it gets old. The bark is dark and scales off in small, irregular flakes. By climbing a large Tetracentron tree growing on the edge of a cliff and chopping off some branches to make a clear space, I manage to take some snapshots of the upper part of the Davidia tree in full flower. A difficult task and highly dangerous. Three of us climb the tree to different heights and haul up axe and camera from one to another by means of a rope. The wood of Tetracentron is brittle, and the knowledge of this does not add to one's peace of mind when sitting astride a branch about 4 inches thick with a sheer drop of a couple of hundred feet beneath. However, all went well, and we drank in the beauties of this extraordinary tree. The distinctive beauty of Davidia is in the two snow-white connate bracts which subtend the flower proper. These are always unequal in size, the larger usually 6 inches long by 3 inches broad, and the smaller 3 ½ inches by 2 ½ inches; they range up to 8 inches by 4 inches and 5 inches by 3 inches. At first greenish, they become pure white as the flowers mature and change to brown with age. The flowers and their attendant bracts are pendulous on fairly long stalks, and when stirred

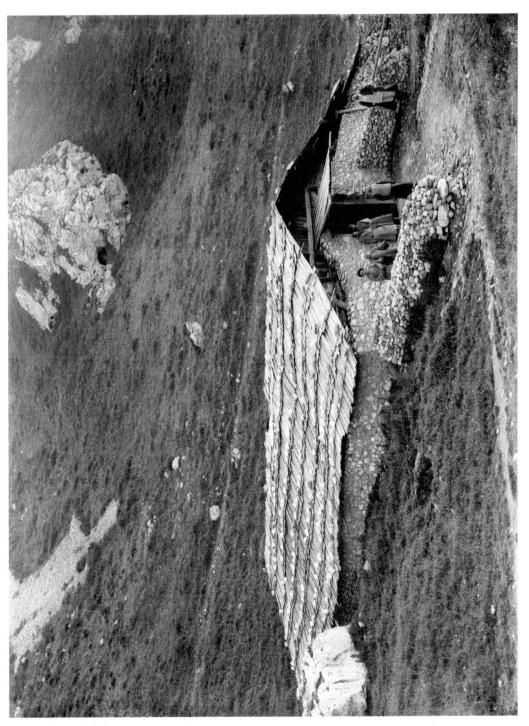

MY LODGINGS ON THE HSUEH SHAN PASS

by the slightest breeze they resemble small doves hovering among the trees. The bracts are somewhat boat-shaped and flimsy in texture, and the leaves often hide them considerably, but so freely are they borne that the tree looks, from a short distance, as if flecked with snow. On dull days and in the early morning and evening the bracts are most conspicuous. The fruit superficially resembles a small walnut, but the inner shell is absolutely unbreakable. To my mind Davidia involucrata is the most interesting and beautiful of all trees of the north temperate flora.

"With the Davidia is a good-sized tree of the Horse-chestnut (Aesculus wilsonii), 50 feet in height by 4 feet in girth. Higher up Hornbeam and Tetracentron are common, and Birch, white, red, and black, luxuriate.

"Maples are a feature of these woods; all are tall trees, but of no great thickness. Unfortunately very few are flowering, and indeed this is true of the forest trees generally this year.

"Perhaps the commonest tree in these forests is the Beech; parts being formed entirely of these trees. So light-demanding are they that they suffer no competitors or even undergrowth. For the first time it is possible for me to say definitely that two distinct species of Beech exist in this region. One forms a tree with a single trunk, the other always has several trunks. The former species has glabrous, shining green leaves, a large, dense, much-branched head; it makes a tree 40 to 50 feet high with a trunk 5 to 10 feet in girth, and, save for its smaller stature, very strongly resembles the European Beech. This has been named Fagus lucida. The second species is F. engleriana, which grows much taller, but never attains the girth of the other. It generally has six to twelve trunks, averaging 2 to 5 feet in girth, arising closely together and slanting away from one another as they grow. The bark is light gray and the leaves sub-glaucous and hairy below; branches somewhat ascending but with the young branchlets slender and pendulus. A local name for the Beech is Peh Litzu. Small plants are common, but no flowers are to be discovered.[1]

"In the shade of trees, Ribes longeracemosum Wilsonii, a remarkable Black Currant, with racemes 1 to 1 ½ feet long, is common,

[1] In 1910 I succeeded in introducing young plants of these and of a third species (F. longintiolata) into cultivation from this region.

48

while Rodgersia aesculifolia, with large, erect, thyrsoid panicles of white flowers is rampant.

"Five species of Oak, three deciduous and two ever-green, occur. Meliosma veitchiorum and many species of Pomace and Cherries are common, whilst the Varnish tree is everywhere abundant. In dense shade various ever-green Barberries occur, and in open country Neillia sinensis forms dense thickets.

"Of Conifers, Pinus armandi and P. sinensis are scattered over the cliffs; Picea wilsonii and a flat-leaved Spruce (P. brachytyla) are rare, whilst the Hemlock Spruce (Tsuga chinensis) is fairly common on the cliffs—neat, dense trees of no great size with their young leaves just unfolding and old cones abundant. The White Pine (P. armandi) is more common higher up on the mountains; with its long needles, graceful port, and light gray bark this tree is strikingly handsome; the cones are pendulous, borne at the ends of the glabrous branches. The very resinous wood is used locally for torches, burning with a clear, bright flame, and giving a good light."

CHAPTER VI

FOREST AND CRAG

ACROSS THE HUPEH-SZECHUAN FRONTIER

O N leaving Wen-tsao a sharp descent for a couple of hours brought us to the upper waters of the Hsingshan River, which we left several days ago. Crossing this stream by a covered bridge we reached the hamlet of Li-erh-kou, around which trees of the Hardy Rubber (Eucommia ulmoides) and Magnolia officinalis (Hou-p'o) are cultivated for their bark. A steady ascent from Li-erh-kou through occasional woods of Oak and Birch, interrupted by areas where people were busy ploughing the fields and sowing maize, brought us to the hamlet of Chin-tien-po, where we lunched. Near this place is a fine new Meliosma (M. beaniana), a tree 60 feet high. It was leafless, but one mass of creamy white flowers borne in pendulous panicles. Near by this tree I discovered one small specimen of Judas tree (Cercis racemosa). Prior to this discovery I knew of only two trees some fifteen days' journey southwest of Ichang. This new tree was about 25 feet high, with a stem half decayed through at the base, and a mop-like head. In spite of its partial decay the tree appeared in vigorous health, and was one mass of silvery rose-colored flowers, borne in short racemes. The leaves of this species are hairy below. Varnish and Walnut trees occur in abundance, and we met several coolies laden with cakes of fat, expressed from the fruits of the Varnish tree (Rhus verniciflua). The double-flowered form of Spiraea prunifolia is commonly planted on graves, and the bushes were wreathed in flowers.

Soon after leaving Chin-tien-po we commenced a precipitous ascent, and after climbing for several miles reached the neck of a ridge where Viburnum rhytidophyllum luxuriates. From this neck the ascent is more gradual, and but few crops are grown, as it is nearing the limits of cultivation in these regions. Near some limestone cliffs are two magnificent trees of Maackia chinensis, each 65 feet tall and 7 feet in girth. The bark of this tree is smooth, of a gray-green color, and the unfolding leaves are silvery gray. Here, too, are numerous small trees of Staphylea holocarpa and Peach bushes. These were in full flower, and flitting amongst the flowers and drinking in the honey were many beautiful little sun-birds (Aethopyga dabryi). Azalea simsii was left behind at 5500 feet altitude.

A few hundred yards beyond the limestone cliffs we crossed over at 7000 feet altitude, into Fang Hsien, and traversed a narrow moorland valley clothed with grass and bounded by rounded hills covered with thickets. In this moorland are acres of Astilbe davidii and A. grandis, with several Senecios and other ornamental herbs. The thickets are composed chiefly of Birch and Willow, with a few Poplar and Silver Fir, and an occasional flat-leaved Spruce. The vegetation was scarcely in leaf, and it was evident from the appearance of the ground that snow had only just melted away. We flushed a solitary snipe and secured a cock pheasant for the larder, but very little life of any sort was visible in these uplands. At the head of this moorland valley we entered a narrow defile and, after skirting the side of a mountain through thickets in which various Maples and Currants were prominent, reached Hung-shih-kou. This is a miserable hut of wood in a half-ruinous condition, kept by a family clothed in rags. It is situated at an altitude of 6300 feet, by the side of a considerable torrent, and is walled in by precipitous, well-wooded mountains.

At night some of the coolies slept in a loft above the room I occupied, and every movement they made caused dust and dirt to fall over my bed. On waking in the morning I found myself covered with this filth, and nearly choked with the dust into the bargain. The owner of this hovel is a hunter, and he has shot the serow of this region, which is known as "Ming-tsen Yang." He had a couple of pairs of horns and a flat skin which we secured, and, judging from this fragmentary material, the beast must be larger than any known species. (In 1907 my associate, Mr. Walter R. Zappey, made several trips after this animal, but to no purpose, though he secured a tantalizing glimpse of just one specimen).

The name Hung-shih-kou signifies "Red stone mouth," and has reference to the outcropping of red standstone which occurs here and extends to Hsao-lung-tang, 20 li distant, which we made our halting-place for the next day. Though we had only 20 li to cover we started early, glad to escape from the miserable lodgings into the woods again. Ascending a stream, through brushwood thickets composed of Willow, Birch, Spiraea, and Roses, we twice crossed the stream by rotten bridges of roughly hewn tree-logs before reaching our destination. On the way we passed several fine trees of Picea Wilsonii, beneath which old graves nestle.

The largest trees are about 70 feet tall and 6 feet in girth; the leaves bright green, and the habit distinctly stately; the cones are borne in large clusters, and many still remained on the trees. Here also are small trees of the White Pine (Pinus armandi) with cones 9 inches long. A new Poplar (Populus wilsonii) was discovered in flower, and Veitch's Viburnum and Spiraea were common with their young leaves just unfolding. The handsomest tree in these parts is, however, Betula albo-sinensis, a Birch with orange red bark, which on exfoliating exposes the glaucous waxy bloom of the layer below. Trees 40 feet high are still pyramidal in habit, much branched, with slender, ascending branches on which the lenticels are very prominent. The older trees, as seen on the tops of the mountains, are mop-headed, 60 to 80 feet tall, with a clean trunk for 40 feet more, and are still strikingly handsome though blown and battered by the wind.

The hamlet of Hsao-lung-tang (Small Dragon-pool), alt. 7400 feet, consists of two dilapidated wooden huts pitched on opposite sides of a lovely burn, which flows through a narrow sloping valley lying almost due east and west. This valley is flanked by steep ridges clad only with grass and scrub. Odd patches of Birch and Silver Fir attest to forests which have been all destroyed by fire. From the numerous old graves and abandoned fields it is evident that formerly more people dwelt in this valley than do so to-day. Tiny patches of cabbage and Irish potato occur around the huts; and also plantations of Tan-kuei

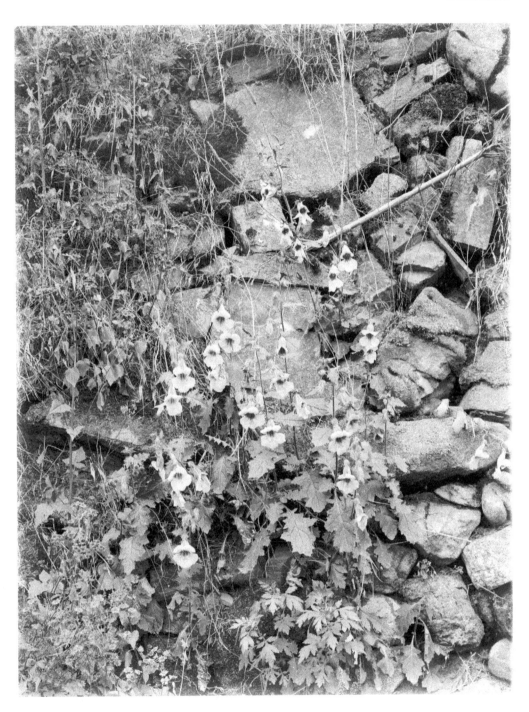

REHMANNIA ANGULATA

CHINA — MOTHER OF GARDENS

(Angelica polymorpha sinensis), a valued Chinese medicine. The people declare the valley too cold for wheat or barley.

On the occasion of my first visit to this place in 1901, and again in 1907, I had to retrace my steps owing to dearth of supplies. Since then no white man had visited this region. In the direction in which we were bound these are the last inhabited houses for over a hundred li.

I took a photograph of the hostel on my arrival, but what I should have liked to photograph was the interior. This was impossible, since, even at midday, a light was necessary to see into the farthest corners. Dirt and filth in many forms abounded, and although plenty of timber is to be had for the felling, the house, through the idleness of its owner, has been allowed to fall into a most ruinous state. Of one low story, the house is partitioned into four compartments, and is provided with no outlet for the smoke or for the ingress of light, save through the doorway and holes in the roof; the floor, of course, is mother earth. Pigs were quartered in one section, into which our arrival also forced the owners. Cows and goats occupied a hovel 6 feet from the door, the floor of which was fully a foot deep in filth. Luckily, the weather continued gloriously fine, and the surroundings were less miserable in consequence. (In passing, I might record the fact that this was the only occasion on which I enjoyed fine weather in this place. Twice previously I had been marooned here for days, and either stayed in bed or shivered by the doorway watching the rain.)

Bee-keeping is one of the principal industries of the peasants in these wilds, and around this hostel are scores of bee-hives. The hives are hollowed-out logs of Silver Fir, about 3 feet 6 inches long by 1 foot wide, two pieces of wood fixed crosswise in the centre, and opposite these three or four holes bored to allow the bees ingress and egress. Rude boxes often take the place of these logs. The beeswax is not separated from the honey, the honeycomb being eaten as removed from the hives. Though the climate is rigorous, the bees are healthy and strong, and disease is unknown among them.

The morning following our arrival we ascended the Sha-mu-jen range behind our lodgings. The first 500 feet was steep going, but afterwards the climb was easy. At about 8000 feet woods of Silver Fir

FOREST AND CRAG

(Abies fargesii) occur. The trees at first are of no great size, but their dimensions increased as we ascended. Most of the larger trees have been felled and converted into coffins; the remains of thousands of them are scattered everywhere around. On the decayed trunks of many of these trees large bushes of Rhododendron are growing, thereby proving that the trees have lain there these many years past. Some of the prostrate trunks measured over 130 feet in length and 6 feet in diameter. None of this size is now standing, but plenty that are over 100 feet tall occur. The upper part of the ridge is a cliff some 200 feet high, under the lee of which Birch and Maple are common and wild Rhubarb is also found. We discovered a more or less easy path up the cliff, and crossed over at 9700 feet altitude. The highest peak in this range is probably a couple of hundred feet higher. The summit is of hard limestone with rare outcroppings of red sandstone. Stunted wind-swept Silver Fir and various kinds of Currant extend to the summit. Rhododendron and a dwarf Juniper (J. squamata) are also common. The descent was through woods of Birch and Bamboo to an open, grassy, scrub-clad, sloping moorland, through which a considerable torrent flows. The Bamboo, so common here-about, is very beautiful, forming clumps 3 to 10 feet through. The culms are 5 to 12 feet tall, golden yellow, with dark, feathery foliage; the young culms have broad sheathing bracts protecting the branchlets. Taken all in all, this is the handsomest Bamboo I have seen. In 1910 I successfully introduced it into cultivation. It has been named Arundinaria murielae in compliment to my daughter, Muriel.

In the vicinity of the stream shrubs in great variety abound; of these the Willows, Roses, Spiraeas, Philadelphus, Hydrangeas, odd bushes of Rhododendron fargesii, and clumps of Aralia chinensis are the principal features. The Rhododendron referred to is one of the most beautiful, with compact trusses of white or, more commonly, rosy red (occasionally deep red) flowers; the leaves are small, displaying the trusses of flowers to great advantage. This species is usually a bush 5 to 8 feet tall, and of about the same dimensions through the head; more rarely it is 15 to 20 feet high. The steep grassy slopes are almost devoid of trees; the fine pasture land and the typical moorland character of this narrow valley constitute a region that is very different from all others in central China.

In the afternoon we visited Ta-lung-tang (Large dragon-pool), a deep, silent pond about a stone's throw across, nearly circular in outline with reedy margins, walled in by steep grassy mountain-slopes. In short, in situation and appearance the very kind of pool that in any country legends would be wrapped around, and so in this case many curious stories concerning elves and demons are centred round this water. The day was gloriously fine and sunny, but the wind, which swept through the valley in considerable force, was very cold. Whether it be due to local conditions or to the altitude I could not determine, but the tree flora is comparatively poor and of little interest, and very unlike the belts that occur between 4000 and 6500 feet. The altitude, however, favors coarse herbs, and these are rampant. Many interesting shrubs also occur, but with the exception of Silver Fir, Birch, and Poplar, trees are rare.

With a prospect of 60 li of unknown road before us we planned a daylight start, but this scheme did not mature, as the men had to prepare and cook their morning meal before starting. The entire absence of food supplies makes travelling hereabout extraordinarily difficult. Yesterday four of the men journeyed back 45 li in order to buy food-stuffs, and returned only after dark; several of them were up most of the night grinding maize and preparing cakes for the march.

On leaving Hsao-lung-tang we ascended the lesser branch of a stream through a narrow valley flanked by bare grassy mountains having here and there small patches of Silver Fir and Birch forest. The road is one steady climb, never steep but often difficult owing to the Bamboo scrub. The decaying stumps and stark tree-trunks speak eloquently of the magnificent forests which must have formerly existed here until destroyed by axe and fire. To the botanist and lover of Nature this vandalism is painful, but presumably it was necessary for economic reasons. The unwitting cause of it all has been the Irish potato. But Nature took her revenge when the potato disease devastated the crop and ruined the country-side, causing a general exodus of all the people. Nature is fast reclaiming the whole region, but reafforestation is a slow

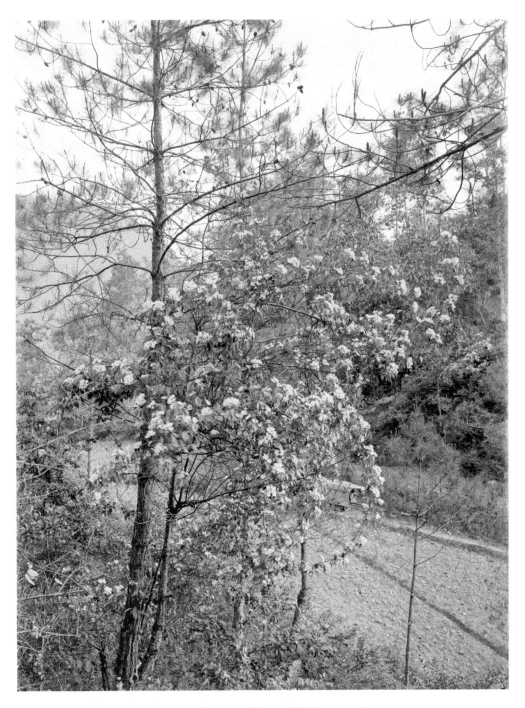

MUSK ROSE (ROSA HELENAE)

process.

Nearing the head of the pass we entered a fragment of the virgin forest, composed exclusively of large trees of Silver Fir and Birch with a dense undergrowth of Rhododendron. The last named comprise four species R. fargesii, R. maculiferum, R. sutchuenense, and R. adenopodum, most of them bushes 10 to 20 feet tall, their flowers making one blaze of color. The Silver Fir (Abies fargesii) and Birch trees (Betula albo-sinensis) are of huge dimensions, but none was fruiting. On emerging from this patch of forest we entered a rolling moorland covered with Bamboo scrub which merges gradually into areas clad with the dwarf Juniper, coarse grasses, and herbs, amongst which a species of Onion was abundant. This moorland extends across the rounded saddle of the range and for several miles down the other side. The crest of the saddle I made 9500 feet altitude, and from this point we obtained a fine view of the series of bare, savagely jagged peaks from which the range (Sheng-neng-chia) takes its name. The highest peaks probably exceed 11,000 feet altitude, and the lower slopes are forested, but the country is not attractive. Animal life is remarkable by its absence, and hardly a bird was to be seen. The solitude which reigned in this remote, inaccessible region was broken only by the noise of rushing waters and the low whining of the wind amongst the tree-tops. In shady places blocks of ice still remained, and about the head of the pass the grass was only just beginning to show green. Save for an alpine Primula and a Dandelion no flowers of any sort were to be seen.

On crossing the pass we again entered Hsingshan Hsien, and after wandering across moorland for a few miles a short steep ascent led us across a lateral spur into Patung Hsien. From this point a precipitous descent of 2000 feet brought us to a ruined and deserted but at a place called Wapeng, the only accommodation the country-side affords. In the descent we passed hundreds of curious rock-stacks—bare blocks of shale standing erect, with acute edges, like gaunt sentinels guarding the neighborhood. The mountain-side was formerly under cultivation, but is now abandoned and covered with grass and coarse herbs. Around the hut a little medicinal Rhubarb and much Tang-shen was growing, telling of former plantations of these and other medicines. The country on all sides is very steep and much cut up, but stark decaying tree-trunks, the sole remnants of former forests, mar the beauty of the landscape on all sides.

We reached Wapeng, alt. 8400 feet, fairly early in the afternoon, and the men were busy till nightfall collecting fuel and rigging up a bamboo shelter beneath which to pass the night. The day had been gloriously fine and the night proved equally so, with a distinctly frosty nip after sundown. A roaring fire made things look cheerful, and everybody was in the best of health and spirits. The sides of the but were airy and the wind played about one all night. The roof was partially wanting and afforded a good view of the starry heavens above. It was a lonely place, yet one felt peculiarly happy and glad to be privileged to visit a region so remote from the world in general.

There was no difficulty in getting the men up next morning, and we were off just as the sun's rays broke over the landscape. Dark mists obscured the view for an hour or so, but as the sun rose these disappeared and we enjoyed another gloriously fine day. A steep and precipitous, nay breakneck, descent of 1000 feet brought us to a narrow well-wooded valley, walled in by forest-clad mountains. The Silver Fir does not descend more than 500 feet from Wapeng, below which its place is taken by Hemlock Spruce. This tree (Tsuga chinensis) is not plentiful, but giants 80 feet tall by 12 feet in girth occur. The forests as we descended quickly became of mixed character, and finally Conifers completely disappeared. The variety of trees and shrubs was astonishing, and nearly all the more interesting trees of western Hupeh were to be found and in quantity. Maples are particularly abundant, and I gathered specimens of a dozen species in flower. Four species of Rhododendron occur scattered, but not in quantity. On rocks in places an interesting Orchid (Pleione henryi) abounds and was one mass of flowers. The Davidia is fairly plentiful, and the curious Euptelea franchetii and Tetracentron sinense are common trees. A feature in these woods was Staphylea holocarpa, a small tree covered with pendulous trusses of white and rosy pink flowers. A Horse-chestnut (Aesculus wilsonii), Chinese Yellow-wood (Cladrastis wilsonii), Hemsley's Styrax, and Pterostyrax hispida, all of them large trees, were fairly frequent; Cherries, Birdcherries, and many Pomacea abound. Birch is one of the commonest constituents of these forests; in the more open areas Bamboo scrub forms dense thickets, and high up in the woods Rhododendron maculiferum forms trees 25 feet tall with a trunk 1 foot in diameter.

Here and there clearings have been made for the cultivation of the medicine Huang-lien (Coptis chinensis). In one abandoned clearing were hundreds of Lilium tigrinum luxuriating amongst the grass and tall herbs. In dark shady places the noble Lilium giganteum yunnanense is common. This Lily has tubular snow-white flowers spotted with red within, and glossy green, cordate leaves. An occasional Spruce or Pine tree occurs, and at the edge of the forests Cunninghamia appears. Many of the cliffs are clothed with Hemlock Spruce. Birch is fairly common, but with the exception of one or two evergreen species, Oak is very scarce. Hornbeam is not plentiful and Magnolias are decidedly rare trees; Ash is general, and the Linden, represented by three or four species, abundant. The Laurel family is represented by four species, all of them deciduous, including a handsome kind with young foliage of a bronze-red. Honeysuckles are rare, save for the climbing species Lonicera tragophylla, which has golden yellow flowers. Clematis in variety are common, especially C. montana (white and rosy red forms) and C. pogonandra with its top-shaped yellow flowers. Several species of Schisandra, all of them a wealth of flowers, Holboellia fargesii, and the botanically interesting Sinofranchetia sinensis are the principal climbers.

The road follows the course of a torrent which rises near Wapeng and quickly becomes a considerable stream. The path is narrow, very rocky, and difficult to follow, and how our chairs got through was a puzzle. Both torrent and path ultimately plunge into a narrow ravine shut in by lofty cliffs, unclimbable and bare. In places the rocks are of lime-stone, but from 5000 feet downwards slate and mud-shale predominate.

At 4500 feet altitude we reached the edge of the forest and entered a cultivated area, where there are a few inhabited houses—the first we had seen for two days. Barley and Irish potato are the crops.

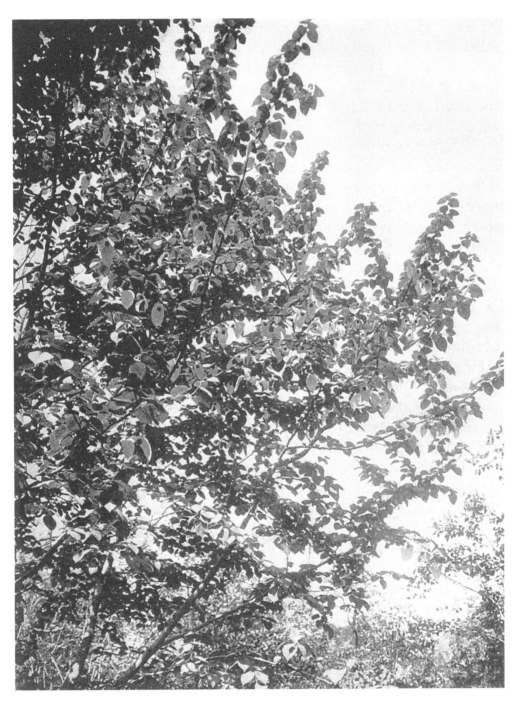

Davidia involucrata in Blossom

CHINA — MOTHER OF GARDENS

Near the edge of the forest the torrent flows underground for about a mile. On rocks here Lonicera pileata abounds as a fluviatile shrub; the curious climber Hosiea sinensis is common, covering rocks fully exposed to the sun. In the open country I noted in full flower a fine specimen of the Chinese Tulip-tree (Liriodendron chinense), 70 feet tall and 5 feet in girth.

A precipitous descent, through fields margined with Tea bushes, led to the tiny hamlet of Sha-kou-ping, where the torrent we had followed joins with a very considerable stream flowing down from the northeast. The united waters plunge at once into a ravine and finally enter the Yangtsze a few miles above the city of Patung. Sha-kou-ping is only 2600 feet above sea-level, and is hemmed in on all sides by lofty cliffs. The flora is that common to the glens and gorges around Ichang, and the wealth of flowers was extraordinary. The Banksian Rose is one of the commonest shrubs hereabout, and was laden with masses of fragrant white flowers. Opium Poppy was abundant and the whole country-side was gay with the color of flowers. Styrax veitchiorurn occurs here, and trees 20 to 40 feet tall were garlanded with ivory-white blossoms.

From Sha-kou-ping we toiled slowly up the rocky ravine down which the main stream rushes. A paper-mill or two are located here, but houses are few and far between. The rocks are of slate shales, often very rotten, and the torrent is a succession of rapids and cataracts. In spite of the turbulent nature of its waters it is full of fish, some of them of good size.

The hamlet of Ma-hsien-ping, our intended destination, proved to be a miserable place of some half a dozen hovels all filled with people engaged in collecting tea. We therefore journeyed on for another 10 li to some farmhouses at Shui-ting-liangtsze, and arrived just as the sun was setting behind the range. We found accommodation in a large farmhouse, alt. 3900 feet. The day's journey proved very arduous, but there was much by way of compensation. The scenery was sublime and the flora wonderfully rich and varied. In all I gathered specimens of upward of fifty new kinds of woody plants, many of them previously unknown. This region is one of the richest I have visited, and I subsequently secured a fine haul of seeds, the great majority of the plants raised from them being now found growing and thriving in many gardens of America and Europe. (Later I again traversed this same region, and owing to heavy rains was over a week in covering the country between Hsao-lung-tang and Shui-ting-liangtsze, a flooded torrent holding us up for three consecutive days).

It was nearly midnight when all was quiet last night, the men being loud in their grumbling against taking the road to Taning Hsien instead of that to Wushan Hsien. The reports we had heard indicated a bad time ahead for all of us and for the men in particular, owing to the extreme poverty of the country-side. I heard them as I lay in bed, but no complaints were brought to me.

It was later than usual when we got away in the morning. After a steep ascent we meandered along the mountain-side, and ultimately crossed over into Fang Hsien again by a low pass, alt. 5600 feet. This is the real watershed of the Han and Yangtsze river systems. The Sheng-neng-chia is a gigantic spur thrust out from the backbone of the chain, and the streams which take their rise from three sides of this spur flow down to the Yangtsze. From the watershed we had a good view of the Sheng-neng-chia peaks bearing E.S.E., and of some equally lofty mountains to the east, evidently in the vicinity of the Yangtsze itself. On both sides of the watershed is a rather broad cultivated valley bounded by razor-edged hills clothed with woods of Oak and Pine. Varnish trees abound on the edges of the fields and Walnut trees are also common. Farmhouses are scattered over the country-side, and the crow of the pheasant, the coo of the wood pigeon, and the notes of the cuckoo were heard on all sides. By the wayside are many fine trees of Sweet Chestnut and Magnolia, and one very fine specimen of Corylus chinensis, 120 feet tall and 12 feet in girth. Many medicines are cultivated hereabout, more especially Rhubarb and Tang-shen. Populus lasiocarpa, with huge handsome foliage, is one of the commonest trees.

After a few miles the cultivated valley ends and we entered a narrow defile flanked by steep, well-wooded mountains. Hereabout the interesting Sinowilsonia henryi is common, forming a small, bushy tree with handsome foliage and long, pendulous racemes of inconspicuous flowers. The most ornamental tree, however, is a fine Crab-apple (Malus baccata mandshurica), which was laden with umbels of pure white fragrant flowers borne on long slender stalks. Issuing from this defile we entered a small cultivated flat and found lodgings at the hamlet of Pien-chin, alt. 5200 feet.

The vegetation during the day's journey was not very remarkable, though I added sixteen kinds of plants to the collection. Noteworthy on the rocks and cliffs was Viburnum rhytidophyllum, with its large flat corymbs of dirty white flowers, which are not very pleasing to the nostril. The defile was rich in shrubs, amongst which various Rhododendrons were prominent; Azalea simsii was common and Rosa omeiensis was just opening its flowers. All day Oak woods were common, but these never contain much that is of more than passing interest. In abandoned cultivated areas a small Poppy, resembling the common Iceland Poppy, with deep yellow (occasionally orange) flowers was abundant and attractive. In shady places the large yellow flowers of Chelidonium lasiocarpum made a fine show, and common on bare limestone cliffs are Corydalis wilsonii and C. tomentosa, both species with yellow flowers and glaucous foliage. Around our lodgings there was much cultivation, maize, barley, pulse, and the Irish potato being the principal crops. Several paper-mills occur by the side of the stream, bamboo pulp being the raw material from which the paper is made.

On leaving Pien-chin we followed a river to a point where it is joined by a tributary stream which we crossed and then ascended the road which skirts its banks. This stream is gentle for a Hupeh torrent, and for 10 li the road is of the easiest. The mountain-sides are covered with shrubs and trees, among which Cercidiphyllum was conspicuous. Occasional houses and small patches of cultivation occur, but the country generally is very sparsely peopled. Populus lasiocarpa is abundant and large branches are commonly driven in the ground to make fences; these branches take root and form groves. A magnificent tree of Ailanthus Vilmoriniana, 150 feet tall and 20 feet in girth, was passed, and I was astonished at the huge size of this specimen. Tangled masses of Actinidia chinensis and various kinds of wild Roses were

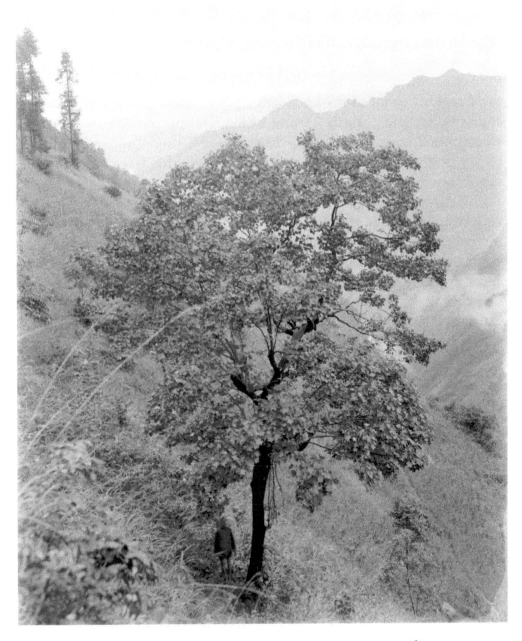

CHINESE TULIP-TREE (LIRIODENDRON CHINENSE), 60 FEET TALL

everywhere abundant, filling the air with soft fragrance. Leaving this delightful mountain stream we made a steep ascent of 900 feet and then, to our great surprise, entered a broad level valley. This valley was evidently in earlier times a mountain lake—to-day the margins are cultivated and the centre is a marsh. The whole district is known as Chu-ku-ping or Ta-chu-hu—the latter name having reference to its former condition as a lake. A flat area of this character is unique in these regions, as far as my knowledge goes. Several roads cross this fiat and we took the one for Taning Hsien. By the wayside strawberries, white and red, luxuriate and were very good eating. Quite a number of horses and cattle were grazing in the valley, and the country could support many more.

After meandering some 15 li over the easiest of roads we made a very steep and fatiguing ascent to alt. 7300 feet, and crossed over into the province of Szechuan. From the neck of the divide, looking away E.S.E., we obtained a good view of the Sheng-neng-chia and the main and subsidiary ranges and peaks—nothing but mountains on every side save the tiny valley at our feet which we had just crossed. In the ascent we passed many shrubs in full flower; particularly striking were the various kinds of Viburnum, Deutzia, Abelia, and Cornus. A precipitous descent through a ravine and we reached the hostel at Hwa-kuo-ling, alt. 6350 feet, where plantations of Rhubarb were common and several other medicinal plants cultivated.

The road we were following is called the great salt road, but we met only four men carrying salt in the day's march. Indeed, on the whole journey we encountered virtually no traffic. This mountainous country supports only a very sparse population and foreign trade has no chance hereabout. Our great difficulty was in securing enough food for the men. At Chu-ku-ping we managed to get one good meal from the local head-man and bought portions of a wild pig recently killed. At the hostel nothing was obtainable and the men had to eke out on the small rations they had with them. Goitre is common in these regions and nearly everyone is affected. It would seem to be hereditary, since I notice children in arms showing unmistakable swellings in the throat.

Boisterous winds and heavy clouds alternating with bright

FOREST AND CRAG

sunshine marked our first day's journey in eastern Szechuan. We were again amongst cliffs of hard limestone and the scenery strikingly resembles that of the Yangtsze gorges and contiguous country. The whole region is too steep for cultivation, and habitations are few and far between and most dilapidated in character. The soil is stiff, clayey loam and the few crops we saw were wheat, rye (Secale fragile), Irish potato, maize, and pulse. The cliffs are for the most part well timbered, and the common trees and shrubs of Hupeh are represented. Pinus armandi is very abundant and P. henryi is also common. Odd trees of Spruce and Hemlock also occur. A fine specimen of Acer griseum, 60 feet tall, 7 feet in girth, with curious cinnamon-red papery bark was the feature of the day's march; unfortunately, it was badly situated for photographing. Beech, Yellow-wood, and Dipteronia sinensis were common trees en route.

The road is one long succession of ascents and descents and most fatiguing. In the afternoon, after a particularly trying ascent, we wandered for an hour or so through woods of Oak (chiefly Quercus variabilis and Q. aliena) and Sweet Chestnut (Castanea mollissima) the latter laden with its white, evil-smelling flowers. Walnut and Varnish trees are everywhere abundant and Campanula punctata is a common weed of cultivation. No foreigner had ever before traversed this region and the people were very timid, locking up their houses and hiding themselves from view at our approach. The cliffs in this neighbourhood are full of caves and many of these are bricked up to form places of refuge in troublous times. We found lodgings for the night at Peh-kuo-yuen, alt. 3750 feet, in the house of the head-man of the hamlet. Foodstuffs were scarce and there was great difficulty in persuading the people to sell, and what little we did obtain was at famine prices.

The following morning we descended by a moderately easy path to a torrent and then commenced a heart-breaking ascent of some 2600 feet. It was excessively hot and I do not remember perspiring so much before. A rugged, precipitous, sparsely populated country is this, and I never wish to see it again. Limestone regions are magnificent from the scenic point of view, but for travelling over they are exhausting and arduous beyond words! Our destination was Hsao-pingtsze and no one knew the distance. Inquiries made as often as possible always elicited the same reply: "Seven or 8 li from Peh-kuo-yuen, 7 or 8 li to Hsao-ping-tsze." Late in the afternoon the distance to go increased to 30 li and did not shorten until we suddenly sighted the two huts which form the hamlet of Hsao-pingtsze!

The ascent was largely under cultivation, but the final stage was through jungle. Lonicera tragophylla is common and was in full flower, but we saw no good plants. A bush of Schizophragma integrifolium, one mass of the purest white, on the cliffs, was conspicuous from afar. But the flora generally is very ordinary, with Rhododendron discolor and R. mariesii common here and there. On reaching the top of the cliffs we entered a cultivated slope where Walnut and Varnish trees abound. The district is called Ta-ping-shan and consists of several scattered farmhouses surrounded by fields of maize, pulse, barley, and Irish potato. At one of these farmhouses my followers managed to secure a good meal and high spirits prevailed in consequence.

On leaving this place we continued to ascend by an easy path skirting rolling downs. A few scattered houses occur for a couple of miles but were mostly deserted, and we soon left all signs of cultivation and habitation behind us. The downs are treeless and clad mostly with grass and scattered bushes of Willow, Barberry, and Spiraea. The depressions between the hills were masses of blue Forget-me-not. The whole region would make excellent grazing ground for cattle. Crossing over at 7950 feet altitude, we descended by an easy road for a mile or so and passed a couple of huts surrounded by extensive plantations of medicinal Rhubarb. Many fine herbs luxuriate hereabout, and among them Iris wilsonii with its yellow flowers was conspicuous, covering large areas. Eventually we reached the edge of a precipice, down which the road fairly tumbles for 5 li to Hsao-pingtsze. This hamlet, as the name indicates, is situated on a tiny flat (probably caused by a landslide) and boasts two miserable, dilapidated houses. We took up lodgings in the smaller and presumably less squalid of the two, but there was little to choose between them in all consequence. On three sides the hamlet is walled in by steep cliffs and the fourth is the edge of

FOREST AND CRAG

a precipice itself. It was only some 30 yards from our but to the edge of this precipice, and the view from this point is one of the most extraordinary and wonderful my eyes have ever beheld. Below me (some 4000 feet the morrow proved) at an acute angle lay a small village with a considerable river flowing past it. Beyond this was range upon range of bare, treeless, sharp-edged ridges, averaging 5000 to 6000 feet in height, with outstanding higher peaks and grander ranges in the beyond. The rocks are mainly of limestone, white, gray, and reddish, giving a bizarre appearance to the whole scene. Never have I looked upon a wilder, more savage, and less inviting region. A storm was brewing and the light rapidly failing, making it impossible to take a photograph, though no photograph could have produced a picture that would give an adequate idea of the savage grandeur of the whole scene. It was indeed sufficient to awe and terrorize one. Such scenes sink deep into the memory and the impressive stillness produces an effect which is felt for many years afterwards. Soon the angry rain-clouds darkened and blotted out the whole scene and the next moment a thunderstorm burst over us. This storm lasted the night through and, the roof of our hovel being like a sieve, the rain soon converted the mud floor of the but into a quagmire. We huddled together and did what we could to keep dry and warm, but the night proved long and cheerless.

Soon after daybreak next morning we made our escape from these wretched quarters, but rain was still falling, and of the wonderful scene of the preceding evening nothing was visible from the gap but an ocean of clouds. The descent is most precipitous and for the first 2000 feet we fairly tumbled down. Afterwards it became more gradual and led over a steep cultivated slope of red clayey soil, making walking difficult. Nowhere is this descent easy, and very glad were we all that our route was down instead of up this mountain-side. At the foot of the descent the road leads through a rocky defile to emerge on the banks of a clear-water river some 60 yards broad. Across this we were ferried to Tan-chia-tien, the village we saw from near our lodgings last night. This village consists of some fifty houses which are huddled together and overhang the river in front and cling to the cliff behind in an extraordinary manner. From this village a kind of long street with houses scattered here and there along its length extends for 2 miles to the village of Chikou, situated at the junction of this river with another of almost equal size. A mile or so from Chikou up the secondary stream are the salt wells of Tan-ing-ching.

The road we struck at Tan-chia-tien is a highway leading northward to Shensi and southward to Kuichou Fu on the Yangtsze River. Hereabout and down to Taning Hsien, 12 miles distant, and northward I know not how far, the cliffs are sheer to the water's edge. The road is well graded and a good 6 feet broad, and has been excavated or blasted from solid rock.

From Chikou to Taning Hsien is said to be 30 li with not a house or hovel between. To cover this we with difficulty engaged boats, long, narrow, lightly built affairs (Sin-po-tzu), turned up at prow and stern, with no oars and steered by long sweeps projected fore and aft. The current was strong and rapids numerous; aided by a freshet we covered the whole distance in half an hour. The brief journey was through one grand chasm, the walls of rock being sheer to the water's edge with no space even for a shingle-bank to lodge. These cliffs are treeless and mostly bare with here and there grassy patches and clumps of delicate, graceful Bamboo (Arundinaria nitida). The road zigzags around the cliffs on the right bank well above high-water mark, and every inch of it has been blasted from the hard wall of rock. Stone gates and barriers occur at intervals, but there are no houses. This road is of such a nature that time and neglect can affect it but little, but it is now scarcely used except by occasional pedestrians and salt-carriers when the river is impracticable. I tried hard to discover when and by whom the road was built but found no one who could tell me. It is evidently one of the ancient arteries of China, and probably dates back to the discovery of the salt-wells. It struck me as being an old military road and may probably have been built centuries ago when Kuichou Fu was a place of infinitely greater importance than it is to-day.

The river I have mentioned, known locally as the Tan-ing Ho, rises near the borders of Shensi, Hupeh, and Szechuan, and after flowing nearly due south enters the Yangtsze at Wushan Hsien. From Chikou boats descend to its mouth, 200 li distant.

MARKET VILLAGE OF TAN-CHIA TIEN

CHINA — MOTHER OF GARDENS

Taning Hsien, alt. 750 feet, the most easterly inland town in Szechuan, is situated on the right bank of the river, here about 100 yards broad, and sweeping from the gorge in a fine curve. The town is wedged in on the side of a mountain-slope up which the city wall ascends for several hundred feet. The river-front is bounded on one side by the city wall, and the shops, houses, and yamens are crowded together near the river. The upper slopes enclosed within the city wall are given over to agriculture. The town, comprising about 400 houses, is the residence of a district magistrate, and boasts a trade in salt and odds and ends. Formerly it was the centre of a large opium traffic

At Taning Hsien the Chinese Banyan (Ficus infectoria), so abundant and characteristic of the central parts of Szechuan, puts in an appearance. Near a temple, a few hundred yards from the north gate of the town, I observed from the boat what appeared to be a Mantzu cave built in the face of limestone rock. On inquiring I was told of four or five similar caves in this neighborhood. Later I may have something to say about these caves, but it is interesting to be able to register their presence at the extreme eastern edge of the province, since heretofore they have been considered a feature of the more western parts. Physically and geologically speaking, the country east of the Taning River belongs to western Hupeh. Almost immediately west of it the characteristic red sandstone of Szechuan commences.

For twenty-two consecutive days my followers and I had struggled through the wild, lonely mountain fastnesses of northwestern Hupeh, suffering much from bad roads, worse accommodation, and scarcity of food supplies. For the first time on record the journey had been accomplished by a foreigner, and one and all of my followers were happy in the thought of the comparative luxury and plenty of the country which was now before us.

CHAPTER VII

THE RED BASIN OF SZECHUAN

GEOLOGY, MINERAL, AND AGRICULTURAL WEALTH

THROUGHOUT the eastern and central parts of the province of Szechuan, from near the Hupeh boundary to the valley of the Min River, the predominant rocks are red clayey sandstones, probably of jurassic age. These rocks are of immense thickness and impart a characteristic red color to the surface, and for this reason the late Baron Richthofen gave the term Red Basin to the whole region. This basin is nearly tri-angular in shape, the city of Kuichou Fu marking the apex. Imaginary lines connecting Kuichou Fu with Lungan Fu in the northwest, and Kuichou Fu with Pingshan Hsien keeping a little to the south of the Yangtsze River respectively mark the northern and southern sides. Another line from Lungan Fu and thence skirting the valley of the Min River to Pingshan Hsien marks the base of the triangle. The entire basin is nearly 100,000 square miles in area, and is surrounded on all sides by lofty mountain ranges, those on the west rising above the snow-line. In the east the boundary ranges are composed principally of upper carboniferous limestone. The western boundary ranges are largely made up of shales. The Yangtsze River traverses the basin from west to east, following a course nearly parallel with the southern limits of the basin itself. Within this triangle there is abundant life, industry, prosperity, wealth, and intercommunication by water. Outside of it on all sides the contiguous country is sparsely inhabited, little productive and no river is navigable save the Yangtsze, where it leaves the basin.

In ancient geological times this region was doubtless a vast inland lake with a fairly even floor. Since the draining off of the waters the Yangtsze River and its network of tributary streams have eroded channels 1500 to 2500 feet deep through these soft sedimentary rocks, and converted the whole basin into a thoroughly hilly country. To-day the only level area is the plain of Chengtu, some 80 miles long and 65 miles wide, with an average altitude of 1800 to 2000 feet above sea-level. The rest of the basin is broken up into a network of low, rolling, or flat-topped mountains averaging about 3000 feet above sea-level, and nowhere exceeding 4000 feet altitude. The whole of this region is under agriculture, the highest development of which obtains on the Chengtu plain, perhaps the richest area in the whole of China.

How great a period of time has elapsed since the disappearance of the waters from this basin is purely conjectural. But that this triangle has long constituted a well-marked boundary is evidenced by the fact that remark-ably few of the plants found in the mountains bordering the eastern limits at 2000 feet altitude and upward are common to the mountains bordering the western limits. The genera are of course the same, but the species are usually distinct. The difference between the flora of the eastern and western border-ranges is too great for a mere 500 miles of longitude to account for solely. The same is true of the fauna in so far as the game birds and animals are concerned.

From evidence presented by the flora to-day it appears doubtful if ever the Red Basin was covered with great forests. Rather would I suppose that subsequent to the disappearance of the waters the region bore some resemblance to the bad lands of certain parts of the United States of America. All this is admittedly pure conjecture. Every-where to-day, trees, shrubs, and herbs are common, but the flora, in contradistinction to that of the contiguous regions, is relatively poor, and the species largely common to the entire basin. Further, the majority of these species are widely spread throughout the warmer low-level regions in China, some indeed ranging to the extreme eastern limits of the country. A theory is apt to become fascinating, and may easily be carried too far. The facts above recorded are best left until the geology of China is more accurately known.

Coming down to historical times we learn that the region previous to the advent of the Chinese was peopled by an aboriginal population divided into the kingdom of Pa in the east, and the

THE RED BASIN OF SZECHUAN

kingdom of Shu in the west. This aboriginal population has entirely disappeared, but records in the shape of well-constructed caves having square en-trances are found scattered all over the Red Basin. These caves are especially abundant around Kiating Fu. A little investigation of these interesting places has been attempted, and fragments of pottery and odds and ends discovered. The entrances to these caves could only be closed from the outside, and from this fact, and other details, it is probable that they served as the burial-places of the chiefs and more wealthy among this extinct people, rather than as dwelling-places or harbors of refuge. Doubtless they have been subsequently used for these latter purposes, but that they were designed for tombs seems to best explain their origin. From Chinese history we learn that as early as 600 B.C. the kingdom of Pa had relations with the Chinese kingdoms of Ts'u, which occupied the regions north of the barrier ranges. Later, Pa princesses married Ts'u kings. Ts'u was in time conquered by Ts'in (another Chinese kingdom), which gradually absorbed Pa, and finally conquered Shu about 315 B.C. A military road was commenced from the neighborhood of modern Hanchung Fu, designed to connect with the region around modern Chengtu, by Ts'in-shih Hwang about 220 B.C. This road, which enters Szechuan from across the barrier ranges near Kuangyuan Hsien, is still in existence as the great highway connecting Chengtu with Hanchung Fu, Sian Fu, and, ultimately, Peking itself. For the next fifteen centuries the history of this region is full of war, rebellion, and internecine strife. Usurpers established petty dominion over the country from time to time, only to disappear among slaughter and bloodshed. There is scarcely a square mile of the whole region but what recalls scenes of valor, treachery, and carnage. In the latter half of the thirteenth century the famous Tartar, Kublai Khan, carried his arms victoriously over nearly the whole of modern China, and formed an Empire which the succeeding Ming and Manchu dynasties maintained more or less intact.

Since the time of Kublai Khan many rebellions have swept over Szechuan, decimating the population and paralysing industry. The present population is mainly derived from immigrants (voluntary and otherwise) who settled there during the early half of the eighteenth century. A census taken in A.D. 1710 returned only 144,154 souls for the whole province. To-day the population is estimated at 45,000,000! In spite of all the long-sustained wars and bloody rebellions, agriculture has managed to subsist, and the whole of the Red Basin is a lasting monument to Chinese genius and industry in matters agricultural. An abundant water-supply and constant tillage are necessary to obtain a full crop from these sandy clays and marls. Fortunately, the whole region is one vast network of streams, all of which drain into the mighty Yangtsze. The Chinese have taken full advantage of this intricate river system, and devised manifold methods of irrigation. These devices, combined with the untiring patient industry of the people, have converted an incipient bad land into a rich and fertile region of terraced fields. In no part of China that I have visited are the people entitled to greater praise for meritorious agricultural accomplishment than throughout this Red Basin.

In many parts of this region the river valleys are so steeply eroded that very little cultivatable bottom-land is formed. Consequently the rice belt is relegated to slopes and summits of the low, flattened hills. In limestone regions the bottom-lands constitute the main rice belt, but in the sand-stone regions the opposite obtains. The climate of the whole region is mild and genial, and during both winter and summer the land is cropped. Rice is the great summer crop with maize, millet, sweet potato, sugar-cane, tobacco, pulse, and various other crops. The principal winter crops are wheat, rape, peas, broad beans, cabbage, Irish potato, etc. Formerly opium was cultivated in enormous quantities as a winter crop, but this has lately been almost entirely suppressed. Cotton does not thrive in the Red Basin, though its culture is attempted in many districts, notably Yilung Hsien and in Tungchuan Fu. Cotton is the one commodity that this region has to import, and nearly all its surplus products go to meet this deficiency. But, if cotton is very little grown, many kinds of hemp are produced in quantity, though very little is used for textile purposes. Silk production is every-where an industry of importance, and in many districts the staple. Only the very poorest are without some silk garment, though such is only habitually worn by the more wealthy. Tea is grown in many

TYPICAL VIEW OF RICEFIELDS IN THE RED BASIN

districts both for local consumption and for export. In the more westerly parts tea for the Thibetan market is a staple product. Wood Oil and many other valuable economic trees are also largely cultivated. Fruit is generally grown, including peaches, apricots, plums, apples, pears, and oranges in variety. Oranges thrive remarkably well in this red sandstone, and the extensive orchards are a wonderful sight during the month of December. Tangerine varieties are most generally cultivated, and the fruit in season can be purchased at the rate of twelve hundred or more for fifty cents! The tight-skinned varieties are less frequently grown, and are more expensive. Around Lu Chou are plantations of Litchi trees. When they came from their original homes the settlers evidently brought with them their favorite trees and grains and planted them around their new homesteads. These introductions, and the favorable climate, explain the presence of such variety of cultivated plants, which is probably greater than that found in any other province in China.

The steeper and rougher country is covered with small woods of Oak, Pine, and Cypress, elsewhere trees are confined to the vicinity of streams, houses, temple grounds, wayside shrines, and tombs.

The streams are navigable for extreme distances, and a perfect network of roads traverses the basin in every direction. These roads are, on the whole, well built for Chinese roads, but are not kept in thorough repair any more than those elsewhere in the land. The streams, however, are well supplied with ferries, and well-built bridges, substantially constructed of stone, and kept in good repair, are a feature throughout the entire region. Large cities, market villages, hamlets, and farmhouses dot the land, which everywhere appears prosperous and its inhabitants contented. Drought occasionally brings famine, but, on the whole, the Red Basin suffers much less from this dread calamity than do other and less favored parts of the eighteen provinces of China.

The mineral wealth of the Red Basin is not varied, but enormous brine deposits occur scattered over the whole area, and are worked at depths varying from almost surface level to 3000 feet. In the eastern parts, Kuichou Fu and Wen-tang-ching, for example, the rivers have scoured the rocks until the brine deposits are practically exposed.

THE RED BASIN OF SZECHUAN

In the west, however, as at Wu-ting-chiao, situated on the left bank of the Min River a few miles below Kiating Fu, the brine is found at about 500 feet down. At Tzu-liu-ching, on the left bank of the To River, where the richest deposits occur, the brine is found at depths from 1000 to 3000 feet.

Salt is worked in some thirty-nine districts in the Red Basin. It is everywhere a government monopoly, and its production and subsequent distribution are rigorously controlled. The annual output is estimated at about 300,000 tons. At Tzu-liu-ching most of the brine is evaporated by inflammable gas; in all other places the brine is evaporated by coal heat. In boring the deep wells, it is uncertain whether brine or gas will be struck, but both are equally valuable. The occurrence of this inflammable gas indicates the probable presence of petroleum beds at still greater depth.

Coal is found in greater or lesser quantities all over the Red Basin, and is always found not very far removed from brine-pits. This coal varies from lignite to anthracite. The average quality is poor, but one or two good seams have been found, notably at Lung-wang-tung, a few miles north of Chungking.

Our early description of the Red Basin needs some amplification to explain the presence of coal and other minerals. Although the sedimentary sandstones are in a state of undisturbed stratification over a great part of this area, yet there is dissecting this Red Basin a number of linear elevations, in which the underlying limestone is bent up from a great depth. This limestone forms in every case an axial core, lined on either side by highly inclined strata, among which there is ordinarily noticeable, next to the axis, a double belt of coal-formation, followed on either side by strata of red sandstone standing on edge. Baron Richthofen estimates that "the area of the coal-bearing ground in Szechuan probably exceeds in size the total area of every other province of China." But probably throughout nine-tenths of this area the coal-measures are buried deep beneath the superincumbent strata, and with trifling exceptions can never become available for mining. In the linear elevations, above referred to, the belts of coal-formations, though narrow, are of great length. They are most readily accessible in those places where rivers have cut through and exposed the ends of the seams. Mining is done by means of horizontal adits working from an exposed surface inwards. Throughout the Red Basin, coal is the ordinary fuel.

Iron ores occur scattered throughout the entire region, but though in the aggregate the iron-smelting industry is a considerable one, in no one place is iron made on a large scale. Sulphate of iron (copperas) is found in combination with coal in one or two districts, notably in Kiangan Hsien.

Lime is common to all the linear elevations mentioned above, occurring in juxtaposition with coal, and is burnt in kilns in the usual way. Gypsum is found and worked in one or two places, notably Mei Chou and Pengshan Hsien, both districts on the Min River, between Kiating and Chengtu.

Mineral oil in small quantity occurs in the district of Pengch'i Hsien, where a native company has made some attempts to develop the industry, but with unsatisfactory results.

Other less important minerals occur in small quantities. The precious metals, gold and silver, are not found in the Red Basin proper but in the mountainous country to the west of this region, where copper, lead, and zinc ores also Occur.

In reference to gold it should, however, be mentioned that rude placer mining is carried on during the winter months, throughout the numerous shingle-banks exposed in the beds of the Yangtsze, Kialing, and Min rivers. On the Yangtsze this precarious industry is first to be noted some 50 miles below Ichang, but it is not general until the region west of the gorges is reached. The industry is carried on by unemployed peasantry, and the returns are most insignificant. This gold is in all probability brought down by the Yangtsze and its larger tributaries during the summer floods. There is no record of any gold-bearing quartz having been found in situ in the Red Basin proper. In the mountains bordering its western and northwestern limits gold quartz is found in greater or less quantities, and all the principal rivers of this region either take their rise in, or flow through, these ranges. This fact explains the presence of small quantities of gold far removed from the gold-bearing strata.

CHAPTER VIII

EASTERN SZECHUAN

NARRATIVE OF A JOURNEY FROM TANING HSIEN
TO TUNGHSIANG HSIEN

HE region described in this chapter was traversed by Lieut.-Colonel C. C. Manifold and Captain E. W. S. Mahon when surveying for a possible route for the proposed Hankow-Szechuan Railway in 1903 or 1904, I am not sure which. There is no record of any other traveller having crossed this part of eastern Szechuan, though it is very possible that missionaries may have done so. I do not know the conclusions arrived at by the surveyors, but the construction of a railway along the route I traversed would be a difficult and costly undertaking.

The following narrative is compiled from my diary, and may, perhaps, convey a brief idea of the nature of the country and the flora found in the more easterly parts of the Red Basin. As will be gathered, I took ten days to cover the distance, but I travelled leisurely, and the journey could be accomplished in six days.

June 28, 1910.—Yesterday we spent the day at Taning Hsien, refitting and preparing for our journey westward to Chengtu Fu. Money exchange proved an involved and difficult business. Ten-cash pieces, both Hupeh and Szechuan currency, are accepted here at 20 per cent discount. This means that the purchasing power of a thousand such cash is only equal to 800 string-cash. Farther west, Hupeh 10-cash pieces are not current, and the Szechuan 10-cash piece is only accepted for two days' journey west of this town. We had therefore to burden ourselves with string-cash, which added considerably to the weight of our loads. A thousand cash in 10-cash pieces weighs less than 2 lbs.; in string-cash the same equivalent weighs over 8 lbs.! If there is one reform more badly needed than another in China it most certainly is in the matter of currency.

Leaving Taning Hsien by way of the west gate we made a slight ascent and entered a narrow highly cultivated valley, flanked on our right by fairly high and on the left by lower mountains, nearly treeless and sparsely cultivated. The town of Taning lies in a depression, and the morning mists obscured the general view. It is a small place, with much of the land enclosed within its walls given over to cultivation. An outer gate, wall, and block-house guards the west gate proper.

Ascending the valley by an easy road which more or less skirts a fairly large tributary stream of the Taning Ho, we reached the village of Che-tou-pa before noon. Rice was abundantly cultivated everywhere, irrigation being effected by means of large Persian wheels. Much cotton is cultivated following wheat, the winter crop. Maize was 5 feet tall and in full flower. Paliurus orientalis, a thin tree 30 to 50 feet tall, is very common, and was laden with white, circular, odd-looking fruits. Weeping Willows, Cypress, and fine specimens of a hairy leaved, small-fruited Hog-plum (Spondias axillaris pubinervis) were noteworthy, with Bamboo groves in abundance.

On leaving Che-tou-pa we deserted the main tributary stream and ascended a small branch. The valley narrows, and the hills are more wooded, chiefly with Cypress. The road is easy, though here and there sadly in need of repair. We journeyed slowly, and eventually crossed over a ridge of low hills to the hamlet of Lao-shih-che, which we reached at 5 p.m. This tiny place, alt. 1950 feet, and 55 li from Taning Hsien, consists of half a dozen houses, scattered through a narrow valley with rice fields on all sides. The people were very nice, but inquisitive.

We were on the edge of the Red Basin and much of the soil had the characteristic red color. Wood Oil trees are commonly cultivated, but cotton was not in evidence during the afternoon. In a grove I noted some magnificent trees of Pistacia chinensis and Sapindus mukorossi. The young shoots of the former are cooked and eaten, and the round fruits of the Sapindus are used as soap. Celtis trees are common, their smooth, pale gray bark rendering them conspicuous. On a ridge we

SOAP-TREE (SAPINDUS MUKOROSSI). 80 FEET TALL, GIRTH 12 FEET

noted many trees of the interesting Button-tree (Adina racemosa). These trees were 30 to 60 feet tall, 2 to 4 feet in girth, and the finest specimens of their kind I have met with. The Chinese Pine (Pinus massoniana) is general, but by far the commonest tree of the day was the Cypress (Cupressus funebris).

The road proved a pleasant change; instead of savage scenery, low rounded hills backed by steeper mountains, all rather treeless, and for the most part cultivated, were the order of the day. Here and there were a few outstanding cliffs of limestone with an occasional temple crowning odd crags. At Taning Hsien we secured a number of new coolies, and these men described the country passed through in the afternoon as Laolin (wilderness). This immensely amused my Ichang men, who recommended these newcomers to try the Sheng-neng-chia before speaking of Laolin!

The day was grilling hot, and all were fairly exhausted on arrival at Lao-shih-che. Whether it was the heat or the after effects of a day's holiday I could not determine, but I was called upon to play doctor to nearly half my followers. The majority were suffering from stomach troubles, several from filthy sores. Epsom salts, permanganate of potash, and iodoform dressings soon improved the majority.

The next day was gloriously fine, but scarcely so hot as the previous day, or perhaps the slightly increased altitude made it more bearable. The whole day we travelled nearly due west through a narrow valley bounded by moderately high parallel ranges. The road continues easy with occasional ascents and descents. We were still on the fringe of the Red Basin, but in the afternoon gray sandy soils were most in evidence. Rice is cultivated wherever sufficient water is obtainable, and was scarcely ever out of our view. Maize is the other principal crop, with various kinds of pulse and the Irish potato. The sweet potato is cultivated here and there, and Wood Oil trees (Aleurites fordii) are even more abundant than before. Much oil is evidently produced in this region, and we noted many oil-presses during the day. The parallel ranges are from 500 to 1000 feet above the valley, sparsely cultivated, and for the most part well timbered with Cypress (Cupressus funebris), Pine (Pinus massoniana), and Oak (Quercus serrata). Poplar is a common tree, and by the sides of streams Weeping Willows abound. Shrubs in variety occur, the most noteworthy being Itea ilicifolia and Torricellia angulata. Nowhere else have I seen this latter shrub so plentiful; it favors the sides of streams, ditches, and rocky gullies, forming a densely leafy bush 8 to 12 feet tall. The fruit when ripe is black, and is borne in large pendulous cymes. The Itea occurs in rocky places, and its pendulous tails of greenish-white flowers are often 18 inches long. The leaves very closely resemble those of the common Holly, and when not in flower it might easily be mistaken for that plant.

Houses are scattered along the route, but the population is sparse. We met a few mule trains, but there was really very little traffic on the road. We found accommodation for the night at Hsia-kou, a prettily situated hamlet, alt. 2800 feet, 65 li from Lao-shih-che. Our lodgings were spacious, but the occupants of the house looked unprepossessing opium sots.

At To-chia-pa, a small hamlet passed a few miles before reaching Hsia-kou, a road branches off to the northward and leads to Chengkou Ting. It was said to be a hard road to travel over.

On leaving Hsia-kou we immediately plunged into a ravine with steep limestone cliffs 300 to 500 feet high; the road follows the dry bed of a torrent. At the head of this ravine we made a slight ascent, and wandered across low mountain-tops for a few miles, then descended and crossed a branch of the Kuichou River by a covered bridge. Up to this point Pine trees and the China Fir (Cunninghamia lanceolata) are common. At the bridge I photographed the largest tree of Platycarya strobilacea I have seen. This specimen was fully 75 feet tall, with a girth of 6 feet. I had no idea it could attain such dimensions. A few miles beyond this point we forded the main branch of the Kuichou River, a broad, shallow, clear-water stream, and about noon reached the village of Chiao-yang-tung. Soon afterwards we were overtaken by a furious thunderstorm, which arose with amazing suddenness. The fury of the storm spent itself in a torrential downpour of short duration, but rain fell steadily during the rest of the day. The rain did not improve the mud road, and our progress was slow and difficult in consequence.

CHINA — MOTHER OF GARDENS

During the whole afternoon we made a steady ascent, skirting the mountain-sides through woods of Pine and Oak. Eventually the road enters a narrow sloping valley, at the head of which we found lodgings for the night in two houses which constitute the hamlet of Shan-chia-kou, having travelled 65 li. Around this place the flora is varied and essentially cool-temperate in character. Bushes of Mock Orange (Philadelphus incanus) were conspicuous on all sides with their wealth of pure white flowers. The Hautboy strawberry is abundant, and around our hostel I gathered in a few minutes enough of these luscious fine-flavored white berries to stew for dinner. The Torricellia was again common. It ascends up to 3500 feet altitude, and often forms a small inelegant tree.

We saw very little rice during the day, maize and Irish potato being the chief crops. There is practically no traffic on this road; the mule-trains seen yesterday evidently came down the road from Chengkou Ting. Population is sparse, and what there is looked strongly addicted to the opium habit. So far, however, we had not seen any signs of poppy.

A magnificent day ushered in the new month. The morning was tolerably hot, but the afternoon scorchingly so. A hundred yards beyond our lodgings we reached the head of a ridge, and an abrupt descent of a couple of thousand feet or so led to a narrow valley where much rice, maize, Irish potato, and a little Hemp (Cannabis sativa) are cultivated. The parallel ranges flanking this valley are of limestone with outstanding bare rocks and cliffs, very little cultivated but with good woods of the common Pine. Here and there in the valley we passed fine trees of Sassafras, Sweet Chestnut, Sweet Gum (Liquidambar formosana), China Fir, and Poplar. At the head of the valley we made a slight ascent to the top of a ridge. Below us, some 2500 feet, flowed a considerable river walled in by lofty lime-stone precipices. It was 10.30 a.m. when we reached the top of this ridge, and the rest of the day's march was a more or less precipitous descent to the river, which we reached at Sha-to-tzu about 3 p.m. In its early stages the descent is as difficult as it well could be—over loose Rowleyrag-like debris, down and up steep steps, and over slopes of greasy clay. We crossed one or two cultivated slopes, but most of the time the road skirts around the sides of cliffs. At the edge of one precipice, 500 to 1000 feet sheer, the road is carried through a narrow tunnel some 50 yards long and 3 ½ feet broad at the exit. This tunnel is partly natural and partly made by blasting the hard limestone. It was quite dark within the tunnel save for a faint glimmer of light at the exit. Both chairs and loads were with difficulty carried through this tunnel. This roadway is of recent date, and is unique in my experience of Chinese roads. Rough as it is it saves about 10 li and a very steep ascent and descent.

From the tunnel-way the road skirts the tops of the cliffs with many exasperating and wearying ascents and descents. Finally we descended to a small tributary of the main stream and, crossing over, reached Sha-to-tzu, a busy market village and, for the nature of the country, of considerable size. Up the tributary stream some 10 li, iron is mined and smelted, the quality being described as good. Around Sha-to-tzu, coal is worked and lime burnt.

The river we had with so much fatiguing travel reached enters the Yangtsze at Yunyang Hsien, distant 150 li. It is a clear-water stream of considerable volume, and is navigable for small boats from just below Sha-to-tzu to within 15 li of its mouth. Salt and a little peddling traffic was noticeable on the road; also odd loads of medicines, including Tu-chung, the bark of Eucommia ulmoides. The salt is a product of Yunyang Hsien, and is not allowed to enter Taning Hsien. The quality is said to be superior to that found within the latter district.

The flora of the day's journey was not particularly interesting, being very much the same as that found in the glens and gorges around Ichang. A new Stachyurus and Abelia engleriana were collected. The Heavenly Bamboo (Nandina domestica) was particularly abundant in rocky places, its elegant foliage and large erect trusses of white flowers with conspicuous yellow anthers making it very attractive. In autumn and winter the masses of scarlet fruit render it extremely beautiful. Wood Oil trees were general in rocky places, and Hypericum chinense, a wealth of rich golden yellow, was strikingly handsome, nestling on the cliffs everywhere. Quite a little Ramie (Boehmeria nivea) is cultivated, and the people were busy stripping the fibre-containing bark from the stems. The leaves, like those of several other plants, are used for feeding pigs. The stripping and cleaning is all done by hand labor.

The day's march was full of interest, but the intense heat and hard road made the 60 li very trying, and all were glad when the end of the stage was reached. The scenery was magnificent, and forcibly reminded us of the glens and ravines around Ichang. The railway surveyors must have been filled with despair when they encountered this steep limestone country.

Sha-to-tzu is only about 700 feet altitude, and, in spite of the swift-flowing stream which passes its front door, was suffocatingly hot. We managed to find a good inn with quarters removed from the street and remarkably private in character. We had no difficulty in changing silver here, but 10-cash pieces were no longer negotiable. String-cash was the only kind the people would accept.

Just below Sha-to-tzu we crossed the river by a ferry which is assisted by a convenient rapid, and commenced a steep ascent. A few hundred feet up we were afforded a good view of the village we had just left. It contains about a hundred houses, crowded together on a narrow, fan-shaped slope. A few temples shaded by large Banyan trees were conspicuous, and the whole made a decidedly pretty scene. The ascent is through cultivated fields, groves of Wood Oil trees, and finally Pine woods. At 3100 feet altitude we crossed a gap, and 200 feet more led to the top of the range. The rest of the day we followed an undulating, easy road which meanders through rocky, Pine- and Cypress-clad mountain-tops, and finally descends to Che-kou-tzu, which was our destination for the day.

The country is very pretty; farmhouses are scattered along the route, and where possible the land is under cultivation. Rice was of course the crop where water is obtainable, maize and Irish potato elsewhere. Tobacco is grown; a little of this crop has been noted every day since leaving Taning Hsien. Lime-kilns were common all day. In one place we saw a number of men out with guns after muntjac. They fired several times, but did not succeed in killing the animal during the time we watched the sport.

A few li before reaching Che-kou-tzu we passed an unusually

large house of much architectural beauty. It was erected by a rich man named T'ao, who held the purchased rank of Hsien. He died some twenty years ago, and the family has fallen on evil times, thanks to idleness and opium.

The flora was not very interesting. Some fine trees of Cypress and occasional ones of Paulownia fargesii were noteworthy. Pine abounds, and I saw several examples of clustered cones. These cones, a hundred and more crowded together, were all small, and appeared to have displaced the male flowers. Che-kou-tzu, alt. 2050 feet, consists of some forty houses situated above the mouth of a stony stream and backed by low mountains, on the top of which is an ancient fort.

On leaving Che-kou-tzu we immediately entered a pretty valley, highly cultivated with rice and bounded by low, rolling hills. A large number of farmhouses and a small hamlet occur in this small but prosperous valley. Through-out the whole forenoon we traversed a number of such depressions separated one from another by low ridges, always ascending slightly with the valleys narrowing until finally they become mere basins surrounded by rocky limestone mountain-tops. Crossing a final ridge we entered Kai Hsien at a place called Shih-ya-tzu, 35 li from Che-kou-tzu. Up to this point the scenery is very pretty, the rocky mountain-tops being clothed with woods of Pine and Cypress. Oak is common, and in more open places and around habitations we passed fine trees of Spondias, Pistacia, Paulownia, Tapiscia, and Hovenia dulcis; the last covered with masses of white flowers.

The afternoon's journey was all downhill, ending in a very precipitous descent to Wen-tang-ching. The road led through maize plats, odd rice fields, and bare, treeless hill-tops, with no flora of interest. Nearing our halting-place for the day it was fearfully hot, and the absence of shade was severely felt. Here and there the hill-tops are crowned by old forts built of dressed stone. These relics (chaitzu) of turbulent times abound all over the salt districts and more wealthy regions of eastern Szechuan. Lime-kilns, small clay-covered affairs, were common en route, and many of the rice fields had been dressed with slaked lime.

CHINA — MOTHER OF GARDENS

Wen-tang-thing is a town of considerable size, by far the largest place we had met with since leaving Ichang. It is built on steep slopes bounding the two sides of a clear-water stream, and backed by high limestone cliffs. On the southwest side these cliffs are stark and sun-baked. Large quantities of salt are produced here. The brine-pits are situated on the foreshore and immediate neighborhood of the stream. The supply depends on the state of the river, the lower the water the more brine is obtainable. During summer floods the industry is suspended. The salt is white, powdery, of moderate quality, valued at twenty-six cash per 16-ounce catty. It is distributed throughout the north and west of the Hsien, but cannot enter the city of Kai Hsien itself. Dust coal is mined in the neighborhood and used for evaporating the brine.

The town consists of about a thousand houses and boasts several temples and guild-halls, the hall belonging to the Shensi guild being very prominent on account of its large size and ornate architecture. Two small pagodas protect the luck of the place, and many chaitzu crown the surrounding hills. The inhabitants are not prepossessing, being unusually dirty and over curious. Some were not over civil, and there was a slight scuffle between my men and some rowdies. Our inn was dark, suffocatingly hot, and most undesirable in every way. It was the best we could find, and served its purpose, uncomfortable as it was. Behind the inn is a huge cave with vast stalactites and a cool breeze blowing through it. This is the curiosity of the town, and was pointed out with a great show of pride.

All along the route from Taning Hsien there has been much argument over the price of foodstuffs. The natives constantly putting up the price on my men, this led to heated words, but generally ended in the men getting a fair price. Many of them had travelled too far not to know the ropes.

Wen-tang-ching is only 750 feet altitude, and with the heat from stark surrounding cliffs and hundreds of furnaces is a regular inferno. Prosperous it may be, but it failed to appeal to us, and one and all were glad to quit it.

A steep ascent of a few hundred feet and we cleared the town.

ORNATE TOMBSTONE

CHINA — MOTHER OF GARDENS

After passing through a large graveyard we descended to an alluvial valley where much sugar-cane, maize, tobacco, and a little cotton is cultivated. The road is broad, paved with blocks of hard stone, and traverses the valley to its head at Ma-chia-kou, 12 li from Wen-tang-ching. Ma-chia-kou is the coal port for the salt-wells. Coal is carried over-land some 30 li, and at this point put into small boats and conveyed to the brine-pits. This coal is valued at three cash per catty, the carriers receiving one cash per catty for carrying it down. The boats are small, steered by sweeps fore and aft, and can descend this stream to Kai Hsien, 60 li below Wen-tang-thing, and from thence to Hsiao-ch'ang on the Yangtsze, 110 li distant. At Ma-chia-kou the road leaves the main stream, which flows down from the north-ward, and after crossing a neck descends to a broad stony torrent, which it ascends through uninteresting country, eventually leading through a limestone ravine. The coal supply is of primary importance to the salt-wells, consequently the road is kept in good repair. During the fore-noon we met hundreds of coolies and many women laden with coal. Iron is found in this neighborhood, and pigs of this metal were being carried down to the boats.

On leaving the above-mentioned ravine we traversed a valley of rice fields and reached Yi-chiao-tsao about noon. Five li above this hamlet we crossed over, and during the rest of the day's march descended a narrow valley flanked by steep Cypress-clad slopes. The sweet potato is abundantly cultivated, also rice and maize. Houses are frequent, and the people appear fairly well-to-do.

We found lodgings for the night at Wang-tung-tsao, alt. 1350 feet, having covered our usual 60 11. The day was terribly hot, making the journey very fatiguing. The inn is beautifully situated in a grove of Bamboo and Cypress, but is poor and abominably stinking. Really, it is a pity that such a vile house should defile such a charming spot.

The next day was also grilling hot, with no signs of a storm to cool the air. Descending a few li we struck a rather broad stream with many red sandstone boulders in its bed. The road ascends this stream to its source, and steep ascents and descents were all too frequent. We lunched at the village of Kao-chiao, and a more hot, fly-infested, stinking hole, with people more inquisitive, I have not experienced. Savage, snarling, yelping dogs abounded, and these, with the other discomforts, did not add relish to the meal. My followers seemed to share my views of this village, and grumbling and malediction were loud on all sides. Our meal did not occupy long, and we all felt better when clear of this filthy, pestiferous place.

The whole day was spent among sandstone, gray and red, and we were seldom out of sight of rice fields. Pine abounds, but the Cypress does not appear to be at home here, and occurs very sparingly as compared with previous days. Wood Oil trees are common, but the flora generally is not interesting. Elaeagnus bushes are common and were in ripe fruit. The stems of this shrub (Shan-yeh-wangtzu, or Yang-ming-nitzu) are commonly used for making the long stems of tobacco pipes so frequently seen in this region. The Burdock (Arctium major) is common in stony places and often cultivated, being used as medicine under the name Yu-pangtzu.

Three li before reaching our lodgings we crossed a ridge, and passing through a stone gateway, entered the district of Tunghsiang Hsien. We found an inn at P'ao-tsze, a small scattered hamlet, alt. 2650 feet, 65 li from Wang-tung-tsao. The inn is clean and prettily situated in a little valley bounded by low red-stone hills all under cultivation. The host is evidently a man of substance, and amongst other things owns a reclining chair of novel workmanship, of which he is evidently very proud.

There was no breeze last night, and I slept badly, partly owing to the heat and partly to the occupants of the inn talking in high argumentative tones till past midnight. This is a common habit of the Chinese and very exasperating to any one trying to get to sleep.

With only 50 li to do to Nan-pa ch'ang the men were in high spirits and set out in style. The road proved easy—by one o'clock we had covered the distance, and had a couple of long rests into the bargain. On leaving P'ao-tsze we made a short, steep ascent, and then descended by an easy road leading over and among sandstone bluffs. Twenty-five li on we reached the bed of a small stream and followed it to its union with a large, clear-water stream flowing down from the northward. This stream flows past Nan-pa ch'ang and is navigable for small boats down to Tunghsiang Hsien and up-stream some 290 li to Tu-li-kou. Near our destination we passed many coolies carrying down bright anthracite coal. This comes from Fu-che-kou, some 50 li away, and the men receive 200 cash per picul (100 catties) for carrying it down. We also noted iron in flat slabs, which comes from Tung-che-kou, 25 li distant.

Pine was again the common tree, but Cypress also was fairly common. The sandstone is evidently more favor-able to the Pine than to the Cypress. We saw two or three trees of the rare Hung-tou-shu (Ormosia hosiei). The wood of this tree is highly valued and so heavy that it sinks in water. Wood Oil trees continued abundant, and around Nan-pa ch'ang plantations of Mulberry were being made. Evidently seri-culture is about to be attempted in this district.

Nan-pa ch'ang, alt. 1550 feet, is a village of consider-able size, and is built on a flat bordering the stream. Formerly it was one of the most important centres of the opium trade in Szechuan, and its product was of very superior quality. The opium trade is now completely stopped, and this place has suffered tremendously in consequence. It also boasts a trade in general merchandise, supplying a large area of country to the northward. But opium was its real source of wealth, and with the disappearance of the opium traffic all trade has declined. To the northward a lot of tea is grown and the leading people of Nan-pa ch'ang are endeavoring to divert this trade from its present headquarters, Taiping Hsien, to their own village.

Around Nan-pa ch'ang there are a few Mantzu caves. Everything was very quiet in the village and we attracted little or no attention. We saw a couple of uniformed police, odd street lamps, and other signs of modern ideas. Leaving this village the next morning at 7 a.m., in four small boats, we dropped down the beautiful clear-water stream, and reached Tunghsiang Hsien at 3 o'clock. The distance is 140 li by water, 90 li by land. Numerous rapids obstruct the stream, but since the volume of water is comparatively small they are not dangerous. The river is bounded by sand-stone cliffs, often steep and covered with Pine, Cypress, and mixed shrubby vegetation. Chaitzu are common, and here and there we passed villages. Cultivation is general, and the crops were beginning to show signs of suffering from drought. Pulse in variety is abundantly cultivated, together with rice and other favorite articles of food. Ordinarily the whole region is one of plenty and prosperity.

It was a pleasant change dropping swiftly down this beautiful river, and we all enjoyed the journey. On reaching Tunghsiang Hsien a thunderstorm broke and the rain cooled the air delightfully.

We entered the city of Tunghsiang, alt. 1400 feet, through the east gate, and found accommodation in a quiet and moderately clean inn. The city, though not large, seemed a busy place. Formerly it boasted a large traffic in opium, and its general trade was then very considerable. It nestles among low hills on the right bank of the river, and is faced on the opposite bank by steeper and higher mountains. Sandstone cliffs and bluffs abound, and in some respects the whole scene reminded me of the country around Kiating Fu.

Our inquiries into the matter of currency disclosed the fact that Szechuan dollars were accepted, but 10-cash pieces were still useless. The Roman Catholic and China Inland Mission have established outstations here. An Irish missionary belonging to the latter was staying here at the time of my visit, and I enjoyed for an hour or so the pleasure of his company. It was pleasant to hear my own tongue spoken again. Not since leaving Ichang, 35 days before, had I encountered a single foreigner.

CHAPTER IX

THE ANCIENT KINGDOM OF PA

NARRATIVE OF A JOURNEY FROM TUNGHSIANG HSIEN TO PAONING FU

ROM Tunghsiang Hsien the recognized route to Chengtu or Paoning Fu descends the river via Suiting Fu to Ch'u Hsien, then strikes west-ward to Chengtu, northwest to Paoning Fu. I had no fancy for the main route, since, by going due west from Tunghsiang Hsien to Paoning Fu, we should explore new ground. My map (War Office, Province of Ssu-ch'uan, Eastern Sheet) gave no route, but indicated villages, and it was evident, therefore, that these villages were connected by a road of some sort. Chiangkou seemed a good place to start for, so my men were instructed to find a cross-country road to this town. At first the innkeepers, chair hongs, and local officials denied all knowledge of any such road, and indeed of such a place. But any one who has travelled in China values such denials at their proper worth and is not discouraged. The men who had charge of these inquiries were trusted followers of ten years' standing, and though entirely ignorant of the geography of the region could be relied upon to ferret out a route if such existed. After about six hours' investigation, from the magistrate's yamen downwards, I was informed that a small mountain-road did exist, but was over hard and difficult country, affording the poorest of accommodation. This was sufficient; they were told to get an itinerary of this route and engage a few local men as extra carriers. I went to bed about 10.30 p.m., satisfied that by 6 o'clock next morning everything would be ready for our cross-country jaunt. In my travels about China I have been singularly fortunate in never having any trouble with the Chinese. In the spring of 1900 I engaged about a dozen peasants from

THE ANCIENT KINGDOM OF PA

near Ichang. These men remained with me and rendered faithful service during the whole of my peregrinations. After a few months' training they understood my habits thoroughly and never involved me in any trouble or difficulty. Once they grasped what was wanted they could be relied upon to do their part, thereby adding much to the pleasure and profit of my many journeys. When we finally parted in February, 1911, it was with genuine regret on both sides. Faithful, intelligent, reliable, cheerful under adverse circumstances, and always willing to give their best, no men could have rendered better service.

This cross-country journey from Tunghsiang Hsien to Paoning Fu, via Chiangkou, promised to be of more than ordinary interest. There was a novelty about it also, since there was no record of any foreigner having attempted it before. The route lay across the old kingdom of Pa (see Chapter VII, p. 74), and I hoped to find some evidence of this ancient race. Chinese history is dry and difficult reading, and it is hard to dig out solid facts. Wars, rebellions, and massacres deluge everything in blood; the arts of peace are seldom given any prominence. The Chinese historians have always treated the aboriginal races with arrogant contumely, rendering it almost impossible to discover at this late date anything about the arts and life of these lost peoples. That the modern province of Szechuan boasted kingdoms and dynasties of its own before the advent of the early Chinese is historical fact. The first Emperor of the Ts'in dynasty, Ts'in-shih Hwang or Shih Hwang-ti (221-209 B.C.), incorporated part of the kingdom of Pa with the rest of his dominions and nominally also that of Shu, whose capital was near modern Chengtu Fu. The succeeding Han dynasty (206 B.C. to A.D. 25) made the conquest complete. Since this time no aboriginal chief has ruled the Red Basin of Szechuan, though it has been conquered and re-conquered time and again by usurping Chinese and alien races. During the period A.D. 221-265, the Chinese Empire was divided into three kingdoms, one of which, under the Emperor Liu-pei, had its capital at Chengtu. Liu-pei and three of his generals and statesmen are handed down as popular idols, and everywhere in Szechuan stories are told of the doughty deeds accomplished by these heroes of old. With this brief introduction I again take up my narrative :—

My principal men once more proved equal to the occasion, and on July 8th, everything was arranged for our cross-country journey. An itinerary had been made out, and the Hsien provided us with a couple of uniformed soldiers. (He sent six, but I managed to get them reduced to two.) Heretofore on this journey we had managed to avoid taking official escort, although it is the custom to do so in Szechuan. No ordinary traveller desires this honor, but it is thrust upon him and cannot easily be avoided. The presence of this escort renders the officials responsible for the traveller's safety in accordance with treaty arrangements. It is necessary to pay these men a few cash, but often they prove useful in odd ways. Cash is cheap, and an extra hundred per day for each soldier does not amount to any considerable sum. The difficulty is in keeping the escort down to two men. Four and six are common numbers, and if one did not protest continually an almost unlimited number of authorized and unauthorized ragamuffins would attach themselves to one's caravan. If there is cash to be made the legitimate escort is often not above farming in a few extra hands, thus securing more money. The escort is provided with a letter from the official supplying it wherein the number of men dispatched, and their destination, is given, so by examining this it is possible to check any attempt at fraud. On dismissing these men at their journey's end it is necessary to give them a card to carry back to their superior. Their letter is stamped by the official who provides the new escort, and the card signifies that their duty has been satisfactorily carried out. If they return without a card for any reason or other they are liable to be punished.

Leaving Tunghsiang Hsien by the west gate we followed the main road to Suiting Fu for a few li, then branched off to the right. The road is well paved, and we met plenty of traffic. For the first 20 li the road is practically level, winding in and out among low hills. It then makes a steep ascent to the top of some bluffs, where Mien-yueh ch'ang is situated, 30 li from the city of Tunghsiang. Throughout the rest of the day the road was easy, leading through and among low hill-tops and shallow valleys intercepted by hills 300 to 500 feet high. Cypress and

PAULOWNIA FARGESII, 55 FEET TALL, IN BLOSSOM

CHINA — MOTHER OF GARDENS

Pine are abundant, so also are Pistacia and Albizzia kalkora, both making large umbrageous trees. Vitex negundo is the commonest shrub, sometimes attaining to the dignity of a small tree: it was everywhere covered with masses of lavender-purple flowers.

The country is highly cultivated. Rice predominates, with various kinds of beans (especially Lutou, i.e., green beans) next in importance—both crops evidently follow after wheat. We passed odd patches of cotton and very many Plum trees. The region is well populated, bypaths abound, and it was no easy matter for us to keep to the right road At one point the road bifurcates, one branch leading to Shuang-ho ch'ang, the other to Shuang-miao ch'ang, our proposed halting-place for the night. The names of these two villages, when spoken rapidly, sound much alike, even to Chinese ears. My men got somewhat confused, and for a time there was danger of the caravan following two divergent routes.

We passed through the market village of Wang-chia ch'ang (ch'ang signifies market village), a curious little place, dominated by a temple in the middle, the roofs of the houses uniting to form a central covered way, beneath which the road passes through the village.

Shuang-miao ch'ang was our intended destination for the day, but being market day the village was filled to over-flowing. A hundred or more people followed us into an inn, and in a little while there was hardly room to breathe. Many were obviously under the influence of wine. It was too hot to tolerate such overcrowding curiosity, so we pushed on a further 5 li, where we happened on a decent farmhouse, which we commandeered. The owner being away, his wife was at first sorely afraid, but in a couple of hours her confidence was gained and all was well. The men had difficulty in obtaining food and lodging. The majority went back to the village, but none complained: they all realized the impossibility of my remaining the night in such a crowded place.

Our quarters were new and shaded by a grove of Bamboo and Cypress, but mosquitoes were multitudinous, rendering life miserable. The place is called Hsin-chia-pa, alt. 1950 feet. We had covered 80 li, through a rich and interesting country. Lady Banks's Rose was particularly abundant, with stems 2 feet round, festooning trees from 40 to 50 feet tall. Mantzu caves occur sparingly. In several places we passed cultivated patches of Cockspur Millet (Panicum crus-galli frumentaceum).

We parted excellent friends with our hostess at Hsin-chia-pa, a trifling present and 400 cash made her extremely happy, and her thanks were both genuine and profuse. Soon after starting we made a precipitous ascent of 1000 feet and crossed what is probably the watershed of the Suiting and Sanhuei rivers. A descent led to the head-waters of a small river, where is situated the tiny market village of San-cha-miao. Market was in full swing, the one short street with its few hovels being crowded with people. We passed through without stopping to satisfy the curiosity of the crowd. At this village several roads converge, the one we followed continuing to descend the stream, and leading through a rocky jungle-clad defile. The cliffs are of red and gray sandstone, steep, rugged, and crowned with Pine and Cypress. As fluviatile shrubs Distylium chinense, various Privets (Ligustrum) and Cornus paucinervis abound. The last-named is a low-growing Dogwood with spreading branches, and laden with small flat corymbs of white flowers, it formed a most attractive bush by the water's edge. In the jungle-clad slopes through which the road winds, Tea bushes 15 feet and more tall are common. They looked uncommonly like spontaneous specimens, but were probably planted long ago, though some of them undoubtedly have become naturalized. Occasional trees of the handsome Red Bean (Ormosia hosiei), occur; at one time this was probably a very common tree in this region. Its timber is most valuable, and the tree has been ruthlessly felled. There is practically no cultivation in this defile, or room for any, and not a house for 20 li.

After traversing this wild and interesting ravine for several hours we made a steep ascent to the top of the cliffs, and on the way up discovered spontaneous plants of the China Rose (Rosa chinensis) in fruit. These were the first really wild specimens I had met with. Once on top of the cliffs we found that the country all around is under cultivation, chiefly rice, with houses at frequent intervals. After a few li the road descends to the river again, and crossing by stone steps we reached the market village of Peh-pai-ho, where we found accommodation in a large house. This village, alt. 1600 feet, also known as Peh-pai ch'ang, is a small place with unprepossessing residents. Our quarters were dark, fairly filthy, and loafers crowded around until bedtime.

The day's journey of 60 li was through a sparsely populated country, which, considering the low altitude, was unusually wild and jungle-clad. The flora had points of interest, the finding of Tea bushes and plants of the China Rose in the rocky defile being particularly noteworthy. On bare sandstone cliffs large white trumpet-flowered Lilies (Lilium leucanthum) were common, with their stems thrust out at nearly right angles to the cliffs. We met very few people on the road, and most of the women we saw had natural feet. In the early morning we passed quite a lot of Panicum crus-galli frumentaceum, cultivated.

The itinerary my men secured at Tunghsiang Hsien did not err on the side of accuracy. Constant inquiries were necessary and the results were confusing. The river which flows past Peh-pai ch'ang was said to unite with the Chiangkou stream at Chiang-ling-che, 70 li distant.

A heavy thunder-storm occurred in the night, accompanied by a downpour of rain which lasted intermittently into the early forenoon of the next day. The country needed rain badly, and the air was cool and fresh in the morning. Peh-pai ch'ang is a regular warren of dilapidated houses, filthy and stinking, with a loafing and unduly curious population. A loin-cloth belonging to one of my chair-bearers was stolen during the night, and my followers had little that was complimentary to say about the village or its inhabitants.

Following the river down-stream for 5 li, we reached Lei-kang-kteng of the maps. This hamlet (pronounced Lei-kang-t'an, from a fine waterfall on a small river which, flowing from the north, joins the main stream at this point) consists of a deserted temple, a few scattered houses, and an old fort high up on the cliffs. It and Ta-chen-chai, another old fortress, are the only places marked on the map both are of no importance today. The market villages, the real places of importance, are not shown. Maybe these villages have sprung up comparatively recently, and the forts lost their importance. This is the only feasible explanation which occurs to me. This section of the country is only known from Chinese maps, and these were probably compiled during military times long ago.

From Lei-kang-k'eng a steady ascent for 30 li leads to the top of a ridge where is situated the important market village of Peh-shan. This place boasts a fine temple and about a hundred houses. Like all such villages in these parts it consists of one central street, virtually closed over by the nearly uniting eaves of the houses. These market villages are a striking feature of this part of Szechuan. They are situated approximately 30 li apart, and nine markets are held monthly in each. These are arranged in such manner that the three villages lying nearest to one another hold market on different days, thus between them practically covering the month. On market days the country-folk assemble from all sides to buy and sell. Pedlars and itinerant merchants constantly journey from market village to market village. Such markets are of the highest importance in a sparsely populated country, but the denizens of these villages suffer from too much spare time. Market days are what they exist for, and on; the other days are mainly spent in gambling and sloth. This system of market villages dates away back to the very dawn of Chinese civilization, and in the region we are concerned with here, is very little changed from what it was in the earliest times.

Five li before reaching Peh-shan ch'ang we struck a road which comes from Suiting Fu, 120 li distant. The country hereabout is split up in low mountain ranges, averaging 3000 feet altitude, composed of gray and red sandstones. The river-valleys are mere ravines clothed with dense jungle, Pines, and Cypress, with no bottom-lands or cultivated of any sort. Some 500 feet up, the cultivated area begins and extends to the summit. Terraced rice fields abound, tier upon tier, intercepted by low bluffs, the tops of all of which are cultivated. The whole country is very pretty, and in many respects peculiar, so far as my experience goes. Most of the women have natural feet, and many were busy weeding and firming the rice plants.

On leaving Peh-shan ch'ang the road makes a steep descent to a stream and a correspondingly steep ascent to the top of the bluffs again, winding round to the crest of a ridge where is situated the market village of Yuen-fang. This place, alt. 3100 feet, which was our destination for the day, having covered the allotted 60 li, is prettily situated. We found lodgings in a new and clean house boasting a veranda overlooking a grove of Pine and Cypress trees. The crowd which collected was small and though inquisitive kept at a respectful distance.

The flora proved identical with that of the previous day's journey. I again met with sub-spontaneous Tea bushes in the jungle and also saw a number of the Red Bean trees. Perhaps the most interesting objects noted during the day were the tombstones. These are very different from any I have seen elsewhere. They are of freestone, often highly sculptured, the workmanship being superior and the effect both artistic and dignified. One or two old stone mausoleums were magnificently sculptured. The aboriginal population of this region were accomplished workers in stone, and their work may have served as patterns for the Chinese to copy from. In conception the designs are evidently not pure Chinese, and I strongly suspect Mantzu influence, to use the Chinese term for the aboriginal population.

At Fu-erh-tang there is a particularly fine family temple, and nearby a Mantzu cave in an isolated piece of rock. Around many of the mausoleums and family temples ancient stone pillars (wei-tzu, i.e., masts) occur. Wayside shrines and small temples, dedicated to Kwanyin (Goddess of Mercy), and to the tutelary genii are common, the images being carved in stone and mostly colored blue and white. The day's journey was more than usually interesting; somehow one felt instinctively that he was traversing a region closely associated with man from very ancient times.

Leaving Yuen-fang ch'ang soon after 6 a.m., we traversed country similar to that of the day before, and reached Pai- (pronounced P'an) -miao ch'ang at 10 o'clock. Here, contrary to what my map indicated, I found no river. Replies to inquiries gave it as 30 li farther on, and so it proved. The map for this region is hopelessly inaccurate, and it was quite useless attempting to be guided by it. Pai-miao ch'ang is a small village built on the top of a ridge and surrounded in part by woods of Cypress and Pine. Crossing an undulating area we descended by an easy path, finally reaching the T'ungchiang River, 10 li above Chiangkou. This river is fully 100 yards broad, with red-colored water and a sluggish current. Boats were easily secured and we dropped downstream to Chiangkou, which we reached at 3 o'clock, just before a heavy thunder-storm broke. The day's journey was said to be 70 li, the road was easy, with flora and scenery identical with that of the preceding days.

Chiangkou, alt. 1600 feet, is the second town in size and importance in the department of Pa Chou. It consists of about 500 houses, built on the fringe of a promontory between two rivers, backed by low, steep, well-wooded hills. The rivers unite at this point and are navigable downwards to Chungking. The more easterly stream descends from T'ungchiang Hsien, the westerly stream from Pa Chou, each town distant from Chiangkou 180 li. Both streams are navigable for small boats up-stream to these towns.

A Feng Chou (official next below a Chou in rank) re-sides at Chiangkou. From a distance the town looks well-built and prosperous, but it does not improve on closer inspection. The position is admirable and undoubtedly the town is of considerable commercial importance, yet we had great difficulty in exchanging twenty taels of silver. Like other towns we had passed through, Chiangkou was feeling the suppression of the opium traffic severely, and until new industries arise to take the place of the opium trade the re-sources of all these places will be crippled.

We found accommodation in a poor but quiet inn, and, thanks to the thunder-storm, no curious crowd gathered to annoy us. My principal men spent several hours in finding out a cross-country road to Yilung Hsien, and eventually succeeded.

On leaving Chiangkou we ferried across the Pa Chou River and then made a steep ascent of a few hundred feet. The rest of the day we meandered along the crest of a range of low mountains, following an undulating path. In parts the road was good, in others ankle deep in slippery mud. Thunder-showers fell at intervals and it was fairly cool.

CHINA — MOTHER OF GARDENS

The country generally is similar to that traversed during previous days. Tobacco is a rather common crop hereabouts and we saw a little cotton. Maize is very rare, but rice is abundantly cultivated. Shrines and small temples continued common and in good repair. Kwanyin and Tuti are the common deities, the latter representing an old man and his wife, constitute the tutelary genii. Dignified, ornately carved tombstones and mausoleums were everywhere in evidence.

Our intended destination for the day was Chen-lung ch'ang, 60 li from Chiangkou, but on reaching there we found market in full swing, and, to avoid the crowd, we journeyed on another 6 Ii. On market days these villages are impossible, from the foreigner's point of view. I rode through this village in my chair, and the crowd which gathered at the upper end of the place mustered several hundred. Wine appears to flow freely on market days and many were under its exciting influence. Prudence as well as comfort therefore demands that one avoid all crowds as much as possible when travelling in the interior regions of China. Women attend these markets in force and appear to be a power in this part of the Celestial Empire. Their bearing and manners generally are very free for Chinese women: natural, unbound feet are the rule.

Chen-lung ch'ang is clustered on the narrow neck of a sandstone ridge, and in common with all such villages boasts a fine village temple. We lodged for the night in a poor wayside inn at Hei-tou-lean, alt. 3100 feet.

The next day was cool, with showers at odd times but of no consequence. With the exception of one steep descent and an ascent in the late afternoon, the road was more or less level all day, traversing the tops of the low mountains. These sandstone mountains are dissected by innumerable deep, narrow ravines, clothed with Pine, Cypress, and a dense jungle of miscellaneous shrubs. Unlike limestone country no bottom-lands are formed, and cultivation is relegated to the higher parts of the ranges. Farmhouses are scattered here, there, and everywhere, but the villages are all situated on the tops of the mountains, most frequently on the divide of a ridge.

Fourteen li from Hei-tou-k'an we passed through the village of

THE ANCIENT KINGDOM OF PA

Tai-lu ch'ang, where market was in progress and many pigs on sale. Thirty li from this place we passed Ting-shan ch'ang, a village of considerable size, charmingly situated on the neck of a ridge, backed by a chaitzu and a fine Cypress grove. Chaitzu, of which frequent mention has been made, are a feature of these parts. They are old forts, said to have been mostly constructed during the great sectarian rebellion of A.D. 1796-1803. A small official (Hsao-shoa-tang) resides at Ting-shan ch'ang. In spite of its fine situation this village was unusually filthy and was dominated with strong odors of a wine-distillery. The usual crowd of loafers followed us for some distance on quitting this village.

In the late afternoon we arrived at Lung-peh ch'ang, alt. 3000 feet, after travelling 74 li. We lodged in a rambling, dilapidated inn, fairly clean, with rooms removed some little distance from the street—the village sewer. Market not being in progress the crowd of inquisitive idlers was relatively small.

The flora was not particularly interesting, but we passed a number of fine Camphor trees (Cinnamomum camphora). The crops, however, were rich and varied. Rice and sweet potato predominate, odd patches of cotton were noted and also others of Indigo (Strobilanthes flaccidifolius). In the afternoon coolies laden with salt passed us. This salt is pure white and granular and comes from Nanpu Hsien. From our lodging Ting-shan ch'ang was visible, 30 li distant and nearly due east. The map shows a river flowing past this village, but the only one we could get tidings of was 50 li from that place.

After a comfortable night's rest we continued our journey through country similar to that of foregoing days, but less well-wooded and more inclined to be arid, with broader valleys more under cultivation. Our route followed the boundary between Pa Chou and Yilung Hsien. We passed through two market villages and stayed for the night in a farmhouse 1 li before reaching Fu-ling ch'ang, alt. 2800 feet. We purposely stopped at this place in order to escape market day at the village, but did not avoid a constant crowd until after dark, when the doors were closed. We found all these crowds quiet and orderly enough, but a continuous mass of faces, with wooden expression, blocking the doorway, obstructing light and air, is very trying.

CHINA — MOTHER OF GARDENS

Immensely useful as these markets are to the country-side, they have decided drawbacks from a traveller's point of view. A good police force is really more necessary in these villages than in the cities. The more lawless element fears a Hsien (Magistrate), but has little respect for a Ti-pao (Village Head-man). Local produce is mostly in evidence in these markets; a few needles, aniline dyes, trumpery odds and ends, chiefly of Japanese origin, are about the only foreign goods met with.

We saw more cotton during the day than we had elsewhere observed on this journey, and the crop looked flourishing. Kao-liang (Sorghum vulgare) was a common crop, but rice and sweet potato again preponderated. The sorghum and rice were bursting into ear. Wood Oil trees occur, but are not plentiful, and commercially this crop is unimportant hereabout. Mixed with the cotton were odd plants of the oil-seed yielding Sesamum indicum (Hsiang-yu).

In the late afternoon we traversed country which some-what resembled that around Tunghsiang Hsien—on all sides, as far as the eye could see, nothing but ridge upon ridge of low sandstone mountains. These ranges average about 3000 feet in altitude, those to the east and north being higher than those to the west and south. The map is all wrong for the region, so I could not definitely place our route. The river Sheng-to, so boldly indicated, escaped us, though we should have crossed it had the map been correct. The market villages passed were smaller than heretofore, very filthy, and stinking, yet most charmingly situated on the neck of low ridges, and well shaded with trees. Camphor trees are very common, and Pride of India trees (Melia azedarach) particularly abundant. The stage said to be 70 li proved very easy, the weather being dull and cool.

Our stay at the farmhouse was scarcely a success; we had a full crowd until bedtime, and in spite of fair promises four of my men who remained in the house with me had neither dinner nor bedding. As a punishment I paid only half our usual rate, much to the householder's chagrin. Fu-ling ch'ang was quite deserted when we passed through in the early morning. It occupies the narrow neck of a sandstone ridge, after the usual manner of these villages. The same is true of Shih-ya ch'ang, 30 li farther on. Ten li beyond this latter village we passed a

REDBEAN TREE (ORMOSIA HOSIEI), 60 FEET TALL, GIRTH 20 FEET

nine-storied pagoda and sighted the town of Yilung Hsien, to the northward, about a mile distant as the crow flies and at equal altitude, 2500 feet. Yilung is a very small town, situated on the mountain-top, backed by a steep bluff and surrounded by a wall of dressed sandstone. Two-thirds of the land enclosed within the city wall is given over to cultivation. We passed to the southwest of the town by a road which makes a steep descent and ascent and then meanders along the tops of the mountains until Tu-men-pu is reached. The mountains are lower, more flat, the valleys wider, and the whole country more treeless. Cotton is abundantly cultivated throughout this region, and it is evident that the district of Yilung produces a very considerable quantity. Rice and sweet potato are the common crops, the latter thriving on the hot almost soilless rocks. The earth is drawn into ridges, often leaving bare rock between, and cuttings are inserted. These cuttings, leafy shoots about 6 inches long, quickly take root and form plants that produce an abundant crop. Sorghum is fairly common in places, but maize is very scarce. Stone monuments were less in evidence, but we passed a fine 0-mi-to Fu stone surmounted by a hideous T'engkou. Six old hats protected this stone from the rain and sun; in front was a huge mass of ashes and the remains of many joss sticks. We were informed that the tutelary genius of this spot is renowned for his benevolence, and that it was hoped shortly to erect a shrine over the spot.

We had been unfortunate in the matter of market days all along, and found another in progress at Tu-men-pu. Seemingly having gained nothing by staying the night a little beyond or before reaching these villages, we experimented and stayed at one. It was not a success. A mob rushed our inn and bedlam reigned for a couple of hours. Eventually the crowd thinned, but the more insistent and curious remained until bedtime. There was much noise, but the crowd was friendly enough; nevertheless, I was glad it proved to be the last market village of its kind we encountered before reaching Chengtu.

Tu-men-pu or ch'ang, alt. 1950 feet, 70 li from Fu-ling ch'ang, is a large and prosperous village boasting much trade on market days. Something of everything in the way of native produce was on sale, and the narrow street was thronged to overflowing. Five li before reaching this place our road converged with one leading to Pa Chou city by way of Yilung Hsien.

I had a poor night's sleep in consequence of loud talking being carried on far into the early hours, a woman (as usual) being the principal offender. This was an emphatic reminder of the hubbub of the crowd which besieged us on arrival, and I was really glad to quit Tu-men-pu. A few li beyond this village we branched off from the main road, which goes to Nanpu Hsien. Much salt comes from this township, and during the last two or three days we had met many carriers laden with this commodity.

Forty li beyond Tu-men-pu we passed the poor village of Shui-kuan-ying, protected by dilapidated gates which denote its former military character. In years gone by it was a barrier of some considerable importance. Twenty li farther on we reached the village of Chin-ya ch'ang, alt. 2150 feet, which differs from all we had met with heretofore in having a broad main street fully exposed to the heavens. To our great joy market was not in progress. We found lodgings in a new and quiet inn, which proved a welcome change; the people, too, were courteous and much less inquisitive. The day was exceptionally hot, and all were glad to reach the end of the allotted stage of 60 li. Twelve li before reaching Chin-ya ch'ang we struck a main road leading from Nanpu Hsien, and following it entered the village through an isolated ornate gateway. Beyond the village is a bluff of gray sandstone studded with square-mouthed caves. These caves are crude imitations of Mantzu caves, and are of recent origin, and purely Chinese.

The day's journey was through less interesting country than usual. The broad valleys and nearly treeless mountains are all under cultivation. Cotton was again common in the forenoon, but much less so afterwards. This crop looked as flourishing as Chinese cotton usually does. Tobacco is sparingly cultivated. The tobacco leaves are merely sun-dried before using, and the quality is therefore poor. Sweet potato was more plentiful than ever; the arid sand-stone rocks evidently suit this crop. Rice was, of course, everywhere abundant, sorghum common, but maize was very scarce and suffering from drought. The Irish potato is very little cultivated in these parts. Around Tu-men-pu white-wax is produced in small quantities on the Privet (Ligustrum lucidum), but the cultivation is slovenly carried out, the trees being dwarf and ill-cared for. A few Cypress trees were noted, but Paulownia is a common tree. and Wood Oil trees rather plentiful. A little silk is raised. but the industry is unimportant hereabout. Odd trees of the Banyan (Ficus infectoria) occur near houses and shrines. We passed a few fine tombs, but the average headstone is less ornate than those formerly met with.

We experienced a brief but terrific thunder-storm during the early hours of the morning, and rain continued to fall slightly when we set out from Chin-ya ch'ang. For 20 li we followed an abominable road of mud. This was very greasy, and caused many of us to come croppers. Ultimately, we reached a paved road, and, 6 li farther, a tributary stream of the Kialing River. This tributary is broad, broken by cataracts and rapids, and quite unnavigable at this point. It unites with the Kialing River, locally known as the Paoning Ho, at Ho-che kuan. This is a small riverine port boastng a remarkably fine shop where coal, lime, and especially Chinese wine (sam-shu), were on sale. On the paved road we met several men carrying Bombay cotton yarn—the first example of foreign goods we had encountered on the whole journey!

At Ho-che kuan the Kialing River is smooth and placid, and when in flood is fully 400 yards broad. We ferried across the river to the right bank, and then traversed an alluvial flat of considerable size, highly cultivated with rice and sorghum, with here and there a little abutilon hemp. At the head of this fiat, some 10 li from the river, we crossed over some levelled hillocks into a basin—evidently an old lake bed—surrounded by bare mountains 200 to 500 feet high. This depression was a lake of luxuriant padi (rice), with houses here and there, nestling in clumps of trees. From this basin we passed through a low, narrow gap between the hills, and came abruptly to the Paoning River a little below the city itself. We were ferried across and found lodgings in a large and fairly comfortable inn. The flora of the day's journey was without special interest, Cypress being the only kind of tree really common. But shading some graves, opposite Ho-che kuan, occurs the largest specimen of the Pride of India (Melia azedarach) I

112

have met with. This tree is 70 feet tall, and 10 feet in girth.

Paoning Fu is a city of past rather than of present great-ness. It is still a most important administrative centre, but its real interest lies in its great historic past. From the early days of Chinese conquest it has been a strategical point of vast importance. During the Ming dynasty (A.D. 1368-1644) a generalissimo of forces had a palace here. The terrible rebel, Chang Hien-tsung (A.D. 1630-46 circa), ravaged the country roundabout, but spared the city itself. The result is that many of the official residences and temples date back to ancient times.

Formerly Paoning was the centre of a lucrative and thriving silk industry, but this has steadily declined during the last twenty years, and to-day it is of little consequence. Attempts are now being made by the officials to rejuvenate and foster this industry, which apparently failed more through lack of business ability and tenacity than anything else. On the neighboring hills I was told wild silk is produced, the worms feeding on the leaves of a scrub Oak, Ching-kang (Quercus serrata).

The city occupies an extensive alluvial flat on the left bank of the river within an amphitheatre of low, bare, often pyramidal, hills, 300 to 600 feet high. Viewed from the opposite bank there are no outstanding architectural features visible, save a pavilion, which is virtually the only building breaking the monotony of level roofs. The area within the city walls is largely occupied by yamens, temples, and residences of the more wealthy. Business is mostly carried on outside the city proper, and is confined mainly to one street. Umbrellas were the most noticeable articles on sale, but the city is famous for its superior vinegar, great jars of which were on view.

Hedges of the thorny shrub, Citrus trifoliata, are a prominent feature of this city and its suburbs, giving to the quieter streets a country-lane-like appearance. The water supply of the city is from wells, which are often very deep. This water is said to be good, but that supplied to our inn had a very earthy flavor. From what I saw of the city during a day's stay there, I received the impression of its being clean, its people very orderly and courteous, but the decline in prosperity was marked. The Paoning Ho is a shallow river, and opposite the city about 500 yards broad when in flood. It is navigable for boats of considerable size downward to Chungking. Up-stream small boats ascend to Kuangyuan Hsien. A certain amount of merchandise descends in small boats from Pikou, in Kansu, to Chaohua Hsien. These rivers are most important to Paoning Fu, for, in addition to export trade, the coal and wood used in the city itself are conveyed over these waterways. On the right bank facing the city is a ledge or cliff, on which nestle several temples and pavilions, sheltered by groves of Cypress. In a gap in this cliff is situated the busy little village of Nan-ching kuan. Timber is very scarce around Paoning. Cypress wood is commonly used in house-building; Alder wood (Alnus cremastogyne) occasionally being employed for window frames, but its chief use is as fuel. Pine occurs, but, save as fuel, is worthless. Cunninghamia, that most useful of Chinese Conifers, does not grow in this neighborhood. The wood of the Hungtou tree (Ormosia Hosiet), so highly esteemed for carpentry, was formerly fairly common and cheap. To-day, however, it has to be brought from a distance, and, in consequence, is expensive. Oak and Huanglien (Pistacia chinensis) are the only other timber trees of note. Paoning is an important missionary centre, and the seat of a Protestant bishopric. During my brief visit I had the pleasure of spending a few hours with the kindly and energetic Bishop Cassels, and certain of his coadjutors, who did all they could to render my stay pleasant.

Leaving Paoning Fu and following the main road via Tungchuan Fu, by easy stages I entered the city of Chengtu Fu nine days later, having occupied fifty-four days on the journey from Ichang.

The journey from Tunghsiang Hsien to Paoning Fu fully bore out my expectations. The crowds on market days were a decided drawback, but not once was I insulted or called (in my hearing) uncomplimentary names. The avaricious greed and cunning of the inhabitants were most marked. They were constantly putting up the prices of foodstuffs on my followers, which led to much argument and high words, and several times I was called upon to settle such disputes. The greed of the Szechuanese peasant and small shopkeeper is a byword amongst the Chinese of other provinces. The term Szechuan Lao-ssu (Szechuan rat) is applied derisively to the whole population by the Chinese from other provinces. Niggardly and avaricious they undoubtedly are, but they are great agriculturists, and the question of the "mote and beam" may well be left open. As mentioned before, the province is largely peopled by descendants of immigrants, and these folk almost invariably style themselves men of the provinces their ancestors came from.

The outstanding features of this ancient part of Szechuan are:—

1. The elaborate system of market villages situated at equal distances of 30 li apart, each with its nine market days per month, and alternating with the markets of neighboring villages. Each village is situated on the mountain-top and usually on the neck of a divide, with one central more or less covered street.

2. The rice belt is confined to the mountain-slopes and summits, the valleys being ravines, jungle-clad as a rule, with little or no cultivatable bottom-lands. The highly cultivated nature of the region and the presence of cotton in quantity around Yilung Hsien.

3. The numerous fine mausoleums with remarkably good sculpturing: the peculiar, dignified style of headstones and mural monuments generally. The number of wayside shrines and deities all in excellent repair.

4. The independent bearing and buxom appearance of the women. and their evident influence in general market business. Throughout the whole region natural, unbound feet are the rule.

5. The region is far from being thickly populated, and cannot be termed wealthy, but apparently it is largely self-contained and self-sufficient.

6. The intense curiosity of the people, due to the fact that few before had ever seen a foreigner.

CHAPTER X

THE CHENGTU PLAIN

THE GARDEN OF WESTERN CHINA

HE plain of Chengtu is the only large expanse of level ground in the great province of Szechuan; it is also one of the richest, most fertile, and thickly populated areas in the whole of China. Its extreme length from Chiang-kou in the south to Hsao-shui Ho beyond Mienchu Hsien in the north, is about 80 miles as the crow flies; its extreme width from Chao-chia-tu in the east to Kuan Hsien in the west about 65 miles, in a straight line. From Kiung Chou in the extreme southwest to its northeast limits beyond Teyang Hsien is about 80 miles. The circumferential boundaries are very irregular, the total area being under 3500 square miles. Chengtu Fu, the provincial capital, and seventeen other walled cities, are situated on this plain, together with very many unwalled towns of large size. Farmhouses dot the plain in every direction; the total population probably exceeds 6,000,000.

This plain is really part basin, part sloping alluvial delta, having an elevation ranging from about 1500 feet above sea-level in the south and east to 2300 feet in the northwest and west. It is bounded to the west and north-west by the steep descent of a high mountainous region, which at very little distance from it reaches above the snow-line. In the extreme north-west the snow-clad Chiuting shan actually overlooks the plain. On its other boundaries the sandstone hills of the Red Basin rise sharply in bluffs 1000 to 1500 feet above the level of the plain. The high barrier ranges protect the plain from the cold northerly and westerly winds, but to these must be ascribed the rapid changes in temperature, the fogs, raw atmosphere, and the overcast skies so characteristic of Chengtu Fu.

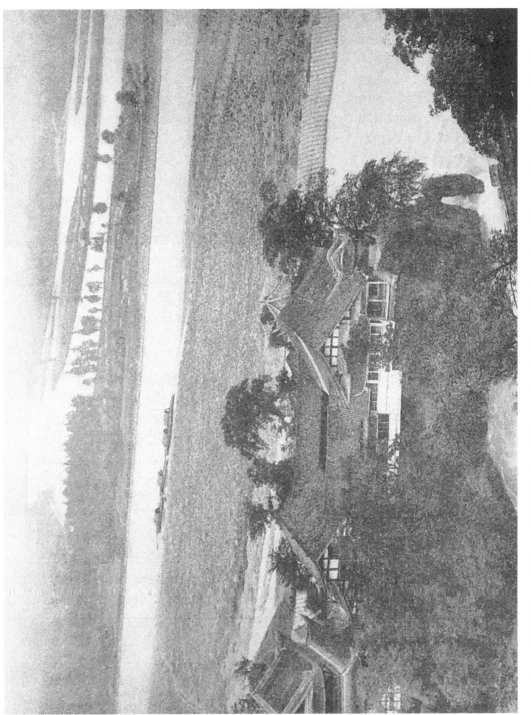

IRRIGATION WORKS AT KUAN HSIEN, INAUGURATED MORE THAN 2,000 YEARS AGO

CHINA — MOTHER OF GARDENS

The plain owes its abundant fertility to a complete and marvellous system of irrigation, inaugurated some 2100 years ago by a Chinese official named Li-ping and his son. The headquarters of this irrigation system is Kuan Hsien, a city situated on the extreme western edge of the plain, where the Min River debouches from the mountains. The principle on which the system is based is simple in conception, but very intricate in detail. An obstructing hill called Li-tiu shan was first cut through for the purpose of leading the waters through and distributing them over the plain. The passage having been excavated, the waters of the Min River were divided, by means of an inverted V-shaped dyke, a little distance above the canal into two main streams, the South and North rivers, as they are called. The waters of the north stream are carried through the Li-tiu shan cut, and after passing through the city of Kuan Hsien are divided into three principal streams. The most southerly of the three, called The Walking Horse, flows directly east, and irrigates the districts of P'i Hsien and Chengtu. The central stream, called the Cedar Stem River, flows northeast, and is utilized to irrigate the western and northern parts of the above-named districts. Branches of these two streams flow past the south and north walls of Chengtu, uniting near the east gate of the city. The third, or northern branch, known as the South Rush River, flows north toward the city of Peng Hsien, and then southeastward past Han Chou. All the sub-divisions of this branch and its anastomosing canals and ditches unite near Chao-chia-tu to form the head-waters of the To River, which flows due south past the famous salt-wells of Tzu-liu-ching, and finally enters the Yangtsze at Lu Chou. The South Rush River is fed by numerous torrents which descend from the ranges bounding the northwest edge of the plain These streams—broad, stony, irresponsible things with no defined banks—exist only during rains or the melting of the snow in spring. In crossing the northern parts of the plain the traveller can form some estimate of what the whole was like before the irrigation canals were dug and dykes erected. But to return to the system at Kuan Hsien. The south river, which occupies the original bed of the Min River, is divided into four principal streams almost immediately opposite the Li-tiu Hill. The most easterly branch, named the Peace-ful River, irrigates the districts of Kuan Hsien, Pi Hsien, and Shuangliu Hsien. The next branch, called the Sheep Horse River, irrigates other parts of the above-named districts, uniting with the Peaceful River, at Hsinhsin Hsien. The third stream, called Black Stone River, irrigates the department of Chungching Chou, and unites with the other streams at Hsinhsin Hsien. The fourth stream, called Sand Ditch, flows southwest through Tayi Hsien and Kiung Chou, joining the other streams at Hsinhsin Hsien. All the streams which intersect the Chengtu plain, save those forming the upper waters of the To River, unite at Chiangkou, a village at the extreme southeastern edge of the plain, some 45 English miles south of Chengtu city.

This system of anastomosing canals, ditches, artificial and natural streams, forms a complex yet perfect network. The current in all is steady and swift, the bunding secure, and floods unknown. Not only are all these streams and canals available for irrigation, but they are also utilized to generate power required in various industries. Flour-mills abound, driven by vertical or horizontally fixed water-wheels. Similar mills are used for crushing Chinese rape-seed, preparatory to pressing for the extraction of the oil.

It must not be supposed that Li-ping and his son completed the system which obtains to-day. They were the originators, and the lines they laid down have been followed and enlarged upon by succeeding generations. These famous irrigation works are perhaps the only public works in all China that are kept in constant and thorough repair. Every year the bunding is repaired and all silt removed from the bed of the channels. An official styled Shui-li Fu—Prefect of Water-Ways—residing at Chengtu, has charge of the system. In late winter the water is diverted at Kuan Hsien from the North River to admit of the removing of silt. In the early spring, conducted with much pomp, there is an annual ceremony of turning on the waters. The motto of Li-ping, "Shen tao t' an, ti tso yen" (Dig the bed deep, keep the banks low), has become an established law in these parts, and is rigorously carried into effect. Amidst so much that is decaying and corrupt in China it is refreshing to find an old institution maintaining its standard of excellence and usefulness through century after century. The originators of this work have been deified, and two magnificent temples overlooking their work at Kuan Hsien bear witness to the gratitude of the millions who have enjoyed, and continue to enjoy, prosperity from the labors of the famous Li-ping and his son. The hero-worship here exemplified would do credit to the people of any land.

The larger of the two temples merits some description. It is by far the finest example I have seen in my travels, and is probably not excelled by any temple in all China. It nestles midst a grove of fine trees, facing the river on the side of a hill, with broad flights of steps leading from terrace to terrace. The buildings are of wood, finely carved and lacquered. The courtyards of stone are broad and spacious, with ornaments in bronze and iron of old and unique workmanship. There are figures representing Li-ping, his wife, and son, also many finely gilded and inscribed votive boards, gifts of a long line of succeeding emperors, viceroys, gentry, and guilds. Not a weed is allowed to grow, the whole place being kept scrupulously clean by the Taouist priests in charge. In the courtyards are many interesting trees and shrubs, trained in Chinese manner with consummate skill. Two magnificent specimens of the Crepe Myrtle (Lagerstroemia indica), trained into the shape of a fan some 25 feet high by 12 feet wide, and said to be over 200 years old, are finer than anything of the kind I have seen elsewhere.

The whole of the plain is subdivided into small fields, every field or series of fields having its own level, differing (sometimes only by one or two inches) from that of its neighbors. This arrangement necessitates a complicated code of regulations, which, sanctioned by custom and usage, determines the proportions in which the water of any one canal is distributed into its branches, and the order of succession in which proprietors of different fields are allowed to make use of it. The system has been so far perfected that each rice field receives, exactly at the right time, a sufficient supply of running water. So complete is the whole arrangement, that scarcity, much less famine, is virtually unknown on the Chengtu plain.

There are no extremes of climate in this region. In summer the temperature seldom reaches 100° F., in the shade; in winter it seldom falls below 35° F. It is humid at all times and essentially cloudy, more especially in winter, when the sun is rarely seen, owing to banks of mists. The land is always under cultivation, yielding two main crops that ripen in April or May, and August or September respectively. Catch crops are obtained between these two main harvests. Rice is the chief summer crop, but certain districts produce millet, sugar, pulse, indigo (Strobilanthes flaccidifolius), and tobacco in quantity, P'i Hsien being noted in particular for the latter crop. Wheat and Chinese rape are the chief winter crops with Broadbeans (Vicia faba), peas, barley, and Hemp (Cannabis sativa), common in certain districts. Wen-chiang Hsien is famous for its hemp, which is grown in quantity as a winter crop and exported largely to other parts of Szechuan and down river. This product, known colloquially as Huo-ma, has been wrongly identified by many travellers. As summer crops, Ramie or Hsien-ma (Boehmeria nivea) and Abutilon Hemp or Tuen-ma (Abutilon avicennae) are both cultivated more or less in quantity. The only Jute or Huang-ma (Corchorus capsularis) I ever saw was in July, 1910, growing near Yao-chia-tu. In the northern parts of the plain, Mienchu and Teyang hsiens, a little cotton is raised, but commercially the crop is unimportant. Opium was never cultivated in quantity on the plain.

All the Chinese vegetables and culinary oil-producing plants are cultivated in quantity in the Chengtu plain, and their general excellence is not excelled elsewhere. To enumerate them it would be necessary to give a complete list of such plants cultivated in all but the coldest parts of China. This enumeration is reserved for a subsequent chapter.

A striking feature of the plain is the enormous number of large houses and farmsteads dotted here, there, and every-where, and shaded by groves of Bamboo, Nanmu, and Cypress. The frequency of these houses, with their enveloping groves, gives a well-wooded appearance to the entire region, and the general view is broken up in such a manner that from no point can many miles of the plain be seen at one time.

The variety of trees is very great; fully fifty species could easily be enumerated. Alongside the streams and ditches, Alder, Ching-mu (Alnus cremastogyne) abounds, and forms one of the principal sources of fuel. In the more northern parts of the plain the curious

CHINA — MOTHER OF GARDENS

Camptotheca acuminata, with clean trunk, gray bark, and globose heads of small white flowers, displaces the Alder. Around the houses Bamboo, Oak, Pride of India, Soap trees, Cypress, and Nanmu are the commonest trees. The Nanmu is a special feature around temples. Several species of the genus Machilus are called Nanmu, all agreeing in being stately, tall, umbrageous evergreens. The wood they yield is highly valued, and the trees are particularly handsome. The Banyan tree, so abundant a little farther south, is very rare here, and neither Pine nor China Fir (Cunninghamia lanceolata) are common. Occasionally trees of the Red Bean (Ormosia hosiei) occur, always, however, in temple-yards or shading wayside shrines. The great industry of Chengtu Fu is sericulture, consequently Mulberry trees abound, and Cudrania tricuspidata (Tsa-shu), the leaves of which are also used for feeding silkworms, is likewise fairly common.

In such a highly cultivated area the natural flora has, of course, been destroyed. The few indigenous shrubs and herbs that remain are relegated to the sides of streams and grave-yards. In places the Chinese Pampas-grasses (Miscanthus sinensis and M. latifolius) are common; in autumn the fawn-colored plumes are most attractive. Occasionally thorny shrubs like Barberry, Christ's thorn, colloquially Teh-li-pe kuo-tzu (Paliurus ramosissimus), and San-chia pi (Acanthopanax trifoliatus) are used as hedge plants. The commonest fence, however, is made by bending down and interlacing the bamboo culms.

Since the plain is strewn with cities, villages, and farmsteads, a network of roadways necessarily obtains. A main artery extends north-northeast, through the plain and beyond to Shensi province, and ultimately reaches far-distant Peking. This road was commenced from the Shensi end by the great Shih Hwang-ti (he who commenced building the Great Wall) about 220 B.C. It extends from Chengtu in a southwesterly direction to Kiung Chou, and thence to remote Lhassa. Other highways connect the provincial capital with Chungking, the great mart on the Yangtsze River to the southeast; Kuan Hsien in the west, and the Marches of the Mantzu beyond. Roads of secondary importance link these highways with other roads and connect the capital with all the principal cities of the plain and regions beyond.

ROADSIDE BAMBOOS ON THE CHENGTU PLAIN

CHINA — MOTHER OF GARDENS

Most of the roads were originally paved with one or two slabs of stone laid lengthwise down the middle, with bare earth on either side. The constant wheel-barrow traffic, a feature of the entire region, has worn deep grooves into these slabs, All too frequently the slabs have disappeared altogether. leaving unpaved long stretches of roadway. In dry weather these roads are dusty, but easy to travel; in wet weather they are from ankle to knee-deep in sheer mud Often they are practically impassable. and travelling over them in ordinary rainy weather is an experience beyond words to describe. They illustrate admirably the contrariety of things which obtain in China generally. Here in the wealthiest region of the west. if not of the whole of China. the average road is of the meanest width. and in an abominable state of repair. There is much talk of the need of railways in China—true, they are needed badly, but good highways, roads, are an infinitely greater want. The highways and byways on the Chengtu plain are a disgrace to the entire population of this fertile, wealthy region. "What is everybody's business is nobody's business" is a saving that is as applicable in China as in Western lands. The roads exist for the good and welfare of all. but it is nobody's real business to protect them: they are. in consequence. neglected by all—peasants. farmers. officials, and gentry alike.

Mean as these roadways are. they are spanned by hundreds of large honorary portals and memorial arches. mostly constructed of red, or more rarely gray, sandstone, or occasionally of wood. In the vicinity of the more wealthy cities (Han Chou. for example) these portals and arches arc extraordinarily abundant. Many are masterpieces of Chinese architecture. All are well built and covered with sculptures in relief, representing scenes of mythical or everyday life. The ends of the ridge pole and of the gables are usually long drawn out and resolutely upturned, adding additional lightness and beauty to the whole. These long, exaggerated. upturned gable ends are a characteristic feature of the houses, temples, and shrines met with all over this region.

The innumerable ditches, canals, and streams are all well bridged. The bridges are kept in good repair, and refleet the highest credit on the engineers who constructed them. They are built of red or gray sandstone, more rarely of wood, as near Han Chou. The stone bridges vary from one to a dozen or more arches, sometimes hog-backed, but more usually the Roman arch is employed; others are of causeway or trestle design, with or without balustrades, ranging from a single slab laid across a narrow ditch to many such laid on a series of piers built in the bed of the streams. Near Sintu Hsien there is an example of one of these trestle or pier-bridges 120 yards long. Outside the east gate of Chengtu is a red-sandstone bridge of nine arches, which is generally regarded as the bridge mentioned by Marco Polo. A similar bridge exists near Yao-chia-tu, but this has some twenty arches. Immediately outside Han Chou there is a covered wooden bridge, 120 yards long, 6 yards broad, resting on eight stone piers. This bridge, known as the Chin-ying chiao (Bridge of the Golden Goose) , is the handsomest, most ornate wooden structure of its kind I have met with in my travels.

In reference to the bunding of the streams and canals it should be mentioned that cobble-stones enclosed within long sausage-shaped, bamboo-latticed crates are universally employed for this purpose. This system is said to date back to the later times of the Ming dynasty only. Previous to that period the principal abutments and revetments were of iron, fashioned into the shape of gigantic oxen, turtles, pillars, etc. At the places where canals unite or divide, or where the water cascades to a lower level, the earthworks are protected by walls of stones, firmly cemented together.

Another item, and one which astonishes every traveller, is the enormous size of the blocks of stone used in the bridges, more especially those erected on piers. I have no exact measurements by me, but these slabs would average at least 12 yards long by 20 inches square at the ends. Commonly the blocks are of hard limestone, occasionally of conglomerate. The slabs of sandstone when used are shorter. At Chao-chia-tu sandstone slabs are used as fencing.

Any attempt to describe the cities on the Chengtu plain would necessitate more space than is at my disposal. They differ, with the exception of the provincial capital, in no marked particular from other cities of Szechuan. In size they vary considerably, some of the large unwalled towns being commercially more important than the walled cities. Most of the cities and surrounding districts are noted for certain things; for example, Mienchu Hsien for its wheaten flour and paper, P'i Hsien for tobacco, Wen-chiang Hsien for hemp, Peng Hsien for indigo, Shuangliu Hsien for straw-braid, and so on. The majority of these cities are very ancient; all contain fine temples, as becomes such centres of wealth. Chengtu (long. 104° 2' E., lat. 30° 38' N.) was described by Marco Polo, who visited it during the thirteenth century, as a "rich and noble city". Modern travellers, and their name is well-nigh legion, have all agreed with the great Venetian's dictum. In many respects Chengtu, with its population of 350,000 people, is probably the finest city in the whole of China. It is built on a totally different plan from that of Peking, or even Canton, so that comparisons are difficult. The present city of Chengtu is comparatively modern, but occupies much the same site as the capital of the aboriginal kingdom of Shu. This kingdom was conquered by Shih Hwang-ti (the First Emperor) some time between 221-209 B.C., who nominally added it to his dominions. The succeeding dynasty of Han (206 B.C. to A.D. 25) incorporated it as an integral part of China. During the epoch of the Three Kingdoms the site (or thereabouts) of the city was occupied as the capital of the kingdom under Liu-pei. Succeeding dynasties have always made it a most important seat of administration, and princes of the imperial clan or viceroys have resided there. It is still the seat of a viceroy who governs the province of Szechuan and nominally controls all Thibetan affairs.

Great Britain, France, and Germany have each estabfished a Consulate-General there, but on the plea that the city is not an open port, the Chinese have successfully resisted the purchase of land on which to erect suitable houses and offices for the staffs representing these Powers. The result is that these officers are housed in dilapidated Chinese quarters, insanitary, dangerous to health, and unbecoming the dignity of the Powers they represent. It is nothing short of a scandal to thrust men into such abominable quarters. Chengtu Fu is far removed from London, Paris, and Berlin, also from Peking, but is it fitting to make backwoodsmen of these representatives? Missionaries of every denomination are firmly entrenched at Chengtu, and can acquire all the property their funds admit of either for residences, hospitals, schools, or churches.

The city is surrounded by a magnificent wall, some 9 miles in circumference, with eight bastions, pierced by four fine gates. This wall is 66 feet broad at base, 35 feet high, and 40 feet broad at top, along which runs a crenulated balustrade. It is faced and paved with hard brick (the walls of all the other cities on the plain are of sandstone), and is kept in thorough repair. During Manchu times a Tartar garrison was stationed here, a large area on the southwest side of the city being walled off to form a Manchu city. Within the city walls are many fine residences, private and official, temples, a large parade ground, etc. The city is clean, orderly, with an efficient police. To wander through the streets noting the varied industries carried on is a liberal education in Chinese ways of doing things. The wares on sale are of infinite variety, and are themselves indicative of the wealth which is everywhere apparent. The shop-signs, lacquered and gilded, hang vertically downwards, and proclaim in their large artistic characters the titles of the shops and the wares on sale. The city is full of officials, both in and out of office, who move about the streets in sedan-chairs carried at a great speed. The chairs are peculiar in having the long poles curved, with the body of the chair resting on top of the curve. When carried, such a chair is well above the heads of the crowd. The streets are always crowded with pedestrians, chairs, and wheel-barrows. Different trades occupy their own particular quarter. Certain streets are devoted to carpentry in all its branches, boot-shops, shops devoted to horn-ware, skins and furs, embroideries, second-hand clothes shops, silk goods, foreign goods, and so forth. Silk-weaving is the great industry in Chengtu, hundreds of looms being in use.

Evidences of Occidental influence abound. A provincial university and many schools for imparting Western learning exist. Two agricultural experimental farms, an arsenal, mint, bazaar, and many buildings of semi-foreign design. The arsenal and farms are outside the city. An electric lighting plant was operating at the time of my last visit (1910), and the installation of a telephone service was in progress. The Post Office is strongly established here under control of Europeans, and this is the only Western innovation really accomplishing good work. The others (and I have not covered them all) are experiments pure and simple. These are controlled by officials among whom jealousy is rife and peculation not unknown. The good intentions of honest officials are easily nullified by jealous-minded sycophants and ultra-conservatives. The city exhibits numerous examples of blighted experiments, some of them mere follies, but the majority calculated to be beneficial if properly controlled and carried through. The city-fathers and officials have exhibited mad haste to acquire such Western knowledge as they deem useful. They have no real idea of what they want, and there is little co-ordination in any matter. The students rule the colleges; their fathers, the gentry, rule the province. "China for the Chinese," and "away with foreigners and foreign influence" are their slogans. This cry is perfectly legitimate, but they should move slowly. They think they are fully fledged men, whereas they are mere babes in the knowledge of the things they covet so much. The unfortunate rebellion which has spread with such rapidity and brought about so much disaster to the nation, originated with the hot-heads of Chengtu. Primarily it was aimed not so much against the dynasty as against foreign capital. The central government had agreed to a foreign loan, which, amongst other things, had for its object the construction of a railway from Hankow to Chengtu. It was this loan that was the fat in the fire which produced the conflagration—the last straw, if you will, but the primary cause of the rebellion. The dynasty was dethroned (it was effete, anyway, and should have passed fifty years ago), a dictatorship under the guise of a republic cleverly formed by the only man who could save China from anarchy if not disruption—Yuan Shih Kai. But foreign loans have become more absolutely necessary than ever before. The present system of government can only be transient, another dynasty must arise. I mentioned above that the province was under a viceroy, and that the gentry ruled the province. This is the keynote to the whole difficulty. The viceroy has to carry out the instructions of the central government; he has also to please the gentry. The wishes of the two powers became diametrically opposed, and not all the tact of the cleverest diplomats could save the situation. The

THE CHENGTU PLAIN

viceroy (Chao Erh-hsiin) was removed to Manchuria, and his brother (Chao Erh-feng), recalled from the Thibetan Marches (where China's new toy, in the shape of an army modelled on quasi-Western lines was indulging in an altogether uncalled-for war of aggression), appointed to the post. The new viceroy arrived too late to check the revolt, and was ultimately murdered. The gentry declared that no foreign capital, and the necessary supervision of such capital, should enter into the construction of a railway in Szechuan. With Chinese money and Chinese engineers the scheme shall be accomplished, say these autocrats. The central government thought otherwise and made other arrangements. Then came the revolt, fulminated by the gentry of the Chengtu plain, which speedily got beyond their control. The Manchu dynasty, when it ascended the Dragon throne in A.D. 1644, immediately set to work and rescued Szechuan from the bloody grip of the rebel and arch-destroyer, Chang Hien-tsung, and brought peace to the land. Two hundred and sixty-seven years later this dynasty was dethroned by rebellion initiated by the gentry of the Chengtu plain. Dynasties and republics may come and go, but in the future, as in the past, industry, combined with agricultural skill, will continue to win sustenance, derive wealth, influence, and power from this fertile and beautiful region – the Garden of western China.

CHAPTER XI

NORTHWESTERN SZECHUAN

NARRATIVE OF A CROSS-MOUNTAIN JOURNEY TO SUNGPAN TING

FEW days after our arrival at Chengtu in 1910 I determined upon a journey to the border-town of Sungpan Ting, for the express purpose of securing seeds and herbarium specimens of certain new coniferous trees previously discovered by me in that region. During 1903 and again in 1904 I had visited this interesting town. On the first occasion I travelled by the ordinary main road, via Kuan Hsien and the Min valley. The next year I followed the great north road across the plain of Chengtu to Mien Chou, then travelled via Chungpa and Lungan Fu, by another recognized highway. On these journeys I gleaned tidings of a byroad leading from Shihch'uan Hsien across the mountains, finally connecting with both the above routes. This route promised to be interesting as well as novel. Only Roman Catholic missionaries had previously traversed it, so far as I could learn. An Hsien was selected as the real starting-point for this trip.

With this object in view we passed through the north gate of Chengtu city early on the morning of August 8th. Following the north road as far as the city of Han Chou, then branching off and travelling via Shihfang Hsien and Mienchu Hsien, we reached the city of An Hsien, some 300 li from Chengtu, after three and a half days. The road led us right through the luxuriant Chengtu plain to its extreme northwestern limits near Hsao-shui Ho. Afterward we crossed some low foot-hills to a small stream leading to An Hsien. The journey was very easy, though fatiguing owing to the extreme heat of the season.

The city of An Hsien is small, of little importance, prettily situated on the left bank of a stream backed by bare mountains which rear themselves some 2000 feet above the level of the river. Two streams uniting here form a river navigable during high-water season to Mien Chou, a city on the Fou Ho—the western branch of the Kialing River system. An Hsien is a little beyond the northwestern limits of the Chengtu plain, and its river gives it direct communication with Chungking, during the summer at least.

Leaving by the north gate, we took a road that ascends the main branch of the river which is kept from flooding the city by a well-made low bund of stone slabs, firmly cemented together. After traversing a small cultivated valley we plunged into a rocky defile and crossed the river by an iron suspension bridge, 110 yards long. The bridge is old and in poor repair, and it swayed considerably as we walked singly across. A few miles farther on we recrossed the stream by a similar bridge, and reached Lei-ku-ping, our destination for the day, at 6 p.m. A certain amount of rice is cultivated hereabout, but maize is the staple crop. As an undercrop to maize, Amorphophallus konjac (Mo-yu) is commonly cultivated, the tubers being used as food after their acrid properties have been removed by washing in water. We met considerable traffic, mostly coolies laden with sheep-skins and medicines from Sungpan, which they put on boats at An Hsien for conveyance to Chungking; much potash (lye) in small tubs, and oil-cakes, also the residue of Chinese rape-seed after the oil is expressed. Coal of very poor quality, mostly dust, is obtained in the surrounding mountains, and we met scores of mules, ponies, and coolies, engaged in transporting it.

Lei-ku-ping, alt. 2750 feet, is a large market village, possessing one principal street with gates at each end, which are closed after sunset. The centre of a large and important industry in tea, Lei-ku-ping largely supplies Sungpan Ting and the country beyond. The tea is grown in the surrounding districts and brought to the village for sale. Later we shall have more to say concerning this industry.

It rained heavily during the early hours of the morning, and though it was fair when we set out, showers fell the whole forenoon. On leaving Lei-ku-ping we ascended a few hundred feet to the head of a low divide, and then descended to the village of Che-shan, situated on the right bank of a considerable stream. This village shares in the tea industry for the Sungpan market, but is of less importance than Lei-ku-ping.

From Che-shan to Shihch'uan Hsien the road ascends the right bank of the river, which flows between steep precipitous mountains. The path is usually several hundred feet above the stream, broad and fairly easy for the most part, but constantly ascending and descending. The mountain-sides are steep but, where not absolutely vertical, are all under cultivation, maize being the staple crop. There is very little limestone, the rocks being chiefly loose sandstone and mud shales. These shales weather rapidly, and the steepest cultivated slopes are usually composed of these rocks.

The river is broad, and could easily be made navigable for boats during the high-water season. Even in its present condition rafts could be floated down, but we saw no traffic whatsoever on its waters. The water was dirty, and much driftwood was strewn along the shores. This is collected, dried, and stacked, forming apparently the principal source of fuel. Trees are very scarce, but around houses occur Sophora, Pistacia, Pteroceltis, Sterculia platanifolia (Wu-tung), Koelreuteria bipinnata, and Alder. The Koelreuteria was just coming into flower; the flowers are golden yellow produced in large, much-branched, erect panicles; the leaves are very large and much divided. Shrubs are not plentiful, but, much to my surprise, the China Rose (Rosa chinensis) is quite common, and evidently spontaneous, by the wayside, on the cliffs, and by the side of the stream.

A few li below the city of Shihch'uan Hsien the river is spanned by a bamboo suspension bridge, about 80 yards long, supported on cables made of split bamboo culms plaited together. These cables, eight in number, are nearly 1 foot in diameter, and are fastened to stanchions on either side of the river. Two similar cables on either side of the bridge are carried across at higher levels, and have attachments of bamboo rope supporting those which form the base of the structure. A capstan arrangement is used for making the cables taut, and the lower ones are covered with stout wicker-work to form a footway. Like all such structures, this bridge is heavy, sags very much in the middle, and is very unsteady to walk across. The life of these bridges is only a few years, and strong winds often make them very unsafe.

Shihch'uan Hsien is a small city charmingly situated at an altitude of 2800 feet, on the left bank immediately below the junction of two rivers. It is surrounded on all sides by steep, more or less cultivated mountains. Inside the city are many trees, which add considerably to the effect. A pavilion and a small pagoda crown two prominent hills, and assure the luck of the place. A narrow suburb runs ribbon-like between the river and the city wall. This wall is broken down in places, and the gates are low and small. We found accommodation in a large, curiously constructed inn remarkable for the strength of its stinks and the abundance of vermin and mosquitoes it sheltered. The day's journey was given as 65 li, but the li were long, consequently the coolies with their loads arrived late. Cash was needed, but on opening a box to obtain some silver for exchange we found that some one had stolen from it about 30 taels and 5 dollars. The load belonged to a coolie we had engaged at Taning, Hsien, and retained because he had given unusual satisfaction! The previous day he had engaged a local coolie to carry his load, on the ground that he was feeling sick. He was last seen near Che-shan, still unable to carry his load. Evidently he was the culprit, but he was thoughtful enough to leave us about half the amount contained in the box. Since he had about three-quarters of a day's start I concluded it was best to quietly cut the loss, my first and last in China. The delays incident upon lodging a complaint with the official would have involved me in further expense and trouble, with but small chance of recovering the money lost.

The main road to Sungpan continues to ascend the right bank of the river to its source, then crosses over a range and enters the upper Min valley at Mao Chou. I had been over most of this route in 1908 when crossing the Chiuting range from near Mienchu Hsien to Tu-men pu, thence to Mao Chou. The route we had in view leads to the northwest from Shihch'uan Hsien. From Chengtu to this point we had travelled without escort, but with the difficulties of an unknown route before us I thought it best to secure such at this city. Sending my card to the Hsien's yamen, in the ordinary way, I informed this official of my project, and asked for the customary escort. Half an hour afterwards my card was returned with the information that there was trouble at Sungpan and no escort would be supplied! The refusal was as curt as it was insolent, but whether the Hsien was actually responsible I never found out. In the whole of my eleven years' travel in China this was the first and last experience of official discourtesy. Thus two annoying experiences, both unique in their way, yet, happily, trivial and unimportant, marked my visit to Shihch'uan Hsien, a town which, from the commencement of my travels in the western Szechuan, I always had a keen desire to visit.

The next day we left Shihch'uan Hsien at sunrise, glad to escape from the malodorous, vermin-infested inn. No one put in an appearance from the yamen, and no attempt to prevent our taking the route proposed was made. I had rather feared this might happen, but my fears were fortunately groundless. On leaving the city by the north gate we struck a stream nearly equal in volume to the main river. The road ascends the left bank, and almost immediately plunges into a narrow, wild ravine, through which we con-tinued the whole day. Like all such roads it skirts the mountain-side, being usually several hundred feet above the river, but is constantly descending to the water's edge, only to ascend again a few hundred yards farther on. It is in good repair, although the rocks are of soft mud shales, and signs of landslips were frequent. Wherever possible maize is cultivated, but houses are few and far between. The country strangely reminded me of that around Wench'uan Hsien in the upper Min valley farther west. Trees are very scarce, the Wu-tung (Sterculia platanifolia) being perhaps the most common. The shrubs denote a dry (xerophytic) climate, nearly all having small leaves, either thick or covered with a felt of hairs. Of these shrubs, Abelia parvifolia, Lonicera pileata, Ligustrum strongylophyllum, and various kinds of Spiraea, are common. Bushes of the wild China Rose are not infrequent. Five li before reaching Kai-ping-tsen, our destination for the day, we crossed a clear-water tributary by a remarkably well-built stone-arch bridge. During the day we passed several rope bridges, made of a single thick cable of plaited bamboo culms—sure signs of difficult borderland country. Near Shihch'uan Hsien we passed a bamboo suspension bridge, similar to the one already described; at Kai-ping-tsen there is another such bridge. There was a fair amount of traffic on the road. Potash salts (lye), shingles, and oil-cake were the principal loads encountered, all being carried on men's backs, the first-named being the most common.

Kai-ping-tsen, alt. 3200 feet, is a small village of about fifty houses, situated on the left bank of a stream some 50 li north of Shihch'uan Hsien. A new, empty house afforded us comfortable lodgings; the people were courteous, and made our brief stay with them very pleasant. A remarkably fine headstone, recently erected over the tomb of a much-respected widow, was the chief thing of interest in the village.

On leaving Kai-ping-tsen we continued to ascend the left bank of the stream through country similar to that of the previous day, for 30 li to the market village of Hsao-pa-ti. This village, all things considered, is of considerable size (about one hundred houses), with many farmhouses scattered around. The mountains are less rugged and steep, and are given over to the cultivation of maize. The houses are low, built of mud shales and roofed with slabs of slate. Market was in progress; foodstuffs, fuel, and potash salts being the principal goods on sale. A bamboo suspension bridge spans the river and a road leads across country, ultimately joining with the main road between Shihch'uan Hsien and Mao Chou. On leaving Hsao-pa-ti the road deserts the river and ascends through maize fields over a rather low ridge. It then descends to a small tributary, after crossing which a steep climb of 1000 feet leads to the summit of another ridge. From this point we sighted the main stream again, flowing through a smiling valley, at the head of which nestles the village of Pien-kou, which was our destination for the day. This village proved a good 20 li from the ridge, though it looked close at hand. The road led through fields of maize to the valley, and finally across the river by an old and very shaky bamboo suspension bridge, which swayed tremendously and was really unsafe.

Pien-kou (Yuan-kou of the maps), alt. 3800 feet, is a market village of some importance, but a fire had recently destroyed half the houses. We had some difficulty in obtaining lodging, the only decent place being full and the occupants unwilling to move. After a little time persuasive insistence won, and we settled down comfortably, if crowded. One of the occupants was down with fever. I dosed him with quinine, and supplied him with enough to last several days, much to his appreciation. This act got noised abroad, with the result that applications for medicine quickly became too numerous. Quinine is a drug much appreciated by Chinese, being about the only foreign medicine they have real confidence in.

The day's journey was said to be 70 li. It was long and uninteresting. The flora is miserably poor; Alder being the only tree really common.

The road we were following ultimately joined the Mao Chou-Sungpan main road near Chen-ping kuan, about 160 li below the town of Sungpan. We could get no tidings of a road crossing to the Lungan-Sungpan highway, but all the same we felt sure of finding one. Thus far the route indicated on my map was all wrong, and we were left very much in the dark as to our actual whereabouts. However, I was long since accustomed to this state of affairs.

Leaving Pien-kou, a journey of 40 li brought us to Peh-yang ch'ang, a village of a dozen scattered, dilapidated houses. The road was distinctly bad in places owing to landslips. The rocks are mainly mud shales standing on edge. We followed the right bank of the river we had pursued from Shihch'uan Hsien for the first 22 li, then crossed over to the left bank by means of a shaky improvised bridge of two tree logs, the bamboo suspension bridge which formerly crossed the stream hereabout having broken down. At this cross-over point resides a Chinese official, locally styled a Tu-ssu. This official was most courteous, helping us with advice and guidance to cross the stream.

The journey generally was a repetition of the two former days, through a rocky but uninteresting gorge. Wherever possible, maize is cultivated, and we noted two small patches of rice. Houses are few and far between, and we met only a few coolies laden with potash salts, charcoal, and shingles. The flora was not interesting, Alder, Pterocarya,

A MEMORIAL ARCH

and Comas controversa are the only common trees. Buddleia davidii is abundant by the stream-side, and was in full flower. The China Rose also is fairly common. A Lily (Lilium leucanthum) without bulbils, otherwise very like Lilium sargentiae, is plentiful in places. At Peh-yang ch'ang, alt. 4100 feet, we found a road leading off to the right, and connecting with the Lungan-Sungpan highway at Shui-ching-pu; this we decided to follow.

Above our lodgings at Peh-yang ch'ang the river bifurcates, one branch, a clear-water stream, being locally adjudged the larger. It is up this stream the road connecting with the Mao Chou-Sungpan highway ascends. The people told us that this road was similar in character to the one we had followed thus far, but more difficult, especially since the proper bridges had nearly all been recently destroyed by floods. The cross-over to the Min valley is near a place called Hwa-tsze-ling, where fine forests of Silver Fir and Spruce occur. Pien-kou is a considerable wine market, much of the product finding its way to Sungpan over this rough cross-country road.

A fatiguing march marked our first day's journey toward the Lungan-Sungpan highway. We made two long ascents and descents, and commenced a third ascent, putting up for the night at Hsao-kou, after covering 55 li. The second ascent was fully 2000 feet, and very steep, through maize fields, culminating in abandoned herb-clad areas. The descent was mainly through coppice and brush. Houses occur scattered here and there, wherever cultivation is practicable, maize being the staple crop; the Irish potato and peas are also grown. The road proved difficult, but I had traversed worse.

The forests have been destroyed, brushwood now covering the uncultivated areas. Topping the loftier crags, and in inaccessible places generally, a sprinkling of Conifer trees still exist, but we did not get near them. The vegetation generally is that common to the 5000 to 6000 feet belt in west Szechuan, but is less varied than in many parts I have visited. In the valleys Alder was common, and on the slopes the Varnish tree (Rhus verniciflua) and Walnut (Juglans regia) occur in quantity. In coppices the Davidia, both the hairy and glabrous varieties, is plentiful, but no large trees were noted. Throughout the bottom-lands and abandoned cultivated areas Summer Lilac (Buddleia davidii) was a wonderful sight—thousands of bushes, each one with masses of violet-purple flowers, delighting the eye on all sides, the variety magnifica, with its reflexed petals and intensely colored flowers, being most in evidence. I gathered also an albino form, one small solitary bush, the only one I have ever met with. Forming a much-branched bush 4 to 8 feet tall, with rose-purple flowers, Hydrangea villosa was next to the Buddleia, the most strikingly ornamental shrub. On moist rocky slopes plants of Rodgersia aesculifolia occur in millions. It was in the fruiting stage, but when in flower the acres of snow-white panicles must have presented a bewitching sight. Nowhere else have I seen this plant so abundant or luxuriant. The slender arching plumes of white flowers, produced by Spiraea aruncus, covered acres of ground; an apetalous Astilbe (A. rivularis) was also abundant and worthy of note.

The hamlet of Hsao-kou, alt. 5900 feet, consists of three scattered houses, surrounded by maize plats, with remains of other ruined houses near by. It is encompassed on all sides by steep mountains, some of them culminating in lofty limestone crags and rugged razor-like ridges with pinnacled peaks—all of them inaccessible. At the back of the inn are a few Larch trees, and near by several large trees of a flat-leaved Spruce. The Hou-p'o (Magnolia officinalis) is cultivated hereabout, and also around all of the houses we passed during the day. The innkeeper likewise cultivates a medicinal Aconite (Aconitum wilsonii), the tuber of which is valued as a drug in Chinese pharmacy.

We encountered only three men carrying goods during the whole day; two were laden with potash salts, the third with the bark of a Linden, used locally for making sandals. Evidences of forest fires were all too frequent during the day's march.

The next day rain ruined what otherwise would have been a more than ordinarily interesting march. From 7 a.m. until 2 p.m. we struggled up some 4000 odd feet to the summit of the pass leading across the Tu-ti-liang shan; then descended another 4000 feet to the hamlet of Hsueh-po, where we secured lodgings in a large and good house. Rain commenced shortly before 11 a.m., and continued the rest of the day. Our perspective was limited to a few hundred feet; now and again a strong gust of wind would scatter the mists, admitting momentary glimpses of cliffs and inaccessible peaks clothed with jungle and with occasional Conifer trees, but such views were rare.

The hamlet of Hsao-kou is very scattered, and we passed two or three more houses soon after leaving our lodgings. But after about 3 li houses and cultivation vanished, as did also the Buddleia and Hydrangea previously so abundant. The ascent, at first gradual, soon becomes precipitous, through a jungle growth of shrubs and coarse herbs. The latter with the thin brushwood is cut periodically and burnt. The ashes so obtained are placed in wooden vats fitted with sieve bottoms, boiling water is poured over them, and the liquid drains into tubs, where it is evaporated and salts of potash (lye) left as a residue. This product is packed in flasks and carried to market towns for sale. We passed several rude huts where men were engaged in this occupation. The road ascends a small torrent and is nowhere easy. By throwing logs across the stream and boggy places, lumber-men have succeeded in making some sort of a path. But crossing these wet, slippery logs was difficult. At one such crossing I slipped, but by jumping into the rock-strewn torrent somehow managed to avoid a nasty accident. Near the summit, and for some distance down the Lungan side of the pass, are split pieces of wood, arranged to form a long flight of shallow steps that assist the roadway materially. The descent after a few hundred feet becomes gradual, leading through open, park-like slopes, quite unlike anything I have encountered elsewhere in China. Now largely denuded of trees these glades are covered with grass, and horses, goats, and pigs are raised here in some quantity.

Formerly this range of mountains must have been covered with Conifers, but the lumber-man's hands have been heavily laid on these forests. We passed none but small, decrepit specimens of no value. Hemlock, Spruce, and Silver Fir are all represented. The outstanding feature of the march was the abundance of Cercidiphyllum trees. Throughout the moist slopes and park-like areas on both sides of the range this tree is common. Stumps of decaying giants abound, one of these, which I photographed, measured 55 feet in girth! This specimen had been broken off some 30 feet above the ground, and was a mere hollow shell, but still supported many twiggy, leafy branches. These stumps are relics of the largest broad-leaved trees I have seen anywhere in China. Growing interspersed with these remains were many specimens of the same tree, 60 to 80 feet tall, 8 to 10 feet in girth, perfect in outline, with myriads of neat, nearly round, bright green leaves. One of these was in young fruit, and for the first time in my travels I secured specimens of the fruit of this beautiful and interesting tree. (Later I collected ripe seeds, and this tree is now growing in the Arnold Arboretum, where it promises to be quite hardy. It proved to be a variety distinct from the Japanese species).

This tree (Cercidiphyllum japonicum sinense) attains to greater size than any other broad-leaved tree known from the temperate zone of eastern Asia. In size it is only approached by its close ally, Tetracentron, which is also common in the woods on the Tu-ti-liang shan. A local name for the Cercidiphyllum is Peh-k'o, a name strictly applied all over China to the Maidenhair-tree (Ginkgo biloba).

The summit of the range is composed of mud shales, which seem favorable to the growth of vegetation generally. Between 8000 feet altitude and the summit Rhododendron calophytum is extraordinarily abundant, trees 40 to 50 feet tall and 5 to 7 feet in girth, with handsome cinnamon-brown bark, cover many acres. Euptelea pleiosperma and Pterocarya hupehensis are other interesting trees plentiful hereabout. The bark of the last mentioned tree is used locally for roofing purposes. Willows in many species are common; the bark of certain of these and also that of Linden trees is used by the peasants for making sandals. Viburnum erubescens Prattii, with pendulous panicles of white fragrant flowers, followed by fruit which is at first scarlet and then changes to black, is perhaps the commonest shrub. Various Araliads grow epiphytically on all the larger trees that have a rough humus collecting bark. Maples in variety, Sorbus laden with fruit, and many other interesting trees were striking constituents of these woods. Tall-growing herbs made a grand display, especially the apetalous Astilbe rivularis, Spiraea aruncus, Anemone vitifolia with white and pink flowers like the Japanese Anemone, Artemisia lactiflora with large panicles of milk-white, fragrant flowers, Balsams (Impatiens) with yellow, pink, and purple flowers; mixed with them also were Meadow Rue, Aconites, many Senecios, and Meconopsis chelidonifolia growing about 3 feet tall with clear yellow flowers, saucer-shaped and 2 ½ inches across. Acres of the country-side are covered by these various herbs.

There was indeed plenty to interest one; the flora of this region is undoubtedly rich, and it was most unfortunate that the rain prevented an exhaustive investigation. Hsueh-po, alt. 6000 feet, consists of a few houses surrounded by high mountains with a good-sized torrent, which rises near the head of the pass, and flows through the narrow valley. Maize is cultivated as the staple crop. The Hydrangea and Buddleia previously noted ascend to this altitude, and were a wealth of blossoms. Alder also extends to this point; Poplar likewise. This latter tree has a very graceful port and the leaves have red petioles and veins when young.

Our lodgings were good and weather-proof, which was fortunate, since it rained heavily the night through, and until eleven o'clock in the forenoon of the next day. Afterwards it was fair, but threatening, heavy clouds and mists obscured the countryside from our view. Around the inn are several trees of a handsome, flat-leaved Spruce (Picea ascendens) with pendulous branchlets. This tree, known locally as Me-tiao sha or sung, is the most esteemed timber tree in these parts. The trees are felled, hewn into planks about 25 feet long, 5 inches thick, and 12 inches broad, and carried on men's backs to a point on the river whence it is possible to float down rafts. Lumbering is a very considerable industry in these mountains, the timber finding its way to Chungpa. This fine Spruce was fruiting freely. (Later I secured plenty of seed, and successfully introduced it into Western gardens).

On leaving Hsueh-po, we crossed the torrent and descended the left bank. At K'ung chiao the torrent is joined by another of equal size, the united waters forming a fine clear-water stream. From this point downward rice is cultivated. The stream continues to receive affluents, a very considerable one joining it at Tu-tien-tsze. At Peh-mu chiao, 10 li above Tu-tien-tsze, the timber logged in the surrounding mountains is made into rafts and floated down. Just below Shui-ching-pu the stream unites with the main branch of the Lungan River (the Fou Ho), and the rafts are floated down past the city of Lungan to Chungpa, a large village of vast commercial importance, in direct water communication with distant Chungking, it being within the Kialing River system.

Tu-tien-tsze is a small market village and a Roman Catholic Mission centre. This Church has a strong following throughout the region we had traversed from An Hsien. The country folk everywhere in this part were most courteous and civil. This, I think, is probably due to the influence wielded by the self-sacrificing priests of the Roman faith. But whatever the cause, I shall always retain pleasant memories of the people encountered everywhere in this little-known region.

The road proved easy all day, usually skirting the mountains well above the stream. At Tu-tien-tsze a cross-country road leads to Lungan Fu, some 130 li distant. Ten li below Tu-tien-tsze we crossed to the left bank of the stream by a covered bridge. Descending a few miles and crossing a promontory we reached the main river (Fou Ho) opposite Shui-ching-pu. Ferrying across to this village, we found lodgings in a large house owned by a Shensi man of the Mohammedan persuasion.

Shui-ching-pu, alt. 4200 feet, is a market village of about 200 houses, situated on an alluvial flat, surrounded by mountains largely under cultivation. A river of considerable size, which brings down an unusual quantity of detritus, joins the main stream on the left bank immediately below the village. A road ascends this stream, leading to Wen Hsien in Kansu province. It was said to be difficult, traversing a mountainous region peopled with Sifan. Iron is a local product of some importance hereabout. Gold is also mined in the neighborhood. The quartz, after it has been broken into small pieces, is pounded into dust in stamping mills, like those commonly used for hulling rice. The dust is washed and the gold separated by aid of quicksilver. Placer mining is carried out all along this Lungan River by unemployed peasants, but the yield is small. In 1904, when I first journeyed to Sungpan by way of Mien Chou, Chungpa, and Lungan, the officials were endeavoring to put a stop to placer mining. Placards were posted forbidding the people to wash for gold, on the ground that landslips were caused through the removal of the rocks on the foreshore.

From Hsueh-po to Shui-ching-pu is said to be 60 li. The valley which we traversed is all under cultivation, and farmsteads are frequent after Peh-mu chiao is reached. Alder, Walnut, and Poplar are the common trees, with Pear, Plum, and Peach trees around houses. In a garden I saw one magnificent specimen of the Crepe Myrtle (Lagerstroemia indica), 25 feet tall, 2 ½ feet girth, just one luxuriant mass of carmine red flowers. Here and there the moist rocks are beautifully carpeted with ferns, Woodwardia radicans, Blechnum eburneum, and Maidenhair being particularly rampant. The Buddleia and Hydrangea previously mentioned are abundantly present, and were a wealth of pleasing flowers.

At Shui-ching-pu we joined the highway between Lungan Fu and Sunpan. The intrepid Captain W. J. Gill,[1] in June, 1877, was the first Occidental to traverse this route. Since that date several travellers and missionaries have been over this road, but the total is small.

My first journey over this highway was, as mentioned above, in 1904. At that time I had no camera, and the recollection of the wonderful scenery had much to do with my second journey to these parts in 1910. I saw the country through the eyes of a botanist, and for this reason I hope a continuance of this narrative will prove justifiable.

Leaving Shui-ching-pu about 7 a.m., we saunteringly covered the 50 li to Hsao-ho-ying by 4 p.m. The road ascends the left bank of the stream for some 20 odd li to a point just above the small village of Yeh-tang. At this place the river is joined by another of nearly equal size on its right bank. A byroad ascends this tributary and leads across the mountains through country sparsely peopled with Sifans, and connects with the Mao Chou-Sungpan highway a few miles below Sungpan Ting. The road we followed crosses the left affluent of the Fou River by means of an iron suspension bridge 24 yards long, erected immediately above the union of the two streams. A few li beyond this place the road plunges into a wild gorge. The scenery is wonderful. Limestone cliffs clad with vegetation rear themselves 1000 to 2000 feet above the torrent which here-about rushes headlong over huge rocks. Wherever possible, maize is cultivated on the slopes and rice in the bottom-lands.

[1] River of Golden Sand.

NORTHWESTERN SZECHUAN

We crossed to the right bank by a covered wooden bridge just below a place where landslips have produced a series of cataracts. About 3 li below Hsao-ho-ying the gorge suddenly opens out, leaving room for a small circular valley, in the middle of which the walled village above named is situated. Viewed from this point where there is an old gateway, the village presents a charming picture of peace and plenty locked in by precipitous mountains. On entering the village, however, one is quickly disillusioned. Abject poverty is only too apparent. The one main street is broad, flanked by more or less ruined houses, with much of the land within the walls given over to maize plats. The people are in keeping with their dilapidated surroundings.

Hsao-ho-ying, alt. 5300 feet, signifies Camp on the Small River. It is an ancient garrison village. Eighty years ago some 700 soldiers were quartered here. This number was speedily reduced as the surrounding country was conquered. Today the garrison is put down at 40 men, but it is doubtful if even this number exists. Three yamens belonging to military officials of low rank are the only respectable buildings in the place.

At Shui-ching-pu we were assured we could exchange silver at Hsao-ho-ying. This proved a fable and landed us in an awkward dilemma. However, "Mo-li-to" (Fata viam invenient), as the locals have it!

The flora of the day's journey was not particularly rich, though we passed many plants of interest. Around Hsao-ho-ying, the Walnut (Juglans regia), Varnish (Rhus verniciflua), Poplar, Apple, Pear, Plum, Peach, and Tu-chung (Eucommia ulmoides) are commonly cultivated. By the side of the torrent the Buddleia was again a wonderful sight. In a temple yard near Yeh-tang is a magnificent tree of Meliosma beaniana, about 60 feet tall and 12 feet in girth, the head being fully 80 feet in diameter. The pinnate leaves produce abundant shade. This tree was covered with small pea-like purple fruits which later afforded me a supply of ripe seeds. The pinnate-leaved members of this small family are all handsome trees, and none was in cultivation previous to my explorations. I have succeeded in introducing three species, all of them promising to thrive under cultivation. One, M. veitchiorum, is now

145

CHINA — MOTHER OF GARDENS

flourishing just within the main entrance to Kew Gardens.

From Hsao-ho-ying to Shuh-chia-pu, 30 li, the road ascends a narrow valley which is without special interest, the bottom-lands and lower slopes being cultivated with maize and buckwheat. Houses occur at intervals. Just above Shuh-chia-pu, a poverty-stricken hamlet of about a score of houses, the river bifurcates. The road ascends the left and larger branch, plunging immediately into a narrow gorge. The track, all things considered, is good, though there is room for improvement. The scenery in this gorge, for magnificent, savage grandeur, would be hard to surpass. The cliffs, chiefly limestone, are mostly sheer, and 2000 to 3000 feet high. Wherever vegetation can find a foothold it is rampant, and a luxuriant jungle of shrubs clothes all but the most vertical walls of rock. By the side of the torrent coarse herbs, shrubs, and small trees abound. The mountain crests and ridges are covered with Spruce and Pine. Now and again glimpses of vicious-looking, desolate peaks, towering above the tree-line, were obtainable. The waters of the torrent roar and dash themselves into foam in their passionate endeavor to escape to more open country. In more peaceful stretches the river describes a series of S-curves with shingly areas covered with Myricaria germanica and Hippophae salicifolia (Sallow-thorn) jutting out into the current. In one place the cliffs recede somewhat, leaving room for a narrow valley, where three or four peasants' huts are pitched. Around these cabins forlorn patches of maize, buckwheat, cabbage, Medicinal Rhubarb (Rheum palmatum tanguticum), and Tang-kuei (Angelica polymorpha sinensis) are cultivated. The abandoned clearings were covered with coarse herbs, among which Senecio clivorum, growing 4 to 5 feet tall, with its golden yellow flowers, was prominent. Astilbe davidii also abounds; like-wise the Buddleia. A sub-shrubby Elder, growing 3 to 5 feet tall, with masses of salmon-red fruits, was a pretty sight in all the more open moist places. (The species proved to be new and has been named Sambucus schweriniana Rehder, in Plantce Wilsoniance, II. p. 306 [1912]). The vegetation indeed is rich and varied, and a large harvest of specimens rewarded the day's labors. After scrambling some 30 li along this gorge we reached the hostel of Lao-tang-fang just as night was closing in. We encountered considerable traffic on the road. Coming from Sungpan were coolies laden with medicines, sheep-skins, and wool. Journeying thither the coolies were laden chiefly with wine in specially constructed tubs, preserved pork, and rice. Lao-tang-fang, alt. 7600 feet, consists of one large new hostel, not quite completed at the time of our visit; a long row of bunks are built along one side, with benches for the accommodation of loads on the other. The whole structure is of wood, the roofing being of shingles badly laid. The mud floors were very damp, and vegetation was springing up in the corners and under the bunks. Skins of serow and budorcas served as mattress on the bunks, or settees, and no two of these skins exhibited the same coloration. Both animals are said to be common in the neighborhood, the serow more especially. The parti-colored bear or giant panda, also occurs here in the Bamboo jungles.

The hostel was full to overflowing and undoubtedly supplies a much-needed want. For the sake of future travellers, if for no other reason, I heartily hope success attends the landlord's venture. Formerly a most miserable structure occupied this site, and I have unpleasant memories of a night spent there in 1904. Except for a tiny cabbage-patch there was no sign of cultivation around the hostel, but clearings were being made for the purpose of cultivating Tang-kuei and other medicines. The view from this spot is savage and grand beyond power of words. On all sides are precipitous mountains, towering 3000 feet and more above the torrent, all more or less densely forested. Almost facing the river is a limestone cliff with upturned strata on edge, sheer and bare of vegetation. Behind this is another nearly vertical slope covered with stark, dead Conifer trees. In the distance, looking back on the road we had followed, bare, vicious-looking peaks, probably 14,000 to 16,000 feet high, were visible. All around the hostel the lesser slopes are covered with impenetrable forest of broad-leaved deciduous trees. The higher parts and the crags are clothed with Conifers, tall, slightly branched trees of no great size—altogether a wonderful scene of natural beauty, at present undefiled by the hand of man.

It was cold during the night; the wind playing freely through the unfinished structure, and the thickest of clothing was needed in order to keep warm.

The next day we made a later start than usual, and travelling most leisurely covered the 40 li to San-tsze-yeh before 5 p.m. The journey was one long scramble through a continuation of the savage ravine. The chairs had to be carried piecemeal, and all of us reached our destination very much fatigued. We enjoyed a gloriously fine, sunny day, the narrow streak of sky visible from the bed of the ravine being of the purest Thibetan-blue. The camera was kept busy and I secured a fine set of views, but so steep is the country and so dense the jungle that it was impossible to photograph trees.

The rock-strewn torrent, with its thundering, seething waters, occupies virtually the entire bed of the ravine, leaving scant room for the road which winds along its banks. We crossed this torrent many times, either by fording it or by means of half-rotten log bridges. Luckily the waters were low and caused us no trouble. In 1904 I ascended this ravine shortly after heavy rains, and have the liveliest recollections of the difficulties encountered. Much of the road and many of the bridges had been washed away, making it necessary to hew a pathway through the jungle and improvise bridges by felling trees in several places.

No words can adequately depict the savage, aweinspiring scenery of this wild ravine. Stupendous limestone cliffs, 3000 to 4000 feet high, often too steep for the scantiest of vegetation to find a foothold, but more generally sparsely or plentifully forested, wall in the torrent and its accompanying roadway. Waterfalls abound, but lateral torrents are few. The flora is very rich, but largely inaccessible. Practically all the trees, shrubs, and herbs common to the 7000 to 9000 feet belt occur here. Conifers are the principal trees. Silver Fir (Abies faxoniana), Spruce, Hemlock Larch, White Pine, Juniper, and Yew are all represented. The Pine (P. armandi) is the commonest tree up to 8500 feet, clinging to the sheer cliffs in a remarkable manner. With its stunted branches and short leaves it was hardly recognizable, suggesting a green maypole rather than a Pine tree. Many of the Spruce and Silver Fir were fruiting freely, the erect, violet-colored symmetrical cones of the latter being very handsome. Larch (Larix potaninii) abounds, overtopping all the other Conifers, but the trees are small. All the Conifers are hereabout designated Sung-shu (literally Pine trees), but the timber of the Larch, flat-leaved Spruce, and White Pine, valued in the order given, are most prized for building purposes generally. Of the broadleaved deciduous trees, Maple, Linden, and Birch are the most common. A few Poplars occur, but Oak is exceedingly rare, the few noted being scrubby evergreens of no great beauty. The variety of shrubs is very great, all the more woodland genera being rich in species. Sorbaria arborea, with large panicles of white flowers, was one of the most attractive, Spiraea, Viburnum, Lonicera, Rubus, Philadelphus, Sorbus, and many other families, made a fine display either with their flowers or fruit. Strong-growing herbs, like the various species of Senecio, Astilbe, Aconitum, and Anemone cover miles of the roadside. In shady places that handsome Maidenhair Fern, Adiantum pedatum, was a charming picture; in sunny spots the lovely Gentiana purpurata with intense carmine-red flowers, was a sight never to be for-gotten.

About 10 li below San-tsze-yeh the ravine widens out into a narrow valley, with the mountain-slopes on the left bank of the torrent less precipitous and grass-clad. We passed the ruins of some old forts, and shortly afterwards a Sifan hamlet consisting of three or four farmsteads, with numerous prayer-flags fixed on the roofs. In the tiny valley wheat, barley, buckwheat, oats, peas, and broadbeans are cultivated, and the crops were ready for harvesting.

San-tsze-yeh, alt. 9200 feet, consists of ruinous hovels built on a level with the infant stream which at this point breaks up into three equal branches, all of which have their source in the near neighborhood. Looking back on the route we had traversed we saw that all the higher peaks are barren and desolate, the highest of all being flecked with snow. The whole plexus is made up of the spurs and but-tresses of the mighty snow-clad Hsueh-po-ting. To the northeast from San-tsze-yeh are other tremendous peaks, bare, barren, and uninviting in appearance. The aspect of the country around this hamlet is purely Thibetan. The scant crops and abject poverty of the inhabitants speak plainly of a country where altitude and climate set agricultural skill and industry at defiance. Such regions the Chinese abhor and cannot colonize. The pastoral Sifan, with their herds of cattle and sheep, remain masters of the soil though politically subject to Chinese authority. The conquest of this wild region must have been a most difficult task and speaks volumes for the military genius which accomplished it.

During the night at San-tsze-yeh I had a violent attack of ague, probably caused by a chill, which culminated in a fit of vomiting. This seizure and the howling of many dogs were against a good night's sleep. In consequence we took things very gently the next day, and I used my chair much more than usual.

Twenty-five li above San-tsze-yeh, to the right of the stream which descends the narrow valley, there is a most interesting place. A torrent heavily surcharged with lime descends from the eternal snows of the Hsueh-po-ting, depositing along its course thick lime encrustations of creamy white. The place is considered holy by the Sifan, to whom any natural phenomenon strongly appeals. A temple has been erected here and a series of some fifty tarns constructed by leading the waters from the stream and making small semi-circular dams. All are at slightly different levels, and the waters as they flow from one to another continue to build up the dams by leaving deposits of lime behind. The bed of each tarn is creamy white, but owing to the light being reflected in different colors, according to the varying depth of each, an attractive scene of many-colored waters is presented. Some are clear azure blue, others creamy white, pink, green, purple, and so on. The temple is called Wang Lung-ssu (Temple of the Dragon Prince), and it is fitting that the Sifan, children of nature as they are, consider the place holy. Near the temple the waters have built up a wonderful series of waterfalls, and every fallen tree and bush obstructing the waters is speedily encrusted with lime. Above the temple the stream is fully 80 yards wide, and the bed is creamy white with soft encrustations of lime, the ripple marks being beautifully defined. These lime deposits extend for a mile or two and present a most striking scene.

From the bed of this stream, a short distance above the temple, a fine view of the snow-clad Hsueh-po-ting is obtainable. The face visible carries but little snow, and immediately below the glaciers are

LOOKING EAST-SOUTHEAST FROM HSUEH SHAN PASS. RUINED FORT IN FOREGROUND wonderful cliffs of red colored rock. In contrast the color effects are most remarkable. There was said to be another temple some few li higher up toward the snows, but I was too fatigued to visit it.

All around Wang Lung-ssu are fine forests of Spruce (Picea asperata), Silver Fir (Abies faxoniana), Birch, with miscellaneous trees and shrubs. In the vicinity of the lime deposits the trees look very unhealthy, many are bleached and dead, others yellow and dying. From the vegetation it is evident that these lime deposits are recent and spreading rapidly. A few Rhododendrons occur on the margins of the stream and in the woods, but are not happy. Right by the water's edge I gathered Arctous alpinus ruber, a tiny alpine shrub with red fruit closely allied to the Blueberries, and found also near the glaciers in British Columbia! This pretty little plant, only some 4 to 6 inches high, is quite common hereabout, but had not before been recorded from China. Near the tarns Cypripedium luteum, a yellow-flowered counterpart of the North American Moccasin flower (C. spectabile), is very abundant. (Later I succeeded in introducing live roots of this species to the Arnold Arboretum).

The forests of this immediate neighborhood are rich in fine Spruce timber, trees 80 to 150 feet tall, 6 to 10 feet in girth, with short branches producing a spire-like effect, are characteristic of the region. The Silver Fir are less note-worthy, but, like the Spruce, were fruiting freely. (Both were subsequently introduced to cultivation). Larch over-tops all other trees, reaching its limits at about 12,000 feet altitude. The vegetation of the ranges flanking the narrow valley, up which the main road ascends, presents a remarkable contrast. The range to the left of the stream, above 10,000 feet altitude, is covered only with scrub and grass; whereas the range on the right bank is heavily forested up to an altitude of 12,000 feet. Early in the afternoon, after covering 40 li, we reached the lonely hostel of San-chia-tsze, alt. 12,800 feet, situated some 600 feet below the head of the pass. During the first 25 li of the day's march we passed several large farmhouses, but nearly all are deserted and falling into ruins. Around these houses a few plats of wheat, barley, flax, and Irish potato are cultivated; also cabbage, garlic, and other vegetables in minute quantities. A Tobacco (Nicotiana rustica), in small quantities for household use, is grown around San-tsze-yeh, and the crop looked very happy. These sporadic attempts at cultivation represent the vain and futile efforts of the Chinese settlers to eke out an existence from the inhospitable soil. This side of the pass is evidently much colder than the Sungpan side, since there, at greater elevations, good crops of wheat, barley, and peas can be raised.

Apart from the forests already mentioned, herbs dominate the flora. A great variety were still in flower, the various species of Senecio and Gentiana being most striking. Gentiana detonsa, a slender plant a foot and more tall, with numerous large deep blue flowers, looked particularly happy, flaunting its blossoms in the sun. On rocky screes the yellow-flowered Clematis tangutica is abundant and was covered with its top-shaped blossoms. The hedges bordering the fields are composed chiefly of Wild Gooseberry (Ribes alpestre) and Sorbaria arborea; the latter was in full flower. In copses by the stream, up to 11,500 feet, Horn-beam, Cherry, Red Birch, Willow, Maple, and Hazel-nut are common. The Hazel-nut is mainly Corylus tibetica, a species having a spiny fruit closely resembling that of the Sweet Chestnut.

The hostel of San-chia-tsze is maintained for the accommodation of travellers, and a posse of soldiers is stationed here to keep down banditti. The hostel is a roomy but miserable cabin, built of shales and roofed with shingles held down by stones. The floor is of mud and is very uneven; there is no outlet for smoke, save the doorway, and no windows. At midday a candle was necessary to avoid falling over things when moving about indoors. During different visits I have suffered many days and nights in this lonely spot, on one occasion being snowed in for three consecutive days. The cabin is situated on a narrow sloping valley running nearly east and west, a mile or so above the tree-limit, flanked on the northern side by a ridge of stark, crumbling rocks. To the south the range culminates in bare peaks and eternal snows of the Hsueh-po-ting. The moorland country all around is typical of eastern Thibet, so perhaps a few details are permissible. The treeless spurs and valleys are covered with extensive heaths of scrub, made up of several species of Spiraea (including S. mollifolia, S.

alpina, and S. mytilloides), Sibiraea laevigata, Lonicera hispida, L. chaetocarpa, L. prostrata, L. thibetica, and others, several Barberries, Currants, shrubby Potentillas, Astragalus, Sallow-thorn, small-leaved, twiggy Rhododendrons, and Juniper. As the altitude increases, one by one these shrubs give out until only the Juniper is left. This ceases about 15,000 feet; alpine herbs ascend another 1000 feet, and the limit of vegetation is roughly 16,000 feet. The Juniper scrub is from 1 to 2 ½ feet tall, very dense, and difficult to traverse, but furnishes excellent fuel. Mixed with this scrub are herbs in great variety, the Poppy-worts (Meconopsis) being particularly abundant. Possibly the commonest herb between 12,500 feet and 14,000 feet is Meconopsis punicea, a lovely species having large, dark scarlet nodding flowers. It was from near this vicinity that I succeeded in introducing this plant in 1903). The violet-blue flowered M. henrici is common between 13,000 feet and 14,000 feet, but much less so than around Tachienlu. The prickly M. racemosa, with blue flowers, is plentiful in rocky places between 13,000 feet to 14,500 feet. From 11,500 feet to 13,000 feet the gorgeous M. integrifolia, growing 3 feet tall, with its peony-like, clear yellow flowers 8 to 11 inches across, occurs, but is not plentiful. The intense colors among alpine flowers everywhere is well known and this region is no exception. The yellow is mostly supplied by Senecio, Saussurea, with other Compositae, and slender growing Saxifraga. The blue and purple by various Aconites, Larkspurs, and Gentians; among the latter Gentiana veitchiorum, with large erect flowers, covers large areas. The Louseworts and Fumeworts are represented by many species, having flowers embracing all the cardinal colors. Primulas occur, but not in many species. Androsace, Sedum, Cyananthus, and other alpine genera abound in species.

Large flocks of sheep are pastured on these uplands, but yak are not kept in quantity hereabout. There is not much variety of game. Blue sheep are common. Budorcas are found near the timber line; on the higher crags occasional flocks of goa, or Thibetan gazelle, occur. Snow-partridge, Thibetan hazel-hen, snow-cock, and allied game-birds, together with Thibetan hares, are fairly numerous. The wolf is the only carnivorous animal really common.

NORTHWESTERN SZECHUAN

The liseuh-po-ting snows are visible on clear days from the wall of Chengtu city, and are accounted the "Luck of the Plain". The Chinese claim that so long as snow covers this peak the prosperity of Chengtu and its surrounding plain is assured. It was a perfect moonlight night as on the occasion of my last sojourn at San-chia-tsze, and late in the evening I beheld the Luck of Chengtu, with its crown of eternal snow lit by the radiant moonlight. The loneliness of the region, the intense stillness on all sides, and the wonderful peak with its snowy mantle, made a most impressive scene.

A glorious morning followed a perfect night. From the head of the pass, alt. 13,400 feet, I obtained further good views of the Hsueh-po-ting, bearing west-south-west and secured some photographs. The peak is probably 22,000 feet high, in shape an irregular tetrahedron, the southwest slopes carrying enormous snow-fields. The northeast face is very steep and carries but little snow. The surrounding peaks are bare and desolate looking; no vestige of life was discernible, and the whole scene was lonely, forbidding, even awesome, though bathed in brilliant sunshine.

Below San-chia-tsze are the stone ruins of an old fort and stockade, relics of ancient warring times, but now covered with various herbs, especially Saxifraga, which were masses of yellow, and other colored flowers. The head of the pass is marked by a ruined tower and fort, from the summit of which Thibetan prayer-flags waved. That robbers still haunt these regions was brought home to us by the sight of a partially covered coffin near the head of the pass. A few weeks before, a poor coolie, bound towards Dungan Fu to purchase rice, was attacked here, robbed, and killed. The bandits got clear away. The coolie's pai-tzu (framework for carrying loads on) and various appurtenances lay on top of the coffin and remain to tell the story of the crime. All around are grassy areas, covered at the season of our visit with blue and yellow alpine flowers.

At the head of the pass small boulders of sandstone, marble, granite, and other rocks lay scattered around. Just below are beds which resemble coal-ashes, probably of volcanic origin.

From the pass we dropped down into a valley which quickly led to fields of golden wheat and barley. The crops were ripening, and here and there the reapers were busy. Passing a ruined fort, several Sifan farmsteads, and a lamasery, the road led to the summit of a grassy ridge. Descending a few hundred feet we sighted the city of Sungpan nestling in a narrow, smiling valley, surrounded on all sides by fields of golden grain, with the infant Min, a clear, limpid stream, winding its way through in a series of graceful curves. In the fields the harvesters were busy, men, women, and children, mostly tribesfolk, in quaint costume, all pictures of rude health, laughing and singing at their work. Under a clear Thibetan-blue sky, the whole country-side bathed in warm sunlight, this busy scene of agricultural prosperity gladdened the hearts of all of us, fatigued and exhausted as we were from the hardships of our journey through savage mountains with their sublime scenery and wonderful flora.

CHAPTER XII

SUNGPAN TING

THE LAND OF THE SIFAN

THE city of Sungpan is situated on the extreme northwest corner of Szechuan, about long. 103° 21' E., lat. 32° 41' N., at an altitude of 9200 feet, and is the farthermost outpost of Chinese civilization in this direction. The surrounding country, more especially to southwest, west and north-west, is inhabited by Sifan, a people concerning which very little is known. Originally established as a military post after the conquest of the neighboring regions by the Emperor Kienlung about A.D. 1775, Sungpan has developed into a most important trade entrepot. It is a city of the second class (styled Ting), but the head civil official has the local rank of prefect, his full title being Fu-I-Li Min-Fu, which signifies the barbarian-cherishing, Chinese-governing prefect. This fanciful title has reference to the official's control over the neighboring Sifan tribes—a control which is purely nominal. The military importance of this strong-hold is still fully recognized, and its strategic value is beyond question. A Chinese general (Chentai), in command of ten regiments, has his headquarters here, with jurisdiction extending south to Kuan Hsien, east to Lungan Fu, and northeast to Nanping in Kansu province.

The town is most picturesquely situated, occupying-considerable space in a narrow, highly cultivated valley flanked by steep mountain-slopes 1000 to 1500 feet high. The Min River, which takes its rise some 35 miles to the north, winds a circuitous course down the valley and flows through the town in an S-curve, entering and leaving the city at unfordable points. On the western side the town is backed by a steep slope, up two sides of which a wall is carried. The west gate of the city is situated at the top of this slope, and is exactly 1000 feet above the river. Save for a yamen and a temple or two the whole of the mountain-slope within the walls is given over to terraced cultivation, the city proper being clustered in the valley alongside the river. The wall surrounding three sides of the city is very substantially built of brick, being fully 20 feet thick and more high, but that which ascends the mountain-sides is in places only 2 feet thick and 4 feet high; a steep ravine, however, immediately outside this wall affords additional protection. Since the Chinese first established themselves here the town has undergone many vicissitudes. Time and again the Sifan have swept down upon it, captured it, and massacred all who fell into their hands. So frequent have been these attacks, and so great is the Chinese dread of treachery on the part of the Sifan, that it is only within the last few years that any of these people have been allowed to remain overnight within the city walls.

In 1910 Sungpan had a resident civil population of about 3000 people, and a floating population equalling, if not exceeding, this number. The houses are nearly all of wood, generally well built, with rather curiously carved porticoes; the timber employed for building is mostly Juniper (Juniperus saltuaria), which is floated down the Min River from a point some 15 miles to the north-northeast. In October, 1901, the city was two-thirds destroyed by fire, but on the occasion of my last visit in 1910 the devastated area had been practically rebuilt. The streets are badly paved, ill-kept, and the city possesses no buildings of architectural beauty. Near the south gate the military section of the town is situated, and a considerable amount of market-gardening is carried on there. The people are very fond of flowers, nearly every house boasting some in pots, on the walls, or in borders. Stately Hollyhocks, with multi-colored flowers, are a feature. With these are generally planted Tiger Lilies, China Asters, and small-flowered Poppies, the whole making a bright and pleasing effect. The China Aster (Callistephus hortensis) is wild in the neighborhood; the Poppy is a species closely allied to Papaver alpinum. The population is mainly Mohammedan Chinese, who carry on a remunerative barter-trade with the surrounding tribes. Tea is the all-important medium employed, this

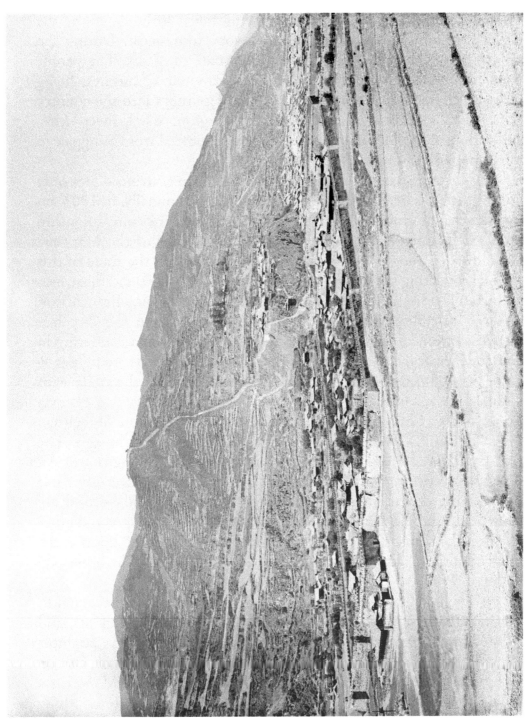

TOWN OF SUNGPAN TING

commodity and a few odd sundries being taken in exchange by the tribes-men for their medicines, skins, wool, and musk. During the month of July a fair is held annually for trade purposes. The people from far and near attend this fair, a vast amount of business being transacted. Trading caravans also make long journeys into the country northwest to the borders of the Kokonor region. Wool, sheep-skins, and various medicines in great quantity are exported from Sungpan to different parts of China.

The trade passing through Sungpan is, I am convinced, not only greater than has been estimated, but is increasing annually. In 1903, on the occasion of my first visit to this town, I enjoyed the companionship of W. C. Haines-Watson, Esq., then Commissioner of the Maritime Customs at Chungking. This gentleman investigated the trade of this region, estimating the exports to Thibet at Tls. 801,000, and those into China at Tls. 512,000 ("Journey to Sungp'an," Jour. China Branch Roy. Asiat. Soc., 1905, xxxvi.). Our visit occurred before the city had recovered from the disastrous fire of 1901, and trade was suffering in consequence. In 1910 trade was evidently booming. I have no figures to guide me, but comparing the two visits I would put the trade with China alone at a million taels. This trade has three outlets: one, east, via Lungan Fu to Chungpa; another, southeast, via Mao Chou, Shihch'uan Hsien to An Hsien; the third through Kuan Hsien to Chengtu. The first two routes afford water communication from Chungpa and An Hsien respectively, with Chungking on the Yangtsze River. By these routes most of the goods intended for Chungking and beyond are conveyed. The trade via Kuan Hsien is mainly with Chengtu and other cities on the plain. This latter trade route has been looked upon as the most important, whereas it is really less so than either of the other two outlets.

The late Captain W. J. Gill in 1877 was the first Occidental to visit Sungpan. Since that date several foreigners have paid visits, and missionaries of Protestant denominations have made abortive attempts to establish stations there. I have visited this place three times, and on each occasion enjoyed the stay and departed with regret. Did the Fates ordain that I should live in western China I would ask for nothing

SUNGPAN TING

better than to be domiciled in Sungpan. Though the altitude is considerable the climate is perfect, mild at all times, with, as a general rule, clear skies of Thibetan-blue. During the summer one can always sleep under a blanket, in winter a fire and extra clothing are all that is necessary. Excellent beef, mutton, milk, and butter are always obtainable at very cheap rates. The wheaten flour makes very fair bread, and in season there is a variety of game. Good vegetables are produced, such as Irish potatoes, peas, cabbages, turnips, and carrots, and such fruits as peaches, pears, plums, apricots, apples, and Wild Raspberries (Rubus xanthocarpus). Nowhere else in interior China can an Occidental fare better than at Sungpan Ting. With good riding and shooting, an interesting, bizarre people to study, to say nothing of the flora, this town possesses attractions in advance of all the other towns of western China.

The valley, which varies from ¼ to ½ mile in width, and the mountain-slopes, rising from 1000 to 1500 feet above, are given over to wheat and barley cultivation, with occasional fields of peas and flax, the latter being valued for its seeds, which yield an oil used as an illuminant. In the latter half of August the whole country-side is one vast sheet of golden grain bending to the wind. This grain is reaped, leaving a generous stubble, which is immediately ploughed under. The ploughs are simple, consisting of an iron-shod shear, a straight handle of wood, and a long shaft, to which is harnessed a couple of oxen or half-bred yak.

In harvesting the grain, tribesfolk (chiefly Po-lau-tzu), who come from the upper reaches of the Tachin Ho, many days' journey to the west-southwest, play an all-important part. Every year these people visit this region for the express purpose of this work, and are, in fact, indispensable. As the crop is reaped it is tied into little sheaves and stacked ears downwards on high hurdle-like frameworks (Kai-kos) to await threshing. The threshing is done by wooden flails, both men and women taking part in the work. The corn is ground in mills driven by water power.

The name Sungpan has reference to forests of Spruce and Fir and the circuitous course of the river Min. The river still pursues its winding course, but the forests have long since disappeared. It is only in temple grounds and among tombs that any trees remain. The mountains are absolutely treeless, where not under cultivation they are covered with scrub and long grass. The outer crust of the mountains consists of a rich flaky loam, probably of glacial origin, rather heavy, but specially adapted for cereal cultivation. In the grass and scrub pheasants are very plentiful in the neighborhood of cultivation, so also is a long-eared, light-gray-colored hare. Musk deer, wapiti, and white deer occur in the neighborhood. On the moorlands a marmot, called Hsueh-chu (snow-pig), burrows in large colonies.

Northwest of Sungpan is the Amdo country, a region of grasslands. The Chinese designate it Tsaoti, which may be interpreted prairie. This region is made up of rolling country above 11,000 feet altitude, where herds of cattle and sheep, and many ponies are reared. A great part of this region is peopled with pastoral Sifan, but the more remote parts are in the hands of nomads belonging to Ngo-lok and Nga-ba tribes, of evil reputation as robbers and bandits, dreaded alike by Chinese and the more peaceably inclined Sifan. These robber tribes are of Tangut origin, having their headquarters about the Kokonor region. Being of nomadic habit they wander far afield, and rob caravans and kill travellers weaker in numbers than themselves. When I arrived in Sungpan in 1910 I found there some 200 soldiers from Chengtu bent on a punitive expedition against these banditti. About a year previously a Chinese official had been murdered in the Amdo country, not many days' journey from Sungpan, and no redress had been obtained. Nine persons were held guilty for this crime, but in spite of demands on the part of the Chinese the clan would not give up these people. The affair ended in the Chinese killing as many members of this robber clan as the small army sent on the expedition could capture. It is from the Amdo region that Sungpan derives most of its wool, skins, and medicines, consequently the trade depends very largely upon peace obtaining there.

The Sifan (Western people) are unquestionably of Thibetan origin. They are not nomads, but essentially a pastoral and agricultural people. In dress, speech, and facial characteristics they agree closely

SIFAN TRIBESMEN

163

with the inhabitants of Anterior Thibet. Their houses are similarly constructed, and Lamaism dominates their lives. As a people the Sifan are divided into several tribal clans: those around Sungpan style themselves Murookai; those a little to the southwest of this town Lappa. Immediately around Sungpan the Chinese language is generally understood, but away from the town colloquial Thibetan only is spoken, each hamlet having an interpreter to conduct all affairs with the Chinese. These people are ruled by headmen who are held directly responsible for the proper maintenance of law and order. The Chinese policy is one of non-interference in so far as is consistent with the status of China as the paramount power.

The Sifan men as seen in the streets of Sungpan and the immediate neighborhood are swarthy in appearance and average 5 feet 6 inches in height or rather more; in walking they have a clumsy gait and are generally awkward and sullen when approached. Their dress is a sort of cover-all made of gray or claret-colored serge, confined around the waist by a girdle; the right shoulder is generally uncovered. This garment is often edged with fur; sometimes it is made entirely of sheep-skins, with the wool worn inside. Short pants and high felt boots cover the legs and feet, though in the streets they frequently go barefooted. The head-gear is either a low, stone-colored, soft felt hat, with turned-up brim bordered with black, or a high, cone-shaped, light gray felt hat edged with white sheep-skin. Occasionally those living near Chinese settlements affect a dirty turban. The hair is worn long and gathered up inside the hat. The Lamas have their heads close-cropped or shaven, and when seen in the streets are usually hatless. In ceremonial dress they wear a sort of cocked hat made of gray serge covered with a mass of fluffy yellowish wool-like stuff. Muleteers and men generally, when travelling, go armed with swords, knives, and long guns, the latter fitted with a fuse and a fork to rest the barrel on when taking aim. All wear charm-boxes on their chests, and carry flint-boxes and tinder suspended from their girdles; somewhere about their person a wooden, often silver-lined, eating bowl is also carried. The wealthy prize a leopard-skin garment most highly.

The young girls are occasionally passing fair to look upon, but from hard work and exposure lose all charm of youth very early. The women are generally flat-faced, very dirty, and far from prepossessing. They have, however, considerable character and an important voice in household and all business matters. Toward foreigners they are timid, but amongst themselves their manners are playful, free and easy, and they laugh and sing at their work. Their outer dress consists of one shapeless piece of serge, which envelops them down to their ankles. Sometimes this is gray, more usually it is blue in color, with a fancy bordering of dark red or yellow in front and around the bottom. High boots of untanned leather encase their feet and lower legs. Their hair is long and black, worn parted down center and collected into one large plait behind; around the forehead it is worn in a series of tiny plaits ornamented with coral-beads, amber-colored stones, and small shells. The large plait is usually wound around the head, together with a piece of cloth to form a kind of padded turban, the whole being decorated with shells and beads. Occasionally saucer-shaped felt hats are worn. In holiday attire, silver rings and gaudy red and yellow tassels are added to their coiffure. They are very fond of silver rings, bracelets, and large earrings ornamented with beads of turquoise and coral. In gala costume the dress is decidedly picturesque.

The men assist in tilling the soil, sowing and harvesting the crops, but the women do the bulk of the work around the homestead, the men being away herding the flocks or on journeys. Though they lead hard lives they seem a happy and contented people in spite of the fact that they are almost without exception afflicted with goitre. Their houses are built of wood and shale-rocks, being either one-storied, flat-roofed, with or without a raised part behind it, or, as is more usual, two-storied and similarly roofed. They count their wealth in head of cattle, horses, and sheep. Wheat, barley, and peas are the staple crops. Meat, butter, and milk enter very largely into their diet. Buttered tea is generally drunk, but they are very partial to a kind of small beer which they brew from barley; they are also fond of Chinese wine.

Monogamy is the rule, but polygamy is common, it being merely a question of wealth. Polyandry is not practiced, but their morals are lax, as is the case everywhere else under Lamaism. Marriage is by

165

consent on part of the girl, presents of oxen and sheep being made on behalf of the bridegroom to the girl's parents; children are appreciated, but the Sifan are not a prolific people. The second son generally enters a lamasery, as is customary throughout Thibet. Widows are permitted to remarry. The dead are disposed of by burial or by being thrown into the rivers.

Abundant signs of Lamaism are everywhere apparent. Prayer-flags flutter from the housetops, mountain-peaks, across streams, and surmount cairns of rocks. Mani-stones are heaped by the wayside; praying-wheels, turned either by hand, by the wind, or by the current of streams, occur on all sides. From the people at their work, either in low crooning tones or in loud chorus, the mystic hymn, "Om mani padmi hom," is continually ascending unto heaven. The chant of the Sifan is decidedly musical, rising and falling in soft rhythmic cadence. I have often listened to them with much pleasure, though from a distance, since if one tried to approach closely they ran helter-skelter away. They are naturally very superstitious, being fond of charms, afraid of evil spirits, and reverence unusual natural phenomena. Although my associations with the Sifan were brief I always received the utmost courtesy at their hands, and found much that was pleasing and interesting among these happy, unsophisticated children of Nature.

CHAPTER XIII

THE CHINO-THIBETAN BORDERLAND

THE MARCHES OF THE MANTZU

T is impossible to define, with any approach to accuracy, the political boundary between Szechwan and Thibet. Indeed, no actual frontier has ever been agreed upon, except at one point, on the highway leading from Tachienlu, via Batang, to Lhassa. There, on the Ningching shan, three and a half days' journey west of Batang, stands a four-sided stone pillar, some 3 feet high, having been erected in A.D. 1728. The guide-book to Thibet says: "All to the east is under Peking; the territory to the west is governed by Lhassa." As to the regions north and south of this stone, nothing is said.

For all practical purposes the Min River, from Sungpan Ting in the northwest to Kuan Hsien, may be regarded as the frontier thereabouts. From Kuan Hsien southward an imaginary line drawn through Kiung Chou, Yachou, Fulin to Ningyuan Fu, and thence to the Yangtsze River, may be accepted as completing the frontier line. This constitutes a well-defined ecclesiastical boundary between the peoples; also it corresponds very closely with the western limits of the Red Basin, which constitutes an unmistakable physiographical frontier. It is true that at certain points, such as Lifan Ting, Monkong Ting, Tientsuan Chou, and Tachienlu the Chinese have succeeded in establishing trading-centres and military depots. But in all these places the population is mixed and the centres themselves surrounded on two or more sides by non-Chinese people. West of the boundary here indicated the Chinese occupy a very limited agregate area, being confined to the high roads and a few valleys suitable for rice and maize cultivation. The largest of these areas is the region known as the

CHINA — MOTHER OF GARDENS

Chiench'ang valley, of which the city of Ningyuan Fu is the capital. This narrow strip extends down to the upper Yangtsze River, being bounded on the east by the independent kingdom of Lolo, which occupies the higher slopes of the Taliang shan and has never been conquered by the Chinese. Immediately to the west of the valley the country is peopled by semi-independent tribes akin to the Thibetans. Indeed, the Min River, with such land to the immediate west suited to rice-culture, may well be regarded as the real boundary of west-ern Szechuan from Sui Fu on the Yangtsze River to Sungpan Ting, in the extreme northwest corner of the province. An arc-line, commencing at Sungpan Ting and connecting with the boundary stone west of Batang, thence south-ward, skirting the right bank of the Drechu (upper Yangtsze,) would form roughly the boundary of Thibet proper. Nominally the whole of this region is considered by the Chinese part of Szechuan province. In certain books and maps parts of this region are referred to as eastern Thibet, and much confusion has arisen from this misnomer.

The country included within the boundaries here given constitutes the hinterland between Szechuan and Thibet, and failing a more lucid term it may be designated the Chino-Thibetan borderland, a title which, if clumsy, has the merit of being both descriptive and accurate. Several trade routes traverse this borderland, but with one exception these have been little travelled by foreigners—the exception being the great highway between Chengtu Fu and Lhassa De, which crosses this region from Yachou, via Tachienlu and Batang to the boundary, and is closely controlled by Chinese. Apart from this highway and the country in its immediate vicinity as far west as Tachienlu, the whole borderland is very much a terra incognita. It is made up of a series of stupendous mountain ranges, separated by narrow valleys, well forested in the lower parts with all the higher peaks extending above the snow-line. These ranges are comparable only with the Himalayas, of which, indeed, they constitute a northeast extension. This rugged region is populated by many independent or quasi-independent tribes, all more or less Thibetan in origin, with the exception of the Lolo.

168

TACHIENLU RIVER, A TYPICAL TORRENT

CHINA — MOTHER OF GARDENS

It is a region where altitude and climate, rather than longitude and latitude, define the frontiers. In the north-west the highlands of Central Asia abut more closely on the Red Basin than they do in the southwest, and form uplands suitable as grazing-grounds for herds of yak, cattle, horses, and sheep. These areas are peopled by nomadic Thibetans, with whom agriculture is relatively unimportant. The broken country, made up of mountain-crag and valley, which forms the greater part of this hinterland, is occupied by various tribes, with whom agriculture is the paramount industry, and wheat, barley, and buckwheat the staple foodstuffs. The forests of this region contain much game, of which these people are skilled hunters. Lastly, in the more fertile valleys, where rice and maize can be successfully grown, Chinese settlers are found, but, as mentioned earlier, away from trading-centres and the great highway between Chengtu and Tachienlu, they are not much in evidence.

In a former chapter brief reference to the mountain chains and rivers of this region has been made, but perhaps a few of the more striking features may be given in detail here. Unlike the mountains bordering the eastern limits of the Red Basin, which are mainly of hard carboniferous and ordovician limestones, those of the west are principally of mudshales and granitic rocks. Here and there, for example Mount Omei and its sister mountains Wa and Wa-wu, hard limestones have been forced up through the older rocks and form bold peaks and stupendous precipices. There is indeed plenty of limestone throughout the hinterland, but pre-cambrian rocks preponderate enormously. These and the shales (probably silurian) disintegrate very readily in their exposed parts and erosion is rapid. In the deforested parts landslides are general. The region is fairly rich in gold, silver, copper, lead, iron, and other minerals, but little mining is carried on. Coal is very rare, except in a few localities where limestone predominates as near Mount Omei and the surrounding region. Salt is known from one locality only (Pai-yen-ching in the Chiench'ang valley). Around Tachienlu hot springs of calcareous and chalybeate waters, more or less rich in sulphur, are common. These springs are usually found in close proximity to torrents, very often occurring in the actual bed of such streams. In many the waters are actually boiling, and I have several times cooked eggs in them. These hot springs are much resorted to by the people of the surrounding regions for bathing purposes, the waters being esteemed as a cure for rheumatism, skin affections, and other complaints.

Three large rivers, Tung, Yalung, and Drechu, flow through this borderland, mainly from north to south, as necessitated by the direction of the mountain axes. These rivers have tributaries in abundance, and the majority of them, draining from eternal snows, carry down enormous quantities of water and detritus. None of these rivers is navigable save for rafts, specially constructed boats, or skin coracles, over very short and interrupted stretches. Bridges and ferries are few, nevertheless the highways and byways of this region skirt the banks of these rivers and their main tributaries.

The valleys of all these streams, and for the purpose of what follows the Min above Kuan Hsien may be included, are deeply eroded, the waters flowing between steep slopes or precipices. These valleys are all very similar, being narrow, shut in by lofty treeless mountains, and all enjoy a much hotter, drier climate than their altitude warrants. Long stretches are barren and desert-like, more especially when the outcropping rocks are solely granitic. Owing to this dry, hot, climate, interesting anomalies obtain in these valleys. At Hokou, on the Yalung, maize can be cultivated up to nearly 9500 feet altitude, whereas at Tachienlu, in the same latitude and 1000 feet less altitude, it is impossible to bring this cereal to maturity. Green parrots (Palaeornis derbyana salvadori) occur as summer migrants in the valleys of the Yalung and Drechu up to 10,000 feet altitude. Rock pigeons occur in multitudes throughout all these valleys above 4000 feet altitude. Monkeys also are common. The flora generally is specially adapted to withstand drought, and is more closely allied to that of the Yunnan plateaux than to the contiguous country. Doubtless at one time the mountain-slopes flanking these valleys were wooded, though it is improbable that the lower slopes were ever heavily forested; but such timber as grew there has long since disappeared, and to-day these slopes are clothed only with coarse grass and scrub. Landslides are a feature of these regions, especially during the melting of the snows or after heavy rains in the surrounding high mountains. At such times travelling hereabouts is highly dangerous, as nearly every traveller can testify from ocular proof. I have witnessed several disastrous landslides, involving loss of life and much destruction of property. In 1910, when descending the Min valley, I unfortunately got involved in a minor one, and sustained a compound fracture of the right leg just above the ankle. In many places rockslides are constantly occurring, and warning notices to travellers not to tarry are frequently displayed throughout the upper Min valley and elsewhere.

Small villages and farmsteads are scattered through these valleys where, goaded by stern necessity, the inhabitants maintain a grim struggle to win a sustenance from the inhospitable soil. Where rice and maize can be cultivated Chinese settlers are found, but above the altitudes admitting of this the tribes are in full possession and cultivate crops of wheat, barley, buckwheat, peas, and linseed—the latter for its oil, which is used as an illuminant. Exceptionally good chilli peppers are grown in these valleys, and certain regions, for example Mao Chou, in the Min valley, are renowned for this produce. Around habitations a few trees, chiefly Poplar, Alder, and Willow, are always present, affording a welcome shade. Cupressus duclouxiana, a handsome timber tree, often 80 to 100 feet tall, is very much at home in these valleys and probably at one time covered quite considerable areas hereabout. This tree is well worth the attention of those engaged in reafforestation work in dry, warm temperate regions. Other trees partial to these same conditions are Sophora japonica, Diospyros lotus, Pistacia chinensis, Erythrina indica, Koelreuteria apiculata, Ailanthus vilmoriniana, Celtis spp., and the Soap trees (Sapindus mukorossi, Gleditsia spp.). Many fruit trees occur, including the Pear, Apple, Peach, Apricot, and Walnut; the latter (Juglans regia) is the commonest tree up to 8000 feet. The natives hack the lower trunk to make the tree fruitful, so they claim, showing that the old adage—"beating the Walnut tree"—is known outside of Europe. Mulberry trees, Cudrania tricuspidata, and tall-growing Bamboos are common up to 4500 feet altitude.

Many of the shrubs found growing in these valleys are spinescent and nearly all are adapted to withstand drought. In the majority the leaves are small or covered with a dense felt of hairs. These shrubs are usually scrubby in appearance yet many produce ornamental flowers or fruit. The Southernwood (Artemisia spp.), with silvery gray, elegantly dissected foliage and yellow flowers, are perhaps the commonest shrubs met with hereabout. Barberries are another special feature, and when laden with masses of red fruit and autumn-tinted foliage present a most attractive picture. This same remark applies to various species of Cotoneaster, all having ornamental fruit. Many kinds of Rose occur, but often the species are local. Common to all these valleys, though most abundant in that of the Yalung, is Rosa soulieana, with fragrant flowers, opening sulphur yellow and changing to white. So also is Miss Willmott's charming Rose (R. willmottiae), with its abundant straw-yellow prickles, neat glaucescent leaves, rosy pink flowers, and orange-red fruit. The beautiful R. Hugonis is confined to a narrow stretch of the Min valley between 3000 to 5000 feet. This is the only Rose with yellow flowers I have met with in China. The fruit is dark scarlet and falls very early. R. multibracteata, an odd-looking species having pretty pink flowers, is very common in the upper reaches of the Min valley and less so in that of the Tung. Forms of the Musk Rose and of R. omeiensis occur but are local. With the exception of the Southernwood, all the above shrubs confine themselves closely to water-courses. In more arid places Caryopteris incana and other species, with intense blue flowers opening in late July, are very abundant, so also are different species of Indigofera, with pink to red-purple flowers. Several species of Buddleia and two varieties of the lovely Clematis glauca, with glaucous foliage and top-shaped, yellow, passing to bronze-colored flowers, ought not to be overlooked. The shingly and sandy foreshores are covered with Willow, Sallow-thorn, and False Tamarisk (Myricaria germanica). In the Tung valley, between 4000 and 5000 feet altitude, a Prickly Pear (Opuntia dillenii) has become naturalized. This American colonist has made itself very much at home, covering many miles of barren, rocky slopes. It grows from 6 to 10 feet tall, and when covered with its yellow or pale orange flowers is very ornamental. The edible nature of the fruit is well known to the natives but is little esteemed. An extract obtained by boiling the fleshy stems is locally employed as a supposed cure for haemorrhoids.

Amongst the coarse grass and scrub, the dominant features of these regions, a variety of showy herbs occur, nearly all having bulbous or thickened rootstocks in some form or other. To garden lovers everywhere these valleys are of special interest, inasmuch as they are the home of many beautiful Lilies. Each of these valleys has species or varieties peculiarly its own, which range up to about 8000 feet altitude, yet while very local these Lilies are numerically extraordinarily abundant. In late June and July it is possible to walk for days through a veritable wild garden dominated by these beautiful flowers. In the Min valley the charming Lilium regale luxuriates in rocky crevices, sunbaked throughout the greater part of the year. It grows from 3 to 5 feet tall, and has slender leaves crowded on stems bearing several large funnel-shaped flowers, red purple without, ivory white suffused with canary yellow within, often with the red purple reflected through, and is deliciously fragrant. In the Tung valley, Mrs. Sargent's Lily (L. sargentiae), a taller grower species than the foregoing, with broader leaves, having bulbils in the axils, equally handsome flowers of similar shape, but varying from green to red-purple without and from pure white to yellow within, is very abundant in rocky places amongst grass and scrub. The flowers of this species are collected, boiled, and dried in the sun, then minced, fried with salt and oil, and eaten in the same way as preserved cabbage. The bulbs of the Tiger Lily (L. tigrinum) and its elegant relative, L. davidii, which are white, are cooked and eaten.

A herb very common in the Tung valley is Thalictrum dipterocarpum. This Meadow-rue grows 6 to 8 feet tall, has elegant, much-divided foliage, and multitudinous, large, lavender-purple flowers—by common consent the hand-somest member of its family. In the Min and Tung valleys, but very local, Incarvillea wilsonii, which grows nearly 6 feet tall and has handsome flowers very like those of I. delavayi, occurs. This plant is monocarpic and has not yet flowered in cultivation. Although I introduced it into the Veitchian nurseries as long ago as 1903. Salvia przewalskii, with large purple flowers, is another striking herb common in the valleys above 8000 feet altitude.

REGAL LILIES (LILIUM REGALE)

CHINA — MOTHER OF GARDENS

This list of ornamental herbs could easily be extended if any useful service would be served thereby. On bare rocks various species of Selaginella abound; the Mullein (Verbascum thapsus), Deadly Nightshade (Hyoscyamus niger), and Thornapple (Datura stramonium) are common weeds by the wayside. The poisonous properties of the two last named are well-known to the natives. From this brief sketch it will be seen that these narrow, dry, almost desert-like valleys, with their abnormally warm climate, possess a flora which, if limited in number of species, contains many plants of more than passing interest and horticultural value.

As mentioned earlier (p. 167), this hinterland is peopled by various independent and semi-independent tribes about which little is known. The whole region is analagous with that separating India and Thibet, and this statement of fact will perhaps convey a more intelligible idea than the most voluminous details. These tribes are divisible into four distinct groups, in accordance with their official status and form of government.

1. States independent, non-tributary, hostile to both Chinese and Lama authority, as the Lolo kingdom. I have no intimate acquaintance with the Lolo—a people once spread over much of Yunnan, but now confined to the region of the Taliang shan, where they have never been conquered by the Chinese. This race possesses a written language peculiar to itself and is probably indigenous.

2. States really independent and even hostile towards China, directly controlled by the Dalai Lama and council, whose policy is supposed to be modified by high commissioners appointed by China, as, for example, Chantui, Derge, and Sanai. The territory occupied by these tribes is west of the Yalung River and contiguous to that of Thibet proper; the people are indistinguishable from those inhabiting anterior Thibet generally. These more western regions have been styled the Thibetan Marches. Some years ago, an acting viceroy of Szechuan, one Chao Erh-feng, was appointed warden of these marches. With an army of Chinese soldiers he indulged in a most aggressive policy and speedily subjected the whole region to Chinese control. He broke the Lama power, destroyed the principal lamaseries, and beheaded the

abbots and other dignitaries. His task was rendered fairly easy owing to affairs in Lhassa, consequent upon the British expedition to that city, and the flight of the Dalai Lama, the whole making impossible any concerted action by Lhassa de in support of their adherents in the marches. (In 1911, Chao Erh-feng was appointed viceroy of Szechuan and was subsequently murdered in Chengtu city by Chinese revolutionists).

3. States tributary-controlled, governed by hereditary native princes and subject to the viceroy of Szechuan in temporal affairs, but more or less strongly influenced by the Dalai Lama, owing to Lamaism being the accepted religion. Of these the kingdom of Chiala, the Horba states, and the Chiarung tribes are the chief. They occupy most of the territory between the Min and Yalung rivers north of a line connecting Yachou with Tachienlu and Hokou. The Chiala kingdom I shall deal with separately when describing Tachienlu, the capital city. The Chiarung are dealt with in the next chapter.

4. A number of very small states, governed by quasi-independent chiefs, indirectly controlled by Chinese officials appointed for that purpose and by the surrounding tributary kingdoms. They are, in fact, tiny buffer areas very useful to the Chinese in maintaining the balance of power among the larger, more independent kingdoms. Many of these principalities are made up of people who may reasonably be looked upon as remains of the aboriginal population of parts of Szechuan and this hinterland. These petty states are scattered through the more easterly parts of this hinterland from Mao Chou in the north through the Chiench'ang valley to borders of Yunnan province. The power exercised by the chiefs varies according to their proximity to thickly populated Chinese districts or otherwise. In the former it is almost nominal, whereas in the latter case it is very considerable.

In addition to the above are certain feudal states whose overlord owes his office directly to Chinese influence, and is bound, if called upon, to render military service to China. These feudal chieftainships are hereditary and were originally bestowed as rewards for assistance rendered to the Chinese in breaking up the Chiarung confederacy during the reign of the Emperor Kienlung. Many of these, for example the Tsa-ka-lao chief, have very considerable power and influence in the temporal affairs of the surrounding tributary-controlled kingdoms. The people are mainly of the same stock as the Chiarung tribes. All the chiefs of these feudatory states and tributary kingdoms are closely related by intermarriage.

The Chinese designate the inhabitants of this borderland Mantzu, a contemptuous term signifying Barbarian and of no ethnological value whatsoever. But the policy they have pursued in dealing with these people has been shrewdly wise if unscrupulous. With arms and money the Chinese have displayed their power and obtained what practically amounts to a suzerainty over the whole borderland. A former emperor said: "Wardens of the Marches should seek to checkmate the native tribes by becoming intimately acquainted with them and their customs and thus able to prevent any united action. In this way the tribes will remain weak and easy to manage. They should be encouraged to appeal to Chinese authorities for advice and protection in their disputes with one another. These authorities will, of course, be in no hurry to settle their cases. If the tribes are taught to fear the Chinese, and the officials act with energy, all trouble will be avoided." This crafty advice has long been acted upon by the Chinese, with much success from their own view-point.

From this brief and very incomplete general account it may be gathered that this hinterland is a fascinating region, presenting ethnological and other problems of great interest, the solution of which is worthy of the attention of Western scientists. It is hoped that a properly equipped expedition will at no very distant date be organized and dispatched to survey and investigate fully this little-known Chino-Thibetan borderland.

CHAPTER XIV

THE CHIARUNG TRIBES

THEIR HISTORY, MANNERS, AND CUSTOMS

ITHIN the limits of the Chino-Thibetan borderland, as defined in Chapter XIII, from Sungpan Ting southwards to Yachou Fu, and west to the valley of the upper Tung or Tachin (Great Gold) River, the territory is divided among numerous cognate tribes collectively spoken of by Chinese as the Chiarung. These people are essentially agriculturists, making their homes in the upland valleys. They are all, though tributary to China, ruled by their own hereditary chiefs, each tribe occupies a properly defined area, with its own capital town, the political centre for the entire region being Monkong Ting. These tribes are non-Chinese and are not indigenous to this region. They are also distinct from the people found in anterior Thibet. They speak a difficult and at first sight unpronounceable jargon, which, if it be the mother of Thibetan dialects, is widely different from that spoken in Thibet to-day. But Thibetan letters have, without difficulty, been applied to it, and scholars, priests, officials, and merchants both read and speak the Lhassa-Thibetan language with greater or less fluency.

The origin of these people is obscure, yet there is good reason to believe they come originally from the region around the head-waters of the Tsang-po (upper Brahma-putra River), and probably have common origin with the people of Nepal and Bhutan. Personally, I am of the opinion that they came over with Genghis Khan, or his son Ok-ko-dai, at the commencement of the thirteenth century, and assisted in the conquest of western Szechuan. As a reward for military services rendered they were given the territory they occupy to-day. During the course of time they waxed powerful, menacing the territory to the east

179

of the Min River, and even taking possession of certain parts. In Ming times the Chinese made war with them on many occasions. They were a source of trouble to the Manchu dynasty until the famous Emperor Kienlung determined upon crushing their power. After a very fierce struggle this was accomplished by a Chinese general named A-kuei. First he subjugated the region of the Hsaochin Ho (Little Gold River), then, after much difficulty, he captured Lo-wu-wei (modern Hsuching), the capital of the Tachin Ho (Great Gold River), took the king prisoner, and made a map of the entire region. The king, named Solomuh, was sent to Peking, where, after a grand court ceremony, he was sliced to pieces. The conquest was completed early in A.D. 1775. Military colonies were then established by the Chinese in strategic places, the more fertile regions were confiscated, and Chinese settlers induced to take up possession. In crushing this confederacy the Chinese were assisted by the tribes, being to some extent divided amongst themselves. Some of them fought on the Chinese side, and as a reward certain areas situated at strategic points were fiefed out and established as feudal states for the benefit of these allies, an overlord with hereditary control being appointed to each. The Chinese handled this campaign with consummate skill, and the administrative system established has remained unchanged down to the present day. The power of the tribes was completely broken: the feudal states and the miltary colonies have safeguarded the Chinese from any concerted action on the part of these people ever since. It will, however, be readily understood that the tribes farthest removed from regions occupied by Chinese enjoy to-day greater independence than those in close contiguity.

Originally the Chiarung had one common language, but time, isolation, and the dividing up into clans has produced many very dissimilar dialects. These people are now split up into eighteen tribes, occupying very unequal areas of territory, and though all are interrelated by marriage they are by no means at peace with one another. Feuds are constant, and fighting amongst themselves is very much the rule. Since this keeps them weak in power the Chinese policy is to intervene as seldom as possible. On the map are indicated as

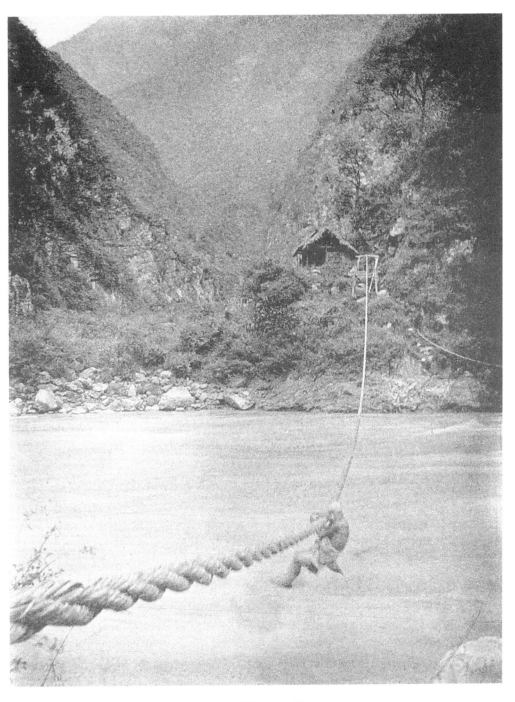

BAMBOO CABLE BRIDGE

accurately as our knowledge admits the positions occupied by some of these tribes and feudal states. It is almost impossible to render into English the guttural sounds denoting the names of many of these tribes. But, fortunately, the more important, namely, Mupin, Wassu, Somo, Damba, Bati-Bawang, Wokje, are the least difficult to pronounce. The whole territory occupied by these people is about 250 miles from north to south, and 200 miles east to west at broadest point. The population is about half a million.

Two main roads, one from Kuan Hsien, the other from Lifan Ting, cross this region, and unite near Monkong Ting. In addition, a network of cross-country byways connects the various villages and states.

The Chiarung are essentially agriculturists, cultivating with much skill crops of wheat, barley, peas, buckwheat, maize, Irish potatoes, and miscellaneous vegetables. Sheep, cattle, ponies, and goats are kept by the more wealthy, often in quantity. The horses are sold to Chinese traders, but the wool is woven into cloth for their own use. Milk, butter, and meat enter largely into their diet. They are also skilled gun and sword-smiths, more especially the Somo people, who manufacture most of these weapons in use among the tribes themselves and the people of eastern Thibet generally. Many are also highly skilled masons, builders, and well-sinkers, and as such have a reputation even amongst the Chinese. During August many visit the upper reaches of the Min River every year to take part in harvesting the crops; indeed, for this purpose they supply most of the labor in that region. Often they are in request in Chengtu and other cities for sinking wells.

The Chiarung live in settlements of from several to a hundred families or even more, always in positions admirably suited for defence. These settlements usually crown some bluff or eminence; very often they are perched like an eagle's aerie high up on the steep mountain-side. The architecture which obtains throughout is characteristic and peculiar. Each settlement is dominated by one or more tall, chimney-like towers, either square, hexagonal, or octagonal in shape, 60 to 80 feet high, and resembling from a distance the stack of some large factory in Western lands. The exact significance of these towers it is difficult to fathom, but it is evident that they can serve as storehouses, watch-towers, and harbors of refuge in times of stress and war. Also they have some obscure connection with religious matters, possibly in this they have remote affinity with the pagodas of China and Burmah. The houses are more or less square, flat roofed, solidly built of shale-rock and mud. Those belonging to the chiefs and men of property are three to four stories high. The walls are thick, pierced with loopholes and several narrow latticed windows. At all four corners of the roof turrets 3 to 4 feet high are built, sometimes there are more in different patterns. From these prayer-flags are displayed, often with the green branches of Juniper. Also on the roof is fixed an incinerator for the sacrificial burning of fragrant Juniper branches as incense. Part of the roof is frequently occupied by a hurdle-like framework called Kai-kos, 10 to 15 feet high, which is employed for drying grain. The rest of the roof is used for religious exercise, eating, sleeping, and recreation; in harvest-time it serves as a threshing-floor. The ground story is made up of a court-yard surrounded by sheep and cattle-pens, the kitchen, and usually a guest-room.

The turrets, upper rim of the walls, edges of the window-spaces, base and base angles of the walls, are washed white, commonly white lines stretch diagonally up the walls, and the swastika cross, with other devices and symbols, are displayed in white on these walls. Crowning the edges of the roof, or arranged on separate structures, symbols denoting a globe, upturned crescent, and the swastika are commonly displayed. The lamaseries are similarly constructed, only larger, and usually with more stories. The houses of the peasants also are on the same plan, but of one or two stories only. All these structures are closely packed together with one to several towers reared above the whole assemblage. The different emblems and symbols of nature worship may occur in the structure of Thibetan houses and lamaseries, but the tall tower is peculiar to the Chiarung.

The bridges are another interesting feature of these regions. All these structures are of designs differing from those found throughout China proper, but agreeing closely with those in use throughout Sikhim, Bhutan, and Nepal, thus furnishing additional evidence as to the affinity of these peoples. All the smaller streams and torrents are bridged by logs arranged on a semi-cantilever principle, and call for no special remark. But the larger streams are crossed by suspension bridges constructed of split and plaited bamboo cables. These bridges are very similar to the cane bridges of Sikhim and Bhutan. They are found throughout the territory occupied by these tribes and the narrow strip of territory wedged in between the Min valley and the western limits of the Red Basin. This latter strip was formerly occupied by these tribes, and is to-day largely peopled by their descendants or half-caste Chinese. As mentioned in Chapter XI, pp. 131, 144, iron suspension bridges occur in one or two places in the northwest corner of Szechuan. This style of bridge is common from the valley of the Ya River, and the Tung at Luting chiao, southward to the frontier of Burmah, and is probably of Shan origin. Similar bridges of iron rods and chains are met with in Bhutan, where they are considered to be of Chinese origin (White, "Sikhim and Bhutan," p. 191). Throughout the Chino-Thibetan borderland iron and bamboo are equally common, yet it is a singular fact that their use in bridge-building is restricted to definite areas.

Cable or rope bridges are abundant throughout the entire region, and extend much farther west and south than the Chiarung territory. These simple but extremely useful structures consist of a bamboo hawser stretched across the stream usually from a higher to a lower point; if the stream is moderately narrow the question of incline is of less importance. The hawser may be anything from 8 inches to 1 foot thick, and being heavy sags considerably in the middle, unless the stream is very narrow, as around Tachienlu, where a rather different method of crossing than that about to be explained is in vogue. To cross one of these cable bridges a person is supplied with a length of strong hempen rope hanging free from a saddle-shaped runner of oak or some other tough wood. The runner clips the cable, and the hempen rope is fastened under and around the legs and waist to form a cradle. When all is properly secured the person throws one arm over the top of the runner, gives a slight spring, and glides down the inclined cable at increasing speed. The impetus obtained in the downward rush carries

DRESS OF A BADI-BAWANG MAIDEN

185

the passenger over the central dip and more or less up the lesser incline on the opposite side. If the momentum is insufficient to land the person, the remaining distance has to be traversed by taking hold of the hawser and hauling hand over hand. Crossing these bridges is fearsome work until accustomed to it. It is speedily accomplished, and there is practically no danger so long as one keeps a cool head and the ropes do not break. It is a common sight to see men with loads and women with children on their backs cross these bridges. But heavy loads are usually fixed to the runners and hauled across by a rope attached to them.

None of the rivers traversing Chiarung territory is navigable in the ordinary sense of the term, but skin coracles, broadly oval in shape, descend certain stretches of the upper Tung River. Also these frail boats serve to ferry over goods and people at certain necessary places. They are made of cattle hide stretched over ribs of tough. light wood. The whole coracle is very easily carried by one man. and closely resembles pictures of the boats used by ancient Britons prior to the Roman invasion. They are steered by a man seated in the stern operating a paddle, and accommodate about two passengers. A passage down or across stream in one of these coracles consists very largely in describing. more or less rapidly, a series of wide circles and half circles. As a novelty, productive of excitement, not unmixed with danger, these coracles and cable bridges can with confidence be recommended to World's Fair promoters and showmen generally. The skin coracle is in general use at ferries throughout eastern Thibet and the Marches. and is not strictly a Chiarung specialty.

In build the tribesmen average about 5 feet 7 inches or rather more; the face is usually oval. with rather pointed chin, straight nose, sometimes inclining toward aquiline. They dress ordinarily in undyed serge cloth of local make, worn in the same manner as that of the Sifan. The legs are swathed in felt putties: the headgear is either a turban or black pudding-basin-shaped felt hat. Those living near Chinese settlements and the highways have their head in part shaven, and wear their hair in a queue Chinese fashion. On holiday occasions their garments are brightened with red borderings. and high felt boots are worn. The women are short in stature (about 5 feet). sturdy and

THE CHIARUNG TRIBES

buxom, somewhat gipsylike, with dark olive complexions. and when young are often good looking. Their ordinary outer dress is a garment of gray native serge of no definite shape, reaching to just below the knee and bound around the waist with a scarf. The legs and feet are bare or encased in top-boots. Commonly they go bare-headed with their long black hair parted down the middle and hanging down the back in one large plait. They are fond of large bangles, earrings, etc., made of silver with turquoise and coral imbedded. On festive occasions garments edged with red and very often made of blue cloth are worn. The more wealthy dames decorate themselves very lavishly with silver ornaments, and wear covering their heads a piece of cloth held down by means of their large plait of hair, which is wound around and decorated with silver and beads of coral and turquoise; the lower part of the piece of cloth hangs free over the back of the neck and shoulders. These dames are women of character, and have a ruling voice in household and family matters generally; also, from what I saw of them, they appear to conduct most of the business. These women lead a strenuous life; they cultivate the fields, tend the flocks, take the farm produce to market, hew wood, and carry water. The domestic duties of cooking, making and mending clothes and general household work devolve upon the men. Yet the women are not unkindly treated, and are far from being down-trodden. Being of cheerful disposition, they seem well suited to the free outdoor life they lead, and laugh and sing as they ply their task. Among themselves these people are frank and easy in manner, and the women enjoy a freedom of position unknown amongst the Chinese. A party of dames and men were fellow-travellers with me once for a couple of days. When the time came to separate they made merry over cups of wine; the women officiated, and cordially invited me to join them. With their laughter and song they made cheery companions, and I was sorry to part from them.

The families are small, but the children are usually strong and healthy. Girls marry between the ages of seventeen and twenty, polygamy is common, but polyandry is unknown except, perhaps, in the upland regions bordering Thibet proper. Temporary marriages, so general in Thibet, are also unknown amongst the Chiarung.

CHINA — MOTHER OF GARDENS

Nevertheless, the standard of morals in vogue amongst these people is a low one. In certain states hetazrism precedes maternity. In Badi-Bawang the unmarried girls and childless women wear only two sporran-like fringes of woollen threads or pieces of fur, suspended from a girdle passed around the body above the hips. The legs are exposed, but the upper parts of the body are usually covered by a coarse serge garment. Only after their first child is born may they wear skirts, since the gods have then purified them. A pregnant damsel selects from among her lovers a husband, who thus becomes the accepted father of her child, her word in this matter being final. Maternity alone ratifies marriage, and indeed saves women from promiscuity. The defloration of virgins is the prerogative of chiefs and headmen, but is not always exacted. In many ways these people are apparently shameless, according to Chinese and Occidental ideas. It is no uncommon sight to see women of all ages, quite nude, bathing in streams by the wayside. This same custom is also common at Tachienlu, where the hot springs are favorite bathing places for both sexes. But after maternity the women are said to remain constant; divorce or legal separation after ratified marriage are not practiced.

The explanation of the above and other curious customs of these interesting people is found in their religious beliefs. Although orthodox Lamaism is more or less paramount the mysterious Bonpa religion, with its marked tendency towards phallic worship, lurks throughout the lonely valleys of the Chiarung tribes. In Badi-Bawang it is the recognized state religion. Also it should be remembered that these regions constituted the famous matriarchal kingdoms of Chinese historians. Indeed, even to-day, certain states have queens holding nominal or actual authority, and in these in some capacity a woman must always rule. Occasionally the difficulty is overcome by styling the ruling head a queen quite irrespective of sex!

Lamaism appears in three forms, the Yellow, Red, and Black, the latter representing the Bonpa cult. The religious centre is Tsong-hua on the Tachin River, about 60 miles west of Monking Ting. But lamaseries are scattered over the land, either separately or in association with the residences of the hereditary chiefs. The Yellow or orthodox sect is first

IDOLS IN A BONPA TEMPLE

in importance and numbers, and is controlled directly from Lhassa. The ritual differs in no way from that practiced throughout the hierarchy of Lamaism. The same remark applies to the unorthodox Red sect, which is of much less importance, and whose priests are allowed to marry.

The Black or Bonpa sect has a ritual bearing an outward resemblance to orthodox Lamaism, but apart from this there is little else in common. In many things the Bonpa are the avowed enemies of the orthodox. They turn their praying wheels from left to right instead of from right to left; they pass sacred objects on the right instead of on the left; also they refuse to repeat the mystic mantra, "Om mani padmi ham," replacing it with one peculiarly their own. As to the origin of this Bonpa it is difficult to say. My friend, Mr. J. Hutson Edgar of the China Inland Mission, who has travelled among and studied these Chiarung tribes more closely than any one else living, inclines to regard it as the remains of the old Nature worship of Thibet, which probably underlies all the religious systems of eastern Asia.

In the state of Wassu are several temples belonging to this Bonpa sect. Through the courtesy of the chieftain I was allowed to inspect some of these temples, and succeeded in obtaining fair photographs of the idols: These latter, made of stone, wood, straw, and plaster, represent giants and demons with their female energies; the walls are decorated with paintings depicting erotomania. Hideous and disgustingly obscene are the contents of these temples, where phallic worship holds unblushing sway. The Wassu chief informed me that the mantra used by these Bonpa priests is "Hom ma-te ma-tsi ma-yoor tsa-lien doo." He kindly gave me a copy of this hymn, but I have not yet succeeded in getting it translated into intelligible English. The principal symbol in use is the fylfot or swastika, which they call yungdrung. A mystical bird, chyong or garuda, is also regarded with great favor as an emblem of fruitfulness. In the Bonpa temples at Tung-ling sham near the residence of the Wassu chief, I also recognized the image of Kwanyin (Goddess of Mercy), the God of Wealth, and many demons similar in appearance to those found in ordinary Buddhist temples throughout China proper. It would thus appear from the

THE CHIARUNG TRIBES

catholic nature of the contents of their temples that these people accept a measure of Buddhism, and Lamaism both orthodox and unorthodox, and the Bonpa in its entirety. An atmosphere of secrecy and mystery enshrouds the Bonpa temples, which are frequently built in places difficult of access. The cult has been subjected to much persecution at the hands of Lamaists, yet, notwithstanding, it retains a firmer hold on the people of most of the Chiarung states than any other form of religion. In their hearts children of nature, their daily life one constant struggle against an inhospitable soil and climate to win a crop necessary for their sustenance, these people very naturally incline most towards the gods of Increase and Fecundity.

CHAPTER XV

ACROSS THE CHINO-THIBETAN BORDERLAND

KUAN HSIEN TO ROMI CHANGO: THE FLORA OF THE PAN-LAN SHAN

URING the summer of 1908, when in Chengtu, I determined upon a journey to Tachienlu. Previously, in 1903 and again in 1904, I had visited this town by three different routes. This time I decided upon traversing the road leading from Kuan Hsien via Monkong Ting and Romi Chango. The only published account of this route that I have knowledge of is in a report by Sir Alexander Hosie,[1] erstwhile H.B.M.'s Consul-General at Chengtu, who returned from Tachienlu over this road in October 1904. What is written in this report about the forests of that region created an appetite within me which nothing short of actual experience could satisfy. Again, this route promised further acquaintance with the tribesfolk inhabiting the hinterland. Sir Alexander's description of the road portrayed a difficult journey, but I felt sure that by taking time and but lightly burdening my men I could get through all right. This confidence was fully justified, as events proved, and what I saw of the forests and mountain scenery, together with the quantity and variety of plants discovered and collected, abundantly repaid for the hardships experienced. The journey is estimated at 1326 li, approximately 330 English miles, but, whilst mere mileage is of little moment in mountainous countries, I should consider 250 miles a more accurate figure.

With Tachienlu as my goal I left the city of Chengtu on the morning of June 15th, and at noon the next day reached the city of Kuan Hsien. An afternoon sufficed to complete my arrangements. The caravan consisted of eighteen carrying coolies, and one head coolie, two chairs, two handy men, an escort of two soldiers, my boy, and self,

[1] Journey to the Eastern Frontier of Thibet, presented to both Houses of Parliament, August 1905.

192

making a party of thirty all told. The journey occupied twenty-three days from Kuan Hsien.

What follows is compiled from my diary: —

The famous bamboo bridge, known as the An-Ian chiao, over which the road to Monkong Ting passes, was having its annual overhaul; in consequence, on leaving Kuan Hsien we had to journey down stream some 5 li to a point where it was possible to cross the various arms of the Min River by improvised bridges and ferry. In so doing we had an opportunity of realizing, somewhat hazily be it confessed, what this area must have been like before Li-ping's wonderful irrigation works came into existence. Without counting the streams flowing Chengtu-ward we crossed five distinct arms of the Min River proper scattered over an area a mile wide, covered with sand, shingle, and coarse grass (Miscanthus sinensis). The detour involved 15 li, and it was not until 9 o'clock that we were opposite the An-lan chiao. This remarkable structure is about 250 yards long, 9 feet wide, built entirely of bamboo cables resting on seven supports fixed equidistant in the bed of the stream, the central one only being of stone. The floor of the bridge rests across ten bamboo cables, each 21 inches in circumference, made of bamboo culms, split and twisted together; five similar cables on each side form the rails. The cables are all fastened to huge capstans, embedded in masonry, which are revolved by means of spars and keep the cables taut. The floor of the bridge is of planking held down by a bamboo rope on either side. Lateral strands of bamboo keep the various cables in place, and wooden pegs driven through poles of hard wood assist in keeping the floor of the bridge in position. Not a single nail or piece of iron is used in the whole structure. Every year the cables supporting the floor of the bridge are replaced by new ones, they themselves replacing the rails. This bridge is very picturesque in appearance, and a most ingenious engineering feat.

From the An-lan chiao the road ascends the right bank of the Min River, and is broad, in good repair, but with many awkward gradients. We found lodgings for the night at Hsuan-kou, alt. 2640 feet, a market village of some 300 houses, situated on a tributary immediately above its union with the main stream which described a very sharp turn on leaving a narrow gorge. The Min River from the An-lan chiao to this point is full of minor rapids, and the current is very swift. Near Hsuan-kou timber is made into rafts and floated down to Kuan Hsien, thence to Chengtu and elsewhere.

During the day's march we passed some good-sized trees of Black Birch, Nanmu, Hog-plum (Spondias axillaris), and small trees of Cryptomeria japonica, the latter obviously planted. A large trumpet-flowered Lily (Lilium sargentiae) was abundant in rocky places by the wayside. Rice occurred sporadically, but the principal crop was maize. Around the inn Tea-bushes are abundantly planted.

On leaving Hsuan-kou we crossed the tributary by a small bamboo suspension bridge, and ascended the left bank by an easy road for 30 li to Shui-mo-kou. Through-out this stretch Cryptomeria is common. All the trees are small and certainly planted. Shui-mo-kou is an ordinary Chinese market village of some 350 houses lining either side of the main street. It is interesting, however, as being the last purely Chinese village in this direction, also the last place wherein supplies can be purchased or silver exchanged until Monkong Ting is reached. I hired an extra man, and all my followers laid in a stock of rice and foodstuffs generally. At Kuan Hsien, appreciating fully the difficult road before us, I had reduced all loads to two-thirds the normal weight. In spite of this the carriers were heavily laden with extra supplies, and could hardly stagger along on leaving Shui-mo-kou.

A short distance beyond the above village there is a steep ascent, but after a few li the road becomes easy and winds around the mountain-side. Scrub Oak and unhappy-looking trees of Cunninghamia are abundant, but the flora generally is poor. Wild Strawberry plants cover the more grassy slopes, and were laden with white and red luscious fruit. We passed a few houses, and finally reached the top of the ridge, alt. 5600 feet, which is known as the Yao-tsze shan. Crossing over we entered the territory under the jurisdiction of the Wassu chieftain, who resides at Tung-ling shan, near Wench'uan Hsien in the Min valley.

Descending by a path, which at first easy soon becomes very precipitous and difficult owing to the abundance of loose rocks, we

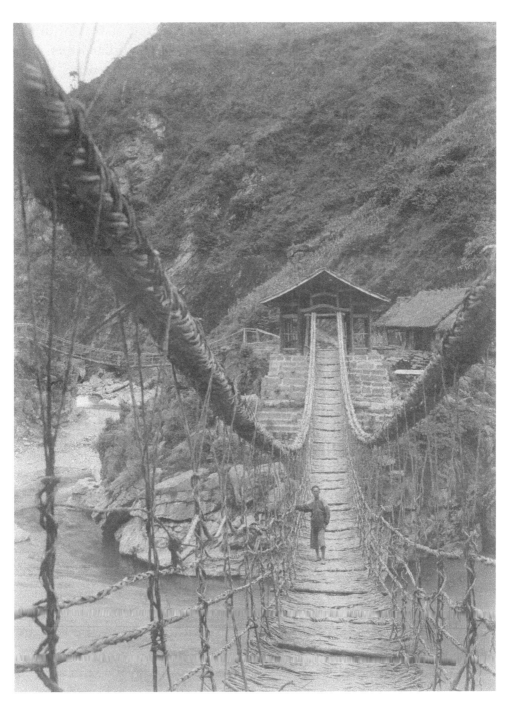

BAMBOO SUSPENSION BRIDGE, 70 YARDS LONG

reached Hei-shih ch'ang, our destination for the day, at 6 p.m. In this descent, near the head of the pass, the Yang-tao (Actinidia chinensis) is abundant, and was a wealth of large white, fragrant flowers. By the wayside, Rosa microphylla is very plentiful, and bushes 2 to 4 feet tall were covered with large pink blossoms. One small tree of Carrieria calycina, with curiously shaped, waxy white flowers borne in erect panicles, was also worthy of note. But the flora generally has been destroyed to make way for crops of maize, oats, and pulse.

Hei-shih ch'ang, alt. 4000 feet, is considered to be 60 li from Hsuan-kou, and consists of three or four houses, situated in a ravine alongside a torrent, with wild mountains on every side. Our lodgings were roomy, and the people both courteous and attentive.

Rain fell heavily next morning when we started out, but ceased about 9 a.m.; the weather remained dull the rest of the day until 4 p.m., when rain recommenced to fall and continued far into the night. Crossing the torrent by means of a covered wood bridge the road immediately ascends a steep mountain called Che shan from the abundance of Varnish trees growing thereon. The ascent, though very steep, is brief, and afterwards for the next 30 li the road skirts the mountain-sides until the summit of the Chiu-lung shan is reached. Descending this ridge it ultimately enters a narrow grassy valley. Here we found lodgings for the night in the solitary hostel of Hoa-tzu-ping, alt. 6100 feet, having covered 50 li during the day.

Until reaching the valley the country was either under maize or covered with a dense jungle. The flora was of passing interest only, being similar in character to that found everywhere in western Szechuan between 4000 and 6000 feet altitude. The more interesting shrubs collected were a yellow-flowered Schisandra, a white-flowered Clem-atoclethra, and the Yunnan Holly (Ilex yunnanensis) with small, neat leaves, clusters of purplish, fragrant flowers, and hairy shoots. Actinidia kolomikta, a large climber with white, fragrant flowers and added beauty in the shape of a multitude of white leaves, is excessively common. Nearly all the species of Actinidia and the allied genus Clematoclethra, other than those clothed with rufous hairs, have these white leaves, which usually become pinkish as the season advances. All the species are handsome climbers, and the majority bear palatable, juicy, edible fruit.

The trees of this region, though not numerous or of any great size, include such remarkable subjects as Davidia, Pterostyrax, Tapiscia, Tetracentron, Beech, and Horse-chestnut. Occasional trees of Cornus kousa chinensis occur, and were a wealth of white flower-heads enlivening the country-side. Walnut trees are common around houses and wild strawberries by the wayside. In the grassy valley and the beautiful Ilex Pernyi occurs with Rodgersia aesculifolia and Lilium giganteum yunnanense in quantity. Around Hao-tzu-ping odd patches of maize are cultivated but where clearings have been made the ground is mostly covered with grass and coarse herbs. During the day we met many men laden with huge logs of Teih-sha (Hemlock Spruce) and Hung-sha (Larch) timber. These logs were dressed, and carried on a wooden framework. I measured one with a tape; it was 18 feet 6 inches long, 7 inches thick, and 9 inches broad. It is astounding how such loads are carried over vile mountain roads. As fellow-travellers during the day we had some tribesmen in charge of a small mule caravan of tea, bound for the state of Wokje.

On leaving Hoa-tzu-ping we soon reached the head of the valley which merges into a narrow jungle-clad ravine. After a precipitous climb of 30 li we reached the summit of the Niu-tou shan, alt. 10,000 feet, where dense mists blotted out the landscape. A similarly precipitous descent of 20 li brought us to Chuan-ching-lou, where we put up for the night.

The flora was very interesting, but owing to a thick pall of mist I was able to observe only the plants immediately alongside the pathway. Perhaps the commonest shrub of the day was Salix magnifica, which is abundant everywhere, but more especially near the water-courses. This extraordinary Willow has leaves up to 8 inches long and 5 inches wide, with catkins 1 foot or more long. It forms a straggling bush 5 to 20 feet tall and, except when in flower or fruit, would scarcely be taken even by the closest observer for a Willow. (I first discovered this plant in 1903, and in 1908 succeeded introducing living plants into cultivation). Many other kinds of Salix, varying from prostrate shrubs to small trees, occur on the Niu-tou shan; indeed, this mountain is remarkable for its wealth in Willows (subsequently I succeeded in introducing into cultivation about a dozen species from this locality). The Actinidia and Clematoclethra previously noted were again abundant. Clematis montana grandifiora, with large white flowers, was a pleasing sight; so also was a Deutzia (D. rubens) with pretty rose-tinted flowers. I saw no deciduous broad-leaved trees of any size, but herbs were luxuriant everywhere, especially the Rodgersia, which covers acres of the mountain-side. The Conifers were the most interesting plants of the day. In the ascent, save for odd trees of Silver Fir and Yew, I saw nothing but Hemlock Spruce (Tsuga yunnanensis). This tree delights in rocky country, clinging to the cliffs in a most remarkable manner. In the descent, however, Silver Fir, Spruce, Larch, Hemlock, and White Pine all occur, but the trees are being rapidly felled, and no large specimens were to be seen. From this place come the logs of timber noted yesterday. The Larch (L. mastersiana) is first met with below T'ang-fang, alt. 9400 feet, where it is common more especially to the right of the road, and descends to 7200 feet altitude.

Chuan-ching-lou, alt. 7000 feet, 50 li from Hoa-tzo-ping, consists of one large, dirty hostel, and three other houses, situated in a narrow ravine, walled in by lofty mountains. A noisy torrent which descends from the Niu-tou shan flows past the inn, and vegetation is rampant on all sides. The road over the Niu-tou shan is difficult, and in many places dangerous. Here and there steps have been cut in the hard rock to assist the traveller, but in the main the road is strewn with loose stones and boulders vile to walk on or over.

We were unfortunate in the matter of weather, for it again rained as we continued our journey. Following the torrent through a narrow ravine for 5 li we reached Erh-tao chiao, where the torrent connects with a very considerable stream which flows from the Pan-lan shan. The united waters form a river which, after traversing very wild country, joins with the Min near the foot of the Niangtsze-ling on the Wench'uan Hsien side of the pass. Turning sharply to the left at Erh-tao chiao we ascended the stream, which is called Pi-tao Ho, and soon crossed over by a wooden semi-cantilever bridge to the left bank. From

ACROSS THE CHINO-THIBETAN BORDERLAND

this point the next 25 li to Wu-lung-kuan is easy, going through a narrow valley where occasional houses occur and a certain amount of cultivation obtains. Above Wu-lung-kuan the road becomes increasingly difficult, and in many places it is execrable. The river is joined by numerous lateral torrents, some of large size, and as the valley narrows into a ravine becomes an untamable, roaring torrent. The scenery, such as the mists permitted of our seeing, is savage and grand. Here and there perpendicular cliffs of limestone cropped out through the mists, their summits covered with Pine trees. We crossed and re-crossed the torrent many times, and after covering 65 li reached Ta-ngai-tung, which was our des-tination for the day. This hamlet, alt. 7600 feet, consists of one large hostel, which was in moderately good repair, and is completely surrounded by steep mountains heavily clad with mixed shrubs and small trees, the upper parts being covered with forests of Conifers. The flora generally is very similar to that of the Niu-tou shan, though scarcely as rich. All the Conifers except Silver Fir are present, though Larch only puts in its first appearance near the hostel. At Erh-tao chiao I photographed a magnificent Juniper (Juniperus squamata Fargesii), a tree 75 feet tall, 22 feet in girth, with graceful pendent branches. Also a Black Pine which retains its cones over many years. (It proved to be a new species, and has been named Pinus wilsonii). This Pine is common on the cliffs, but White Pine (P. armandi) is rare, although we passed the largest specimens of this tree I have met with. Deutzia longifolia with lovely rosy lilac-colored flowers, Spiraea henryi with yard long, flat sprays of pure white, and Neillia longeracemosa with rose-colored blossoms were perhaps the commonest shrubs in blossom. Poplar is the only large deciduous tree hereabouts. Maple is not uncommon, and near Ta-ngai-tung I gathered a Black Birch (Betula insignis) having short, stout erect catkins.

Early next morning we continued our journey, spending the whole day toiling up the ravine through savage, yet wondrous, scenery, with a profusion of vegetation on all sides. Coniferous trees preponderate, the species being the same as those previously mentioned, with a couple of new Spruces added. Yew is less abundant, but Larch (Larix potaninii) much more so, though large trees are very scarce. To my astonishment the Larch cones were ripe, and I collected a quantity of seed. A Poplar (Populus szechuanica) with large leaves, silver gray on the under side, is very common, and we passed some very large specimens. A Rose with large bright red flowers made a fine display, so also did the pink flowered Deutzia mentioned above. Two Lady-slipper Orchids (Cypripedium franchetii and C. luteum), with rosy purple and yellow flowers respectively occur, but are rare. In the bed of the torrent Hippophae salicifolia (Sallow-thorn) is common, and varies from dwarf spiny bushes to trees 25 feet tall, the long slender foliage silvery gray below forming a pleasing contrast to the brighter greens of surrounding trees and shrubs. Many kinds of Maple, Linden, and Mountain Ash are plentiful, and Tetracentron sinense, an interesting tree exceeding in size all other deciduous trees of this particular region, occurs sparingly. Hydrangeas, Spirxas, Honeysuckles, Mock-oranges, Brambles, Roses, Actinidia, Clematoclethra, Viburnum, and other ornamental shrubs struggle for possession of every available spot. The variety and wealth of bloom was truly astonishing, and I know of no region in western China richer in woody plants than that traversed during the day's march.

The weather continued exasperatingly showery, but luckily no great quantity of rain fell, otherwise the route would have been impassable. Heavy mists limited our view, but whenever the clouds lifted we saw nothing but steep mountain-sides, beetling crags or cliffs, bare here and there but mostly clothed with mixed vegetation; giving place ultimately to forests of Conifers. The road is vile beyond the power of language to describe. In several places poles have been fixed horizontally into holes made in the face of the cliffs and decaying planks laid on these to form a roadway. Such bridges as exist are of logs, often rotten, and were always difficult to cross. The river is simply a roaring torrent, cascading over huge boulders in mad endeavor to escape to less savage regions. At one point it receives a torrent, which, judging from the color and temperature of the waters, evidently comes from eternal snows.

During the day we passed a few miserable hovels, but there is no room for cultivation, and the people are wretchedly poor. We stayed for the night at Yii-yii-tien, alt. 8800 feet, 42 li from Ta-ngai-tung, where there are two poor hostels. These useful if squalid structures are all alike on this route, being one-storied, constructed of wood, roofed with shingles held down by stones. A portion is sectioned off as private quarters for the family in charge, and nearby the kitchen is located. A series of bunks is built around all sides of the place, the central part being occupied by benches for the accommodation of loads. Travellers furnish their own food supplies, since nothing is obtainable at the hostel except, perhaps, some green vegetables in minute quantities. Shelter for the night and a fire to cook food and dry clothing are all these places afford. But the foreign traveller enjoys a welcome quietude and freedom from curious crowds. A sound night's sleep rewards the labors of the day, and he awakens refreshed, perfectly fit, and all eager to drink in more of the wondrous scenery of woodland, crag, and stream.

At Teng-sheng-t'ang, 8 li beyond Yu-yu-tien, the ravine widens out into a shallow valley, and the road boldly ascends the grassy, scrub-clad mountains to the left of the stream. Hereabouts Barberries in great variety luxuriate. After a severe ascent we crossed over a shoulder, and for the rest of the day skirted the side of a grassy ridge carpeted with brilliantly colored alpine flowers.

The main stream takes its rise in some snowclad peaks, of which we obtained a glimpse and a photograph, but a considerable tributary flows down from the Pan-lan shan pass. The mountains to the right of this affluent, and also to the right of the main stream, are forested up to 11,500 feet altitude with Spruce, Silver Fir, and Larch. The bed of the valley is covered with bushes of Willow, Hippophae, and Barberries. Up to 10,000 feet altitude Cypripedium luteum is not uncommon on humus-clad boulders and in the margins of woods.

The flora of the grassy ridge leading up to the Pan lan shan pass is strictly alpine in character, and the wealth of herbs was truly amazing. Most of the more vigorous growing had yellow flowers, and this color predominated in consequence. Above 11,500 feet altitude, the gorgeous Meconopsis integrifolia, which has huge, globular, incurved, clear yellow flowers, covers miles of the mountain-side. Crowning plants from 2 to 2 ½ feet tall the myriad flowers of this wonderful Poppywort presented a magnificent spectacle. Nowhere else have I beheld this plant in such luxuriant profusion. The Sikhim Cowslip (Primula sikkimensis), with deliciously fragrant pale yellow flowers was rampant in moist places. Various kinds of Senecio, Trollius, Caltha, Pedicularis, and Corydalis added to the over-whelming display of yellow flowers. On boulders covered with grass and in moderately dry loamy places, Primula veitchii was a pleasing sight with its bright rosy pink flowers. All the moorland areas are covered so thickly with the Thibetan Lady-slipper Orchid (Cypripedium tibeticum) that it was impossible to step without treading on the huge dark red flowers reared on stems only a few inches tall. Yet the most fascinating herb of all was, perhaps, the extraordinary Primula vincaeflora, with large, solitary violet flowers, in shape strikingly resembling those of the common Periwinkle (Vinca major), produced on stalks 5 to 6 inches tall. This most unprimrose-like Primula is very abundant in grassy places. The variety of herbs is indeed legion, and the whole countryside was a feast of color. Silence reigns in these lonely alpine regions, a silence so oppressive as to be almost felt and broken on rare occasions only by the song of some lark soaring skywards. We flushed an occasional snow-partridge and saw one or two flocks of snow-pigeons, but bird-life generally was extremely sparse Save a few voles and mice we saw no animals, but bharal and wolves were said to occur here, the former in quantity.

After travelling 38 li we reached the hostel at Hsiang-yang-ping, alt. 11,650 feet, and remained there for the night. This place is part temple, part inn, and is kept by a priest, to whose clothing and person water was evidently a stranger. The medicine Pei-mu (Fritillaria roylei and other species) is common in this region, and as fellow-guests for the night we had a number of people engaged in digging up the tiny white corms of this plant. Some Chinese traders also were there buying up this medicine at 60 cash per ounce. In Chengtu it is worth, wholesale, 400 cash per ounce, so their profit is a handsome one. Among the medicine gatherers were several Wokje tribesfolk, about 5 feet 8 inches tall, sturdily built, with straight noses and fearless

YELLOW POPPYWORT (MECONOPSIS INTEGRIFOLIA)

expression. Two of their women were with them, and had they been clean and decently dressed they would have been decidedly handsome. We enjoyed during the day a certain amount of sunshine, interrupted by occasional showers, but soon after our arrival at Hsiang-yang-ping it commenced raining in torrents, and continued so to do far into the night.

It ceased raining before daylight, to our great joy. Making an early start we toiled slowly over the dread Pan-lan span, crossing the pass in a dense, driving, bitterly cold mist. The ascent is nowhere difficult, and none of us suffered seriously from the effects of the rarefied atmosphere, in spite of the evil reputation this pass has for mountain-sickness. The ridge is narrow, razor-edged, the summit being composed of sandstone, with marble embedded, piled up at an acute angle and devoid of vegetation. Snow, unmelted from the winter, lay in odd patches immediately below the pass, and on all sides there was much fresh snow. The dense mists prevented any extended view, but what little of the region was viible was bare and desolate. Two or three of the lovely snowbird Grandala coelicolor, were flitting around the snowy patches, their intense blue plumage contrasting remarkably with the white carpet around. I made the pass, 14,250 feet altitude, and the tree-limit about 11,800 feet.

The flora above 12,000 feet altitude is purely alpine and similar in character to that of the region around Sungpan and elsewhere throughout the Chino-Thibetan border-land at the same altitude. Meconopsis integrifolia occurs in countless thousands, also, to my pleasant surprise, the dark scarlet-flowered M. punicea. Although by no means so plentiful as around Sungpan, there were many thousands of this beautiful herb scattered around. Primroses are most abundant; Primula vincaeflora ascends to 13,000 feet, where its place is taken by the lovely P. nivalis and another closely allied species.

On crossing over I photographed the pass and then descended with all possible speed to the miserable hostel of Wan-jen-fen, alt. 13,700 feet, where our lunch awaited us. A little below this hostel a few bushes of Willow, small-leaved Rhododendrons, and Caraganas first appeared and became abundant as we descended. Soon Larch and occasional Spruce appear, and at 11,300 feet altitude trees are fairly numerous. A shrubby, evergreen prickly Oak (Quercus aquifolioides) is characteristic of these wind-swept mountain-sides, the golden brown undersurface of its leaves rendering it most conspicuous. (This Oak is almost as beautiful as the celebrated Golden Oak of California (Castanopsis chrysophylla), and I am very pleased to report its successful introduction to cultivation).

In addition to the shrubs mentioned above, dwarf Juniper, Spiraea, and Sallow-thorn also abound. This moorland country is very interesting and shows unmistakable signs of a drier climate than that enjoyed by the regions on the opposite side of the pass.

A torrent which rises near the head of the pass is soon augmented by tributaries and quickly becomes a roaring unfordable stream. The mountain-slopes close in, and at the tiny hamlet of Kao-tien-tzu the road plunges into a ravine. The sides of this ravine are wooded, Larch and Spruce being abundant, with miscellaneous shrubby vegetation. The elegant Syringa tomentella, a Lilac with branching panicles of fragrant flowers, is very common. On issuing from this ravine we crossed a tributary torrent, more turbulent in character than even the main stream, and found in front of us open country largely under cultivation.

Our caravan was to have stopped for the night at the hamlet of Kao-tien-tzu, but with greater zeal than knowledge pushed on 20 li farther to Reh-lung-kuan. This blunder upset my plans and put all things awry. The collecting work had to be curtailed; it was 10 p.m. ere I got any sup-per, and much of our work had to remain over until the morrow.

The Pan-lan shan is the boundary between two Chiarung states. On crossing over we quitted the state of Wassu and entered that of Wokje. The Wassu territory is wildly mountainous, well forested, and but little suited to agriculture. In consequence it is sparsely populated, and we encountered very few of the inhabitants en route. The hostels and houses on the main road are in the hands of Chinese or half-castes. The men of Wassu are tall (5 feet 8 inches or thereabout), with large, muscular frames, frank, open countenances, and are noted hunters of the beasts of forest and crag. The women are sturdy, buxom, and engagingly frank. Both men and women are darker complexioned than the Chinese, and, I am sorry to say, infinitely less cleanly in appearance. They are very fond of jewellery, both sexes wearing bangles of silver and copper, and silver rings studded with coral and turquoise. The women also wear large silver ear-rings, usually having insets of coral and turquoise. The men are addicted to opium-smoking, though possibly this is strictly true only of those engaged near the main roads as porters and muleteers who have come in close contact with the Chinese.

Reh-lung-kuan, alt. 10,900 feet, is a Wokje village consisting of about a score of houses, a small lamasery, and a tall square tower. We found here a spacious and very fair inn; the people were courteous and obliging. Our carrying coolies were able to purchase opium and a certain amount of foodstuffs. This explained their anxiety to cover 75 li, instead of stopping 20 li short at Kao-tien-tzu.

On leaving Reh-lung-kuan we descended the right bank of the river, which rises near the Pan-Ian shan pass, for 33 li to the hamlet of Kuan-chin-pa, a short day's march being necessary in order to accomplish the work left over. The day was fine and warm, with a strong, cool breeze. Looking back on our route the snows of the Pan-lan shan were visible the whole day. The road was in good repair, and skirts the mountain-sides well above the stream. In ancient times this valley was filled with glacial detritus, through which the strong torrent has cut a deep, narrow bed. This stream, known locally as the Neichu, is really the principal branch of the Hsaochin Ho (Little Gold River). Formerly gold in considerable quantities was mined throughout this valley, and we passed many old workings during the march.

The country generally reminded me forcibly of the upper Min valley, near Sungpan, above 8000 feet altitude. On the left bank of the stream the mountain-sides are very steep and largely covered with woods composed of Spruce, Silver Fir, and a few Pine trees. On the right bank the mountains are more sloping and mainly under cultivation. Wheat is the staple crop and ripens in early August; buck-wheat ranks next in importance, followed at a respectable distance by peas, beans, and Irish potato. The Wokje people are evidently skilled agriculturalists and in their own way fairly well-to-do. The prosperous condition of this state was evidenced by the plenitude of large houses, lama-series, and a relatively dense population. The hostels, how-ever, are all in the hands of half-breeds, derived from early Chinese colonists. The larger houses and lamaseries are usually perched on some bluff composed of glacial mud, grits, and boulders. They are more or less square, two-storied, with flat mud roofs, having small turrets at each corner, from which prayer-flags flutter; a branch of some kind of Conifer is usually in evidence near these flags. Chortens and other Lamaist monuments occur here and there, whilst inscribed mani-stones are common. The peasants' houses are low, one-storied, built of sandstone shales, the roofs either flat or with very slight slope.

That the climate of this valley is relatively dry and warm is clearly shown by the flora, which is markedly xerophytic. Two species of Cotoneaster, several Clematis, the Sallow-thorn, prickly Oak, Barberries, and Roses are the chief constituents. A curious and new bush Honeysuckle (Lonicera tubuliflora), with small leaves and tubular, white, fragrant flowers borne in pairs, is locally abundant. Another common plant is the shrubby Clematis fruticosa, with simple oblong leaves and golden yellow, nodding flowers. A Lilac (Syringa potaninii), with erect panicles of rose-purple flowers, is another interesting shrub, plentiful in this valley. Poplar, a Hard Pine (Pinus prominens), with almost prickly cones, and a White Birch, the bark of which is used for lining straw hats, are the more common trees by the wayside. I also gathered a few late flowers of Incarvillea wilsonii. In a general way this Incarvillea resembles Delavay's, but averages 4 to 6 feet in height. Another new plant collected was a Primrose akin to Primula sibirica, but having taller scapes and longer pedicels. Kuan-chin-pa, alt. 9500 feet, consists of two small and rather poor inns, with the ruins of a large square tower near by.

Twelve li below Kuan-chin-pa, and also on the right bank of the river, is the village of Ta-wei, a considerable place for this region, boasting a large lamasery. This place has an evil reputation, but no ill-will was displayed toward me. Many Lamas clad in claret-colored serge crowded around and watched me as I photographed the village, and displayed much interest in my camera, dog, and gun. Nevertheless, the reputation of this village is well-founded, and I would advise travellers to avoid staying overnight there. From Ta-wei a road leads across the river and over the mountains to Mupin.

On continuing our journey we followed the right bank of the stream for a further 27 li to Mo-ya-ch'a, where, owing to an old landslide, it was necessary to cross over to the left bank. This was accomplished by means of a wooden semi-cantilever bridge. Such bridges have been fairly common en route, but this was the first our road had led over. From this bridge the road descends the left bank, keeping high up above the river to Kuan-chai, which was our destination for the day. The whole valley is very arid, though a considerable area was under wheat. A few Poplar and Willow trees occur near the river, otherwise only high up on the mountain-sides were any trees discernible. The flora is similar to that of all the principal river-valleys of this hinterland, as described in Chapter XIII. Rosa soulieana is very abundant. I gathered several new plants, but the country is too arid to be of much interest botanically.

Situated at an altitude of 8500 feet, Kuan-chai is a small village and the residence of the Wokje chieftain. The chief's house is very large, the upper structure, all of wood, is well built, and the whole is dominated by several tall towers, and fine Walnut trees occur scattered around. The prosperous condition of this little state was further evidenced during the day's march. Large houses are frequent, many being perched high up on the steep mountain-sides. Wheat is the principal crop grown, and at Kuan-chai was just bursting into ear. Maize and the Irish potato are like-wise commonly cultivated. A little flax and Hemp (Cannabis sativa) also occurs, the oil expressed from the seeds of these plants being in general use as an illuminant. We passed odd fields of Opium Poppy, the plants being only a few inches tall. On the fan-shaped slope, at the head of which the village of Kuan-chai is situated, all the crops were remarkably luxuriant.

At Ma-lun-chia a considerable torrent joins the Nei-chu on the right bank. A by-road ascends this tributary, leading to Fupien and thence to Lifan Ting. Our road was for the greater part good and we easily covered the 67 li, enjoying bright sunshine the whole day.

Immediately beyond the chief's residence the road mounts over a steep bluff, where is situated the hamlet of Hsao-kuan-chai. This place is reputed to have offered stern resistance to the Chinese in their conquest of this valley a hundred odd years ago, and was only captured after a long siege. The remains of the sangars and old forts are still to be seen. From this point the road continues to wind along the left bank of the river for 40 li to the town of Monkong Ting. Both sides of the valley are very arid, the flora poor and uninteresting. Very few houses occur in the valley, but high up on the mountain-sides we saw many scattered about and surrounded by wheat fields. At Laoyang the river is joined on the right bank by another of almost equal volume. The main road from Lifan Ting, via Fupien, descends this tributary stream and joins at this point the road we were following. From what little we could see of the valley of this Fupien stream it appeared to be equally arid and barren as the one we had descended from Reh-lung-kuan. Continuing our journey and on rounding a bend in the river, we suddenly sighted, perched on a rocky promontory, the town of Monkong Ting. After passing through a gateway we noticed a separate township, rather prosperous looking, situated in a lateral valley a little to the left of the main road. This is the official town of Monkong Ting, where reside the principal officials, civil and military. Crossing a torrent by a wooden bridge we entered the place first sighted from the bend in the river. This proved to be an old military camp of poverty-stricken, dilapidated houses, scattered alongside a street about 100 yards long. Two hundred yards beyond this camp we reached the thriving business town known as Hsin-kai-tsze. Monkong Ting, therefore, consists of three distinct towns or villages: (1) the official town, (2) old military camp, (3) the business town. All three are unwalled, though a gateway has to be passed on entering each. The situation is most picturesque and strategically very strong. Monkong Ting is the political centre of this region and a place of very considerable importance. The two Chiarung states of Wokje and Mupin have their boundaries at this point, and the rest of the valley to Romi Chango is divided into feudal states.

CHINA — MOTHER OF GARDENS

The streets of Hsin-kai-tsze were thronged with people, chiefly tribesfolk, selling medicines and buying various sundries for their own use. They made a very picturesque crowd, the dames being especially noticeable by reason of their display of silver dress-ornaments, bangles, and ear-rings. The inns were all crowded, but the head official obligingly secured a couple of rooms for us and treated us with much courtesy and good-will. The people were naturally curious and grouped themselves around us, but their manners were deferential.

Hsin-kai-tsze, alt. 8200 feet, is a most important medicine-mart, being famous for its Pei-mu (Fritillaria spp.), Rhubarb, Ch'ung tsao (a caterpillar infested with the fungus Cordyceps sinensis), and Chung-hoa (an umbelliferous plant, possibly Ligusticum thomsonii). All of these are collected and brought in for sale by the tribesfolk. Musk and deer-horns also figure in the trade.

Several roads radiate from this centre; one of these leads from the official town to Mupin, over the pass of Chia-chin shan, which was said to be higher than that of the Pan-lan shan and surrounded by snow-clad peaks.

The Wokje state preserved its prosperous appearance to the end, and is evidently a thriving, happy little country. The people strongly resemble the Wassu folk, though possibly they are scarcely as tall and have slightly sharper features. The Chinese language is understood and in common use along the main road, where the people imitate the Chinese in shaving their heads and wearing a queue. Lamaism evidently has a strong hold on these people, judging by the number of lamaseries we saw.

I had intended remaining a day at Monkong Ting, but owing to the crowded condition of the town decided to defer this holiday until we reached Romi Chango. The inn in which rooms were provided for us was crowded with people who were noisy over their cups and business dealings, rendering sleep well-nigh an impossibility.

Just outside Hsin-kai-tsze the road crosses over by a log bridge to the right bank of the stream. This bridge was being repaired, and only two very uneven logs were in position. A thin rope was stretched across to serve as a hand-rail on the left side. Crossing was really dangerous,

THE WOKJE VILLAGE OF TA-WEI

the waters below being deep and turbulent. The official kindly provided local experts to carry our gear over, and the way these men accomplished the task filled me with admiration. I rewarded them with 1000 cash, to their astonished delight. My dog was lashed firmly to a flat board and carried across on a man's back. He struggled violently, and the man only just managed to get him over before he got half loose. I walked over behind the dog and was relieved when the 30 yards across the yawning gulf were safely passed. Everything came over all right, but my followers clung to the local men like grim death, the majority shaking in their nervous fright. Such dangerous entertainments are not desirable, and I heartily hoped that we had no more such bridges to cross. From this bridge we descended 60 li to the hamlet of Sheng-ko-chung, alt. 7600 feet, through arid country and over a bad road. The river is here a broad and turbulent stream, flowing between steep banks composed of loose rocks. A few Poplar, an occasional Cypress (C. duclouxiana) and Koelreuteria apiculata (the latter was covered with masses of small yellow flowers) are the only trees of note. The region is very sparsely populated, but high up, on the left bank more especially, are a few houses of the same architecture as those of Wokje. As travelling companions during the day we had a party of tribesfolk, chiefly women in holiday attire. They were very cheerful, laughing and singing most of the time. On parting company at Sheng-ko-Chung they made merry over cups of Chinese wine, the dames officiating as to the manner born. It rained heavily during the night, and it was cool and delightfully fresh in the morning when we recommenced our journey down the valley of the Hsaochin Ho. Thirty li below Sheng-ko-Chung we passed the large lamasery of Gi-lung, colored white and picturesquely situated on the right bank of the river. Over a hundred Lamas reside here and exercise considerable authority over the neighborhood. About 10 li beyond this lamasery the river suddenly develops into a series of boiling, roaring cataracts. The fury of the waters was most fearsome to behold, and a wilder stretch of river is scarcely imaginable. Earlier in the day we had crossed to the left bank, and just below the very worst bit of this savage waterway we recrossed to the right bank over a rotten and most unsafe wooden bridge. Some 7 li below this point we reached the hamlet of Pan-ku chiao, alt. 7100 feet, where we found accommodation for the night, having covered 70 li. Just above the hamlet a torrent joins the river on its left bank, and up this lateral valley mountains clad with snow were plainly visible. Bridges are scarce and the few that exist look as if they have not been renewed since this region was conquered, well over a hundred years ago. One thing is certain, they cannot possibly last much longer: the two we crossed during the day were all askew and decidedly dangerous.

The district is rather less arid than that around Mon-kong Ting, yet the flora is very poor. Poplar is a common tree, so also is the Koelreuteria, which was a fine sight, with a wealth of flowers, and evidently enjoys a dry, hot situation. The sub-shrubby Incarvillea variabilis and Amphicome arguta, both with large, tubular, pink flowers, are very abundant by the roadside. Other common shrubs are Bauhinia, Sophora viciifolia, Ceratostigma willmottiae, with lovely blue flowers, Ligustrum and Rosa soulieana. On the cliffs Cupressus duclouxiana is dotted about. Maize is the principal crop, occupying in season almost every inch of available land. Houses are fairly numerous, but most of them are relegated to the higher slopes well above the valley. The scenery in places is rugged and grand. In front of the inn at Pan-ku chiao limestone cliffs rear themselves some 2000 feet, abutting on a cultivated slope where Walnut trees are scattered around. Crowning a bluff is a tall tower and near-by another in ruins, telling of glories now departed.

On leaving Pan-ku chiao we descended the right bank of the Hsaochin Ho, some 42 li to the point where it joins the Tachin Ho or Upper Tung River. This final stretch is little else than one long succession of cataracts and strong rapids, the turbulent waters being thick with brown mud. High bare cliffs predominate, but here and there occur more or less flat fan-shaped areas under cultivation, with houses shaded by Poplar, Willow, and Walnut trees. Diospyros lotus, Hovenia dulcis, and the large-leaved Ligustrum lucidum are other trees common hereabout. Maize is evidently the chief summer crop in these regions, but wheat is grown, a red, beardless variety, having stout ears, and harvesting was in progress. Rock-pigeons are very abundant, and were busily engaged in exacting their toll of the ripening grain.

After passing the hamlet of Yo-tsa we sighted on the opposite (left) bank a large lamasery sequestered midst a fine grove of trees. A little beyond this is the village of Tsung-lu, a curious-looking place, boasting a score or more tall towers. Skin coracles are employed to ferry over to these places.

The Hsaochin Ho is prevented from joining the Tachin Ho at right angles by a rocky spit which at times is evidently flooded over. Marble and granite are common rocks hereabout, the latter being full of mica flakes which glistened in the sun. Ascending the left bank of the Tachin Ho for a couple of li, then crossing over a bamboo suspension bridge 90 yards long, we soon reached the small town of Romi Chango. The whole day's journey was only 45 li, but owing to the heat and rough road we all arrived very much fatigued and in sore need of a day's rest.

From all I could learn it would appear that the region in the vicinity of the river from Monkong Ting to Romi Chango, after its conquest by the Chinese about A.D. 1775, was divided into feudal states, and certain chieftains installed in possession as rewards for services rendered during the struggle. The chiefs, styled Shao-pes, hold hereditary office and are directly responsible to Chinese authority for the good behavior of the people under their rule, also, if necessity arises, they are bound to supply armed men to assist the Chinese cause. Lamas alone are exempt from such military duties; ordinarily the people of these feudal states are agriculturists. These shao-pes are subordinate to the Chinese military commander stationed at Monkong Ting. The two chief shao-pes reside, one at Monkong Ting, the other at Che-lung, a village in the mountains, 20 li removed from the left bank of the Hsaochin Ho and 60 li below Monkong Ting. Another shao-pe resides at Ta-ching, 120 li to the northeast of Monkong Ting, a fourth at A'n-niu, a place in the mountains to the southwest of the region controlled by the Che-lung shao-pe. Beyond the original grant of territory these feudal chiefs receive no rewards, monetary or otherwise, from the Chinese. The system has much to recommend it and evidently works very well. It keeps the Chinese authority supreme, whilst allowing the native folk to be governed by their own recognized chiefs. The difference between the chieftain of a semi-independent Chiarung state and a shao-pe appears to be that, whereas the former is an absolute ruler over a territory long hereditary to his tribe, the latter is more in the nature of an alien ruling over a tract of country fiefed to his forbears by the Chinese, after they conquered this region and broke up the Chiarung confederacy. The territory occupied by these feudal states formerly belonged to the Chiarung tribes, and the people are in the main derived from that stock. Chinese settlers have intermarried with the natives, and in the vicinity of the main road the population is mixed. The people living in the lower stretches of the Hsaochin Ho are an inferior race, of poor physique, and most abominably filthy.

CHAPTER XVI

ACROSS THE CHINO-THIBETAN BORDERLAND

ROMI CHANGO TO TACHIENLU; THE FORESTS
OF THE TA-P'AO SHAN

OMI CHANGO, or Chango, as it is commonly called, is a poor, unwalled, straggling town of about 130 houses. It is without rank, but a magistrate, subordinate to the Tachienlu Fu, and a military official, controlled from Monkong Ting, reside there. The town is really a Chinese settlement, situated in the extreme northeast corner of the state of Chiala. It is built on the right bank of the Tachin Ho, at a point where the river, making a right-angled turn from the north, is joined by a very considerable torrent from the west. The Tachin, a river 100 yards broad, with a steady current and muddy water, sweeps round majestically. High cliffs on the left bank, steep mountain-slopes on the right, lofty mountains to the east and west wall in the town, at the western entrance to which a massive square tower stands sentinel. Chango is a very poverty-stricken place, with a small trade in medicines and sundries. It draws its supplies of rice, paper, and Chinese commodities generally from Kuan Hsien, and everything is phenomenally dear. This is only natural when the distance and difficulties of the journey are duly considered.

A small road descends the right bank of the Tachin Ho, by means of which Luting chiao may, with great difficulty, be reached. A road ascends the right bank of the Tachin Ho and leads to the interesting Chiarung states of Badi and Bawang, where the Bonpa religion holds full sway. Badi the capital of these now united principalities, is only 60 li from Romi Chango. The chieftain is dead, but his widow, assisted by a steward, acts as regent for her infant son. Badi-Bawang is one of the

216

ancient matriarchal kingdoms of Chinese historians, and at all times a woman holds an important place in its government. Badi, the larger of the two states, is very rich in gold, which, though unworked during recent years, is jealously guarded. Chinese visitors, rich or poor, are cross-questioned as to their business and closely watched during their sojourn in this state. The Badi-Ba-wang folk often visit Chango on business, and during our stay there we saw several. Most of them were peasant girls and women, dressed so scantily as to scarcely hide their nakedness. They were short in stature, and apparently unwashed from birth! However, since these were "hewers of wood and drawers of water" of the poorest class, it would be unfair to judge the whole race accordingly.

In Chango we lodged at a comfortable inn, having a clean room, well removed from the street and overlooking the river. We spent a quiet day resting and refitting for the final stage of our journey to Tachienlu. The people were not over-inquisitive and those in charge of the inn were exceedingly obliging. Soon after our arrival the magistrate sent me word that he was suffering from pains in the stomach and vomiting, and would be grateful for some medicine to relieve his suffering. I sent him some Epsom-salts and an opiate. The next day word came that he was much better, only too tired to leave his room. A traveller gets many such requests for medicine, and I have generally found quinine, Epsom-salts and opium pills most useful cures, for which the people were always grateful.

On leaving this lonely town of Chango, which I made 6700 feet altitude, the road to Tachienlu ascends the right bank of the tributary torrent. We were warned that the road was very difficult, leading through forests and over high mountains. It was not long before these statements were verified. The torrent quickly developed into an angry, irresponsible stream; the road in many places had been washed away and much wading was necessary. Our carriers had great difficulty in getting along, and had the waters of the torrent been a few feet higher the road would have been quite impassable. All the bridges were rotten and insecure. High up on the mountain-sides we saw several large hamlets, but there are very few houses in the valley—quite sufficient, however, for whenever the road led past a house we had to traverse an open sewer, often a foot deep in dung and refuse. Such filthy surroundings are characteristic of Thibetan houses. The Chinese would collect all this sewage for their fields, but the Thibetans, who are but poor agriculturists at best, have not yet learned the value of manure. At such places I usually climbed over the fences and walked through the crops, but my men waded through the filth and gave vent to their wrath in loud, angry imprecations The people of Chiala are typical Thibetans and use the lower stories of their flat-roofed houses as pens for horses and cattle. A few li above Chango the flora begins to lose its purely xerophytic character, and becomes more and more luxuriant as the ascent proceeds. The higher slopes are well forested with mixed trees, but nearby the road trees are scarce. The mountain-sides flanking the stream are very steep, being often sheer cliffs. Such places are dotted with Cypress (Cupressus duclouxiana) and prickly leaved ever-green Oak.

After journeying 60 li we reached the village of Tung-ku, alt. 7800 feet, where there are several large Thibetan houses, decorated with prayer-flags, but only two or three hostels, and these poor in character. The owner of the one we stayed in is a noted hunter, and many pelts of the budorcas, serow, and black bear were in use as bed-mat-tresses. His family told us the hunter was away after musk-deer; they also informed us that both the Thibetan-eared and Lady Amherst pheasants are common hereabout. Around the village Walnut trees are most abundant. Wheat is a common crop and was just ripening. Maize, too, was plentiful and is evidently the staple summer crop every-where in these regions.

The next day we covered another 60 li, putting up for the night at the poor hamlet of T'ung-lu-fang. We crossed the river four times by wooden bridges, each more rotten than the other. The river was in partial flood, and a goodly portion of the road was either washed away, obliterated by landslides, or under water. Often we had to make a path for ourselves up the mountain-side. The under-water portions of the road I traversed on the back of one of the soldiers we had with us from Chango, until he stumbled and gave me a ducking. After this I waded.

ACROSS THE CHINO-THIBETAN BORDERLAND

There was no traffic on the road so-called, and I marvelled how my coolies managed to get their loads along. Our chairs were carried piecemeal and even then with difficulty over the worst places. The river was a roaring torrent throughout the whole day's journey, in places really awesome to behold, dashing itself headlong over enormous boulders, or boiling as if forced by some malignant spirit. In many places our path actually overhung this torrent, and one false step meant death.

About 10 li above Tung-ku the river makes a right-angled turn and is joined at this point by another stream of almost equal volume from the west. From this place the road skirts the river through a narrow, savage, magnificently wooded ravine. Maple, Ash, Hornbeam, Birch, Poplar, Hemlock Spruce, and prickly Oak are the chief constituents of these woods, followed by Evodia, Rhus, Cypress, Willow, Elm, Sallow-thorn, Bamboo, and miscellaneous shrubs. The Maples (Acer davidii and A. pictum parviflorum) are larger trees than I have seen elsewhere. The Ash and Hornbeam are all fine trees, and the Hemlock Spruce (Tsuga yunnanensis) in many cases over 100 feet tall, with a girth of 12 to 15 feet.

On leaving this magnificent fragment of virgin forest the country became less interesting. Where the cliffs are not sheer and bare the mountain-slopes have been cleared to a very large extent. The ravine widens into a narrow valley which is covered with scrub. The cliffs and mountain-slopes high up are sparsely clad with Cypress, White and Hard pines, Spruce, Silver Fir, and Hemlock. The scenery is sublime.

We passed few houses and these of the meanest description. Very little land is under cultivation; maize is the chief crop, with patches of wheat and oats here and there. The country is not suited to cultivation, and one marvels how the few people living there manage to find even the most miserable subsistence. Yesterday we noticed herds of a small breed of cattle. The people are shorter in stature than the average, and perfectly proportioned dwarfs are fairly common. Since leaving Monkong Ting, goitre has been manifest among the inhabitants, and in this river valley it is very prevalent.

219

CHINA — MOTHER OF GARDENS

T'ung-lu-fang, alt. 8800 feet, consists of about half a dozen scattered houses. The one we stayed in is of Thibetan architecture, fairly clean, and owned by a Chinese settler. None of these houses affords any bedding for the coolies, and of course nothing is purchasable—all supplies have to be carried by the travellers themselves.

The people at T'ung-lu-fang informed us that we should not be able to reach Mao-niu, as the road had been washed away in several places, and under the lee of some cliffs was flooded to a depth of 4 feet or more. This gratuitous and discouraging information proved, luckily for us, to be scarcely accurate, since, after a struggle, we managed to get through. My head coolie declared it was the very worst road we had ever traversed, and I was inclined to agree with him. Worse it could not have been and constitute a roadway at all! For fully half the distance the track was under water or washed completely away, and we were forced to wade or make a new path over the mountain-side. Just how we got over the 30 li I cannot describe, but we all came through with nothing worse than a severe wetting.

Mao-niu is a fair-sized village for the country, and is mainly perched on a flat 200 feet above the torrent, and surrounded by a considerable area under wheat—a veritable oasis, in fact, surrounded by high mountains. Formerly it was the principal village of a petty state to which it gave its name. It now belongs to the state of Chiala. As far as Mao-niu the scenery and flora is similar to that around Tung-ku and calls for no special remark. The outstanding feature is the woods of Hard Pine (Pinus prominens). The steeper the country the happier this Pine appeared to be. The bark on the trunk is deeply furrowed, often red in the upper parts of the tree; the cones are quite prickly, and are retained for many years. The wood is very resinous, and is evidently much esteemed for building purposes. The Hemlock Spruce is common, and all the trees are of great size.

At Mao-niu the main stream leads off in a westerly direction to Th'ai-ling, a large village of over 100 houses and several lamaseries. It is also the centre of a considerable gold-mining industry, and has the reputation of being a lawless district. We were informed that the road

PRIMULA VEITCHII

thither was in a dreadful state of disrepair, and that most of the bridges had been washed away by recent floods.

On clearing the cultivated area around Mao-niu we plunged immediately into a narrow, heavily forested ravine, down which a considerable torrent thundered. Conifers preponderate in these forests, Spruce being particularly abundant. We noticed some huge trees, but the average was about 80 to 100 feet tall. White and Red Birch are common, and I was fortunate enough to secure seeds of the latter. The Sallow-thorn (Hippophae salicifolia) is exceedingly common, forming trees 30 to 50 feet tall with a girth of 4 to 10 feet. The size of these trees very much surprised me. Willows, Cherries, and different species of Pyrus, are also plentiful. Deutzia, Hydrangea, Philadelphus, Rosa, and Clematis are the principal shrubs, and many were in flower. Primula Cockburniana, which has orange-scarlet flowers, is the most noteworthy herb hereabout.

After wandering several miles through the forests we reached the hamlet of Kuei-yung, alt. 10,100 feet, and 60 li from T'ung-lu-fang. This place consists of half a dozen houses, purely Thibetan in character, built on a slope and surrounded by a considerable area under wheat, barley, and oats. The mountains all around are heavily forested with coniferous trees, and in the far distance a snow-capped peak glittered on the horizon.

The house we lodged in is three-storied with the usual flat mud roof. The walls built of shale-rock are most substantial. Entering through a low doorway we had first to traverse a yard filled with cattle dung, then a piggery where a steep ladder led upward to a couple of dark empty rooms in which we installed ourselves. A ladder from these rooms led to the roof, where I should have preferred to sleep had it not been raining. The house boasts neither table, stool, nor chair, and we had to improvise as best we could. The Thibetans squat on the floor for their meals, and therefore have no use for tables or chairs. The housewife, a most cheery if dirty person, had a very musical laugh. Things generally appeared a joke to her, and incited her to frequent laughter, which it was pleasant to hear. My followers were oddly amused at the strangeness of things, and appeared to enjoy the novelty.

ACROSS THE CHINO-THIBETAN BORDERLAND

Yet it was not out of love for our quarters that I stayed over a day at Kuei-yung, but to photograph various trees and investigate the Conifers. Photography in the forests is no mere pastime. It took over an hour on three occasions clearing away brushwood and branches so as to admit of a clear view of the trunk of the subject. I secured a dozen photographs, which entailed a hard day's work. The trees of Larch and other Conifers, Birch, and Poplar are very fine. The Larch (L. potaninii), though not plentiful, is of great size, and trees 100 feet by 12 feet in girth occur. But the most astonishing feature of these forests is the large trees of Sallow-thorn (Hippophae salicifolia). I had never imagined it could attain to the size of specimens I saw during the day. I photographed two old trees 50 feet tall, 12 and 15 feet in girth respectively. I saw others taller but less in girth. Another interesting tree hereabout is a Cherry (Prunus serrula tibetica), which has a short, very thick trunk clothed with lustrous chestnut-brown bark, and a wide-spreading head. The leaves are willow-like, 3 to 4 inches long; the fruit is red, ovoid, on pendulous stalks. The tree averages about 30 feet in height, the head being 60 feet and more through.

The next morning we bade farewell to our cheery hostess at Kuei-yung, and continued our journey. The road immediately plunges into the forest, and winds through and among magnificent timber. The forests are very fine, and coniferous trees 100 to 150 feet tall, with a girth of 12 to 18 feet, are quite common. The latter consist of four species of Spruce, three of Silver Fir and one of Larch. The handsomest of the Silver firs is Abies squamata, which has purplish brown bark, exfoliating like the bark of the River Birch. The Larch becomes general in the ascent, and ultimately overtops all other trees and extends to the tree-limit. White and Red Birch, Poplar and Sallow-thorn are the only broad-leaved deciduous trees really common. An evergreen Oak (Quercus aquifolioides rufescens), with prickly leaves like a Holly, is abundant. In the shelter of the forests this Oak makes a good-sized tree, but in the more exposed places it is reduced to a small shrub. The wood is very hard and makes the finest of charcoal. Shrubs are not rich in variety, but bush Honeysuckles, Barberries, Spirxaeas, and Clematis are plentiful. Herbs, especially the Sikhim Cowslip (Primula sikkimensis),

CHINA — MOTHER OF GARDENS

P. involucrata, Anemone, Caltha, Trollius, and various Compositx luxuriate on all sides, and the glades and marshy places were nothing but masses of color. The men who were in front of me saw several troupes of monkeys and some eared-pheasants, but I saw no animals and very few birds.

We camped near the tree-limit, at about 12,000 feet altitude, and erected a small but of Spruce boughs under a large Silver Fir tree (Abies squamata). My boy preferred to pass the night in his chair, and the men arranged themselves around a log fire. The neighborhood has an evil reputation for highway robbers, but we felt sure there was small possibility of any attack on us being made. It rained a little during the day, and a sharp shower fell in the early evening, but the night proved fine. The altitude, however, affected our sleep; it was also very cold, and we were all glad when morning broke. My dog suffered as much as any of us; he refused to eat his supper, and I never saw him so utterly miserable. The coolies looked a most woebegone crowd, shivering with cold and generally wretched. They seemed to have no idea of making themselves comfortable; it would have been a simple matter for them to have rigged up a shelter of Spruce boughs, but they were too indifferent for this or even to collect firewood. We brought with us from Kuei-yung, as guide, a Thibetan, and it was he who got together all the wood required for a fire.

There was a slight frost and a heavy dew, but the sun, which rose like a ball of fire, soon warmed us and dispersed the dew. The road is of the easiest, winding through timber and brush alongside a small stream, up to within 1000 yards of the head of the Ta-p'ao shan pass, where the ascent becomes steeper. It is, however, only the last 500 feet that make any pretence of being difficult. Above the place where we camped the Conifer trees rapidly decrease in size, Larch becomes more and more abundant, and ultimately forms pure woods. It overtops every other kind of tree, and extends up to 13,500 feet altitude. Just below the limits of the Larch a dwarf Juniper appears and ascends to near the head of the pass. The scaly-barked Silver Fir (Abies squamata) ascends to 12,500 feet and two species of Spruce to 13,000 feet. This side of the pass enjoys a moist climate, and the tree-line (13,500 feet approximately) is remarkably high. Above the tree-line the mountain-sides, to within a few hundred feet of the pass, are covered with scrub composed, as usual in these regions, of Willow, Berberis, small-leaved species of Rhododendron, Spiraea, Juniper, Potentilla veitchii, P. fruticosa, and Rhododendron kialense, the latter being here the most alpine of all the large-leaved members of the family. Herbs, of course, made a wonderful display of color. In addition to those previously mentioned, other species of Primula, the yellow and violet-blue Poppy-worts (Meconopsis integrifolia and M. henrici), various Stone-crops (Sedum spp.), and Saxifrages are abundant. But the most striking of all the herbs is a Rhubarb (Rheum alexandrae), an extraordinary plant, with a pyramidal inflorescence from 3 to 4 feet tall, arising from a mass of relatively small, ovate, shining, sorrel-like leaves, and composed of broad, rounded, decurved, pale yellow bracts overlapping one another like tiles on a house-roof. The local name of this plant is Ma Huang (Horse Rhubarb); it prefers rich boggy ground where verdure is luxuriant and yak delight to feed. Such places were studded with its most conspicuous tower-like spikes of flowers. The Rhubarb and yellow Poppywort (Meconopsis integrifolia) are always most rampant around places where yak have been herded.

Unmelted snow of the preceding winter was lying in patches just below the summit of the pass, a bare, narrow ridge crowned by a cairn of stones surmounted with many prayer-flags, and 14,600 feet above sea-level. This narrow neck is composed of slate and sandstone, with a certain amount of marble rock scattered around, and connects two massive ranges clad with eternal snows. The day was gloriously sunny, and we had a rare opportunity of enjoying and appreciating the delights of this alpine region. Except for a feeling of giddiness when stooping, and a general shortness of breath, I suffered no inconvenience from the altitude. In spite of their loads only two or three of my men were seriously affected; the gradual ascent was, I think, responsible for our good fortune in this matter. From past experience I had rather dreaded the effects this pass might have on my followers, and was pleasantly surprised at the ease with which they negotiated it.

With the weather conditions so favorable the view from the

summit of the pass far surpassed my wildest dreams. It greatly exceeded anything of its kind that I have seen, and would require a far abler pen than mine to describe it adequately. Straight before us, but a little to the right of our viewpoint, was an enormous mass of dazzling eternal snow, supposed to be, and I can well believe it, over 22,000 feet high. Beneath the snow and attendant glaciers was a sinister-looking mass of boulders and screes. In the far distance were visible the enormous masses of perpetual snow around Tachienlu. In the near distance, to the west-north-west of the pass, another block of eternal snow rears itself. Looking back on the route we had traversed we saw that the narrow valley is flanked by steep ranges, the highest peaks clad with snow, but in the main, though bare and savage-looking, they scarcely attain to the snow-line. On all sides the scenery is wild, rugged, and severely alpine. A cold wind blew in strong gusts across the pass, and we were glad when our photographic work was finished, so that we could hurry down. Several eagles and lammergeiers were soaring aloft, but we saw no animals, though wild sheep and Thibetan gazelle were said to frequent this region.

Descending by a precipitous, break-neck path, over loose slate, sandstone shales and greasy clayey-marls for 15 li, we reached the head of a broad valley. The pass on this side offers a far more severe climb than the side we had ascended. On reaching the valley the track we followed connects with the main road to Th'ai-ling, Chantui, and Chamdo. Commercially speaking this is the highway into Thibet from Tachienlu. It leads through grasslands, affording good pasturage for animals, and though the mean elevation is very considerable the passes are less steep than those on the political highway via Litang and Batang. This Ta-p'ao shan region is notorious for its highway robberies. We met five tribesmen who told us that the previous night their camp had been rushed by an armed band and everything they possessed carried off. Every Thibetan is by nature a robber, and behaves as such when he can do so with more or less impunity. They rob one another freely, but the tribesmen are their favorite victims.

From the head of the valley to Hsin-tientsze, the first habitation, is reckoned as 30 li. The road is broad but uneven, winding through a

YA-CHIA-K'AN, PEAKS 21,000 FEET HIGH

valley, and keeping close to a torrent which descends from the Ta-p'ao shan snows. The mountains on either side of the valley in all their higher parts range above the snow-line; their lower slopes are covered with grass, small Conifer trees, and brushwood. In the valley itself shrubs of large size, chiefly Willows, Honey-suckles, Barberries, and Sallow-thorn abound. Occasional trees of Larch and Spruce occur, all of small size. Flocks of snow-pigeons were plentiful, and I shot several of these birds for our larder.

From Kuei-yung, 120 li, there is no house of any description save Hsin-tientsze, alt. 10,800 feet, a filthy and miserable hostel. Near Kuei-yung we passed a charcoal-burning camp where a few men were engaged, otherwise we did not meet a living soul, until we crossed the pass. It is indeed a most lonely region, but of great interest to a nature lover. I count myself particularly fortunate in being favored by perfect weather for crossing the pass, more especially as it was the first day without any sign of rain since leaving Kuan Hsien.

The thermometer registered 36° F. when we turned out next morning, and our ears and fingers tingled with cold, even though it was July 8th. The smoke inside the inn was too much for my eyes, so I breakfasted in the middle of the roadway. I think everybody was glad to quit Hsin-tientsze with its vermin and stinks. There was an odd patch of wheat around the hostel, but it looked miserable; the season is too short and the climate too severe for cultivation here-about at this altitude.

We followed a broad, uneven road, which had suffered much from animal traffic, for 60 li to Je-shui-t'ang (Hot-water pond), alt. 9800 feet. The descent is gradual, and the day's journey proved a delightful loiter through a shrub-clad valley. We met several hundreds of yak and ponies, all laden with brick tea encased in raw hides and bound for interior Thibet. The Thibetans in charge were an unkempt, wild-looking lot of men, with long guns, swords, and conspicuous charm-boxes. Many of them wore their hair in a long plait with a sort of black yarn braided in, the whole being wrapt around their heads to form a turban; a few wore felt hats with high conical crowns. One or two women were with these caravans tending the animals exactly in the same way as the men. Ability to whistle and heave rocks with sure aim seemed to be the essential parts of a yak-muleteer's profession. Yak are slow, phlegmatic animals, and on sighting any unusual object they stand stock-still for a little time, and then make a mad rush forward. They appear to be docile enough, but their long horns look dangerously ugly, and we got out of their way as much as was possible. Each caravan was accompanied by one or more large dogs. These animals trot alongside the caravan and take no notice of any one, but when tethered and on guard in camp will allow no stranger to approach. They are massively-built dogs, and their savage appearance is heightened by a huge red-colored collar of woollen fringe, with which they are commonly decorated.

The flora was merely a repetition of that of the previous afternoon's journey. The valley and contiguous hillsides are covered with scrub, except for clearings here and there which serve as yak-camps. In addition to the shrubs mentioned as occurring around Hsin-tientsze, prickly Oak, Juniper, several kinds of Rose, and the Thibetan Honeysuckle (Lonicera thibetica) are common; Barberries in variety are a special feature. Conifers are scarce and all of small size; all the larger timber has been felled and removed long ago. At the hamlet of Lung-pu, reckoned 40 li from Hsin-tientsze, crops of wheat, barley, oats, and peas put in an appearance, and became more general as we descended the valley. Around Je-shui-t'ang the cereals were just coming into ear.

During the day, which was beautifully fine, we had grand views of the snowclad peaks around Tachienlu and the steep ranges with pinnacled peaks to the east-southeast of that town. Around Je-shui-t'ang there are several hot springs, in some of which the water was actually boiling. These springs are rich in iron, but in those I examined no sulphur was evident.

Our quarters at Je-shui-t'ang were a considerable improvement on those of Hsin-tientsze, but we were, never-theless, glad to leave soon after daylight dawned. It is considered to be 90 li from this place to Tachienlu, but I should say 60 li is a nearer estimate. We enjoyed another sunny day. The road is easy and leads through a continuation of the valley that we entered on descending from the Ta-p'ao shan pass. The valley and mountain-sides for some 300 to 500 feet above it become more and more under cultivation. Cereals, peas, and Irish potatoes are the principal crops. The potatoes were being harvested, and I noticed that red-colored ones predominated. The region generally has been denuded of its trees, and where not under crops is covered with scrub and coarse herbs. In rocky places small trees of White and Hard Pine (Pinus armandi, P. prominens) occur, also a few comparatively large trees of a very distinct-looking Peach having narrow, lance-shaped, long pointed leaves, rather small fruits, downy on the outside.[1]

Around habitations tall trees of Poplar are common, and an occasional Spruce and White Birch occur. The Spruce (Picea aurantiaca) is a particularly handsome species, with square, dark green needles on spreading branches and red brown pendulous cones clustered near the top of the tree. The Apple, Apricot, Peach, Plum, and a few Walnut trees are cultivated. The fields are fenced with hedges of wild Gooseberry (Ribes alpestre giganteum) and the handsome Sorbaria arborea, which has large erect masses of snow-white flowers. Over these and other shrubs various species of Clematis trail, the most common being C. rehderiana which was laden with a multitude of creamy yellow nodding flowers. The most beautiful shrub, however, was a Lilac (Syringa tomentella) growing from 12 to 15 feet tall, and covered with huge panicles of pink or white fragrant flowers. We crossed the stream by a wooden cantilever bridge and, on rounding a bend, the goal of our long journey came into view. We were all well-nigh dead beat, and it was with thankful and joyous hearts that we greeted the cluster of closely packed houses, which, nestling in a narrow valley, constitute the important border town of Tachienlu.

---

[1] At the time I paid no further attention to this Peach, but in 1910 I secured ripe fruit, and found to my astonishment that the stones were perfectly smooth, free, and relatively very small—characters denoting a distinct species of Peach. It proved to be new, and has since been named Prunus mira. I regard this as among the most remarkable of the discoveries I have been privileged to make. This new Peach is now in cultivation, and by cross-breeding with the old varieties of the garden Peach (P. persica) may result in the production of entirely new and improved races of this favourite fruit.

CHAPTER XVII

TACHIENLU, THE GATE OF THIBET

THE KINGDOM OF CHIALA, ITS PEOPLE,
THEIR MANNERS AND CUSTOMS

HE town of Tachienlu is situated in long. 102° 13' E., lat. 30° 3' circa, at an altitude of about 8400 feet. By the most direct route it is twelve days' journey from Chengtu Fu, the provincial capital, on the great highway which extends westward to Lhassa. It is the Ultima Thule of China and Thibet, where a large and thriving trade is done in the wares of both countries. It is also the residence of the king of Chiala, who governs a very considerable tract of country and exercises strong influence over conterminous states peopled with Thibetans. The first Occidental other than Roman Catholic priests to visit Tachienlu was the late Mr. T. T. Cooper in 1868. Since that date it has been visited by many scores of travellers, and has become fairly well known to the outside world. It is a more than ordinarily interesting place, and though much has been written concerning it the subject is far from being threadbare.

The present town is built on the narrowest of valleys at the head of a gorge, down which the River Lu cascades, falling some 4000 feet before it joins the River Tung, 18 miles distant. A branch of the Lu River bisects the town, being crossed by means of three wooden bridges, and is joined immediately below the north gate by another stream, which flows from the Ta-pa'ao shan snows. The town is hemmed in on all sides by steep, treeless mountains whose grassy slopes and bare cliffs lead up to peaks culminating in eternal snow. On the whole, the situation is about the last in the world in which one would expect to find a thriving trade entrepot. Formerly, Tachienlu occupied a site about half a mile above the present town, but about 100 years ago it was totally destroyed by a landslip, due to a moving glacier. Some day a similar fate will doubtless over-take the existing town.

Notwithstanding its great political and commercial importance Tachienlu is a meanly built and filthy town. It is without a surrounding wall, save for a fragment which runs across near the south gate, and it has no west gate. The narrow, uneven streets are paved with stone in which pure marble, largely figures, though this is only evident after some heavy downpour has washed away the usual covering of mud and filth. The houses are low, built of wood resting on foundations of shale rocks. The principal shops are by no means of imposing appearance, and, indeed, the only places noteworthy are two Chinese temples and the palace of the local king. The latter consists of several lofty semi-Chinese buildings of wood with sloping roofs and curved eaves surmounted by gilded pinnacles, the whole structure is situated in a large compound, and is surrounded by a high stone wall. The residences of the Chinese officials are poor, ramshackle places, and the same is true of the various inns. In the latter most of the business is transacted. Some inns that I visited contained valuable collections of porcelain and bronze-ware, and an extraordinary number of old French clocks. Very few of the clocks were in working order, but many were of large size, and how they all reached this remote place is a mystery to me.

The population of Tachienlu consists of about 700 Thibetan and 400 Chinese families and, with its floating members, is reckoned at 9000 people. In and near the town are eight lamaseries boasting 800 lamas and acolytes. The inhabitants are very mixed, comprising pure Thibetans, pure Chinese, and half-breeds. Very few purely Chinese women are to be found in Tachienlu.

As seen in and around Tachienlu the Thibetans are a picturesque people. Of medium height, and lithely but muscularly built, they have an easy carriage and independent mien. The young women are usually sprightly in manner, always cheery, with dark brown eyes and finely cut features. Both sexes are fond of jewellery ornamented with turquoise and coral, but they are strangers to soap and water, and personal cleanliness is neither appreciated not practiced. Meat, milk, butter, barley-meal, and tea constitute the favorite food of

TOWN OF TACHIENLU

these people; they are also fond of Chinese wine. Everybody carries on his or her person a private eating-bowl, and the average Thibetan disseminates an odor strongly suggestive of a keg of rancid butter. The everyday dress of these people is a loose, shapeless garment of dull red or gray woollen serge, sometimes sheep-skins are substituted in part. Top-boots of soft hide with the hair inside usually encase the feet and lower legs of both sexes. The men wear their hair in a queue wound around the head and ornamented with beads and rings of silver, coral, and glass. A large silver earring with a long silver and coral pendant usually decorates the left ear. The women have their hair parted down the middle and made up into a number of small plaits, which are gathered into a queue, bound at the end with a bright red cord, and wound around the head. Silver and coral are lavishly used in their coiffure and about their person generally. When in holiday attire these people are more gaily dressed, red-colored trimmings to their garments being then much in evidence, whilst the wealthy affect silk and fur robes. Ornaments of silver and gold, inset with coral and turquoise, are most profusely worn. The lamas shave their heads and wear a raiment of coarse serge of a dull red or brownish color. This has no shape, being simply a large piece of cloth thrown over the right shoulder, leaving the left bare. A similar piece of cloth is wound two or three times round the waist and reaches down to the ankle, forming a kind of pleated skirt. They are usually bareheaded and barefooted, and each lama carries in his hand a rosary and a small praying-cylinder. They swagger through the streets with an insolent mien, and lack the good manners so delightful in the ordinary unsophisticated Thibetan. The lamaseries are usually very richly endowed with land, and most charmingly situated midst groves of Poplar and other trees. Nearly all Thibetan families of affluence maintain a lama on the premises to perform by proxy their religious duties. Many other lamas find employment as temporary chaplains to less wealthy families on occasion of marriage, illness, or death.

Commercially, Tachienlu is a most important centre, enjoying a monopoly of the trade between this part of China and Thibet. The value of the trade is estimated at about one and three-quarter million taels. The Thibetans bring in musk, wool, deer horns, skins, gold dust, and various medicines, and take in exchange brick tea and miscellaneous sundries. The trade is largely one of barter, but much less so than that of Sungpan Ting. Sycee and Indian rupees were formerly the only coinage current, but the Chinese during the last few years have been minting in Chengtu a rupee of their own for the special purposes of this trade-centre. Its use has been insisted upon, and, in consequence, the Indian coin has been ousted from the field. Most of the trade is in the hands of the lamaseries on the one hand and Chinese from the province of Shensi on the other. About 30 li to the northeast of Tachienlu gold is found at an altitude of about 11,000 feet, and placer-mining is carried on there. The gold washing is done in exactly the same way as else-where in western China, but the method of paying the miners is peculiar—the arrangement being six baskets for the owner of the mine and a seventh for the miners. Silver also occurs at this same place. The Thibetans hold the view that gold and other precious metals grow, and that their death may result if too much is removed at any one period. How far they actually believe in this superstition is a moot point, but at times it serves as an unanswerable argument. Some years ago a difference of opinion in the matter of assessing the profits arose between the Chiala chieftain, owner of the mine, and the head Chinese official at Tachienlu who was apparently over-avaricious in the matter. The chieftain very quietly advanced the above theory, and closed down the mines for an indefinite period. Gold in great quantity occurs in the state of Litang, west of Tachienlu; much also is mined around Th'ai-ling to the north of this town.

Being on the great highway from Peking via Chengtu to Lhassa, officials are constantly passing through Tachienlu, and the political importance of the town is very great. Although only a town of the second class the head Chinese official has the local rank of prefect (Chiung-Liang Fu), and holds the post of commissary for the Chinese troops stationed in Thibet. Although Batang, 18 days' journey westward, is more accurately the frontier town, Tachienlu is actually the gate of Thibet. The country around and beyond is physically purely Thibetan in character, and is ruled by native chieftains. Garrisons of soldiers and a few resident Chinese officials protect the interests of the Celestial empire and keep a sharp eye on the actions of the local rulers.

It was stated at the commencement of this chapter that the king of Chiala resides at Tachienlu, and perhaps a few details concerning this kingdom and its people may be of interest. According to the Guide Book of Thibet this state came under Chinese influence during the Ming dynasty, about A.D. 1403, and its chief was given the rank of a second-class native official, with control over the tribes west of the river Tung and southward to Ningyuan Fu. The Manchu dynasty, in consideration of the above, made the then chief a third-class native official, with power over three trading companies. New chiefs, chiliarchs, and centurions to the extent of fifty-six were created. This illustrious chief now controls six subsidiary chiefs, one chiliarch, and forty-eight centurions. Since the date of this appointment the Chinese have increased their grip over these regions to the curtailment of the chief's power and authority. Nevertheless, the Thibetans of this region acknowledge this chief as their supreme ruler, and in domestic affairs his authority is absolute. His native title is Chiala Djie-po (King of Chiala); his Chinese title, Ming-ching Ssu, which may be translated Bright-ruling official. The king and Chinese prefect (Fu) are supposed to be colleagues, but in reality the king is subordinate, and when paying official visits must make obeisance before the Fu. In what dealings I had with them I found both to be courteous and obliging, but suspicious and jealous of one another.

The king in 1908 was a slimly built, intelligent man, about forty odd years of age. He took considerable interest in our collecting work around Tachienlu, and with his brother, who is a hunter of much renown, paid us many unofficial visits. He was never tired of watching my companion, Mr. Zappey, fixing up the bird's skins. My own work amongst flowers interested him but little. As a parting gift Mr. Zappey stuffed and mounted a hoopoe for the king, who evinced almost childlike pleasure on receiving it. In return, he made Mr. Zappey and myself several presents, and urged us to visit his country on a future occasion. We found that these Thibetans possessed keen and accurate knowledge of the birds and animals of their country, which made them

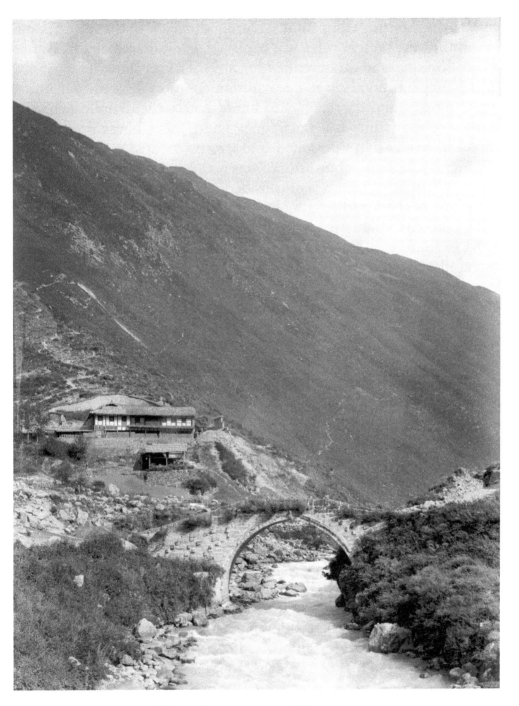

THE GATEWAY OF THIBET

enthusiastic hunting companions. During the reign of the former king, his brother, the present ruler, was banished, and suffered dire hardships during his exile, and often wanted for food. The missionaries stationed in this neighborhood on more than one occasion assisted him, and I understood from them that he had not forgotten their kindly help. The history of the family is a tragic one. The present king's brother was supposed to have been poisoned, and two sisters died early deaths, the result, it is said, of immoral associations with lamas.

The state of Chiala is of considerable size, comprising practically the whole of the territory lying between the Tung River, Chienchʼiang valley, and the Yalung River from lat. 28° to 32° N. The five Horba states in a measure also come under the influence of the king of Chiala. From all I can learn this region has best right to be considered the kingdom of Menia, or Miniak, of European maps. The whereabouts of Miniak has considerably puzzled geographers, but the evidence seems to point to the kingdom of Chiala as representing it in the greater part. Northeast of Chiala is the large and prosperous state of Derge, famed for its copper, silver and swordsmiths. Monsieur Bons d'Anty, when French Consul-General at Chengtu, visited Derge in the autumn of 1910, and on his return gave me a most interesting account of this region. He informed me that Derge is a region of much cultivation, surrounded on three sides by snowclad ranges. The various industries for which the state is famous are not carried on in towns, but by the peasants individually in their homes, and from thence carried to towns for sale. In the valley of the upper Yalung, abutting on the northwest frontier of Chiala and the south-east frontier of Derge, is a wedge of country known as Chantui, peopled by a race of Ishmaels, whose hands are ever turned in conflict with their neighbors. A similar people occupy a wedge of country in the Drechu valley north of Batang, where they are known as the Sanai tribe. Monsieur Bons d'Anty considers that these people are of Shan origin, and remnants of an aboriginal population of this region. This authority has spent many years in studying the ethnological problems of this borderland, and is most competent to express an opinion. It is well known that the Shans formerly ruled in western Yunnan, and there is no reason why they should not, in the distant past, have ascended the valleys of the Yalung and Drechu and established themselves there. But whatever the origin of these people of Chantui and Sanai, they are dreaded by their neighbors, who regard them all as robbers and murderers (Ja-ba) quite beyond the pale.

The religion of the people of Chiala is Lamaism, both the orthodox yellow and unorthodox red sects being represented, but the former are the more numerous and powerful. Some one has described Lamaism as mechanical, a most descriptive term, since the religion consists in the main of turning praying-wheels by hand, water, or wind, counting beads, and the continued muttering or chanting of the mystic hymn, "Om mani padmi hum." Lamaism draws its inspiration from Lhassa, where all the priests repair for study, the head of the sect being the Dalai Lama. Aided and abetted by Chinese authority, the king of Chiala has never submitted to the Dalai Lama in temporal affairs; he has maintained his freedom and right to govern his own people untrammelled by Lhassa interference, in spite of the dire threats and treachery on the part of lamaseries within his jurisdiction. In 1903 the Dalai Lama issued an ultimatum to the king of Chiala threatening to take from him and the Chinese by conquest all the territory west of the Tung valley. The British expedition prevented the carrying out of this threat. The Dalai Lama undoubtedly had designs of territorial expansion at the expense of China's vassal states. The Chinese knew this, and it was fortunate for them that Great Britain stepped in and broke the power of Lhassa De. I was in Tachienlu during 1903 and 1904, and from what I saw and heard there it was plain that the British were unwittingly pulling China's chestnuts from the fire. The Chinese were not slow to perceive the advantageous position they were in after the power of the Dalai Lama was dissipated. Almost immediately a wardenship of the Thibetan marches was established, and a war of conquest engaged upon against certain wealthy lamaseries in Litang and other states, who owned direct allegiance to Lhassa, and heretofore had boasted their independence of China. This war was relentlessly and victoriously pursued under the leadership of Chao Erh-feng, and resulted in the extension of Chinese authority over a very considerable tract of country. Indirectly the king of Chiala's position has been very much weakened as the outcome of these conquests.

The state of Chiala is made up of mountain, dale, and plateau, being essentially a highland country affording good pasturage for yak, sheep, and horses. A chain of snowclad peaks traverse its eastern boundaries. It is a region where altitude regulates the mode of life, the wealth, and marriage customs of its people. The inhabitants are less nomadic than the people to the north and west, but, in common with all other Thibetans, their wealth is represented by herds of yak, horses, and cattle, and flocks of sheep and goats. They are great hunters of musk-deer, wapiti, bear, and other animals, the commercial products of which they trade to the Chinese. The same is true of the medicinal roots and herbs, which grow abundantly in these uplands. Where altitudes admit, agriculture is practiced, but is supplementary to grazing and relatively unimportant. Wheat, barley, oats, buckwheat, peas, and Irish potato are the chief crops. During the winter months these Thibetans live in well-built houses situated in the valleys, and in the spring they migrate to the uplands. The nomads do not move about aimlessly, but have clearly defined boundaries and are subject to responsible headmen. Where agriculture is carried on the womenfolk mostly remain to look after the crops and to do other work pertaining to the farmstead.

Wealth and convenience decide which form the matrimonial alliance shall assume amongst these people, and polygamy, monogamy, and polyandry obtain. Above 12,000 feet altitude polyandry is the rule, and in many places women so united wear distinguishing and honorary badges. Such women are usually the business and ruling heads of their establishments. This custom of polyandry is characteristic of Thibet, and the following note on the subject, written by a friend who has spent many years of his life among these people, is worthy of much thoughtful study:—

So many able men have written about polyandry that what follows will be without interest to those who have studied the system; but to the great mass who are comparatively unacquainted with Thibet and her customs these notes may be of some value. The writer has spent several years among Thibetans and cognate tribes, and has lived for months alone on the wild steppes as well as in the more civilized and well-cultivated valleys.

"The term 'polyandry' is here applied (a) to women living permanently, and cohabitating legally, with more than one man; (b) to those who have been, or are, married temporarily to more than one man or companies of men.

"The former, true polyandry, is confined to the pastoral nomads of the grassy plateaux; the latter, quasi-polyandry, is rampant in all the commercial and political centres on the border and throughout Thibet. In both cases a low conception of the relation of the sexes has made it possible, and climate and political conditions have made it desirable.

"The past hints, and the present proves, that indifference to female virtue connotes the people known as Thibetans and tribes of common origin, and I understand it to be the indirect cause of polyandry. From time immemorial the Thibetan has been taught that the female is a kind of Pandora's box, in which are all the evils that have cursed mankind. All down the ages woman seems to have been the slave of man: dangerous because of latent evil, but also valuable on account of her ability to render him service. In the old barbaric days, when prowess was the prime virtue and a thoroughgoing communism the rule, woman was only a tribal asset, like the animals she tended. Then came religion, a deification of all that rude minds could not explain. It was probably the mysterious Bonpa of to-day which lingers in the lonely valleys where nations meet, and which could have been no friend of virtue if the accounts of orgies in its temples before indecent idols are true, and the unseemly dress of young women and barren wives either demanded or sanctioned by it. Explain it as we may, the fact remains that Thibetan women are today, as they seem to have been in the time of Marco Polo, the most immodest of their sex, and the Thibetan men strangely indifferent about matters which other races demand as essentials.

"All outside work is done by the women, who represent the coarser element of Thibetan society, and their language is often filthy in the extreme. The domestic arrangements make no provision for privacy. Men and women must eat, live, and sleep perforce in the same apartment, and there is no effort on the part of the male to shield the female from conditions which are inimical to virtue.

"The morality of the Thibetans has made such a system possible. This will not be denied by any one who knows them even slightly; but it will sound strange to many when I say that the climatic and political conditions are such that the reformer is puzzled to think of anything to offer as a substitute! To the untutored Thibetan mind it must seem absolutely necessary. Undoubtedly the high altitudes are unfavorable to women. The Thibetan views woman very much as he does an animal, i.e., she can do so much work. Living and working at 12,000 feet altitude and upward requires the strongest material. Woman very imperfectly fulfils these requirements, and maternity and nursing, apart from unfitting her for work, would be well-nigh useless, since infant mortality would be abnormally high. On the relatively thinly populated plateaux the conditions obtaining are emphatically against woman being wanted in numbers. Here robbing and escaping from robbers is the normal condition. It will be evident at once that family duties are not only inconvenient, but interfere with the woman's efficiency personally, and at the same time misdirect the energies of the male portion of the community.

"The nomad is a herdsman, continually moving to and fro with his flocks and belongings. The woman, and the centre she forms, would impair the necessary freedom of movement; it would also follow that she and her belongings would often be unprotected for long periods. Polyandry, by not encouraging permanent settlements and at the same time being the best security against marauding bands, must seem eminently rational to the nomad.

"Polyandry also entails the family property. This is very important, as division of the flocks or grazing-grounds would soon ruin every one. Whatever the ideal system for these Thibetans may be, the one which provides one wife, one family, and one flock for all the male members of the family is the most convenient. Anything else would be suicidal. Both polygamy and monogamy presuppose racial increase and the formation of new and independent centres, but polyandry promises

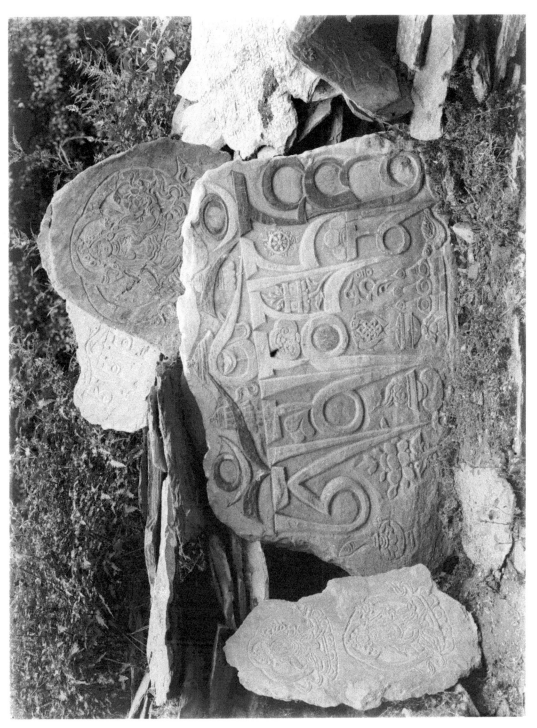

the great desideratum of the Thibetan—an almost stationary community and an intact patrimony.

"In a land of polyandry, priestly celibacy, and nonde-script roving, the number of unmarried women must be large. This class, with the Chinese, Lamas, and Thibetan merchants, is responsible for the quasi-polyandry of the plain, which only differs from prostitution inasmuch as it has the sanction of the country and carries with it no odium. The priest is a celibate, as a rule, by profession, but an inveterate roué in practice. Quite a large number of women are required wherever lamaseries exist. In Lhassa, where thousands of students from all parts of the country study for years, the number of women married temporarily, openly, or in secret, to individuals or small communities is very great. The wandering Thibetan merchants form another class who demand a supply of temporary wives for longer or shorter periods. These may often be men who have formed polyandrous unions in the mountains, but the exigencies of circumstances demand their presence on the plain. In other words, there is no reason why a man may not be a polyandrian legally, and in practice a polygamist.

"But the most interesting phase of this system arises from peculiarities of Chinese domination. Chinese soldiers, officials, and merchants residing temporarily in Thibet form a very large body. These victims of circumstances leave their wives in far-away China. There is a legend that the Lamas have put an embargo on the dainty Chinese woman; but, more probably, her lord and owner has neither the mind nor the money to introduce her to the dangers and hardships of a Thibetan journey. But he rarely, if ever, pines for the wife of his youth. Polyandry and polygamy meet, and temporary marriages, from one month to three years, are the rule. The highest official and the meanest soldier take advantage of the system. With the former it is temporary monogamy or polygamy, but with the latter, owing to pecuniary limitations, one woman often becomes, pro ternpore, the wife of a small community of soldiers. These wives or their children, for obvious reasons, are seldom, if ever, brought out from Thibet; the former make new alliance and the children are claimed by the Lamas.

"The question of Thibetan morality is a very complex one, and it is almost impossible to disentangle the cause from the effect. True polyandry is due, indirectly, to a low moral perception, but it might be incorrect to blame it for the more degenerate quasi-polyandry. Whatever we may think of the former, from the standpoint of absolute morality, it is relatively a moral system and solves many problems. To change it without changing the conditions would be tantamount to driving the brave nomad women into the towns to become the temporary wives of Chinese rabble, priestly roues, and perpatetic Thibetans. Perhaps my hinting that polyandry as a system is in many ways well suited to the plateaux will evoke much unfavorable comment, but there are good men, Roman Catholic and Protestant, priest and layman, who have noticed the same difficulty.

"The effect of the system on the women is another question about which we cannot afford to be dogmatic. When young the Thibetan women are often very pretty, but they age quickly and become as weirdly ugly as the mediaeval witches. To say that polyandry is alone responsible for this change would be sentiment unsupported by facts; but undoubtedly this system, combined with hard work, loathsome uncleanliness, and often grotesque head-dress tends to give a great many women an inhumanly vile expression.

"The families on the plateaux are very small and many women are barren. This is a blessing in disguise, owing to the impossibility of the nomad country supporting more than a very limited population, and the small amount of arable land capable of relieving the congested centres. Polyandry is both directly and indirectly the cause of this limitation of offspring. A glance at the system will show how these uncultured Malthusians obtain their end: Three men, for instance, centre their affections on one woman, who in her lifetime rears two or three children. As monogamists each of these men would have had his own wife and probably a total of fifteen children. But another factor has to be taken into consideration: polyandry not only limits a woman's natural fecundity, but in a great number of cases is the direct cause of barrenness.

"About the domestic arrangements I cannot speak authoritatively, but I have never heard internal discord used as an argument against polyandry. It must often happen that one or two husbands are away tending flocks, worshipping at holy mountains, or robbing travellers. But this is an accident; the domestic equilibrium is rarely disturbed by petty jealousies. The defloration of the bride or brides for there is no reason why two or more sisters should not come into the community—is the right of the elder brother, and the first child is, by courtesy, assigned to him; but the child or children of the union are, in reality, a joint possession. The girls in the community either follow their mother's example, or go into the towns and become the temporary wives of Chinese, Lamas, or wandering merchants. In the former case a dowry is given to the parents, but in the latter the fair one makes the most of her time and in the simplicity of her husband or husbands.

"Polyandry in one form or other is probably practiced whenever Thibetan communities are found. Its existence may be denied emphatically, but closer investigation will only prove the wide distribution of the Miinchausen family. However, an exception may be allowed in the deep, populous valleys of eastern Thibet. Here individualism is the rule, and new centres are formed and thrive without the shadow of a grim Frankenstein disturbing them. So completely has the old dread of offspring been effaced that marriage is always preceded by a tentative period, and maternity alone establishes a girl's right to be admitted into her husband's family. Here the quondam upholder of polyandry, realizing that the fruitful earth and the fruitful woman bring wealth and strength respectively, becomes a confirmed polygamist. To the student of ethnology this metamorphosis suggests the permanency of the valley Thibetan and the gradual absorption or total extinction of his mountain brother."

CHAPTER XVIII

SACRED OMEI SHAN

ITS TEMPLES AND ITS FLORA

THE lofty and sacred eminence known as Mount Omei, or Omei shan, is situated about long. 103° 41' E. lat. 29° 32' N., one day's journey from the city of Kiating. A gigantic upthrust of hard limestone, it rises sheer from the plain, alt. 1300 feet, to a height of nearly 11,000 above sea-level. From the city of Kiating a fine view of this remarkable mountain is obtainable during clear weather, the mirage of the plain seemingly lending it additional height. Viewed from a distance it has been aptly likened to a couchant lion decapitated close to the shoulders, the fore-feet remaining in position. The down-cleft surface forms a fearful, well-nigh vertical precipice, considerably over a mile in height. It is one of the five ultra-sacred mountains of China, but the origin of its holy character is lost in antiquity. We are told that in a monastery here the patriarch P'u (an historical person-age) served Buddha during the Western Ts'in dynasty (A.D. 265-317). P'u-hsien Pu'ssa (Samantabhadra Bodhisattva), Mount Omei's patron saint, descended upon the mountain from the back of a gigantic elephant possessed of six tusks. In one of the temples (Wan-nien-ssu) there is a life-sized elephant cast in bronze of splendid workmanship which commemorates this manifestation. Upward of seventy Buddhist temples or monasteries (either word is applicable, since the buildings are really a combination of both) are to be found on this mountain. On the main road to the summit there is a temple every 5 li, and they become even more numerous as the ascent finally nears the end. These temples are controlled by abbots and contain upward of 2000 priests and acolytes. The whole of the mountain is, or rather was, church property, much of the land on the lower slopes suitable for cultivation having from time to time been sold away from the church. Voluntary subscriptions are now the chief sources of revenue of the religious houses, though many of the temples have money as well as land endowments.

Many thousands of pilgrims, coming from all parts of the Chinese Empire, visit this mountain annually. At the time of my visit there were several pilgrims who had walked all the way from Shanghai, some 2000 miles distant, for the express purpose of doing homage before the shrines of Mount Omei. Thibetans and even Nepalese make pilgrimages here. The images and sacred objects are numberless, many of them being of pure bronze or copper. Three mummified holy men, lacquered, gilded, and deified, the elephant above mentioned, and a tooth of Buddha are among the more interesting objects. The tooth is about a foot long and weights 18 English pounds, and is in all probability a fossil-elephant's molar. On the extreme summit of the mountain, the Golden Summit, as it is called, are the ruins of an ancient temple which was built of pure bronze. It is said to have been erected by the Emperor Wan-li (A.D. 1573-1620), and was destroyed by lightning in 1819. Since this catastrophe nine or ten abbots have come and gone, but none has been able to collect enough money to rebuild it. The mass of metal at present heaped around, consisting of pillars, beams, panels, and tiles, is all of bronze. The panels are particularly fine pieces of work. I measured one panel which had dimensions as follows: 76 inches high, 20 inches wide, 1 1/2 inches thick; some of the panels are slightly smaller than this. All are ornamented with figures representing seated Buddhas, flowers, and scroll-work, and on the reverse with hexagonal arabesques. Many of the panels have been incorporated in one of the two small temples which now stand on the crest of the precipice. Wan-li's tablet, which was contained in the ancient bronze temple, is to-day accommodated in an outhouse along with fuel. The crown-piece is detached and lies outside. This tablet is of bronze, but is hollow. With crown-piece and pedestal it measures 90 inches high, 32 inches wide, and 7 inches thick. Another grand relic left to the tender mercies of the elements is a huge bell which stands 54 inches high and is 120 inches round the middle. On the edge of the cliff are two bronze pagodas, each about 12 feet high, and the remains of a third, which formed part of the ancient temple. It is a saddening sight to see most interesting relics so ignominiously neglected.

From the summit of Mount Omei, when the sky is clear and clouds of mist float in the abyss below, a natural phenomenon similar to that of the Spectre of the Brocken is observable. I have never seen it myself, since rain fell almost continuously during the week I spent on the summit, but it has been described as a "golden ball surrounded by a rainbow floating on the surface of the mists." This phenomenon is known as the Fo-kuang (Glory of Buddha). Devotees assert that it is an emanation from the aureole of Buddha and an outward and visible sign of the holiness of Mount Omei. The edge of the precipice is guarded by chains and wooden posts, but pilgrims in a state of religious fervor have been known to throw themselves over on beholding the Fo-kuang. From this cause the point is called Sui-cide's Cliff. It is the highest and most vertical part of the precipice, which extends in a nearly southerly direction for a couple of miles.

The first foreigner to ascend this famous mountain was the late E. Colborne Baber, who visited it in July 1877, and whose incomparable and accurate account of this region has never been equalled.[1] Unfortunately Baber paid little or no attention to the flora, nor did the equally distinguished traveller and writer Hosie,[2] who ascended Omei shan in 1884. It was not until 1887 that any plants were collected on this mountain. In that year it was visited by a Rhenish missionary, who was also an industrious botanical collector—the late Dr. Ernst Faber. During a fortnight's stay this enthusiast made a most interesting collection, which was found on critical examination to contain no fewer than seventy novelties. In 1890 an English naturalist, Mr. A. E. Pratt, visited the mountain and collected a few plants. Since Baber's visit many hundreds of foreigners have ascended Mount Omei, but with the exception of Messrs. Faber and Pratt, there is no record of any one having collected plants during their visits. For this reason alone I hope this chapter will find justification. The mountain and its temples have been well described by Baber and others, and I have no

[1] Royal Geographical Society, Supplementary Papers, vol. i.
[2] Sir Alexander Hosie, K.C.M.G., H.B.M.'s Consular Service in China.

desire to attempt to repeat descriptions which have been made by abler pens than mine. With this prelude I append the following record of my visit:—

It was on the morning of October 13th, 1903 that I set out from the city of Kiating intent on investigating the flora of this famous mountain. Traversing the highly cultivated plain, which is intersected here and there by low hills, charmingly wooded, the little town of Omei Hsien, alt. 1270 feet, was reached at the close of the day. The next morning, after journeying 10 li across the plain along a road shaded with trees of Alder and Nanmu, we reached the village of Liang-ho-kou, situated at the foot of the sacred mountain. Here the road bifurcates and both paths lead by different routes to the summit. They are paved with blocks of stone throughout, an undertaking that must have entailed a vast expenditure in labor and money, but it would be impossible to traverse certain of the steeper parts unless paving existed. I ascended by one of the routes and returned by the other, so that I saw as much as was possible of the mountain and its rich flora.

Between Omei Hsien and Liang-ho-kou are a number of truly magnificent Banyan trees (Ficus infectoria), known locally as Huang-kou-shu. These trees shelter some old temples and are of enormous size. I measured one, which appeared to be the largest specimen; it was about 80 feet tall, and had a girth of 48 feet at 5 feet from the ground. We also passed some fine trees of Oak (Quercus serrata) and Sweet Gum (Liquidambar formosana). The sides of the rice fields are studded with thousands of pollarded trees of the Chinese Ash (Fraxinus chinensis) on which an insect deposits a valuable white wax. The ditches were gay with the spikes of cream colored, fragrant blossoms of a species of Hedychium, the golden flowered Senecio clivorum, flowers of many kinds of Impatiens, and other moisture-loving herbs.

On leaving Liang-ho-kou the ascent began, and journeying slowly three days' hard climbing brought us to the Golden Summit.

For the purpose of grouping the flora it is convenient to divide the mountain into two regions—(1) from the base to 6000 feet, and (2) 6000 feet to the summit (10,800 feet). Thus divided the flora falls into two well-defined altitudinal zones. The lower zone is made up of such plants as enjoy a warm-temperate climate. Evergreen trees and shrubs predominate, and in the shady glens and ravines Selaginellas and Ferns luxuriate. Of these latter I, in one day, collected over sixty species! The upper zone consists entirely of plants requiring a cool-temperate climate. With the exception of Rhododendron and Silver Fir (Abies delavayi) it is composed almost entirely of deciduous trees and shrubs and herbaceous plants. The belt between 4500 feet and 5500 feet may be termed the hinterland. Here the struggle for supremacy is keen and the fusion of the zones most marked. At 6000 feet the boundary line is unusually well defined.

Cultivation extends up to 4000 feet, maize and pulse being the principal crops, with rice relegated to the valleys and bottom-lands. Plantations of Ash trees for the culture of insect-wax extend up to 2600 feet. The foot-hills around the base of the mountain are covered with Pine (Pinus massoniana), Cypress (Cupressus funebris), and Oak (Quercus serrata). The sides of the streams which meander among these hills are clothed with Alder (Alnus cremastogyne), Pterocarya stenoptera, and the curious Camptotheca acuminata. Around the temples and farmsteads Nanmu (Machilus Bournei) and tall-growing Bamboos abound; on the more exposed hillsides a climbing Fern (Gleichenia linearis) forms impenetrable thickets, and Onychium japonicum, Melastoma candida, Musscendra pubescens, are common road-side plants. At 3000 feet all these plants drop out and give place to others. Cunninghamia lanceolata, which occurs sparingly in the valleys, gradually increases in number, and between 2500 and 4500 feet large areas are covered solely with this invaluable Conifer. Apart from the Cunninghamia, the family of Laurinece forms, between 2000 and 5000 feet, fully 75 per cent of the aborescent vegetation. This Laurel zone, as it may be termed, is composed chiefly of evergreen trees and shrubs, the genera Machilus, Lindera, and Litsea being exceptionally rich in species. Within this zone also occur the following interesting monotypic trees: Tapiscia, Carrieria, Itoa, Emmenopterys, and Idesia. The evergreen Viburnum coriaceum, with blue-black fruits, and five species of evergreen Barberries are also met with.

In ascending any high mountain, more especially in these

latitudes, it is most instructive and interesting to note the aggressivenes of the temperate flora. Mount Omei offers special facilities for studying this phenomenon. Everything around us looks so smiling that all Nature seems to be at peace. In these days, however, every one is alive to the fact that a stern and relentless war of conquest is being continually waged on all sides, and that every inch of ground is contested. It is well that plants cannot speak, or the exultations of the victors and groans of the vanquished would be too much for humanity to withstand. But to note the struggle: The large-leaved Cornet (Cornus macrophylla) manages to extend its area nearly to the base of the mountain, being closely attended by several species of Maple, among which Acer davidii, with white striped bark, is particularly prominent. A Black Birch (Betula luminifera), several species of Viburnum, Pyrus, Malus, Rubus, and Prunus are also well to the fore; but it is in the hinterland (4500 to 5500 feet) that the main battle between the zones is fought. This narrow belt is extraordinarily rich in woody plants. Of those peculiar to it I may mention Pterostyrax hispida, Pterocarya delavayi, Euptelea pleiosperma, Decaisnea fargesii, Horse-chestnut (Aesculus wilsonii), and the monotypic genera Tetracentron, Emmenopterys, and Davidia. At least five species of Maple occur with many fine specimens of each. Several species of Evonymus, Holboellia, Actinidia, and Holly are also common. The bulk of the Laurineae have given up the struggle, their place being taken by evergreen Oak and Castanopsis. In this belt monkeys are common, and are fond of the blue pod-like fruit of the Decaisnea, the shining black, flattened seeds of which, how-ever, I noticed they cannot digest.

On clearing a dense thicket and emerging on to a narrow ridge, 6100 feet above sea-level, an extraordinary view presented itself. Above towered limestone cliffs nearly a mile high; below spread valleys and plains filled with a dense, fleecy cumulus, through which the peaks of mountains peered like rocky islands from the ocean's bed; to the westward the mighty snowclad ranges of the Thibetan border, 80 miles distant as the crow flies, presented a magnificent panorama stretching northward and southward as far as the eye could range. The contrast between the floral zones was equally startling and impressive. Below,

HYDRANGEA XANTHONEURA WILSONII, 15 FEET TALL

until lost in the clouds, was a mass of rich, sombre green vegetation; above were autumnal tints of every hue, from pale yellow to the richest shades of crimson, relieved by clumps of dark green Silver Fir. The whole scene was bathed in sunlight, a gentle zephyr stirred the air, and gorgeous butterflies flitted here and there seemingly unconscious of winter's near approach. The solemn stillness and quiet was broken only by the warbling of an occasional songster in some adjacent tree or bush. It was indeed a never-to-be-forgotten scene.

At 6200 feet the Cunninghamia gives up the fight, having struggled nobly until reduced to the dimensions of an insignificant shrub. A Silver Fir (Abies Delauayi) next assumes the sway, and right royally does it deserve the sceptre, for no more handsome Conifer exists in all the Far East; its erect, symmetrical cones are violet-black in color and are usually borne in greatest profusion on the topmost branches. The temples on the higher parts of the mountain are constructed almost entirely of the timber of this tree. It is first met with on Mount Omei, at 6000 feet, at which altitude it is of no great size and unattractive in appearance but at 6500 feet it is a handsome tree. It is, however, between 8500 and 10,000 feet that this Silver Fir reaches its maximum size. In this belt hundreds of trees 80 to 100 feet tall, with a girth of 10 to 12 feet, are to be found. Hemlock Spruce (Tsuga yunnanensis) occurs sparingly, but always in the form of large and shapely trees. An occasional Yew tree (Taxus chinensis) and, on the summit, dwarf Juniper (J. squamata) complete the list of Conifers growing on the higher parts of this mountain. The unspeakably magnificent autumnal tints already referred to are principally due to numerous species of Viburnum, Vitis, Malus, Sorbus, Pyrus, and Acer, together with Enkianthus deflexus, which surpasses all in the richness of its autumn tints of orange and crimson.

At 6200 feet the ascent becomes increasingly difficult, and having surmounted a formidable flight of steps, 800 feet high, we were glad to rest at the temple of Hsiah-hsiang-chiih. All the temples on Mount Omei occupy lovely and romantic situations, but none more so than this, which has one side flush with the edge of a precipice, and the others sheltered by a grove of Silver Fir. The hospitable priests regaled us with tea and sweetmeats and entertained us with much that was curious and amusing. They claimed that it was at this particular place that P'u-hsien Pu'ssa alighted from his elephant to allow the footsore animal to bathe in a near-by pool, the spot to-day is marked by a cistern.

Immediately on leaving this temple two steep flights of steps, followed by a slight descent, led us to a small wooded plateau which shelves away from a vertical precipice. Here-about Sorbus munda, with white fruits, was a most con-spicuous shrub. A climbing Hydrangea (H. anomala) reaches to the top of the tallest trees. Several other species of Hydrangea grow epiphytically on the larger trees and so also do two or three species of Sorbus. Rhododendrons are fairly abundant, more especially near the edge of the precipice. The first few Rhododendron bushes were noted growing at 4800 feet, and altogether I gathered thirteen species on this mountain. But as compared with the region to the west Mount Omei is poor in Rhododendrons. The same is true for Primulas, of which four species only were met with.

At 9000 feet the most difficult stairway of all occurs, and I was fairly exhausted when the top of it was reached at 10,100 feet. Winter had laid his stern hand heavily here, and most of the woody plants were leafless. At 10,000 feet Bamboo-scrub puts in an appearance and increases as the summit is neared until finally it crowds out nearly every-thing else and forms an impenetrable jungle about 4 to 6 feet high.

From the top of the last stairway an easy pathway of planking leads to the summit, which we reached just as the sun was setting behind the snowclad ranges of the Thibetan border.

A perfect night succeeded the day, and our hopes were high for the morrow. Alas! a thick fog and drizzle was what we awoke to find. A terrible precipice in front and a more or less shelving away behind was all we could make out of the lay of the land. To find out what the summit is really like, a long walk was undertaken, but resulted in little beyond a thorough drenching. The mountain-top is somewhat uneven, sloping away from the cliffs by a fairly easy gradient. It is everywhere covered with a dense scrub, composed mainly of dwarf Bamboo

CHINA — MOTHER OF GARDENS

(Arundinaria nitida), with bushes of Willow, Birch, Sorbus, Barberry, Rhododendron, Spiraea, and Rosa omeiensis interspersed. Near the watercourses these shrubs are more particularly abundant. Trailing over the scrub Clematis montana Wilsonii, is very common. At least five species of Rhododendron grow on the summit, but, judging from the paucity of fruits, they flower but sparingly. In places sheltered from the winds fine groves of Silver Fir remain, but in the more fully exposed sites these trees are very stunted and weather-beaten. The dwarf Juniper (J. squamata), with twisted, gnarled stems, is also plentiful in rocky places.

Around the temples small patches of cabbage, turnips, and Irish potato are cultivated, and several favorite medicines are grown in quantity, such as rhubarb, Huang-lien (Coptis chinensis), tang-shen, and tang-kuei.

Here and there on the mountain we passed hucksters' stalls, on which various local products were exposed for sale. These consist chiefly of medicines, porcupine quills, crystals of felspar, sweet tea, and pilgrim staves. The latter, made from the wood of an Alder (Alnus cremastogyne), are carved in representation of dragons and Buddhas. The sweet tea is a peculiarity of Mount Omei, being prepared from the leaves of Viburnum theiferum, a species very ornamental in fruit and which I successfully introduced to gardens.

CHAPTER XIX

THROUGH THE LAOLIN

NARRATIVE OF A JOURNEY FROM KIATING TO MALE, VIA WA-WU SHAN

EAVING the city of Kiating, on September 4th, 1908, we followed the main road to Yachou Fu and stayed for the night at Kiakiang Hsien, a small city, altitude 1200 feet, 70 li from our starting-place. It had rained heavily in the early morning, but cleared just before we set out, and was cool and fine, although dull the whole day. The road is broad, mostly well paved, and leads through a rich and highly cultivated region. Around Kiating the rice had been harvested, much of the land reploughed, and another crop, chiefly buckwheat and turnips, planted. A few miles beyond this city, however, the rice crop was not so forward, and though a portion was being reaped the bulk would not be ripe for some weeks.

Around the margins of the rice fields trees for the culture of insect white-wax are abundantly planted. Pollarded Ash (Fraxinus chinensis) were chiefly noticeable, but in places trees of Privet (Ligustrum lucidum) are used for this industry. Much of the wax had been collected, but in one place we were fortunate enough to witness the process and obtain photographs. Sericulture was very much in evidence, and all the alluvial flats are planted with Mulberry trees, but trees of Cudrania are not common. In this region in particular the silkworms are fed on the leaves of both these trees; the people claim that this mixed diet results in a stronger kind of silk.

The Szechuan Banyan (Ficus infectoria) is the most striking tree hereabout; its widespreading umbrageous head usually shelters some wayside shrine. Venders of cakes, peanuts, and fruit are also to be found occupying some temporary stall under these beautiful trees. The road

257

skirts the sides of low hills of red sandstone for considerable distances, and is mainly parallel with, and in full view of, the Ya River. The hills are clad with common Pine (Pinus massoniana), Cypress (Cupressus funebris), a jungle-growth of low shrubs, and the scandent Gleichenia linearis. Small trees of Oak and Sweet Chestnut, and larger ones of Alder are also common. Groves of tall-growing Bamboos, of course, are everywhere abundant. In the sandstone cliffs are very many square mouthed Mantzu caves; the scenery is distinctly pretty and pleasing.

We left Kiakiang at 6.30 a.m. the following day, and quickly reached a ferry, where we crossed over the Ya River, a broad, stony, shallow stream. Quite near this place are two really fine and very large old temples known as Ping-ling-ssu and Kuei-ling-ssu. The first named, in particular, contains some very fine idols; both, however, have a very deserted and neglected appearance, giving the impression of glories departed. The sandstone cliffs at the ferry are highly sculptured, but are rapidly weathering away, much of the work being undecipherable and hidden by vegetation.

The li proved very long, and we did not reach Che-ho-kai until 7 p.m., going steadily the whole day. The distance is 80 li, and three ferries, which hinder considerably, have to be crossed. Near the city of Hungya Hsien, which we sighted in the late afternoon, large plantations of Ash trees for the culture of insect white-wax abound. Rice is everywhere the great crop; the yield was heavier than usual, and the people were busy reaping and threshing it. Fine Banyan trees are plentiful, Alder is abundant, and hand-some Nanmu trees are not infrequent around temples and houses. We also noted a small tree of the Hog-plum (Spondias axillaris) bearing quantities of its oblong, yellow, edible fruits. The vegetation generally is similar to that around Kiating, but the China Fir (Cunninghamia lanceolata) is more common and Pine and Cypress less so.

Che-ho-kai, alt. 1400 feet, is a large and important market village, situated on the right bank of the Ya River. The inn is very fair. I occupied a large room overlooking the river, but, as I discovered later, with a piggery and latrine beneath.

The next day we began our real journey. Instead of following the main route to Yachou Fu by crossing over the river, we ascended the right bank for a couple of li beyond Che-ho-kai, and then crossed a considerable affluent of the main stream. Rafts of good-sized poles of China Fir descend this tributary from Liu ch'ang, a market village, and ordinary bamboo-rafts ascend to this place. After climbing to the tops of some low hills the road zigzags around considerably through fields of rice and wooded knolls, and affords an unusually fine view of the Ya valley. Passing the tiny market village of Tung-to ch'ang we reached Kuang-yin pu (or ch'ang) at 10.45 a.m., having covered 30 li.

From Kuang-yin pu we engaged in a steep ascent over a well-paved if narrow road, and after four hours' climbing reached the summit of the Fung-hoa-tsze, alt. 4100 feet. This ridge is of red sandstone throughout, and is well covered with small trees of the China Fir. This Conifer abounds on the slopes flanking the roadway to the top of the pass and forms pure woods. Though the trees are of no great size the area covered with this Conifer compares favorably with any other I have seen. Where trees are scarce the jungle growth is very thick, warm-temperate in character, and of little interest.

Descending, at first steadily, through knolls covered with China Fir and the densest fern jungle composed of Gleichenia linearis I have ever seen, we soon reached an area under maize. From this point a steep descent led to a cultivated flat, then, after winding through rice fields with tiny wooded hillocks on all sides, we crossed a neck and entered the hamlet of Liang-ch'a Ho, alt. 2350 feet, a long 65 li from our starting-point. We found very decent accommodation, all things considered, but mosquitoes were unpleasantly numerous and hungry.

It rained very heavily during the early morning of the next day, so we delayed our starting until eleven o'clock. We found all the streams in flood, and to cross one larger than the ordinary we had to engage local assistance. After a rather steep ascent of 500 feet from Lian-ch'a Ho we crossed a narrow ridge and descended to the market village of N'gan ch'ang. This is a poor place, partly in ruins, situated on the right bank of the stream which unites with the Ya Ho, 2 li above Che-ho-kai. On leaving N'gan ch'ang we ascended the right bank of the stream to Pao-tien-pa, alt. 2600 feet. This scattered hamlet possesses no inn, but we found quarters in a schoolhouse devoted to the New Learning (i.e., Western Knowledge) . A scholar from this place had recently gone to Japan to increase his store of knowledge, and the dominie was very proud of this success. This hamlet boasts a ruined pavilion, a temple, and a stone gateway, evident signs of former prosperity.

During the short journey of 25 li the road led through fields of rice, bounded by wooded knolls and sandstone bluffs. The flora was of little interest; Idesia polycarpa and Acanthopanax ricinifolius are fairly common in places, but the trees are of small size. Alongside the ditches and road-way handsome Lycoris aurea abounds, and the golden yellow flowers with recurved, wrinkled, perianth-segments made a gay display. Its red-flowered counterpart, L. radiata, also occurs, but is much less frequent. The local name for this plant is Lao-wa-suan, which signifies Crow's foot Onion, a very apt term in so far as the shape of the flower is concerned.

The following day was fine but hot, and more or less cloudy. With only 35 li to cover, we journeyed slowly after making an early morning start. A moderately steep ascent of 15 li brought us to the summit of the Tsao shan, alt. 4100 feet. This ridge is covered with an uninteresting jungle of coarse grass and scrub, with odd trees of Chinese Fir, but in the ascent I gathered specimens of a fine new species of Castanopsis.

From the summit of Tsao shan we obtained our first view of the Wa-wu shan, an extraordinary-looking, massive mountain, singularly like Wa shan in contour, and resembling a huge ark floating above clouds of mist. Following an easy path which led through fine woods of evergreen Oak, Nanmu, and Castanopsis we descended to Ma-chiao-kou, where there is an iron suspension bridge over a wide torrent. This hamlet consists of one large house and a mill, where is made the specially good and tough bamboo paper used at Yachou Fu for wrapping brick tea. The bamboo is obtained from the surrounding mountains, and is a species with dull green culms, each about the thickness of a man's thumb, growing 12 to 15 feet tall. On crossing over the bridge, I photographed a fine specimen of Alniphyllum Fortunei, one of the rarest of Chinese trees. A short steep ascent, then a rather drawn-out descent, ultimately brought us to the banks of a clear-water stream of considerable size, which we crossed by an iron suspension bridge 50 yards long, and soon reached the market village of Ping-ling-shih, alt. 2900 feet. This is a small and dirty place of about 50 houses, situated on the left bank of a stream which joins the Ya Ho, some 10 li below Yachou Fu. It is in Hung-ya Hsien, in full view of Wa-wu, and the most important place in the Laolin (wilderness) , as this region is denominated.

The flora of the day's journey was rather more interesting than heretofore. Wooded knolls are the rule. Evergreen trees, more especially Oak and Castanopsis, are very general, and of large size. I gathered four species belonging to the latter genus, all handsome umbrageous trees. A fine specimen of the curious Hazel-nut (Corylus heterophylla crista-galli), 60 feet tall, 5 feet in girth, was one of the most interesting trees noted. The nut in this variety is hidden within a crested cup. The China Fir is most abundant, being the only Conifer met with. The absence of Pine and Cypress since leaving the valley of the Ya River has been a most remarkable feature. The country generally is very broken, the sandstone bluffs bold, and clad with the usual jungle growth wherever trees are sparse.

In order to ascend Wa-wu from Ping-ling-shih it was necessary for us to make a detour from our intended route. The summit was said to be 70 li distant, but, owing to the steep and difficult road, two days are required to cover this. We left behind all our spare gear and arranged what it was necessary to take into light loads. The road on clearing Ping-ling-shih ascends a rock-strewn tributary of the main stream, through a region given over to rice fields and cultivation generally. At eleven o'clock in the forenoon after traversing 30 li we reached the large temple of Tsung-tung-che, alt. 4000 feet, situated at the foot of the real ascent of Mount Wa-wu. This temple is built of wood, very old, and in poor repair. A priest and one attendant were in charge; the rooms, though dingy and damp, were alive with fleas. But since there is no other accommodation between this place and the summit it was necessary to make the best of things. I had my bed arranged in a large hall where three huge images of Buddha looked down benignly upon me. During the morning occasional showers fell, but in the afternoon a steady downpour set in, which added to the cheerlessness of our roomy but dilapidated quarters.

Just before reaching the temple we passed through the hamlet of Tung-ch'ang Ho, where there is a very large iron foundry employing a considerable number of men. Iron ore is common in the surrounding mountains, and costs 12,000 to 13,000 cash per 10,000 catties. Every 10,000 catties of ore yields about 4000 catties of pig iron, which was said to be of good quality, and sells for 2500 to 3000 cash per picul of 100 catties. The smelting is done in furnaces heated by charcoal, which costs at the foundry 12 to 13 cash per catty. Most of the smelting is done during the winter, the summer months being given to the collecting of charcoal and iron ore. Large iron cooking-pans are also made here in considerable quantities.

Copper is also found in the same range as the iron ore, but on the opposite side. Formerly it was worked and smelted here, the name Tung-ch'ang signifying copper-shop or factory. From what I could learn the industry had been abandoned for some ten years or more when copper mining became a government monopoly controlled by the officials. The people told me that they could not produce copper on paying lines under Tls. 35.00 to Tls. 36.00 per picul. The officials would only pay Tls. 28.00, consequently copper smelting was given up and replaced by that of iron. A hard, smokeless coal occurs in the neighborhood, but is not much used. Altogether this Tung-ch'ang Ho, with its iron foundry, coal mines, and abandoned copper workings, constitutes an interesting mining centre.

Around the temple are many fine trees of Castanopsis, and the finest specimen of the interesting monotypic Tapiscia sinensis I have seen. This tree is fully 80 feet tall, with a girth of 12 feet. Many fine trees of the Kuei-hwa (Osmanthus fragrans) are planted in the temple grounds, and were in full flower, scenting the atmosphere all around. Near streams Alder (Alnus cremastogyne) is abundant, and on the hills the China Fir also.

It rained heavily all night, and drizzle fell when we set out next morning at 6.30 a.m. This drizzle developed into a steady downpour as

HAMLET OF PING-LING-SHIH, MOUNT WA-WU IN DISTANCE

we advanced, and continued with increased violence the whole day. The road is atrocious from the very beginning. For the first 2500 feet there is a semblance of a track, some of it being made by laying pieces of split timber crosswise. The next 2500 feet is a rough scramble upward through cane-brake and brushwood until the summit is reached. The ascent is up the north-northeast angle of the mountain, and though never really dangerous is always very difficult. We dragged ourselves upward by grasping shrubs, and it was a marvel to me how the coolies with their loads managed to overcome the ascent. The foot-hold was precarious, and it was often a case of one foot forward and two backward.

On reaching the summit we followed a winding path for 12 li to the temple of Kwanyin-ping, alt. 9100 feet. The mountain top is undulating, park-like, and covered with an impenetrable jungle of Bamboo-scrub about 6 feet tall arising from a floor of Sphagnum moss. Silver Fir (Abies delavayi), called Lien sha, i.e., Cold Fir (signifying that it is only found in cold regions), is scattered through in quantity, but I saw no really handsome trees, all of them showing the effects of wind-storms, age, and decay. The pathway across the summit is about 2 ½ feet wide, paved throughout with split timbers, though here and there fallen Silver Fir trees, slightly notched and flattened, have been utilized in making this roadway. We passed three temples in absolute ruins, but saw no signs of life of any description. The heavy rain and dense mists obscured all views, and I saw nothing of the country or scenery except what was encompassed in a perspective of 30 yards. Drenched to the skin but mildly describes the plight in which we reached the temple. Our gear arrived equally wet some two hours afterward, and we were some time getting things dry and shipshape.

The temple of Kwanyin-ping is very large, with many outhouses, and is built entirely of wood. It contains many scores of idols, but is in a poor state of repair. The main road hither is from Yungching Hsien, distant 120 li. During the Chinese fifth and sixth moons (June, July) some two to three thousand pilgrims visit this temple, but for the rest of the year it has scarcely a visitant. The priests reside at Yungching Hsien except at the pilgrim season, a novice being left in charge. This novice lives all alone, without even a dog for a companion. As a reward he receives 1 ½ catties of rice per diem as rations and 2000 cash (say, one dollar) per annum salary. In spite of his lonely life, and he has been in charge for three years, this novice was a very cheery person. He moved around quickly, had a ready smile, and chanted hymns and prayers wherever he went. He speedily made a fire for us to dry ourselves and clothing, and made himself generally useful. His cheery influence made itself felt, and my men soon ceased their grumbling over the vileness of the road and my madness in wanting to visit such a place. The novice told us that the first temple was built on this mountain during the eastern Han dynasty (A.D. 25-87.). At one time there were as many as 40 temples here, but during Ming times the majority were destroyed, and the temple ornaments melted down. Today there are only two in any sense tenantable, and in one only is a man kept the year round. This same authority vouch-safed the information that the heavy rains were due to the felling of timber; the country folk holding this view were opposed to further cutting, but the Magistrate at Yung-chin Hsien pooh-poohed the idea, and insisted on the slaughter being continued, with the result that torrential rains fell every day except in winter, when snow took their place.

The next morning opened dull and threatening, but eventually the sun came out and we enjoyed a fine day. The temple stands in Hungya Hsien, and is situated on the edge of a precipice. The views looking northeast over the Ya valley and west to the Thibetan alps are very fine; some almost vertical limestone cliffs near by the temple are covered in a remarkable manner with Silver Fir. The whole surroundings are wildly romantic, and it is small wonder that the place is deemed sacred and holy.

Wa-wu shan or Wa shan, as it is much more frequently but erroneously called, is one of three sacred mountains, forming the three corners of and enclosing a triangular tract of wild, sparsely inhabited country known as the Laolin (wilderness). On even the most recent maps the term Lolo is written across this region, but as a matter of fact no Lolos live there. The few people found here are Chinese—peasants, charcoal-burners, miners, and medicine-gatherers. The other two mountains, Omei shan and Wa shan, have been described by former travellers, but, with the possible exception of some Roman Catholic priest, my visit was the first undertaken by any foreigner to the summit of Wa-wu shan.

Like its sister mountains, Wa-wu is a gigantic upthrust of hard limestone, but of less altitude than they, being only 9200 feet above sea-level. It is a huge oblong mass, composed of a series of vertical cliffs 2000 feet and more sheer, reared on a base of red sandstone rocks. The summit is flat with sand and mudstone shales scattered about, and is said to be 60 li long by 40 li wide, but this is an exaggeration 30 li by 15 li being, probably, nearer the truth. Its appearance from a distance has already been given, and the nearer the approach the more impressive become the perpendicular walls of rock. The similarity in appearance between this mountain and the real Wa shan has been alluded to, and I strongly suspect that the mountain seen from the summit of Omei shan and called Wa shan is really this Wa-wu shan. Their extraordinary vertical sides and flat summits make these two peaks unique among the mountains of western China.

From a botanical standpoint Mount Wa-wu proved disappointing. In the first place, its altitude was some 1500 feet less than I had hoped for. Secondly, all the trees have been felled for making charcoal and for other purposes, leaving only a dense shrubbery in which variety is not great. Thirdly, the paucity of Coniferae on the summit other than Silver Fir, and the impenetrable thickets of slender Bamboo which render any extended exploration impossible. The flora generally is that common to every mountain in this region of similar altitude, but, of course, it has a certain number of species peculiarly its own in the same way as every other mountain in China has. The outstanding feature is its wealth of Bamboo-scrub; its specialty, the abundant carpet of Sphagnum moss on the summit. This moss occurs on Wa shan and on practically all the other mountains of this region, between 8000 and 11,500 feet, but nowhere have I seen it so luxuriantly plentiful as on Wa-wu shan.

The day being fine and clear I obtained good views of everything. The summit is made up of low, wooded hillocks, tiny dales, and glades. Here and there it is a morass, and on one occasion from such a place we flushed a solitary snipe. The feathery bamboo-culms are very beautiful, and the scattered, often sentinel-like, old trees of Silver Fir quite picturesque. A few trees of Hemlock Spruce occur, but their number is infinitesimal. Some of the Silver Fir were 100 feet tall, and 10 to 12 feet in girth, but all such trees contain much dead wood. Here and there saplings are common, but they can scarcely compete with the Bamboo in the struggle for possession. At one time Davidia (both hairy and glabrous-leaved forms), Tetracentron, Magnolia, various species of Acer, Pyrus, Castanopsis, evergreen Oak, and Laurinex covered the lesser slopes, but, to-day, these are represented only by bushes which have sprung up from the felled trees. Rhododendrons are fairly numerous, and I noted about ten species. One of these forms a tree 25 feet tall, and 3 to 4 feet in girth. (It proved to be new, and has been named Rhododendron Openshawianum in honor of the Rev. Harry Openshaw, of Yachou Fu.) Various Aralaids are plentiful, and were mostly in ripe fruit. The China Fir (Cunninghamia lanceolata) ascends to 4500 feet altitude, and very few of the evergreens other than Rhododendron extend above 6000 feet. Herbs, of course, occur, but none of any great value or interest.

A local industry of considerable importance at the season of the year my visit occurred, and for six weeks previously, is the collecting and preparing of young Bamboo shoots for culinary purposes. The species in request is one having culms the thickness of a man's thumb, and growing 10 feet tall. The young shoots are culled when 8 to 12 inches above the ground, stripped of their sheaths and apices, leaving only the white, brittle succulent central part. These are boiled in water, then removed, suspended from rafters in a close chamber and dried by means of heat from steady-burning fires fed from locally made briquettes. When thoroughly dry they are packed in bales and carried to Chengtu and other cities, where they are esteemed a great delicacy. We saw fully a score of rude shanties where this industry was in full swing. On the spot the raw shoots are bought for 6 cash per 16-oz. catty, the collecting being done by contract. The prepared article, known as Tsin-tzu, sells at Ping-ling-shih for 8 to 9 Tls. per 100 catties of 20 oz. each This region is famed far and wide for its product of dried Bamboo shoots, and the industry affords employment for a large number of people.

Many wild animals, including budorcas, serow, goral, leopard, and bear were said to occur on Wa-wu, but hunting them would be almost an impossibility. We saw no animals of any kind, but I do not doubt the reports given as to their presence on this jungle-clad mountain.

A day sufficed for our investigations, and leaving the next morning about nine o'clock, a hard day's march brought us back to Ping-ling-shih at 5.45 p.m.

Our object being to traverse this Laolin country through its greatest width to some point in the valley of the Tung River, we readjusted our loads, and the following day continued our march. Crossing the tributary stream by a rickety iron suspension bridge, we soon left Ping-ling-shih behind. The path ascends the right bank of the main stream frequently high above its waters, and at times some little distance removed. As soon as it enters limestone country the river becomes confined within cliffs. The li were long, the road rough, and it took us five hours to cover 30 li to Yueh-ch'a-ping. This place consists of a single house, situated near where the stream bifurcates. One branch and a companion roadway leads off in a southeasterly direction, and by this track it is possible to reach Huang-mu ch'ang. The path we followed ascends the branch which swings from the southwest, skirting the base of Wa-wu shan. After crossing a cultivated shoulder we plunged into a deep, narrow gorge, traversing a difficult roadway usually high up above the stream. The scenery is very fine—steep cliffs, either bare or clothed with shrubs, on every side. Journeying slowly we reached the solitary house at Chang-ho-pa, alt. 4000 feet, about 5 p.m., having covered 50 li.

During the day's march we saw a number of interesting trees, and obtained specimens and photographs. Carrieria calycina, a widespreading flat-topped tree, is very common in rocky places by the stream side, and was laden with its torpedo-shaped, velvety-gray fruit which was not ripe. The Tapiscia is fairly numerous, but the trees are of no great size. Perhaps the most noteworthy tree of this region is Meliosma kirkii, which has a shapely habit of growth, rigid branches, and handsome pinnate leaves, 2 feet long. Evergreen Oak, various Laurinex, tall-growing Bamboos, and a Fan Palm (Trachycarpus excelsus) are abundant, denoting a mild, moist climate. The China Fir is the only Conifer. The quantity of this useful tree and the many fine and shapely specimens were among the leading features of this trip. We had left rice behind at last, and entered a region where only maize is grown. Every available bit of land is under cultivation, but the district is very sparsely populated. A certain amount of tea is grown around Ping-ling-shih, but the industry is of little importance commercially.

The people at Chang-ho-pa informed us that the road before us was much worse than that which we had traversed. For the first 10 li after leaving our lodgings I thought they had dissembled, but afterwards the truth of their statement was only too evident. The stream flows through a narrow, wild gorge or succession of gorges; the road is either some hundreds of feet above the stream, or down by the water's edge, the ups and downs repeating themselves with monotonous and irritating frequency. The path is very much overgrown with weeds and brush, always very narrow, the ascents and descents precipitous and difficult. It is misleading and foolish to term it a road. Goats would make a better pathway, did they travel it frequently.

The scenery is grand, though mists and drizzle did their best to rob us of its enjoyment. The cliffs are in the main clothed with shrubby vegetation, but alongside the stream large trees are common. The climate is evidently very moist and warm, since broad-leaved evergreens abound. Perhaps the most common shrub or small tree is a Walnut or Butternut (Juglans cathayensis), which has six to twelve fruits arranged in a raceme, and leaves up to a yard in length. The Horse-chestnut (Aesculus wilsonii), Yellow-wood (Cladrastis sinensis), Hornbeam, and various Maples are among the more interesting trees hereabout. Clearings and abandoned cultivated areas are overgrown with the hand-some Anemone vitifolia alba, which was 4 to 5 feet tall, and bore myriads of large attractive flowers. This herb made a wonderful display, and I do not remember having seen it so luxuriant elsewhere in my travels. Beneath cliffs dripping with moisture, Begonias, Impatiens, Ferns, and various Cyrtandrx in masses made pretty effects. The China Fir ceases at 4800 feet altitude, but limestone country is not to its liking, and the trees quickly become scarce on quitting the red sandstone.

Houses and patches of cultivation are few and far between, but it is surprising that any should be found in such a precipitous country. We put up for the night at one of the three small houses which collectively form the hamlet of Peh-sha Ho, alt. 5000 feet, 40 li from Chang-ho-pa. The house is built on a steep bank, overlooking a point where the stream divides, the larger branch flowing from a southerly direction.

On leaving Peh-sha Ho we headed for the source of the lesser of the two streams—a mere mountain torrent. Our difficulty all day was in discerning the track and keeping to it. I lost it early in the morning, and wasted two hours in a jungle of Bamboo; my boy had the same misfortune in the afternoon. The collecting of Bamboo shoots is an industry here as on the other side of Wa-wu, and the tracks made by men engaged in this are many. The path we endeavored to follow was frequently less well-defined than these tracks and, moreover, was overgrown with vegetation. It crossed the torrent many times, but the fords were difficult to discover. We passed neither house nor person, and perforce had to explore our own route. It rained heavily the whole day, increasing our discomfort.

Our objective for the day was some lead mines, but early in the afternoon it became evident that we could not reach them before night was well advanced. Darkness over-took us, and we had visions of spending the night in the woods, which bound the torrent; suddenly, however, the welcome glare from a charcoal-burner's but gladdened our hearts. Scrambling somehow down the steep slope, and across the torrent, we quickly reached this haven of shelter. It proved a wretched hovel, but the warmth from the charcoal pit was comforting since we, and all our belongings, were wet through. My bed was fixed up in a shed where prepared charcoal was stored, the men taking possession of the hut, thankful that a refuge of some sort had been found.

THROUGH THE LAOLIN

Much of the day's journey had consisted in struggling through brush and Bamboo, and by way of variety, wading the torrent was thrown in. Whenever the mists lifted, cliffs and crags, densely covered with vegetation, were to be seen on all sides. The flora is apparently rich, but it was impossible for us to investigate it. All the larger trees have been cut down and converted into charcoal. Davidia, Tetracentron, Cercidiphyllum, and Cornus chinensis are common as bushy trees by the wayside; Maples are plentiful, and stout climbers, such as Actinidia, Clematoclethra, and Holboellia are rampant.

Two men were in charge of the charcoal pits. They told us the place is called Tan-yao-tzu, and that we had only covered 30 li! All the hardwood trees having been felled they are now forced to use the softwood of Silver Fir and Hemlock Spruce, which, they said, grow in quantity on the higher crags. The charcoal is all used for smelting lead at the mines.

The roof of the shed leaked freely, but an arrangement of oil-sheets kept my bed fairly dry, and I enjoyed a good night's sleep. Awaking soon after daybreak we found it was still raining. Leaving the hut, alt. 7250 feet, we crossed two branches of the stream and scrambled up the mountain-side to rejoin the track. Soon afterward we entered a narrow scrub-clad valley, at the head of which a precipitous, circuitous ascent brought us to the top of a ridge where the lead mines are situated. In the ascent, Rhododendron hanceanum and two other kinds are particularly abundant, forming thickets; Lonicera deflexicalyx is also plentiful, and was a wealth of orange-colored fruit. On the humus-clad rocks pretty little prostrate Gaultheria cuneata with snow-white fruits is common. The hovels at the lead mines are miserable structures, but we were glad of their shelter from the rain and cold. The whole mountain appears to be full of lead, the ore (galena) being very rich. Well-shored adits are carried for considerable distances into the mountain-side, and the ore is brought out in baskets fitted on runners. The galena is pounded by hand labor into small particles; the lead is obtained by levigation and stored in large wooden vats. Subsequently it is melted into large oblong ingots, in which form it is carried away to Chengtu and Sui Fu. The freight down to the nearest waterway is very

271

considerable. Lead has been worked in this neighborhood for many years, and the mines are owned by a man who resides at Kiating. The laborers are paid 1800 cash per month. We were told that the previous year's output was 10,000 catties, but little reliance can be placed on this statement. Such an output is very small, but the primitive methods employed are slow and expensive. For smelting and other purposes the mountain has been denuded of its timber, and is now in its upper parts a grassy, scrub-like wilderness. I made the altitude of the mines 9400 feet, that is to say, 2000 feet above the charcoal pits whence the fuel necessary to melt down the lead is drawn. The sides of the workings are bare and gravelly, and were covered with rich yellow flowers of a Sedum-like plant, which was new and is unknown to me.

On leaving the lead mines and crossing a slight dip we reached a babbling brook which forms the roadway for the next few li. On deserting this we made a very steep ascent to the top of a grassy ridge, alt. 10,400 feet, only to find that a deep ravine separated us from the watershed proper. After a most precipitous descent of 1600 feet over a rocky and difficult path, we reached the bed of a torrent, which I take to be the stream we noted at Peh-sha Ho flowing from a southerly direction.

On reaching this stream the rain ceased, the mists cleared away rapidly, and the sun showed itself for the first time in four days. The surrounding country is savage, and is made up of a magnificent series of limestone cliffs, their steepest crags clothed with weather-worn trees of Silver Fir. Everywhere else the trees have been cut down.

From the torrent we struggled up a severe ascent of 1000 feet, and reached the summit of the watershed, alt. 10,100 feet. Here we got a very fine view of the country, which is simply a succession of cliffs and crags capped by rugged trees of Silver Fir, and with a dense growth of broad-leaved trees in the more inaccessible pockets.

The rest of the day's journey was all downhill over a vile pathway. We reached the tiny hamlet of Yang-tientsze, alt. 7600 feet, at 6 p. m., having occupied eleven hours in covering 30 li. Two men who carried our foodstuff arrived just as darkness closed in, and reported the rest of our gear far behind. Our lodgings were poor enough in all conscience, but most acceptable after such a fatiguing tramp. After dinner I tried to sleep on an oil-sheet spread over one of the native beds, but was soon discovered by hungry, tormenting fleas, and, tired as I was, sleep proved impossible. About one o'clock my bed and some other gear arrived. The carriers had been forced to wait after darkness fell until the moon was up in order to see the path. I could not complain; they had done their best over a most heart-breaking road. The rest of our loads turned up soon after daybreak, and we left Yang-tientsze at 7.30 a.m. Descending by a comparatively easy road for 30 li we reached before noon the village of Mali, alt. 5300 feet, a very poor place, situated on the main road between Omei Hsien and Fulin via Wa shan.

Thus had the Laolin been crossed from northeast to southwest, and, personally, I have no desire to repeat the journey. The continued rains increased considerably the difficulties of the bad roads and made what, under the most favorable weather conditions, must always be a fatiguing journey, an exceedingly arduous and miserable one The rain and dense mists robbed the trip of its greatest charm, namely, the scenery. Except on odd occasions I saw nothing outside a radius of 50 yards. The unpropitious weather also prevented any investigation of the flora other than that alongside the pathway. In so far as it came under my observation this region possesses very little in the way of woody plants beyond what are common to the same altitude anywhere in western Szechuan. For richness in species it does not compare favorably with Mount Omei or Mount Wa. However, there are some points of interest. The region evidently enjoys a warm, wet climate, and the belt of broad-leaved evergreens, especially Oak and Laurinx, extends to a greater altitude than usual. The abundance of China Fir and such interesting trees as Davidia, Tetracentron, Cladrastis, Magnolia, Aesculus, Cercidiphyllum, and Butternut (Juglans cathayensis) is perhaps the outstanding feature. Strong-growing climbers such as Holboellia, Actinidia, and Clematoclethra abound, and I obtained seeds of several species. Many kinds of Sorbus with white, red, and purple fruits occur, and seeds of these were also secured Honey-suckles, Brambles, and Rhododendrons are also abundant. The scarcity of

Birch, Beech, deciduous Oak, and sweet Chestnut, and the entire absence of Pine, Cypress and Poplar are marked features of the region. Throughout the higher altitudes Silver Fir and Hemlock Spruce are the only Conifers, although in one place I thought I detected some Spruce trees high up on the cliffs. I saw no fine trees of either of these Conifers; all that now remain grow on the crags and other equally inaccessible places, and have suffered much from the winds and weather generally. The jungle growth of Gleichenia on the sandstone, and the impenetrable Bamboo thickets everywhere between 6000 and 10,000 feet altitude, are the most striking floral characteristics of the entire region. The mining industries have been the cause of the wholesale felling of the timber.

The entire absence of decent roads, the sparse population, wretchedly poor accommodation, the savage cliffs, and jungle-clad mountain-sides sufficiently entitle this region to be termed Laolin, i.e., a Wilderness.

CHAPTER XX

WA SHAN AND ITS FLORA

HE sister mountain to the sacred Omei is Wa shan, situated about long. 103° 14' E., lat. 29° 21' N., six days' journey (roughly 80 miles) from the city of Kiating. The intervening country is very rough, wild, and mountainous. The road is execrable. Baber, the first foreigner to visit and ascend this mountain, as well as Mount Omei, gives its altitude as 10,545 feet above the sea-level, 4560 feet above the neighboring valleys. My readings were 11,250 feet above the sea, 5150 feet above the surrounding country. Allowing for error in the barometer, I think the mountain cannot be less than 11,000 feet. The flora—always a fair guide as to altitude—proves it to be higher than Mount Omei (10,800 feet); and this agrees with the opinion of the natives, who assert that it is the higher of the two mountains.

As seen from the top of Mount Omei it resembles a huge Noah's Ark, broadside on, perched high up amongst the clouds. Viewed from a near distance it is seen to consist of a succession of tiers of vertical limestone cliffs, only seriously broken at one point, with a perculiarly flat sum-mit. From the hamlet of Ta-t'ien-ch'ih (6100 feet) which is situated in a depression at its base, the mountain is remarkably square looking, its four sides being more or less perpendicular. It appears to be no more than 2000 feet above the hamlet, and yet it is really 5000 feet higher. When it was first pointed out to me, 20 miles or so distant, I could not believe it was Wa shan—it looked so like a huge precipice, its massiveness belittling its height.

As stated above, the first foreigner to visit Wa shan was the late E. Colborne Baber, who made the ascent on June 5th, 1878. The description of this mountain, given by him, is so accurate and beautiful that I cannot do better than quote it: "The upper storey of this most

275

imposing mountain is a series of twelve or fourteen precipices, rising one above another, each not much less than 200 feet high, and receding very slightly on all four sides from the one next below it. Every individual precipice is regularly continued all round the four sides. Or it may be considered as a flight of thirteen steps, each 180 feet high and 30 feet broad. Or, again, it may be described as thirteen layers of square, or slightly oblong, limestone slabs, each 180 feet thick and about a mile on each side, piled with careful regularity and exact levelling upon a base 8000 feet high. Or, perhaps, it may be compared to a cubic crystal, stuck amid a row of irregular gems. Or, perhaps, it is beyond compare. Some day the tourist will go there and compose 'fine English'; he could not choose a better place for a bad purpose; but if he is wiser than his kind he will look and wonder, say very little, and pass on."

It was on the afternoon of June 30th, 1903 when I first arrived at the scattered hamlet of Ta-t'ien-ch'ih, from whence the ascent can be made. This tiny hamlet is situated in an oval depression, locked in by high mountains on all sides. The depression is about a mile long and rather less than half a mile broad at its widest point, a small lake surrounded by a luxuriant greensward occupies the lower end. A species of Aconitum, with lovely blue flowers, is very abundant. The Chinese call it Wu-tzu, and say that it is poisonous to man and cattle alike. Around the farm-houses, maize, peas, beans, buckwheat, and Irish potatoes are cultivated. The people here mostly profess Christianity, and a Roman Catholic mission-house is the only decent building in the hamlet.

Having procured a guide, I left the inn at 5.45 a.m. on July 1st, to ascend the mountain. Mists obscured everything as we set out, and it felt very raw and cold. The path is the merest track—very sinuous, steep, and difficult. Rain commenced at 2.30 p.m., and continued during the whole of the descent. We reached our inn at 6.30 p.m., drenched through and through.

At one time a dense forest of Silver Fir covered the mountain, but this has long since been felled, and the majority of the trees still lie rotting where they fell. It is a common sight to see bushes of Rhododendrons, 20 feet or more tall, growing on the decaying trunks.

WA SHAN, 11,200 FEET HIGH

277

CHINA — MOTHER OF GARDENS

Some of these Firs could not have been less than 150 feet in height and 20 feet in girth. On the summit there are still a number of trees left, but none of great size, and nearly all have their tops broken off, either by the wind or by the snow. This mountain, in common with others I have visited, shows only too plainly the destructive nature of the Chinese. Fifty years more, under the present regime, and there will not be an acre of accessible forest left in all central, southern, and western China. The making of charcoal alone imposes a very heavy toll on hardwood trees and shrubs. The preparing of potash salts is a common industry in the mountains west, and is another means of clearing away the vegetation in a ruthless manner. It is to the charcoal-burning industry that I attribute the marked absence of Oak, Beech, and Hornbeam.

Besides the Silver Fir (Abies delavayi), the other Conifers are Tsuga yunnanensis, Juniperus formosana, and Picea complanata. Rhododendrons constitute the conspicuous feature of the vegetation, and their wood is luckily, not esteemed for making charcoal. They begin at 7500 feet, but are most abundant at 10,000 feet and upward. In the ascent I collected 16 species. They vary from diminutive plants 4 to 6 inches high, to giants 30 feet or more in stature. Their flowers, also, are of all sizes and colors, including pale yellow. It was most interesting to watch the displacement of one species by another as we ascended. One of the commonest species is R. yanthinum, which has flowers of various shades of purple.

The ascent of the mountain commences 100 yards or so from the inn; cultivation ceases at 6200 feet. Above this, for 1000 feet, is a belt, which has at some time been cleared for cultivation, but is now densely clad with coarse weeds. Amongst these occur quantities of Rodgersia pinnata alba, Spiraea aruncus, Astilbe, and Pedicularis, with a few bushes of Deutzia longifolia, Philadelphus wilsonii, and Poison Ivy (Rhus toxicodendron) interspersed. Above this, for 500 feet, comes a well-nigh impenetrable thicket of Bamboo scrub. The species (Arundinaria nitida) is of remarkably dense growth, with thin culms, averaging 6 feet in height. Next above this, till the plateau is reached, is a belt of mixed shrubs and herbs, conspicuous amongst which are Syringa komarovii, Hydrangea anomala, H. villosa, Neillia affinis,

Dipelta ventricosa, Ribes longeracemosum Davidii, Enkianthus deflexus, Styrax rosea, Deutzia spp., Rubus spp., Viburnum spp., Spiraea spp., Acer spp., Malus spp., Sorbus spp., Meconopsis chelidonifolia, Fragaria filipendula, Lilium giganteum yunnanense, and the herbs of the lower zone. A few Rhododendrons occur chiefly on the cliffs.

The plateau (8500 feet) is about half a mile across, marshy in places, and densely clad with shrubby vegetation and Bamboo scrub. In addition to those already noted as occurring in the belt below, I found Hydrangea xanthoneura, Rosa omeiensis and Aralia chinensis, also a species of Caltha, and a few Conifers. Rhododendrons became more abundant as we advanced. Crossing this plateau we reached the northwest angle of the upper storey, and scrambled upward by a narrow, rocky, tortuous path through dense thickets of mixed shrubs, which gradually gave place to Rhododendrons as the narrow ledge at 10,000 feet is reached. Rosa omeiensis, which was past flowering below, was here a mass of lovely white. Two or three species of Lonicera and various Labiatae occur within this belt, and on shady rocks at least three species of Primula, including P. davidii.

From 10,000 feet to the summit of the mountain Rhododendron accounts for fully 99 per cent of the ligneous vegetation. A few Conifers, Loniceras, Rosa orneiensis, Clematis montana Wilsonii, Pieris, and Gautheria veitchiana make up the remaining one per cent. Of the herbs, Primula is the most noteworthy. Five fresh species of this genus occur, and amongst them, though uncommon, the lovely yellow-flowered P. prattii. A blue-flowered Corydalis, Cypripedium luteum, with large yellow flowers, Rubus fockeanus and another herbaceous species are other pleasing plants. On shady rocks the curious Berneuxia thibetica abounds. This interesting plant was first referred to the genus Shortia by Franchet, and was later made the type of a new genus by Decaisne. The flowers are small and insignificant, white or pale pink in color. On bare rocks I gathered the pretty white-belled Cassiope selaginoides.

My attention and interest, however, were chiefly taken up with the Rhododendrons. The gorgeous beauty of their flowers defies description. They were there in thousands and hundreds of thousands. Bushes of all sizes, many fully 30 feet tall and more in diameter, all clad with a wealth of blossoms that almost hid the foliage. Some flowers were crimson, some bright red, some flesh-colored, some silvery pink, some yellow, and others pure white. The thick rugged stems, gnarled and twisted into every conceivable shape, are draped with pendent Mosses and Lichens, prominent amongst the latter being Usnea longissima. How the Rhododendrons find roothold on these wild crags and cliffs is a marvel. Many grow on the fallen trunks of the Silver Fir and some are epiphytic. Beneath them Sphagnum moss luxuriates and makes a pretty but treacherous carpet. On bare exposed cliffs I gathered two diminutive species of Rhododendron, each only a few inches tall, one with deep purple and the other with pale yellow flowers.

Dense mists obscured our view, though about ten o'clock the sun broke through and made a temporary rift in the clouds of mist, disclosing a scene which made us hunger for more. In one place we leant over a precipice and could hear the roar of a torrent some 2000 or 3000 feet below. Near the summit three precipices, each 40 or 50 feet in height, have to be ascended by means of wooden ladders. Up these I carried my dog, never thinking of the descent. On returning he became frightened, and though we blindfolded him, he struggled much, and on one occasion his struggles all but upset my balance. I was heartily thankful when safe ground was reached. It requires all one's nerve to mount a ladder with no balustrade, fixed to a cliff 40 feet vertical, and on either side a yawning abyss lost in the clouds. It is at 10,700 feet—a narrow ridge not 8 feet broad—that the first ladder is encountered. From here to within a few feet of the summit the path is terribly steep, difficult, and dangerous. On clearing the topmost ladder and the remains of another, we unexpectedly reached the summit by the easiest path imaginable for all the world like a woodland path at home.

The summit is a slightly undulating plateau, many acres in extent, with thickets of tall Rhododendrons festooned with Clematis montana Wilsonii, and clumps of Silver Fir, the remnant and offspring of giants which once clothed this magnificent mountain alternating with glades carpeted with Anemones and Primulas and tiny streamlets meandering hither and thither. Baber aptly describes it as "the most charming natural park in the world."

In times past several temples existed on the summit, of which ruins only now remain. At present there is but one temple, which contains an image of P'u-hsien P'u-ssa seated on a plaster elephant. It is built of the timber of the Silver Fir (Abies delavayi) and was in excellent repair. Near the temple a small patch of medicinal rhubarb, a few cabbages, and Irish potatoes are cultivated.

The partly shrubby Sambucus adnata and several herbs, including Pedicularis, Microula, Fragaria filipendula, and F. elatior, range from base to summit. Fragaria filipendula is a new strawberry worthy of note; the fruit is red, more or less cylindrical in shape, often an inch in length, and of very good flavor. It is widely distributed in western China, and at Tachienlu I have enjoyed many a dish of this fruit with cream from yak's milk.

Two days later I ascended a lofty spur (10,000 feet) of this mountain and added several fresh plants to my collection. Of these I may mention Paeonia veitchii, Rubus tricolor, Clematis faberi, Ribes laurifolium, Potentilla veitchii, Pyrola rotundifolia, Styrax perkinsiae, Aristolochia moupinensis, Acer, Anemone, Pyrus, Sorbus, Berberis, and Primula. High up on the cliff Leontopodium alpinum and several species of Anaphalis abound. Amongst the Sphagnum at least three species of Lycopodium occur. On dripping, shady rocks and trunks of the Rhododendrons, a filmy Fern (Hymenophyllum omeiense) is abundant.

During the four days I botanized on this mountain I added some 220 odd species to my collection. On each of these days the work was excessively hard, and drenched to the skin but mildly describes our condition each evening as we reached our inn. On one occasion, through treading on some loose debris, I was only saved from being precipitated over a steep cliff by the presence of mind of a coolie who happened to be near me at the moment.

Zoologically, Mount Wa and the surrounding wilderness is particularly interesting as being one of the places where wild cattle (Budorcas tibetanus) are found. I saw their footprints only; they were nearly as large as those of a cow. Ornithologically, it is interesting as being the home of at least five species of pheasant, including the blood and Amherst species.

I have climbed and botanized on many mountains in different parts of China, some much higher than this, but none have I found richer in cool-temperate plants, and more especially flowering shrubs. Altogether, with its rich flora, peculiar fauna, its singular geological formation, and its magnificent natural park on the summit, Wa shan has unique claims on the attention of the naturalist.

CHAPTER XXI

THE FLORA OF WESTERN CHINA

A BRIEF ACCOUNT OF THE RICHEST TEMPERATE
FLORA IN THE WORLD

N previous chapters the mountainous character of western China has been emphasized. Such a region, affording wide altitudinal extremes, a great diversity in climate, and a copious rainfall, is naturally expected to support a rich and varied flora. Yet after making every allowance for the favorable conditions obtaining in this region the wealth of flowers which meets the eye is astonishing and surpasses the dreams of the most sanguine botanist. Competent authorities estimate the Chinese flora to contain fully 15,000 species, half of which are peculiar to the country. These figures speak for themselves and yet fail to give an adequate idea of the profusion of flowers. The remote mountain fastnesses of central and western China are simply a botanical paradise, with trees, shrubs and herbs massed together in a confusion that is bewildering. On first arriving in a new and strange country it is difficult to recognize the plants one is familiar with under cultivation, and many months elapse before one is in any sense familiar with the common plants around him. During the eleven years I travelled in China I collected some 65,000 specimens, comprising about 5000 species, and sent home seeds of over 1500 different plants. Nevertheless, it was only during the latter half of this period that I was able to form an intelligent idea of the flora of China and to properly appreciate its richness and manifold problems.

The Chinese flora is, beyond question, the richest temperate flora in the world. A greater number of different kinds of trees are found in China than in the whole of the other north-temperate regions. Every important genus of broad-leaved trees known from

283

temperate regions of the northern hemisphere is represented in China except the Plane (Platanus) and False Acacia (Robinia). All the coniferous genera of the same regions, except the Redwoods (Sequoia), Bald Cypress (Taxodium), Chamxcyparis, Umbrella Pine (Sciadopitys), and true Cedars (Cedrus), are found there. In North America, excluding Mexico, about 165 genera of broad-leaved trees occur. In China the number exceeds 260. Of the 300 genera of shrubs enumerated in the "Kew Hand-List of Trees and Shrubs" (1902 ed.) fully half are represented in China.

The great interest and value, however, of the Chinese flora lies not so much in its wealth of species as in the ornamental character and suitability of a vast number for the embellishment of parks and outdoor gardens throughout the temperate regions of the world. My work in China has been the means of discovering and introducing many new plants to North America, Europe, and elsewhere. But previous to this work of mine the value of the Chinese plants was well and appreciatively known. Evidence of this is afforded by the fact that there is no garden worthy of the name, throughout the length and breadth of the temperate parts of the northern hemisphere, that does not contain a few plants of Chinese origin. Our Tea, Polyantha, and Rambler Roses, Chrysanthemums, Indian Azaleas, Camellias, Greenhouse Primroses, Moutan Paeonies, and large flowered Clematis have all been derived from plants still to be found in a wild state in central and western China. The same is true of a score of other favorite flowers. China is also the original home of the Orange, Lemon, Citron, Peach, and Apricot. The horticultural world is deeply indebted to the Far East for many of its choicest treasures, and the debt will increase as the years pass.

Our knowledge of the marvellous richness of the Chinese flora has been very slowly built up. Travellers, missionaries of all denominations, merchants, consuls, Maritime Customs officials, and all sorts and conditions of men have added their quota; but, as in geography and other departments of knowledge relating to the Far East, Roman Catholic priests have played the prominent part. The exclusive policy of the Chinese has necessarily increased the difficulties

DEUTZIA WILSONII

of Europeans who sought to acquire an intimate knowledge of the country, and honor is due to the workers who have exploited this field in the past.

On behalf of the Horticultural Society of London and others, Robert Fortune, in the 'Forties and 'Fifties of last century, completed the work of his predecessors and exhausted the gardens of China, to our lasting benefit, but the difficulties of travel were such that he had practically no opportunity of investigating the natural wild flora. With the exception of perhaps half a dozen plants, everything he sent home came from Chinese gardens. But one of his wildings—Rhododendron fortunei, to wit—has proved of in-estimable value to Rhododendron breeders.

Charles Maries, collecting on behalf of Messrs. Veitch, in 1879, ascended the Yangtsze as far as Ichang. He found the natives there unfriendly, and after staying a week was compelled to return. During his brief stay, however, he secured Primula obconica, one of the most valuable decorative plants of today. Near Kiukiang he collected Hamamelis mollis, Loropetalum chinense, and a few other plants of less value, and then hied himself away to Japan. For some curious reason or other he concluded that his predecessor, Fortune, had exhausted the floral resources of China, and, more extraordinary still, his conclusions were accepted! When at Ichang, could he have gone but some three days' journey north, south, or west, he would have secured a haul of new plants such as the botanical and horticultural world had never dreamed of. By the irony of Fate it was left for two or three others to discover and obtain what had been almost within his grasp.

The enormous Chinese population, especially in the vicinity of the lower Yangtsze, and its vast alluvial delta and plains, no doubt misled Maries, as it has done others. So densely is China populated that every bit of suitable land has been developed under agriculture. A Chinese is capable of getting more returns from a given piece of land than the most expert agriculturist of any other country. Dry farming and intensive cultivation, though unknown to the Chinese under these terms, have been practiced by them from time immemorial. The land is never idle, but is always undergoing tilling and manuring. Nevertheless, in spite of the almost incredible industry of the Chinese cultivator, much of the land in the mountain fastnesses of central and western China defies agricultural skill, and it is in these regions that a surprisingly varied flora obtains. These regions are very sparsely populated, are difficult of access, and, until comparatively recently, were totally unknown to the outside world.

The botanical collections of the two French Roman Catholic priests les Abbes David and Delavay, of the Russian traveller, N. M. Przewalski, and of the Maritime Customs officer, Augustine Henry, gave the first true insight into the extraordinary richness of the flora of central and western China. Delavay's collection alone totalled about 3000 species, and Henry's exceeded this number. Botanists were simply astounded at the wealth of new species and new genera disclosed by these collections. An entirely new light was thrown on many problems, and the headquarters of several genera, such as, for example, Rhododendron, Lilium, Primula, Pyrus, Rubus, Rosa, Viburnum, Lonicera, Cotoneaster, and Acer, heretofore attributed elsewhere, was shown to be China.

This truly astounding wealth of species, exists, not-withstanding the fact that every available bit of land is under cultivation. Below 2000 feet altitude the flora is everywhere relegated to the roadsides, the cliffs, and other more or less inaccessible places. It is impossible to conceive the original floral wealth of this country, for obviously many types must have perished as agriculture claimed the land, not to mention the destruction of forests for economic purposes.

In order to summarize the account of this wonderful flora it will be convenient to divide the region into alti-tudinal zones or belts. The mountainous nature of the country lends itself admirably to such an arrangement, and it is perhaps the only feasible way of dealing with a subject so vast and unwieldy. The chart (p. 289) represents an ideal section of the region and may convey a clearer idea of the subject than the text which follows:—

Division 1.—"The belt of cultivation—2000 feet altitude." The climate of the Yangtsze valley, up to 2000 feet altitude, essentially warm-temperate. Rice, cotton, sugar, maize, tobacco, sweet potatoes, and legumes are the principal summer crops; in winter, pulse, wheat, rape, hemp, Irish potato, and cabbage are generally grown. It is a region of intense cultivation and the flora is neither rich nor varied. The following wild plants are characteristic: Bamboos (Bambusa arundinacea, Phyllostachys pubescens and other species), Fan Palm (Trachycarpus excelsus), Pride of India (Melia azedarach), Crepe Myrtle (Lagerstroemia indica), Wintergreen (Xylosma racemosum pubescens), Chinese Banyan (Ficus infectoria), Gardenia (Gardenia florida), Roses (Rosa lavigata and R. microcarpa), Nanmu (Machilus nanmu and other species), Pine (Pinus massoniana), Soap tree (Gleditsia sinensis), Alder (Alnus cremastogyne), Privet (Ligustrum lucidum), Paulownia duclouxii, oranges, peaches, and other fruit trees, ferns, especially Gleichenia linearis, weeds of cultivation, miscellaneous shrubs and trees, including Pterocarya stenoptera, Celtis spp., Caesalpinia sepiaria, Wood Oil (Aleurites fordii), and Cypress (Cupressus funebris); the last two occurring particularly in rocky places.

Division 2.—"Rain forests belt—2000 to 5000 feet altitude." Between 2000 and 5000 feet are found rain forests, consisting largely of broad-leaved evergreen trees, mainly Oak, Castanopsis, Holly, and various Laurineae. The latter family constitutes fully 50 per cent of the vegetation in this zone. Ferns, evergreen shrubs, China Fir (Cunninghamia lanceolata), and Cypress are other prominent components. This belt is interesting also as being the home of nine-tenths of the montypic genera of trees that are so prominent a feature of the Chinese flora. Among the more interesting of these are: Eucommia, Itoa, Idesia, Tapiscia, Sinowilsonia, Platycarya, Davidia, Carrieria, Pteroceltis, and Emmenopterys. Cultivation is less general in this region, and the winter crop especially is of less importance. The crops are similar to those of the belt below except that maize is the staple and displaces rice. In Hupeh this zone is much less extensive and can hardly be said to exist when comparison with its development in western Szechuan is made.

Division 3. "Cool—temperate belt—5000 to 10,000 feet altitude." From 5000 to 10,000 feet is the largest and most important

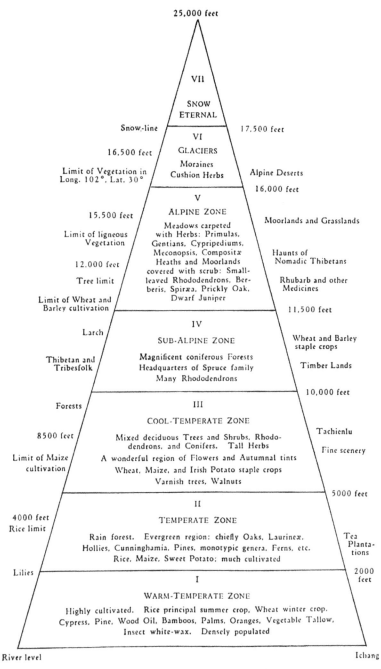

25,000 feet

VII

SNOW
ETERNAL

Snow-line   17,500 feet

VI

16,500 feet   GLACIERS
                     Moraines
Limit of Vegetation in   Cushion Herbs   Alpine Deserts
Long. 102°, Lat. 30°
                                                 16,000 feet

V

15,500 feet   ALPINE ZONE
                                                 Moorlands and Grasslands
                     Meadows carpeted
Limit of ligneous   with Herbs: Primulas,
Vegetation   Gentians, Cypripediums,
                     Meconopsis, Compositæ   Haunts of
12,000 feet   Heaths and Moorlands   Nomadic Thibetans
                     covered with scrub: Small-
Tree limit   leaved Rhododendrons, Ber- Rhubarb and other
                     beris, Spiræa, Prickly Oak. Medicines
Limit of Wheat and   Dwarf Juniper
Barley cultivation   11,500 feet

IV

Larch   SUB-ALPINE ZONE   Wheat and Barley
                                                 staple crops
Thibetan and   Magnificent coniferous Forests
Tribesfolk   Headquarters of Spruce family   Timber Lands
                     Many Rhododendrons
                                                 10,000 feet

Forests   III

                     COOL-TEMPERATE ZONE   Tachienlu

8500 feet   Mixed deciduous Trees and Shrubs, Rhodo-
                     dendrons, and Conifers. Tall Herbs   Fine scenery
Limit of Maize   A wonderful region of Flowers and Autumnal tints
cultivation   Wheat, Maize, and Irish Potato staple crops
                     Varnish trees, Walnuts
                                                 5000 feet

II

4000 feet   TEMPERATE ZONE
Rice limit
                     Rain forest. Evergreen region: chiefly Oaks, Laurineæ.   Tea
                     Hollies, Cunninghamia, Pines, monotypic genera, Ferns, etc.   Planta-
                     Rice, Maize, Sweet Potato: much cultivated   tions

Lilies   2000
                     I   feet

                     WARM-TEMPERATE ZONE

                     Highly cultivated. Rice principal summer crop, Wheat winter crop.
                     Cypress, Pine, Wood Oil, Bamboos, Palms, Oranges, Vegetable Tallow,
                     Insect white-wax. Densely populated

River level   Ichang

CHART ILLUSTRATING ZONES OF VEGETATION

289

zone of all. It is composed principally of deciduous flowering trees and shrubs characteristic of a cool-temperate flora and belonging to familiar genera. To these must be added forests of Conifers and many ornamental tall-growing herbs. It is in this zone that is found the astonishing variety of flowering trees and shrubs so preeminent a feature of this flora: of Clematis 60 species are recorded from China, of Lonicera, 60; of Rubus, 100; of Vitis, 35; of Evonymus, 30; of Berberis, 50; of Deutzia, 40; of Hydrangea, 25; of Acer, 40; of Viburnum, 70; of Ilex, 30; of Prunus, 80; of Senecio, 110; and the enumeration might be further extended. Pyrus (including Malus, Sorbus, Micromeles, and Eriolobus) is a prominent family in the belt, and behaves in China in the same manner as Crataegus does in the United States.

Amongst such botanical wealth it is difficult to make selections, but if any one family has outstanding claims it is Rhododendron. As in the Himalayan region, so in western China, the Rhododendrons are a special feature. The genus is the largest recorded from China, more than 300 species being known. I, myself, have collected about 80 species and have introduced upward of 65 into cultivation. Rhododendrons commence at sea-level, but do not become really abundant until 8000 feet is reached. They extend up to the limits of ligneous vegetation (15,000 feet, circa). These plants are gregarious in habit and nearly every species has a well-defined altitudinal limit. In size they vary from alpine plants only a few inches high to trees 40 feet and more tall. The color of their flowers range from pure white, through clear yellow to the deepest and richest shades of scarlet and crimson. In late June they are one mass of color, and no finer sight can possibly be imagined than mile upon mile of mountain-side covered with Rhododendrons in full blossom.

Division 4.—"Temperate alpine belt—10,000 to 11,-500 feet altitude." Above 10,000 feet in western China the character of the flora undergoes a great change, and the belt between 10,000 and 11,500 feet forms the hinterland between the temperate and alpine zones. This narrow belt is mostly moorland, but where the nature of the country admits, magnificent forests occur. The moorlands are covered with dwarf, small-leaved Rhododendrons and scrub-like shrubs, chiefly

THE FLORA OF WESTERN CHINA

Berberis, Spiraea, Caragana, Lonicera, Potentilla fruticosa, P. veitchii, and Hippophae salicifolia, with Willow, prickly scrub Oak, coarse herbs, grasses, and impenetrable thickets of dwarf Bamboo. The forests are composed almost exclusively of Conifers, chiefly Larch, Spruce, Silver Fir, Hemlock Spruce, and here and there Pine. A few trees of Red and White Birch and Poplar occur, chiefly near streams. Specifically very little is known about the constituents of these forests, but, to illustrate their wealth, I may mention that on my last journey I collected seeds of some 16 different species of Spruce, and 5 of Silver Fir. These forests are, unfortunately, fast disappearing, and are only to be found in the more inaccessible parts. The tree-limit varies according to rainfall, and may be put down as between 11,500 and 12,500 feet.

Division 5.—"The alpine belt—10,500 to 16,000 feet altitude." The alpine zone extends from 11,500 to 16,000 feet. The wealth of herbs in this belt is truly astonishing. Their variety is well-nigh infinite, and the intensity of the color of the flowers is a striking feature. The genus Pedicularis (Louseworts), with 100 species, is perhaps the most remarkable constituent. The Louseworts are large social plants and occur in countless thousands, their flowers being all colors save blue and purple. They are really most fascinating plants, and it is a great pity that their semi-parasitic nature prevents their cultivation. The Ragworts (Senecio), with 100 species, have yellow flowers, and the plants vary in size from low cushion plants to strong herbs 6 feet or more tall. Blue is supplied by the Gentians (Gentiana), of which there are 90 species. These again are social plants, and on sunny days the ground for miles is often nothing but an intensely blue carpet of Gentian flowers. The Fumeworts (Corydalis), with 70 species, supplies both yellow and blue flowers and cannot be denied a place. Then there are the wonderful alpine Primroses (Primula). This family is represented in China by more than 100 species, four-fifths of which occur in the west. These, like Gentians, take unto themselves in season large tracts of country and carpet them with flowers. Sometimes it is a marsh, at other times bare rock or the sides of streams. One of the most beautiful is Primula sikkimensis. Along the sides of stream-lets and ponds this species is as common as the Cowslip in English meadows.

291

CHINA — MOTHER OF GARDENS

Associated with it is its purple congener P. vittata. Other striking species are P. cockburniana, with orange scarlet flowers, a color unique in the genus; P. pulverulenta, a glorified P. japonica, with flower-scapes 3 to 4 feet tall, covered with a white meal, and flowers of a rich crimson color; and P. veitchii, which is best described as a hardy P. obconica. Other striking herbs are Incarvillea compacta and I. grandiflora, both with large red flowers, and Cypripedium tibeticum, a terrestrial Orchid with an enormous pouch, dark red in color. Also we find Meconopsis in half a dozen species, including M. henrici, with violet-colored flowers; M. punicea, with dark scarlet flowers; and M. integrifolia, with yellow flowers 8 inches or more across—possibly the most gorgeous alpine plant extant.

Division 6.—"High alpine belt." The limit of vegetation is about 16,500 feet; a few cushion plants belonging to Caryophyllaceae, Rosaceae, Cruciferae, and Compositae, with a tiny species of Primula and Meconopsis racemosa being the last to give out. Above this altitude are vast mo-raines and glaciers, culminating in perpetual snow. The snow-line cannot be less than 17,500 feet. Although at first sight remarkable, the high altitude of the snow-line is easily accounted for by the dryness of the Thibetan plateau and highlands to the immediate west.

Having briefly outlined the different altitudinal zones and instanced some of the more striking plants characteris-tic of each, it may be of interest to point out the more im-portant absentees. In China there are no species of Gorse (Ulex), Broom (Cytisus), Heath (Erica), Heather or Ling (Calluna); the Rock-rose family (Cistus and Helianthemum) is also unrepresented. The place of Gorse and Broom is inadequately taken by Forsythia, Caragana, Berberis, and various Jasmines; that of Heather by dwarf, tiny-leaved Rhododendrons, of which there are twenty or more species. The Cistus family has no representative group unless Hypericum be considered its substitute.

There is virtually no pasture-land in central and western China, but such open country as would compare with commons in England is covered with bushes of Berberis, Spiraea, Sophora viciifolia, Caragana, Pyracantha, Cotoneaster, Philadelphus, Holly, and various Roses. The

MELIOSMA OLDHAMII, 50 FEET TALL, GIRTH 10 FEET

anomalous conditions obtaining in the river-valleys of the west and the peculiar flora found there have been described in Chapter XIII.

Another interesting fact, and one that has peculiar reference to the flora of western Hupeh, is the number of plants bearing the specific name japonica, which are only Japanese by cultivation and are really Chinese in origin. The following well-known plants are examples: Iris japonica, Anemone japonica, Lonicera japonica, Sophora japonica, Senecio japonicas, and Eriobotrya japonica. Possibly some of these (and there are many more) may be common to both countries, but I am convinced that when the subject is properly threshed out, it will be found that fewer plants are common to both countries than is generally supposed.

The Chinese flora is largely peculiar to the country itself, the number of endemic genera and species being remarkable even when the size of the country is given due consideration. Yet in spite of its generally local character, the Chinese flora presents many interesting problems in plant distribution. Not the least interesting is to account for the presence of a species of Libocedrus (L. macrolepis), seeing that the other members of this genus are found in California, Chili, and New Zealand. Another noteworthy feature is a species of Osteomeles (O. Schwerinae), which occurs in the far west of China, the other member of this family being found scattered through the islands of the Pacific Ocean. But perhaps the most extraordinary fact in this connection is the presence on Mount Omei of a species of Nertera (N. sinensis), the other members of this family being purely insular and relegated to the southern hemisphere.

The affinity of the Chinese flora, with contiguous and distant countries, is an interesting theme and one that could be enlarged upon at length. The Himalayan flora is represented by certain species in western and central China, and there is a considerable affinity between the floras of these regions. This is to be expected, yet it presents problems of exceptional interest, since it is the Sikhim element which comes out strongest. When the flora of Bhutan and the country intervening between western China is properly explored it will probably be found that Sikhim represents the most western point of distribution for certain plants rather than their real headquarters. Of Himalayan plants com-monly met with in the region, with which this work is intimately concerned, the following examples may be given: Euonymus grandiflora, Euptelea pleiosperma, Clematis montana, C. grata, C. gouriana, Rosa sericea, R. microphylla, Primula sikkimensis, P. involucrata, Podophyllum emodi, and Amphicome arguta. In Yunnan there is a decided affinity with the Malay-Indian flora.

The aggressive nature of the Scandinavian flora is evidenced by the following herbs and shrubs which are locally very common: Vervain (Verbena officinalis), Agrimony (Agrimonia eupatoria), Buttercups (Ranunculus acris, R. repens, and R. sceleratus), Silver-weed (Potentilla anserina), Great Burnet (Poterium officinale), False Tamarisk (Myricaria germanica), Bird Cherry (Prunus padus), and Plantain (Plantago major).

In the north and throughout the upland valleys and highlands of the west a few central Asian and Siberian forms occur, such as Sibiraea laevigata, Spiraea alpina, Cotoneaster multiflora, Thalictrum petaloideum, Delphinium grandiflorum, and Lonicera hispida.

At first sight it would very naturally be supposed that the Chinese flora was most closely allied if not to that of Europe at least to that of the Asiatic continent generally. Yet this is not so. The real affinity is with that of the Atlantic side of the United States of America.

This remarkable fact was first demonstrated by the late Dr. Asa Gray when investigating the early collections made in Japan. Modern work in China, and especially central China, has given overwhelming evidence and established beyond question Asa Gray's conclusions. There are many instances in which only two species of a genus are known— one in the eastern United States and the other in China. Noteworthy examples are the Tulip tree, Kentucky Coffee tree, the Sassafras, and the Lotus Lily (Nelumbium). A considerable number of families are common to both countries, and in most instances China is the dominant partner. Usually the U. S. A. have one and China several species of the same genus, but here and there the opposite obtains. Magnolias afford a good illustration of this affinity. This genus, absent from Europe and western North America, is represented by 7 species on the Atlantic side of the North American continent, and by 19 species in China and Japan.

The following brief list still further illustrates this:—

SOME GENERA COMMON TO CHINA, JAPAN, AND THE ATLANTIC SIDE OF THE UNITED STATES OF AMERICA

CHINA AND JAPAN		UNITED STATES OF AMERICA	
Genus	No. of Species	Genus	No. of Species
Magnolia	19	Magnolia	7
Schisandra	10	Schisandra	1
Itea	5	Itea	1
Gordonia	3	Gordonia	2
Hamamelis	2	Hamamelis	2
Shortia	3	Shortia	1
Catalpa	5	Catalpa	2
Negundo (Acer)	5	Negundo (Acer)	1
Wistaria	5	Wistaria	2
Astilbe	10	Astilbe	1
Podophyllum	6	Podophyllum	1
Illicium	6	Illicium	2
Stewartia	5	Stewartia	2
Berchemia	8	Berchemia	2
Nyssa	1	Nyssa	4
Carya	2	Carya	15

In a few cases the same species is common to both countries. The most extraordinary instance of this is Diphylleia cymosa (Umbrella Leaf). This plant occurs in localities separated by 140° of longitude and exhibits absolutely no marked variation.

In the instances mentioned above, the families are absent from any other region in the world. In others—for example, Oak, Hornbeam, Elm, Birch, Ash, Beech, and Sweet Chestnut—where the families range around the whole temperate zone of both Old and New worlds, the individual Chinese species are usually more closely akin to

FORESTS OF SPRUCE (PICEA ASPERATA)

those of North America than to those of Europe.

The explanation of this phenomenon is to be found in the glaciation of the northern hemisphere in prehistoric times. In those far-off times the land connection between Asia and North America was far more complete than it is today, and the flora extended much farther to the north. The ice-cap which gradually crept down forced the flora to travel towards the equator. Later, when the period of great cold was over, and the ice-cap receded, the plants crept back; but the ice-cap remained at a more southern latitude than before, and consequently rendered much of the land formerly covered with forests too cold to support vegetable life of any sort. This rearrangement after the tertiary ice age caused a break between the two hemispheres, and the consequent isolation and cutting off of the floras. Other agencies and factors played a part, but the above explains briefly and roughly why the floras so much alike should today be so widely separated geographically.

That the Chinese flora is an ancient one is evidenced by the number of old types it contains. For example, in ancient times, Ginkgo biloba (Maidenhair-tree) was found, not only in Asia, but in western Europe, northern California, and Greenland, as the fossil remains found in Jurassic beds of these countries testify. Today it exists only in China and Japan as a cultivated tree, being preserved to us by the Buddhist and other religious communities who plant it in the neighborhood of their temples. Cycas, Cephalotaxus, Torreya, and Taxus are other old types, but they occur in a wild as well as in a cultivated state in China today. Many of the older ferns, such as Osmunda, Gleichenia, Marattia, and Angiopteris are common in China and widely spread. In speaking of the older ferns it may be of interest to note that Augustine Henry discovered in Yunnan an entirely new genus of Marattiaceae, which has been named Archangiopteris.

From the evidence before us it would appear that the Chinese flora suffered less during later glacial times than did that of Europe and North America. This may possibly have been due to the greater continuity of land toward the equator which obtains in Asia as compared with that of the continents of Europe and America.

CHAPTER XXII

THE PRINCIPAL TIMBER TREES

HE forested regions of China are today remote from the populous parts of the country, and are to be found only in the more wildly mountainous parts, which are little suited to agriculture, and where the rivers are unnavigable rock-strewn torrents, and roads, as such, can scarcely be said to exist. Such districts are always at considerable elevation and are but sparsely peopled. In all the more accessible regions agriculture has claimed the land, and the trees are only met with around houses, temples, tombs, stream-sides, or crowning cliffs. The scarcity of timber is acutely felt throughout the length and breadth of the land. Dressed logs and poles are carried long distances to navigable waterways and floated either down or up-stream, consequently their cost is high. The ports on the sea-board and lower Yangtsze import timber in quantity for general construction purposes from Puget Sound and British Columbia. A certain amount also comes from Japan. Hardwoods for miscellaneous purposes are imported from various parts of Malaysia, and Jarrah wood for railway work has been recently sent from Australia. The famous blackwood furniture of China is not made of native wood, but of timber imported from Bangkok, Saigon, and other places in Indo-China. Botanically the source of Chinese blackwood is unknown. The so-called Bombay blackwood is derived from Dalbergia latifolia, and possibly the Chinese kind is from a closely allied species. Western China is rather better off for timber than other parts of China, and fortunately so, since the importation of timber as a business is utterly impossible. Nevertheless there is a great dearth of wood for building purposes, and timber prices have doubled during the last decade. The massive timbers to be seen in old Chinese temples and houses are now unobtainable from the native trees of China.

CHINA — MOTHER OF GARDENS

Since the scarcity of timber is so great, every kind of tree found in the thickly populated regions furnishes wood of some value, but for the purpose of this chapter it suffices to give a brief account of the more important kinds and those most generally useful.

By far the most important timber in China is, of course, the stems of the Bamboo. The Jesuit priest, Nicolas Trigault, in a work on China, published in 1615, states "They have a kind of reed called Bambu by the Portuguese. It is almost as hard as iron. The largest kind is scarcely encompassed with two hands. It is hollow inside and presents many joints outside. The Chinese use it for pillars, shafts of lances, and for 600 other domestic purposes."

Although three centuries have elapsed since the above quotation was written it applies equally to the conditions of the present day, for the uses to which the Bamboo is put in China are indeed limitless. It supplies many of the multifarious needs of the people with whose everyday life, from birth to death, it is inseparably entwined. From bamboo stems are fashioned the various household utensils, furniture, the house itself, many agricultural implements, masts and gear for boats, rafts, ropes, bridges, irrigation-wheels, water-pipes, gas-pipes, tubes for raising brine, sedan-chairs, tobacco and opium-pipes, bird-cages, snares for entrapping insects, birds, and animals, umbrellas, raincoats, hats, soles for shoes, under-shirts, sandals, combs, musical instruments, ornamental vases, boxes, and works of art—the pen (brush) to write with, the paper to write upon, everything, in fact, useful and ornamental, from the hats of the highest officials to the pole with which the coolie carries his load. Formerly the records of the race were written on bamboo tablets which were strung together at one end like a fan. Records of this description, dug up in A.D. 281, after having been buried for 600 years, were found to contain the history of Tsin from 784 B.C., and, incidentally, also that of China for 1500 years before that date.

Bamboo shavings are used in caulking boats and for stuffing pillows and mattresses. The young shoots are a valued vegetable. According to popular belief, in times of scarcity a compassionate Deity causes the Bamboo to flower and yield a harvest of grain to save the people from starvation.

The Bamboo flourishes everywhere in the Far East, and is just as beautiful when sheltering the peasant's cottage or beggar's but as when ornamenting the courtyards of temples or the mansions of the wealthy. It is the one woody plant that is really abundant throughout all but the coldest parts of the Middle Kingdom. The Occident possesses no tree or shrub which for all-round general usefulness compares with the Bamboo of the Orient.

The Chinese generic name for the Bamboo family is Chu, the different kinds being distinguished by a prefix. The natives have no difficulty in recognizing the various species, but botanists generally have found Bamboos exceedingly difficult to classify. In the Index Florce Sinensis 33 species are enumerated, but for the purpose of this chapter only 4 or 5 kinds are involved.

Throughout the Yangtsze valley, up to about 2500 feet altitude, the Pan chu (Phyllostachys pubescens) is one of the commonest species. Its young spear-like stems rear themselves 30 to 40 feet, and finally develop into beautiful arched plumes. The stems are about 3 to 4 inches in diameter, dark shining green, becoming yellow with age. The wood is moderately thick and is used for a great variety of purposes. It is largely employed on the Yangtsze, above Ichang, for making tracking lines for the various river-craft. A species allied to this, but smaller in every way, never exceeding 20 feet in height, is the Ch'ung chu (P. heteroclada). This Bamboo is commonly used in western Hupeh for paper-making.

A very common species in the warmer parts of Szechuan is the Tz'u chu (Bambusa arundinacea, often called B. spinosa), the Spiny Bamboo. This magnificent species produces stems 50 to 75 feet tall and 8 to 10 inches in diameter at base. It does not spread very much, but forms compact clumps, which are impenetrable on account of their density and the presence of innumerable, slender, ferociously spiny stems which develop among and around the larger culms. This Bamboo has a small core and very thick wood. It is used in household carpentry, for furniture, ornamental vases and boxes and scaffolding, and has a hundred and one other uses.

Another species is the Nan chu (Dendrocalamus giganteus) , the largest growing of all the Bamboos found in western Szechuan. This is confined to the warmer parts of the province, where it forms wide-spreading groves. The stems grow 60 to 80 feet tall and are 10 to 12 inches thick. The core is very large, the wood thin and light. It is commonly used for constructing the rafts which ply on the shallow but turbulent rivers of western Szechuan. It has also many other uses and is especially prized for making chop-sticks.

Yet another very commonly cultivated species is Bambusa vulgaris, sometimes called the Kwanyin chu, which produces pale-colored stems 30 to 50 feet tall. The wood is thin and used for a variety of purposes, but is less valuable than any of the foregoing. The young shoots of these large-growing Bamboos are cut just as they appear above the ground, and eaten as a vegetable, the flesh being white, firm and crisp.

Apart from Bamboo the most common timber for all-round use is that derived from the Sha shu, or China Fir (Cunninghamia lanceolata). This coniferous tree is widely spread throughout warm-temperate parts of China and is especially partial to red sandstone. It is particularly abundant in the Yachou Prefecture and in the mountains bordering the northwest corner of the Chengtu plain. It grows from 80 to 120 feet tall, and has a straight mast-like stem; after the trees are cut down this Conifer reproduces itself by sprouts from the old stumps. The bark is commonly employed for roofing purposes. The wood is light, fragrant, and easily worked. For general building purposes, house-fittings, and indoor carpentry it is the most esteemed of all Chinese timbers; also it is in great request for coffin-making, the fragrant properties of the wood being considered to act as a preservative. For ordinary coffins several logs are dressed and fastened together laterally to form a thick, wide plank called Ho-pan, four of which, with two end pieces added, make a coffin. All who can afford it have such coffins lacquered a jet black. But the more expensive coffins are those in which each ho-pan is hewn from a single log of timber, and the most valuable of all are those made from Hsiang Mu (fragrant wood), or Yin-then Mu (long-buried wood). For such a coffin 400 to 1000 ounces of silver is

CHINA FIR (CUNNINGHAMIA LANCEOLATA), 120 FEET TALL, GIRTH 20 FEET the usual price. For the most part, Yin-then Mu comes from the Chiench'ang valley, where it was probably engulfed as the result of an earthquake in times past. In 1904 I ascended the Tung valley from Fulin to Moshi-mien, en route for Tachienlu, and near the hamlet of Wan-tung came upon a place where natives were engaged in excavating buried timbers. The work was being carried on in a narrow valley. At the head of the valley a torrent had been dammed and the accumulated waters, released at will from time to time through a sluice, carried much of the overlying debris away. Many of the excavations were fully 50 feet deep. All sorts of timber is found buried in this place, but only the Hsiang Mu is considered of value. I procured a specimen of this wood, and subsequent microscopic examination has proved it to be that of Cunningharnia lanceolate. The Chinese consider that these trees have been buried for two or three hundred years. The timber is wonderfully preserved and is more compact in texture and more fragrant than that of recently felled trees. Ho-pans made from Hsiang Mu average about 30 inches wide and 7 feet in length. In all my travels in western China I have seen only one living specimen of Cunninghamia approaching the size of these long-buried giants.

In Chengtu and neighboring cities, the timber known as Lien sha, derived from Abies delavayi and allied species, is generally employed for all the larger beams, pillars, and planking in house-building. The handsome Silver Fir (Abies delavayi), is common on all the higher mountains of the west, but that growing in the Yachou prefecture is most accessible, and this district is the main source of the timber-supply. The timber is soft and not very durable, but the large size of the logs render it most serviceable. The Pine (Sung shu) is very common, the most widely diffused species being Pinus massoniana. This tree ascends from sea-level to 4000 feet altitude. The timber obtained from the higher altitudes is close-grained, resinous, and durable, but that from low-levels is soft, very open, and of little value. Other Hard Pines, such as P. henryi, P. densata, P. wilsonii, P. prominens are found at higher altitudes (up to 10,000 feet) and yield valuable timber, but unfortunately they occur only in inaccessible places. The Chinese White Pine (P. armandi) is widely spread in the more mountainous parts. This tree never attains any great size, but the timber is very durable and resinous. It is esteemed for building purposes and for making torches.

All the Conifers yield useful timber, but unfortunately few are found today in accessible regions. Around Tach-ienlu the Hung-sha (Red Fir), Larix potaninii, is esteemed the most valuable of all timbers. The Tieh sha (Tsuga yunnanensis and T. chinensis) is converted into shingles for roofing purposes and is also valued for planking. In the Lungan prefecture the Me-tiao sha (Picea complanata) is a most valuable timber for general building purposes. Many other kinds of Spruce occur in the mountains, and with Silver Fir and Larch form the only remaining Conifer forests in western China. A Juniper (Hsiang-peh shay), Juniperus saltuaria, is common north of Sungpan, where it is valued for building purposes. Cupressus duclouxiana (K'an-peh sha) occurs in the arid valleys of the west; Taxus chinensis (Tuen-ch'u sha) and Keteleeria davidiana (Yu sha or Oil Fir) are found scattered all over western China between 2000 and 5000 feet altitude, but are nowhere really abundant.

From Ichang westward, up to 3500 feet altitude, the commonest Conifer next to Pine is the Peh sha or White Fir (Cupressus funebris), and in the more rocky limestone regions it is the more common tree of the two. This hand-some Cypress, with its pendent branchlets, is generally planted over tombs and shrines and in temple grounds. The wood is white, hard, heavy, and exceedingly tough. It enters largely into the structure of all boats plying on the upper Yangtsze, forming the sides, bulkheads, and often the cross-beams and decks. It is also made into chairs, tables, and furniture. The superstructure of the boat is usually of Sha mu, the bottom and main timbers of Oak and Nanmu.

Oak is widely dispersed from river-level to 8000 feet altitude, but large trees are scarce except in the vicinity of tombs, shrines, and other sacred places. A general name for the family is Li, and the Chinese distinguish many kinds, such as Peh-fan, Hwa, Hung, Tueh, and Chu li; botanically about a score of species occur in this region, of which the commonest are Quercus serrata, Q. variabilis, and Q. aliena. All yield close-grained timber, highly valued for a variety of purposes apart from boat-building.

Nanmu (Southernwood) includes a number of species of Machilus and Phoebe. All are evergreen and singularly handsome trees. They are largely planted around home-steads and temples in Szechuan, and are a prominent feature of the scenery of parts of the Chengtu plain and around the base of Mount Omei. They grow to a great size and have clean, straight trunks and wide-spreading, umbrageous heads. The timber is close-grained, fragrant, greenish and brown in color, easily worked, and very durable. It is highly esteemed for furniture-making, and for pillars in the temples and the houses of the wealthy. As planking it is used for boat bottoms. Nanmu is one of the most valuable of all Chinese timbers, and the trees among the handsomest of evergreens. Camphor (Ch'ang shu), Cinnamomum camphora, is found scattered over western Hupeh and Szechuan up to 3500 feet altitude, and it fragrant timber, like that of Nanmu, is made into high-class furniture. The wood furnished by the thick main roots of this tree is known as Ying mu, and is valued for cabinet work.

For high-grade cabinet work, picture frames, and the very best furniture the timber most highly esteemed in Szechuan is the Hung-tou mu, derived from Ormosia Hosiei, a tree allied to the Sophora. In the spring O. Hosiei produces large panicles of white and pink pea-shaped flowers, and at all seasons of the year is a striking tree. The wood is heavier than water, of a rich red color, and beautifully marked. It is the most high-priced of all local timbers, and is now very scarce. In north-central Szechuan it is still fairly common, but on the Chengtu plain it is only found in temple grounds or over shrines. The native name signifies Red Bean tree, the seeds being red and contained in bean-like pods. Allied to the foregoing is Dalbergia hupeana, which yields the valuable T'an mu, a wood whitish in color, very heavy, and exceedingly hard and tough. It is almost exclusively employed in building the wheelbarrows used on the Chengtu plain; for the handles of carpenters' tools, rammers for oil-presses, blocks and pulleys used on boats, and for every purpose where stress and strain obtain. This tree grows tall (80 feet) but is never of any great thickness; it is widely spread in the west up to 3000 feet altitude.

PINUS MASSONIANA, 90 FEET TALL

CHINA — MOTHER OF GARDENS

Three other members of the Pea family that yield useful woods of greater or less value, are the Huai shu (Sophora japonica), Tsao-k'o shu (Gleditsia sinensis), and Yeh-ho shu (Albizzia lebbek). All three species are common, the first two forming a characteristic feature of the vegetation of the more arid river-valleys of the west. The wood of these trees is used in general carpentry and furniture-making.

One of the commonest trees throughout the hot, rather arid river-valleys, up to 8500 feet altitude (but by no means confined thereto), is Juglans regia, the Walnut (Hei-tou shu). It is cultivated for its fruits, which are a valued article of food and a source of oil. The wood has recently become in great demand in the newly established arsenals for making rifle-stocks. The supply is not equal to the demand, and much Nanmu timber is used as a substitute. This latter is lighter and less serviceable for this purpose than the Walnut.

The best rudder-posts are made from the wood of the Huang-lien shu (Pistacia chinensis), a large tree found everywhere up to 5000 feet altitude. A log having a natural fork at one end is in general use for the balance-rudders on all the larger boats. The wood of the Loquat (Pi-pa shu), Eriobotrya japonica, which is red-colored, heavy, and of great strength, is also employed for this purpose. The young shoots of the Pistacia, known as Huang-ni ya-tzu, are cooked and eaten as a vegetable, and so also are the shoots of the Ch'un-tien shu (Cedrela sinensis). This last-named tree furnishes a valuable timber, beautifully marked with rich red bands on a yellowish brown ground. Foreigners call it Chinese mahogany. It is easily worked, does not warp nor crack, and is esteemed for making window-sashes, door-joists, and furniture. The tree grows 80 feet tall, the trunk is very straight, and but little branched. It is quite common in western Hupeh up to 4500 feet altitude, but much less so in Szechuan.

Tea-chests for all the higher-grade teas are made of wood derived from the Chinese Sweet Gum (Feng-hsiang shu), Liquidambar formosana. This is a strikingly hand-some tree, growing 80 to 100 feet tall, with a girth of 12 to 15 feet. It occurs scattered all over the west up to 3500 feet altitude; the leaves turn a rich red brown in autumn and remain on the trees far into the winter.

THE PRINCIPAL TIMBER TREES

The best carrying poles are made from the Tzu-k'an shu (Ehretia acuminata and E. dicksonii), the wood of these trees being light but very tough. Oak and Bamboo are also used for the same purpose and are cheaper. For making the drums used on boats and in temples the wood of the Tzu-ch'in shu (Acanthopanax ricinifolius) is considered best, being easily worked, pliable, and resonant. The two ends of the drum are covered with hide.

The finest joss-sticks (Chinese incense) are composed of the pounded leaves and branches of various members of the Laurel family, all of which are rich in fragrant, essential oils. As an adulterant the pulped wood of Cypress and Birch is commonly employed.

On the barren hills around Ichang and elsewhere the common Pine (Sung shu), Anus massoniana, has been planted as a source of fuel. Along the stream-sides and canals on the Chengtu plain, Alder (Ching shu), Alnus cremastogyne, is generally planted for the same purpose. The Alder and Pine, together with Bamboo, are the only trees planted for the economic value of their timber. In the mountains, Beech, Ash, Poplar, Sweet Chestnut, Horn-beam, Birch, and many other valuable and useful timber trees occur, but are difficult of access and consequently not in general use.

CHAPTER XXIII

FRUITS, WILD AND CULTIVATED

HINA is the original home of several fruits which are now cultivated all over the world, as, for example, the orange, lemon, pomelo, peach, and Japanese plum. In the south a number of tropical fruits, such as banana, pineapple, papaw, arecanut, litchi, longan, and Chinese olives (Canarium), are grown, but only the last three, and these in very small quantities, are found in the regions with which we are concerned. In the north, more especially around Chefoo, apples and pears, introduced from America, are cultivated and excellent fruit is produced. In the north, too, fine grapes are grown, and the fruit generally is of a high order. But, in general, little attention is given to fruit-culture; pruning the trees and thinning the fruit is not attended to, with the result that nearly all Chinese fruit is lacking in quality. Usually it is gathered before it is properly ripe, and this has much to do with the absence of flavor which is unfortunately characteristic. Particularly is this indifference and neglect evident in central and western China, where a very considerable quantity and variety is grown. The oranges, peaches, and persimmons are equal to those obtainable anywhere, but all the other succulent fruits are of low-grade quality. It is to be regretted that more attention is not given to the subject, for the regions could undoubtedly be made to produce the very best of fruits.

In ascending the Yangtsze River, from where the foot-hills commence below Ichang, and westwards to Sui Fu, orange-groves are a feature, attaining their greatest luxuriance between Chungking and Lu Chou. In December, when the trees are laden with ripe fruit, these groves are a remarkable sight. The Orange is happiest when growing on the lee side of rocky escarpments, or at their base, where it is protected from the winds. It is very partial to the clayey marls and sandstones of

310

the Red Basin. In western Szechuan the loose-skinned or Mandarin Orange (Citrus nobilis) is most generally grown. In season the fruit can be purchased on the spot at the rate of 500 to a 1000 for a shilling. Unfortunately this orange does not keep well, but when removed and dried the rind constitutes a favorite medicine known as Chien-yun-p'i. The fibres and pithy substance surrounding the fleshy carpels within the rind also form a medicine which is called Chii-lo. In the gorges a tight-skinned or Sweet Orange, Shan k'an-tzu (C. aurantium var.), is more usually met with. The so-called Ichang orange of this type is noted far and wide in China. It has a higher market-value than the mandarin and keeps well. In Chengtu these oranges are kept fresh and good all through the summer, but by what process I failed to discover.

A Lemon (C. ichangensis) is also grown in the Ichang gorge, but is not common. The fruit of this species is ovoid in shape and of excellent flavor. Pomelos, Yo-tzu (C. decumana var.), are met with, but the fruit seldom contains any pulp worthy of the name, consisting usually of little but pith and seeds. The Kumquat (C. japonica) is sparingly cultivated for its fruits, which, preserved with sugar, are an esteemed delicacy. A Citron (C. medica digitata) is also occasionally grown for its curious-looking fruit which is known as fingered citron, or Buddha's hand.

The Orange and allied fruit trees are propagated by notching the shoots which arise from the base of the tree and fixing earth around the cut. A framework of bamboo or a broken earthenware pan is used to keep the soil in place When many roots have been formed in the heaped-up soil a final severance of the shoot from the parent tree is made, and in due course the new plant is removed to a permanent site. Boring-insects are unfortunately making sad havoc among the orange-groves of western China. No attempt at prevention or control is made by the owners, and nothing but the wonderful vitality of the tree saves it from extinction.

The Peach, Tao-tzu (Prunus persica), is abundantly cultivated in Hupeh and Szechuan from river level to 9000 feet altitude. Freestone and clingstone varieties and oval and flattened kinds occur; those from the vicinity of Ichang are of delicious flavor and are probably not excelled anywhere in the world. The climate more than anything else is responsible for this, since the trees are little cared for and generally covered with the san Jose scale-insect. The trees are grown in orchards or in small groups around houses, but sub-spontaneous bushes are met with everywhere by the wayside and on cliffs. An oil is extracted from the kernels in northern China, but not in the western parts of the Empire, as far as my knowledge goes.

The Peach was introduced into Asia Minor and Europe from Persia somewhere about 300 B.C., but it has been cultivated in China from very remote times and was probably carried to Persia by way of the old trade route via Bokhara. While it is now accepted that China is the original home of this invaluable fruit, it is by no means certain as to what particular plant represents the wild type. A species found in northern China and known as P. davidiana, is generally regarded as the source of origin of the cultivated peach. From this view I, however, dissent. My opinion is that the species are distinct, and that the type of the garden peach is no longer to be found in a wild state. The nearest to it is the sub-spontaneous form, plants of which are abundant on the cliffs and by the waysides all over western Hupeh and Szechuan. In this connection it may be of interest to record that in the neighborhood of Tachienlu I discovered a new species of Peach which has since been named P. mira. This plant is a typical freestone Peach in every respect, but has a small, smooth, ovoid stone.

The Apricot (P. armeniaca) is generally supposed to be a native of Armenia, as its name implies, from whence it was introduced to China, where it has long been cultivated; But Maximowicz regarded it as spontaneous in the mountains near Peking. The Apricot tree grows to a large size (40 to 50 feet), but the fruit, known as Hun-tzu, is fibrous and very harsh in flavor. There is room for the improved varieties of apricot in China, as the dried apricots prepared in northern India, which find their way across Thibet to western China, are highly esteemed by Thibetans and Chinese alike.

Plum trees, Ku-li-tzu, are commonly cultivated, the fruits being round in shape and either green, yellow, red, or purple in color, but all are of indifferent flavor. All these cultivated forms are derived from P.

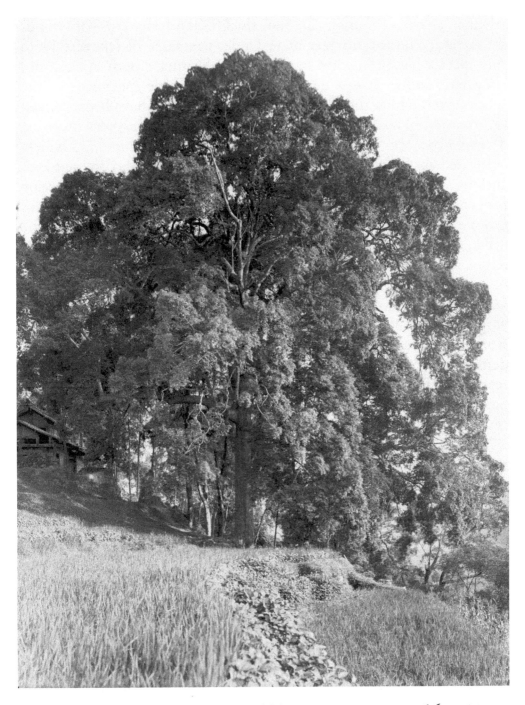

NANMU (PHOEBE NANMU), 100 FEET TALL, GIRTH 16 FEET

salicina, a tree common in the thickets and margins of woods throughout Hupeh and Szechuan. Under the name of Japanese Plum this species has been introduced into California, South Africa, and elsewhere, and is now widely cultivated. Authentic specimens of the species from which the Plums cultivated in Europe have been derived (P. communes) have not been recorded from China, and very probably it does not occur there The Japanese Apricot (P. mume), so widely cultivated in China and Japan, where it is dwarfed and trained into curious shapes and much appreciated for its early flowering propensities, is wild in western Hupeh and Szechuan, being known as Oo-me. The fruit is round, usually red on one side and yellow on the other, of indifferent flavor, and rendered less palatable by reason of its felted, woolly stone.

The common Almond is not grown in China, but in 1910, near Sungpan, I discovered an allied species, since named P. dehiscens, in which the ripe fruit opens and exposes the stone. The kernel of this fruit is eaten and locally is much esteemed. The plant forms a very dense, spiny bush, 5 to 12 feet tall, and is very abundant in the upper reaches of the Min valley. The fruit may be described as dry, since hardly any flesh is developed. This species is now in cultivation, and is certainly an interesting addition to the Almonds hitherto grown.

Cherries, Ying-tao, are abundant in the woods and forests and run riot in species. In Plantoe Wilsonianoe, part II, Koehne describes no fewer than 40 species based on material collected by me alone. The Cherry is, however, rarely cultivated, and such fruit as is on sale at Ichang and elsewhere is small and lacking in flavor. Its chief merit is in being the first stone-fruit of the season, coming into the market the end of April. The Cherry cultivated around Ichang is P. pseudocerasus. The species from which the European cherries have been derived (P. avium and P. Cerasus) are not found in China.

The Pear, Li-tzu, is very generally cultivated and is especially abundant throughout the upper reaches of the river-valleys in the west. It is also common in the higher parts of the glens which lead off from the gorges in western Hupeh. Several kinds are grown, and in some instances the fruit attains a very large size. Usually these pears are as hard as rock, and though very useful for cooking purposes are of little value for dessert. Propagation by crown-grafting is commonly practiced, but little attention is accorded the trees afterward. All the varieties of Chinese pears have been evolved by long cultivation from native species (probably Pyrus serotina, P. ussuriensis, and P. serrulata), and have not common origin with those cultivated in the Occident which have been derived from P. communis. Around Peking the Chinese cultivate a peculiar kind of Pear under the name of Peh-li-tzu (White Pear). The fruit is apple-shaped, about 1 34 inches in diameter, pale yellow in color, and of most delicious flavor. This Pear is probably a superior variety of Pyrus ussuriensis.

Apples are much more sparingly cultivated than pears, with which they are grown in association. They are more frequent around Sungpan Ting and Tachienlu than in Hupeh. The fruit is small, green, or greenish-yellow on one side and rosy on the other in the best variety, with an agreeable bitter-sweet flavor. It is uncertain as to what species these apples belong, but possibly to Malus prunifolia rinki.

The Quince, Mu-kua, is commonly cultivated in central China, but less so in the west. The fruits are oiled and kept as ornaments in houses, being appreciated for the fragrant odor. They are also used as medicine. Two species occur— Chaenomeles sinensis with nearly round leaves and rosy pink flowers and C. cathayensis with elongated leaves and white flowers, flushed pink. Closely allied to the Quince is Docynia delavayi, which is very abundant in Yunnan, where the fresh fruits, known as Tao yi, are used in ripening persimmons. The fruits of each are arranged in alternate layers in large jars and covered with rice-husks, and in ten hours the persimmons are bletted and fit for eating. The Docynia occurs sparingly in western Szechuan, but in that locality the fruit is not utilized.

The Loquat, P'i-pa (Eriobotrya japonica), both wild and cultivated, occurs in quantity up to 4000 feet altitude, and is most abundant in rocky places. This handsome ever-green forms a tree 30 feet tall, and produces its fragrant white flowers in the early winter, the fruit being ripe in April. The fruit is orange-colored, of a pleasant sub-acid flavor, but there is very little flesh surrounding the large, soft brown seeds, which have an almond-like taste and might be used for flavoring purposes.

In different parts of China various species of Hawthorn, Shan-li-hung-tzu or Shan-cha, are cultivated for their fruits. In Hupeh the species thus favored is Crataegus hupehensis; orchards of this tree occur in the neighborhood of Hsingshan Hsien. The fruit is scarlet, nearly 1 inch in diameter, but of insipid flavor.

One of the most delicious of all fruits grown in China is the Persimmon, Tsze-tzu (Diospyros kaki). The Persimmon tree is abundant up to 4000 feet altitude, and usually forms handsome specimens 60 feet or more tall. The fruit may be ovoid or flattened-round, and with or without seeds. It is not really edible until dead ripe, at which stage all the tannic acid is dissipated or changed into sugar. The Chinese have various methods of ripening this fruit to bring out its full flavor. The process, in the main, consists in stratifying and covering them with rice-husks and admitting only a modicum of air. Persimmons are often allowed to remain on the trees long after the leaves have fallen, and the masses of orange-colored fruits on such trees present a wonderful sight.

In the neighborhood of Lu Chou the Litchi (Nephelium litchi) and the Longan (N. longana) are cultivated as orchard fruits. They thrive very well in this district, and the fruits command high prices in the market. The Chinese Olive (Canarium album) is also grown in the same locality. In the arid river valleys of the west the Chinese Date-plum, T'sao-tzu (Zizyphus vulgaris), is frequently cultivated, but the quality of the fruit is poor, and cannot compare in size and flavor with that produced in Shantung and other parts of northeastern China. In the warmer parts the Pomegranate, Tsze-niu (Punica granatum), is commonly met with, but the fruit is scarcely edible. In Yunnan very fair Pomegranates are grown. Although widely spread and naturalized in parts of China, competent authorities consider the Pomegranate to have been introduced there.

Grapes, Chia-p'u-tao, are sparingly cultivated in the west, but the quality is very inferior to those grown around Peking. The only kind I have seen has white fruit. The varieties commonly cultivated are all

MANDARIN ORANGE-TREE LADEN WITH FRUIT

forms of Vitis vinifera, which, according to Bretschneider, was introduced into China from western Asia during the second century B.C. Around Kiukiang the Spiny Vitis, P'u-tao-tzu (Vitis davidii), is sometimes cultivated. This vine produces black, globose grapes of good size and appearance, but the flavor is very harsh. It occurs as a common wild plant in the mountains of the west.

The Walnut, Hei-tao (Juglans regia), is an exceedingly common tree cultivated throughout the regions with which we are concerned, ranging up to 8500 feet altitude. It is especially abundant in the arid river valleys of west Szechuan, and equally so in the mountains and valleys of Hupeh. The nuts vary considerably in size, shape, and in the thickness of the shell. The best are of large size and have very thin shells. They are valued not only as a food but for their sweet-oil, which is expressed and used for culinary purposes. A Butternut, Yeh hei-tao (J. cathayensis), is also common in the woods and thickets. The kernels are eaten, but the shell is very thick and difficult to crack.

The seed of the Maidenhair-tree, Peh-k'o (Ginkgo biloba), after being roasted is esteemed as a dessert nut. The seed of the Lotus Lily, Lien hwa (Nelumbium speciosum), Ground-nut, Lao-hua-tsen (Arachis hypogaea), are similarly valued. The Water-chestnut, Ling-chio (Trapa natans), is abundantly cultivated and the fruit is eaten.

In the woods and thickets many kinds of wild fruits are found which are eaten locally. Brambles (Rubus) in great variety occur, over 100 species being recorded from China. The majority yield edible fruit, and in some cases this is superior to that found elsewhere in the world. I succeeded in introducing about 30 species, and look forward to the day when some one will seriously take up the culture of Brambles and by hybridizing them evolve a new race of berries to add to the soft fruits at present in cultivation. The three best of the new introductions, according to my own palate, are Rubus pileatus, R. amabilis, and R. corchorifolius, all vinous flavored, raspberry-like fruits. The black fruits of R. omeiensis and R. flosculosus are also good eating, as are the orange or red colored fruits of R. biflorus quinqueflorus, R. innominatus, and R. ichangensis. At Ichang in early spring the raspberry-like fruit of R. parvifolius is commonly on sale, being locally

FRUITS, WILD AND CULTIVATED

known as Ts'ai-yang-p'ao-tzu. (The term P'ao-tzu is comprehensive, covering berries generally). At Sungpan in August it is possible to secure fruit of the dwarf R. xanthocarpus in quantity for a few cash pieces.

In the mountains during June and July wild strawberries are plentiful, and the fruit is of delicious flavor. Two kinds occur — the white-fruited Hautboy, Ti-p'ao-tzu (Fragaria elatior), and the red-fruited She-p'ao-tzu (F. filipendula). At Tachienlu, where cream from yak milk is obtainable, I have enjoyed many a dish of strawberries and cream, and also strawberry pie. By the roadsides the Indian Strawberry (F. indica), also called She-p'ao-tzu, is every-where abundant up to 3000 feet altitude. The brightly-colored but flavorless fruit of this plant is considered poisonous by the Chinese.

In the woods species of Currant (Ribes) with both red and black fruit are common. One species (R. longeracemosum) bears large, black fruit of good flavor, on racemes 11/2 foot long. This plant is now in cultivation, and should be utilized as a parent by the hybridist. A Gooseberry (R. alpestre giganteum) is a common hedge-plant throughout the Chino-Thibetan borderland between 8000 and 11,000 feet altitude. The small, round, green-colored fruit is, however, extremely harsh in flavor. A Strawberry-tree, Yang-mei, is common in the margins of woods and thickets between 2000 to 6000 feet altitude, throughout Hupeh, and less so in western Szechuan. The flattened-round red fruit is rough on the exterior, very juicy, and of fair flavor. In the above region the tree so named is Cornus kousa chinensis. In Yunnan the vernacular name is applied to C. capitata, an allied species, but in southeastern China the Yang-mei is Myrica rubra, a relative of our Sweet Gale, and belonging to a widely different family.

A climber, called Yang-tao in Hupeh and Mao-erh-tao in Szechuan (Actinidia chinensis), is very abundant from 2500 to 6000 feet altitude. It produces excellent fruit of a roundish or oval shape, 1 inch to 21/2 inches long, with a thin, brown, often hairy skin covering a luscious green flesh. This is an excellent dessert fruit, and makes fine preserve. In 1900 I had the pleasure of introducing this fruit to the foreign residents of Ichang, with whom it found immediate favor, and is now known throughout the Yangtsze valley as the Ichang gooseberry. I also was privileged to introduce it into European cultivation, and it fruited in England for the first time in 1911. This valuable climber has, in addition to its edible fruit, ornamental foliage and shoots, and large, fragrant flowers, white fading to buff-yellow. It is a good garden plant; the only drawback is that the flowers are polygamous, and it is necessary to secure the hermaphrodite form to insure fruit. Several other species of Actinidia yield edible fruits of fair flavor, one of the best being A. rubricaulis, which is now also in cultivation.

The Chinese eat the white inner pulp of the pod-like, blue-purple fruits of several species of Holbcellia; these plants known as Pa-yueh-cha are stout climbers. The teat-like fruits of several species of Elxagnus, known as Yang-mu-nai-tzu, are also eaten. These have a rather pleasant acid flavor, but are usually astringent in character. The fleshy, thickened fruitstalks of Hovenia dulcis, called Kuai-tsao, are eaten to annul the effects of wine.

Sweet Chestnut trees are abundant in the woods up to 7500 feet altitude, and excellent nuts, known as Pan-li, are produced. Three species occur, one of the most common and widely diffused being Castanea mollissima. As scrub on the hills up to 3500 feet altitude, the Chinese Chinquapin, Mao pan-li (C. Seguinii), is very abundant. Bushes only 2 feet tall produce quantities of small, good-flavored nuts, but the finest are from bushes 5 to 8 feet tall. The best eating chestnuts are, however, those of C. Henryi. This species makes a large tree from 60 to 80 feet tall, and has glabrous leaves and a single ovoid nut within each spiny fruit. It is very distinct from all the other members of its family The acorns of several kinds of Oak and the nuts of different species of Castanopsis are also eaten by the peasants. This is true of different Hazel-nuts, Shan-peh-k'o (Corylus spp.), and Beech-nuts (Fagus spp.).

A Nut Pine (Pinus armandi) is abundant on the mountains from 3500 to 9000 feet, and the seeds are eaten locally. These seeds, however, are not much sought after, and are far from having the economic importance of the Korean Nut Pine (P. koraiensis).

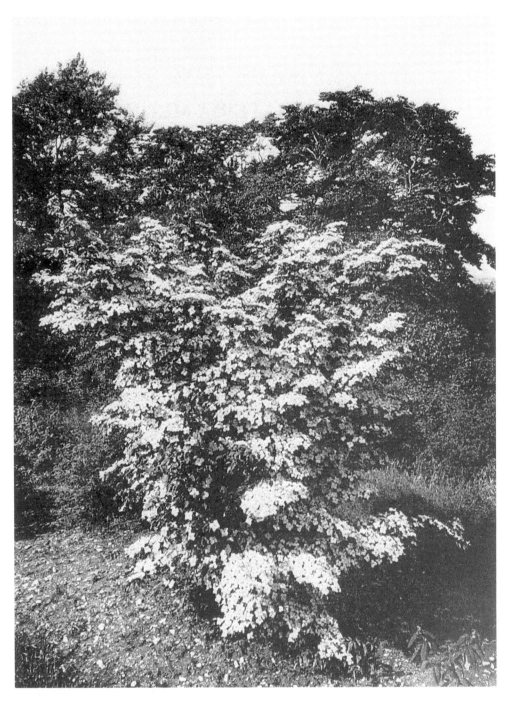

CHINESE DOGWOOD (CORNUS KOUSA CHINENSIS)

CHAPTER XXIV

CHINESE MATERIA MEDICA

ATIVE practitioners in China have very crude ideas of human anatomy, and to be able to read the pulse is proof positive of medical skill. Certain foreign drugs like quinine are highly esteemed, but on the whole the faith of the people is in native medicines. Inoculation for smallpox has long been practiced, so also has acupuncture for rheumatism, and the value of mercury for certain diseases is well known and largely employed. The Chinese materia medica is probably the most varied and comprehensive known. It includes all sorts of most extraordinary things, ranging from tiger bones to bat's dung, and worse. It is, however, principally herbal, and the majority of plants found in China are considered to possess medicinal properties to a greater or less extent. Of all this vast array only rhubarb and liquorice have any real value in Occidental practice. The majority of Chinese drugs are supposed to possess tonic and aphrodisiac properties, and the higher a drug is estimated in these respects the greater its commercial value, as witness ginseng and deer-horns in velvet.

The Father of Chinese medicine is the Emperor Shen-nung, who, according to legend, ruled from 273 7-269 7 B.C. This same Emperor is also the god of agriculture. We are told that Shen-nung went very deeply into the study of herbs, in order to find remedies for the diseases of his people. He is said to have been very successful in his investigations. As an example of his energetic pursuit of this study, it is declared that in one day he discovered 70 poisonous plants and as many antidotes. Tradition is also responsible for the native belief that he had a glass covering to his stomach, in consequence of which he could watch the process of digestion of each herb and mark its influence on the system. A pharmacopoeia, said to have been written by him, formed the nucleus of the Pun-tsao or Herbal, a great work on Chinese materia medica. In every druggist's shop of repute there is an image of Shennung, and he is looked upon as the presiding deity of the business.

The Herbal above referred to was published about A.D. 1590; its compiler, one Li Shi-chin, spent 30 years in collecting the information. He consulted some 800 previous authors, from whose writings he selected 1518 prescriptions, and added 374 new ones, arranging his materials in 52 chapters in a methodical and (for his day) scientific manner. The work, which is usually bound in 40 octavo volumes, was well received, and attracted the notice of the Emperor, who ordered several succeeding editions to be published at the expense of the state. It was, in fact, so great an advance on all previous books, that it checked future writers in that branch, and Li is likely now to be the first and last Chinese critical writer on natural science in his mother tongue.

Many curious statements naturally occur in this extensive old work. For example: "The heart of a white horse, or that of a hog, cow, or hen, when dried and rasped into spirit, and so taken, cures forgetfulness." "Above the knees the horse has night-eyes (warts), which enable him to go in the night; they are useful in the toothache." Another is: "If a man be restless and hysterical when he wishes to sleep, and it is requisite to put him to rest, let the ashes of a skull be mingled with water and given him, and let him have a skull for a pillow and it will cure him."

Some very extraordinary remedies are practiced today. For example: human milk is supposed to give strength to enfeebled old age. It is considered a meritorious filial act for daughters, granddaughters, and others to thus succur their aged relatives. In Chungking in 1908 an extraordinary case came to my knowledge. A native doctor informed a young woman that the only way to save her mother's life was to administer to her a portion of human liver. This daughter took a large knife and deliberately plunged it into her own body and cut away a portion of her liver. Dr. Asmy, a noble, self-sacrificing German doctor, working among the Chinese in Chungking, was informed of the case immediately after it took place, and succeeded in saving the self-mutilated woman's life. Dr. Asmy had the piece of liver preserved in spirit and kept as a memento in his hospital. Among the Chinese soldiers of the old school it was firmly believed that to eat the heart of a brave enemy was a sure way of obtaining the courage he possessed.

These nauseating and nonsensical ideas, however, are not all taken from the Chinese Herbal, and much as we may feel disposed to smile at the advice contained in this work, it is well to remember that Western literature on medicine of the same period contains very much the same sort of instruction. In Europe as late as the end of the sixteenth century, plants were looked upon from a purely utilitarian point of view, not alone by the masses, but by many professed scholars. Just as men lived in the firm belief that human destinies depended upon the stars, so they clung to the notion that everything upon the earth was created for the sake of mankind. In particular they thought that in every plant there were forces lying dormant which, if liberated, would conduce either to the welfare or injury of man. People imagined they discerned magic in many plants, and even believed that they were able to trace in the resemblance of certain leaves, flowers, and fruits to parts of the human body, an indication emanating from supernatural powers, of the manner in which the organ in question was intended to affect the human constitution. The similarity in shape between a particular foliage-leaf and the liver did duty for a sign that the leaf was capable of successful application in cases of hepatic disease, and the fact of a blossom being heart-shaped must mean that it would cure cardiac complaints. Thus arose the so-called Doctrine of Signatures, which, brought to its highest development by the Swiss alchemist, Bombastus Paracelsus (1493-1541), played a great part in the sixteenth and seventeenth centuries, and still survives at the present day in the mania for nostrums.

In ancient Greece there was a special guild, the Rhizotomoi, whose members collected and prepared such roots and herbs as were considered to be curative, and either sold them themselves or caused them to be sold by apothecaries. The Medicine Guild in China today performs much the same work, and its origin is long anterior to the Greek Rhizotomoi. If, then, Chinese pharmacology is today several

MEDICINAL RHUBARB (RHEUM OFFICINALE) CULTIVATED AND IN FLOWER centuries behind that of the Occident, there was a time when it was equally far in front. Marco Polo makes many references to the value of Chinese drugs. For example: All over the mountains of the province of Tangut, rhubarb is found in great abundance, and thither merchants come to buy it, and carry it thence all over the world."

All parts of the Chinese Empire contribute something to the native pharmacy, but, with the exception of ginseng, cassia-bark, camphor, and areca-nut, nearly all the more highly valued drugs come from the forests and scrub-clad highlands of the west. The famous drug, ginseng, the root of Aralia quinquefolia, comes from Korea and Manchuria, and the best quality sells for its weight in gold. To the Chinese this drug is the radix vitoe, restoring strength, vitality, and power to old and young. So precious is this life-giving root that the best plants are, in theory, reserved entirely for the Emperor's use. On the Chinese system this drug unquestionably acts as a strong restorative, tonic, and aphrodisiac, adverse Western opinion notwithstanding. In the forests of the west certain bastard ginsengs occur, but are little valued.

Cassia-lignea, the bark, buds, and leaves of Cinnamomum cassia, comes from certain districts (Luk-po, Lo-ting), in Kwangtung and (Tai-wu) in Kwangsi, provinces in the south, where it is largely cultivated and exported to all parts of the Empire and elsewhere. Cassia-bark (Kuei-pi) is valued as a tonic, stimulant, and condiment. Areca-nut, the seed of a palm (Areca catechu), occurs in the above southern provinces, and also in Yunnan. It is also imported from Cochin-China. Betel-chewing is not in general vogue among the Chinese, who value the nuts more as a medicine (chiefly as an astringent and anthelmintic).

Camphor is in general use all over China. The most valued kind is the Baros Camphor (Dryobalanops camphora), imported from Malaysia (Borneo), the camphor produced in Formosa, and Fokien from Cinnamomum camphora being less esteemed, and chiefly valued for purposes of export to other parts of the world. The Chinese values Baros Camphor as a tonic and aphrodisiac.

The Maritime Customs officials have paid considerable attention to Chinese medicines, and in 1889 a list was published by order of the Inspector-General, the late Sir Robert Hart. This list was compiled from the returns of each treaty port, and an attempt was made therein to identify the plants yielding the drugs and to give their province of origin. The difficulties besetting such a task were enormous, but much good work was accomplished. Consul-General Hosie, in his Report on the Province of Ssuch'uan, compiled a list of Szechuan medicines which very accurately represents the present state of our knowledge on this subject. Not until a complete collection of herbarium material covering flowers and fruits is made, and the whole submitted for identification to some one or other of the great herbaria in Europe, will it be possible to assign correct scientific names to a vast number of these medicines.

Hosie's list comprises 220 different kinds, of which number 189 are of vegetable origin. The trade importance of drugs is enormous; the exports passing through the Maritime Customs, at the port of Chungking, in 1910, being valued at over Tls. 1,540,000; those from Hankow at over Tls. 1,780,000.

I do not propose entering into a detailed account of the Chinese medicines, but will briefly note a few of the more important and their uses, which may not be without interest. Perhaps the most allround useful drug known from China is rhubarb, Ta-huang. The Rhubarb plant occurs throughout the highlands of the Chino-Thibetan border-land, but, as in the days of Marco Polo, the best comes from the "Province of Tangut." This region stretches from Sungpan in a northwesterly direction, and includes part of the modern province of Kansu. Rhubarb is found growing amongst scrub and near rocky watercourses between 7500 feet and 12,500 feet altitude. It is commonly cultivated, but the wilding is esteemed the best drug. The finest rhubarb is obtained from the plant known botanically as Rheum palmatum tanguticum, and this is the variety most commonly met with throughout the extreme northwest of China and the contiguous Thibetan regions. From Tachienlu are exported considerable quantities of a second-grade rhubarb, which is mainly derived from R. officinale, although the variety tanguticum also occurs sparingly in that neighborhood. Other species of Rheum grow in the west, and are used as adulterants. In northwestern Hupeh R. officinale occurs in the forests, and is also cultivated by the peasants, but the quality of the drug is very poor. The so-called Tangut regions enjoy a dry, sunny climate, and curing the drug is a much easier task than in the other districts mentioned. This also probably affects the quality. In China, rhubarb is valued as a purgative, and is employed in the same way as in the Occident.

The best liquorice, Kan-tsao (Sweet-herb), is also a product of the grasslands northwest of Sungpan; inferior kinds grow elsewhere in China. The source of the Sungpan product has been identified as Glycyrrhiza uralensis. It is valued as an emollient, and small quantities enter into nearly every prescription intended for internal application. The drug known in the vernacular as Ch'ung-tsao is a caterpillar infested with the mycelium and the project fructification of a fungus (Cordyceps sinensis). This is another valued product of the western uplands, where it is found at from 12,000 to 15,000 feet altitude. The body of the caterpillar is yellowish, the fructification of the fungus black, the two together being stick-like in appearance and about 5 inches in length. As a medicine it is esteemed for a variety of purposes—boiled with pork it is employed as an antidote for opium-poisoning, and as a cure for opium-eating; also with pork and chicken it is taken as a tonic and mild stimulant by convalescent persons and rapidly restores them to health and strength.

The tiny white bulbs of the Fritillary (Fritillaria roylei, and other allied species), known as Pei-mu or Jen Pei-mu, constitute one of the mostly highly valued medicines from the alpine regions of the west, where the plants grow at from 12,000 to 15,000 feet altitude. Large quantities of this drug are exported from Monkong Ting and Tachienlu. The bulbs are pounded, then boiled with dried orange-skin and sugar. The resultant is taken as a cure for tuberculosis and asthma. In Hupeh the pseudo-bulbs of two terrestrial Orchids, Pleione pogoniotdes and P. henryi, are used for the same purpose, and are known as Ch'uan Pei-mu. These plants grow on moist, humus-clad rocks in the woods between 3000 to 5000 feet altitude.

In clearings in the woods throughout western Hupeh and on

CHINESE MATERIA MEDICA

Mount Omei plantations of Huang-lien (Coptis chinensis) are maintained as a profitable investment. The dried rhizome is an all-round medicine, and particularly valued as a stomachic. An infusion is considered a cure for dyspepsia; used by women nursing children, it is said to promote the flow of milk; pounded and mixed with the white of eggs it is applied as a poultice to boils. Personally I can testify that it makes an excellent and appetizing bitters.

The thickened roots of a number of umbelliferous plants are esteemed for their medicinal virtues, as tonics and blood purifiers generally. One in general use and commonly cultivated is Tang-kuei (Angelica polymorpha sinensis). An extract obtained by boiling the root-stock of Platycodon grandiflorum, a campanulaceous plant known locally as Chieh-k'eng, is a cure for chill in the stomach. The small pods of Gleditsia officinalis, Ya-tsao, sliced and boiled with Tang-kuei, forms an infusion which is considered a certain cure for coughs and colds.

For medicinal purposes an Aconite, Tsao-w'tu (Aconitum wilsonii), is much cultivated, the powdered root being mixed with the white of eggs and applied externally as a remedy for boils. The Ch'uan-wu-tu (A. hemsleyanum, and other climbing species) has uses similar to the foregoing. Also after frequent boilings the root is used in minute quantities as a drastic cure for coughs. Another twining herb, Tang-shen (Codonopsis tangshen), is commonly cultivated in the mountains, the thickened root-stock being valued as an all-round tonic.

The barks of many trees are used in medicine, and the identification of these is not so difficult as in the case of herbs. One of the most esteemed is Hou-p'o (Magnolia officinalis). The best quality bark is worth 1000 cash per ounce. An extract is taken as a tonic, aphodisiac, and certain cure for colds, all in one. The dried flower-buds of this tree, called Yu-p'o, yield an extract on boiling which is taken by women to correct irregularities of menstruation.

The bark of Eucommia ulmoides, Tu-chung or Tsze-mien, is pounded and boiled, the extract being taken with wine and pork as a cure for troubles of the kidney, liver, and spleen. It is also supposed to be a diuretic and aphrodisiac, and is a valuable all-round tonic. The bark of Picrasma quassioides, Ku-lien-tzu, yields, on boiling, an extract which is used in cases of colic and pains in the stomach generally; also as a febrifuge. The bark of Phellodendron chinense, Huang-po or Huang-peh, is a complete materia medica in itself, it being used internally and externally as a general remedy for almost every ailment known to the Chinese, and, being cheap, is a poor man's cure-all.

These selected examples, although few in number, are perhaps sufficient for the purpose of this chapter. Undoubtedly many of the drugs used by the Chinese possess sound medicinal properties, and their proper investigation is well worth the attention of Occidental pharmaceutists.

CHAPTER XXV

GARDENS AND GARDENING

FAVORITE FLOWERS CULTIVATED BY THE CHINESE

RNAMENTAL gardening has been practiced in China from immemorial time, and the people are endowed with an innate love for flowers and gardens. Floral calendars are kept in every house above the poorest, and volumes of poems have been written in praise of the Moutan Paony, Camellia, Plum, Chrysanthemum, Lotus-lily, Bamboo, and other plants. The appearance of the blooms on the more conspicuous flowering shrubs is eagerly watched for, and excursions into the country are taken to enjoy the sight of the first bursting into blossom of favorite trees The dwelling of the poorest peasant is usually enlivened by an odd plant or two, and the courtyard of the shopkeeper and innkeeper always boasts a few flowers of one sort or another. The temple grounds are frequently very beautitful, and attached to the houses of the cultured and wealthy are gardens often of great interest. In the neighborhood of wealthy cities like Soochou, Hanchou, and Canton, are public and private gardens which are famed throughout the length and breadth of China. The finest example I have seen is fittingly associated with the summer palace, a few miles outside Peking. There Chinese gardening may be seen at its best, and it calls forth admiration from all visitors.

Chinese landscape-gardening is represented at its best in the so-called Japanese gardens of today. The Japanese have undoubtedly carried the art to higher state of perfection than the Chinese, but the latter unquestionably originated it. In all these gardens the love of the grotesque predominates, and the landscape effect is essentially artificial; yet in accordance with their own ideals the Chinese are most skillful and accomplished gardeners. Given a piece of ground, no matter if it be

CHINA — MOTHER OF GARDENS

small, and devoid of all natural beauty, or badly situated, they will patiently transform it into a mountain-landscape in miniature. With strange-looking, weather-worn rocks, dwarfed trees, bamboos, herbs, and water, a piece of countryside is evolved replete with mountain and stream, forest and field, plateau and lake, grotto and dell. A network of narrow winding paths traverses the garden, and rustic bridges in various designs are thrown across the infantine streams. The whole effect is often encompassed within a comparatively few square yards, though the perspective is one of seemingly many miles. In all the larger gardens, closely associated with and usually in part overhanging a pool where the Lotus-lily is grown, a small pavilion is erected. Here the proprietor and his guests resort to drink tea or wine, chat, and admire the various flowers. When no male guests are present the garden is frequented by the female members of the family, with whom it is ever a favorite sanctum.

The Chinese do not cultivate a very great variety of plants, and the contents of the various gardens are much the same, though necessarily the selection is modified by climate and locality. To all the flowers grown in Chinese gardens some peculiar significance or aesthetic value is attached. An Orchid (Cymbidium ensifolum), called Lan hwa, is regarded as the king of flowers, the modest appearance of the plant, and the delicate odor of its blossoms, representing the very essence of refinement. The Mei hwa (Prunus mume), owing to the beauty and perfume of its flowers, which are produced in winter when few plants are in blossom, is very highly prized and regarded as a flower of refinement. Around Peking the same vernacular name and attributes are attached to P. triloba and its double-flowered form. The Wintersweet, La-mei hwa (Meratia praecox), is similarly esteemed.

The various Bamboos, emblems of grace and culture, and beautiful at all seasons of the year, are indispensable garden plants. "No man can live without a Bamboo tree in the immediate vicinity of his house, but he can live without meat," is a favorite Taouist saying. The Chrysanthemum (Chu hwa) and Moutan Paeony are other flowers of refinement almost reverently appreciated for the color and beautiful form of their flowers. The Lotus-lily, Lien hwa (Nelumbium

WINTERGREEN (XYLOSMA RACEMOSUM PUBESCENS), 55 FEET TALL

speciosum), is regarded as an emblem of purity, and the Goddess of Mercy (Kwanyin) is always represented seated in the centre of a Lotus flower. The Chinese Luck Lily or Water Fairy (Narcissus tazetta) is cultivated in vast quantities, more especially throughout the eastern part of the Empire, and is in blossom for the New Year festival. It is appreciated for its odoriferous flowers, and its luxurious growth is considered prophetic of wealth and prosperity. This Narcissus is not a Chinese plant, but is a native of the Mediterranean region, from whence it was long ago introduced into China by Portuguese traders, and it, together with the Pomegranate, are virtually the only exotic flowers in high favor with the Chinese.

The Pearl Orchid, Chu-lan hwa (Chloranthus inconspicuus) is valued for the delicate odor of its flowers, which are used in the Anhui province in scenting green teas for the Chinese market. Table grass (Liriope spicata) is admired for its graceful habit, and is placed on a desk or table, to afford rest to the eyes when reading or studying. Lastly in this relation may be mentioned the Hoary Pine, which is emblematical of revered old age. This name is applied to several kinds of Conifers other than Pinus proper.

To complete the list of favorite Chinese flowers we may enumerate Camellia, Heavenly Bamboo, Tien-ch'u (Nandina domestica), Kuei hwa (Osmanthus fragrans), Tzu-ching (Lagerstroemia indica), Tiao-chung (Enkianthus quinqueflorus), Chin-yin hwa (Lonicera japonica), numerous varieties of Azaleas, Roses, Balsams, and Boxwood (Buxus microphylla sinica). Some or all of the above are to be found in every Chinese garden of note. Though the cultured skill expended on many of them is in the direction of dwarfing and training into grotesque shapes, this treatment in no sense robs the flowers of the qualities attributed to them in literature and song. The decoration found on Chinese porcelain well illustrates the nation's love of beautiful flowers and quaint-shaped trees.

China is a land of contrariety —a land whereof no general statement or observation holds good. In spite of their love for the grotesque and the artificial landscapes seen in their gardens, the Chinese have a strong appreciation of natural beauty. This is evidenced

GARDENS AND GARDENING

by the sites chosen for their temples and shrines and for the tombs of the wealthy. Apart from situation, which is usually perfect, such sanctuaries always nestle beneath the shade of magnificent trees, and are approached as a rule through avenues or groves of large trees. Though a few deciduous trees are commonly found, evergreens always have distinctive preference. In the temple grounds around Peking are noble avenues of Juniper (Juniperus chinensis), Elm (Ulmus pumila), and Sophora (S. japonica); in the south, centre, and west of the Empire, Pine (Pinus massoniana), China Fir (Cunninghamia lanceolata), Cypress (Cupressus funebris), Nanmu (Phoebe nanmu and allied species), Yu-la shu (Photinia davidsoniae), Wintergreen (Xylosma racemosum), Banyan (Ficus infectoria), and a few other kinds of trees are always present. Many of these species are extremely rare, except in the precincts of religious sanctuaries.

The world at large does not realize how deeply it is indebted to religious communities for the preservation of many trees. In Europe, for example, most of the best varieties of Pears originated in the gardens attached to religious establishments in France and Belgium and were introduced into England and other countries after the battle of Waterloo. In China, where every available bit of land is devoted to agriculture, quite a number of trees must long ago have become extinct but for the timely intervention of Buddhist and Taouist priests. The most noteworthy example of this benevolent preservation is the Maidenhair-tree (Ginkgo biloba). This strikingly beautiful tree is associated with temples, shrines, courtyards of palaces, and mansions of the wealthy throughout the length and breadth of China, and also in parts of Japan. But it is nowhere truly wild, and is a relic of a very ancient flora. Geological evidence shows that it is the last survivor of an ancient family, which flourished during secondary times, and can even be traced back to the primary rocks. In mesozoic times this genus played an important part in the arborescent flora of north-temperate regions. Fossil remains, almost identical with the present existing species, have been found, not only in North America and Europe, but also in Greenland.

Though today Chinese gardens, nurseries, and temple grounds

335

do not contain anything new in the way of ornamental or economic plants, it was otherwise up to the middle of the last century. Our early knowledge of the Chinese flora was based on plants procured from gardens, notably from those around Canton. The plants were brought to Europe by trading vessels, especially those of the East India Company, at the end of the eighteenth and early in the nineteenth centuries. Different patrons of horticultural and botanical institutions in England lent financial assistance, and collectors were dispatched to investigate and send home all that they could possibly find.

By these means our gardens first secured the early varieties of Roses, Camellias, Azaleas, Greenhouse Primroses, Gardenias, Moutan Paeonies, Chrysanthemums, China Asters, and such-like familiar plants. The Chrysanthemum, for instance, has been cultivated in China and Japan from immemorial time, and its parent forms (Chrysanthemum sinense and C. indicum) are common wild flowers around Ichang and elsewhere in China. In Europe C. sinense was first cultivated in Dutch gardens as early as 1689, no less than six kinds being then known. But these were subsequently lost, and when the plant was again introduced in 1789, through the agency of Sir Joseph Banks, the plant was unknown to Dutch gardeners. The famous gardener, Philip Miller, cultivated C. indicum in the Chelsea Physic Gardens in 1764, it having been discovered in 1751, near Macao, south China, by Osbeck. This species has, however, had much less to do in the evolution of our present-day Chrysanthemum than has C. sinense.

The parent of our Tea Roses (Rosa odorata), and China Monthly Rose (R. chinensis), long cultivated in China and still to be found wild in the central and western parts of the Empire. They were introduced into England through the efforts of Sir Joseph Banks in 1789. The parent of our greenhouse Primroses (Primula sinensis) was introduced from Canton into the garden of Thomas Palmer, Esq., of Bromley, Kent, by John Reeves about 1820. A close relative (P. calciphila) is native of Hupeh, where it occurs in great abundance on the dry, precipitous, limestone cliffs of the Ichang gorge and its lateral glens. This wilding is a true perennial with flowers a uniform mauve-pink color. Another greenhouse Primrose (P. obconica) occurs in the

GARDENS AND GARDENING

same region but in moist loamy situations.

The so-called Indian and Mollis Azaleas and a score of other favorite plants of our gardens all came originally from Chinese gardens through various agencies. It is true we have developed most of these introductions almost beyond recognition, and the Chinese are now acquiring new forms and varieties from us, yet without these early arrivals how much poorer our gardens and conservatories would be today. In bygone times, even only about a century ago, that part of the world which we know as China was loosely spoken of as the Indies, and this geographical blunder is perpetuated in the specific name indica which botanists have attached to some of these plants. In the middle of last century many ornamental plants were received from the gardens of Japan, and botanists, assuming that these were natives of the country, gave the specific name japonica to certain of them. Subsequent knowledge has, however, conclusively proved that a number of the so-called Japanese plants are only cultivated forms of plants originally natives of China. Thus has the geographer and botanist unwittingly obscured China's right to be termed the Kingdom of Flowers.

CHAPTER XXVI

AGRICULTURE

THE PRINCIPAL FOODSTUFF CROPS

 HE Chinese might appropriately be termed a Nation of Shopkeepers, yet, in spite of their commercial enterprise, agriculture is the back-bone of the nation. With a vast population to support, every possible inch of land has been brought under cultivation, and prodigious efforts have been made to obtain the greatest returns from the soil. In spite of it all, millions are ever on the verge of starvation, and almost annually either drought or flood brings famine to some part of the country.

Landed property is held in clans or families as much as possible and is not entailed, nor are overgrown estates frequent. The land is all held directly from the government, no freehold being acknowledged. The conditions of common tenure are the payment of an annual tax, the fee for alienation, with a money composition for personal service to the government. The proprietors of land record their names in the district and take out an original deed (called red deed) which secures them in possession as long as the ground tax is paid. This sum varies very much according to the fertility, location, and nature of the land, but is nowhere heavy or severe. Naturally, good rice-land pays the heaviest tax. The paternal estate, and the property thereon, descends to the eldest son, but his brothers can remain upon it with their families and devise their portion in perpetuo to their children, or an amicable composition may be made; daughters never inherit, nor can an adopted son of another clan succeed. A mortgagee must enter into possession of property and make himself responsible for the payment of taxes levied thereon. The enclosure of recent alluvial deposits cannot be made without the cognizance of the authorities, but the terms in such cases

338

AGRICULTURE

are not onerous. When waste hillsides and poor areas are brought under cultivation ample time is allowed for a return of the capital expended in reclaiming them before assessment is made.

Since the food-supply of the Chinese population has always been supplied from within the Empire, agriculture has rightly been accorded first place among all branches of labor from immemorial time. According to legend, the Emperor Shen-nung (273 7-269 7 B.C.) established agriculture as a science. He examined the various kinds of soils and gave directions as to what should be cultivated in each. He taught the people how to make ploughs, and instructed them in the best methods of husbandry. Immediate results were seen in the improved conditions of the people, and succeeding generations have amply testified their gratitude to him. Under the title of Prince of Cereals he has long since been deified, and is worshipped throughout the length and breadth of the land. In Peking there is an altar dedicated to him, enclosed within a large park. Formerly, at the vernal equinox, the ruling Emperor, assisted by various officials, performed an annual commemorative ceremony of ploughing a portion of the park.

The Chinese nation is to a very large extent vegetarian, flesh being eaten only in small quantities except on festival occasions. Pork, chickens, ducks, and fish comprise the meat-diet, and of these the Chinese are excessively fond, but to the great majority they are luxuries, only to be indulged in on rare occasions. Rice is to them what wheat is to us, the staff of life. So long as the average Chinaman can get rice he is happy; but this would be scarcely true of ourselves if we could only get bread! Next to rice the more important food-stuffs are wheat, maize, pulse, and cabbage. The Chinese fry most of their vegetables, and for this purpose a vegetable oil is nearly always used. The oils expressed from the seeds of members of the Cabbage family, the Soy Bean (Glycine hispida), and Sesame (Sesamum indicum), being most in request.

While the Chinese cultivate a great variety of vegetables the quality of one and all, judged by our standard of quality, is wretchedly inferior. With the exception of maize and sweet potatoes, it is safe to say that not a single Chinese vegetable would command attention in this country. In this chapter I have attempted a fairly exhaustive account of this subject, in so far as it came under my observation during the eleven years I travelled in China. These observations were limited mainly to three provinces, namely, Yunnan, Hupeh, and Szechuan. The estimated area of these territories is about 372,500 square miles—more than that of the Atlantic states from Maine to Georgia or of Texas, Arkansas and Mississippi. Other parts of China have vegetables peculiarly their own. Again, at the treaty ports, where foreigners have settled, varieties of our own vegetables have been introduced and are cultivated for their use. These, with rare exceptions, do not come within our province.

In China the fields are all so small that market-gardening rather than farming best describes the agricultural industry. Long experience has taught the people how to obtain the maximum returns without unduly exhausting the soil, indeed, the extraordinary thing about Chinese agriculture is the fact that, although cultivation has been so long in progress, the soil shows practically no sign of exhaustion. Artificial manures are unknown to the Chinese farmer, and ordinary farmyard manure is scarce and almost a negligible factor. Constant tillage, aided by as much sewage as is possibly obtainable, are relied upon to produce full crops. The sewage from cities and villages is carried long distances away in buckets or in tubs to the fields, and no-where else in the world is human excrement so highly valued or so laboriously collected. In matters of seed-selection, plant-breeding, and the higher arts of agriculture, the Chinese have everything to learn. Rotation of crops and the enrichment of the soil by leguminous crops they under-stand and practice as fully as circumstances permit.

Rice (Oryza sativa) is, of course, the favorite cereal, but being a tropical plant, requiring an aquatic habitat, its area of cultivation is restricted in China, and probably a third of the people never taste this grain save on festival occasions. In southern China two crops of rice are obtainable annually, but throughout the greater part of the land where this cereal is cultivated only one crop can be grown in a season. This occupies the ground from May until early in September.

In the cultivation of rice, the patience, ingenuity, and incredible

IRRIGATION WHEELS

CHINA — MOTHER OF GARDENS

industry of the Chinese are particularly well exemplified. The terraced fields necessary to ensure a flow of water, whether it be on a seemingly flat plain or on a steep hillside, meet the eye of the traveller on all sides. It is little short of marvellous when one reflects on the skillful way in which the entire rice-belt in China is terraced, and the enormous amount of time and labor involved in the undertaking indicate what a hard task-master necessity has been. In matters of irrigation the Chinese are past masters. They have not yet succeeded in making water run uphill, but with their various contrivances they lift it bodily from streams and ditches and convey it long distances to wherever it is needed. The number of devices for irrigation purposes is almost legion, and though simple in principle and efficacious in results they are intricate in detail. Some are operated by hand, others by the foot, and many are automatically worked by the current of the streams. The large skeleton-like water-wheels depicted in the photographic illustration opposite, represent one of the methods commonly in use in central and western China.

Rice-cultivation presents many tedious details and the layman will probably find it difficult to realize that in China the whole crop is planted by hand. The grain is sown thickly in nursery-beds, and when the seedlings are 5 to 6 inches tall they are transplanted in small clumps equidistant in the flooded, prepared fields. Men and women take part in this work and it is surprising how rapidly the fields are planted. The rice plants are made firm in the mud by treading around them immediately they are established. The fields are kept free of weeds and the requisite supply of water is maintained until, as the crop ripens, the fields are finally allowed to get dry. The rice crop is reaped by hand, and without being removed from the field the grain is at once beaten off into wooden bins; afterwards it is dried and stored. The Chinese cultivate three well-marked varieties of rice—namely, ordinary, red, and glutinose. The first two are grown for food only; the red, being the hardiest, is cultivated at higher altitudes than the other, but is by no means confined thereto. This Red Rice, Hung-me (O. sativa praecox), gets its name from the reddish color of the pellicle, which adheres tenaciously to parts of the grain after milling. Glutinose Rice (O. sativa

AGRICULTURE

glutinosa) does not take the place of the other two as a food, being only eaten for a change. It is valued for the weak spirit which is made from it, for sugar which is extracted from it, and for making into cakes and sweetmeats. It is later in ripening than the other varieties, and always commands a higher price in the market. In Yunnan a variety which will thrive without water is grown. This upland rice (O. sativa montana) yields but a poor crop and is very inferior.

Whilst the Chinese are preeminently a rice-eating race, it should be borne in mind that there are millions of Chinese who, save on rare occasions, never eat rice at all. To these people, wheat, maize, and buckwheat are the staple cereals. In the rice-growing districts of China, Wheat (Triticum sativum) is a winter crop, occupying the ground from October to early May. In the mountainous districts and in the colder provinces it is a most important summer crop. I have noted no fewer than five very distinct varieties, comprising both red and white wheats, and both awned and awnless kinds. In late August the mountain-sides and valleys in western Szechuan present a glorious picture of miles and miles of rolling grain fields. In this region 8000 to 10,500 feet represent the wheat-growing belt. The grain is sown by hand in rows, the seeds being dropped in clusters a few inches apart. In the Yangtsze valley, if the wheat crop is late in ripening, it is ploughed in to make way for rice. In the plains of central China the grain is threshed out the moment it is harvested. On the Thibetan borderland it is tied into sheaves and stacked, ears downward, on tall hurdle-like arrangements (Kai-kos) until time and weather admit of its being threshed. (This remark also applies to barley, oats, and other crops). The grain is ground into flour and made into cakes and vermicelli. Chinese flour is usually gritty and of bad color.

Barley is sparsely cultivated throughout the Yangtsze valley, and it is only in the mountainous Thibetan border-land that it is largely grown. The Chinese do not care for the meal, and the grain is chiefly used for making spirit and for feeding pigs and other domestic animals. The Thibetans, on the other hand, highly esteem barley. Roasted and ground into meal and mixed with tea and rancid butter it forms tsamba, their national and staple food. Since it is hardier than wheat its culture extends to a greater altitude; the highest point at which I noted it was 12,000 feet. Both Chinese and Thibetans cultivate several varieties, but the six-rowed species, Hordeum hexastichon, is most in favor. Around Sungpan a variety of the above, having purple paleae, is largely grown, being considered hardier than the type. This variety is apparently peculiar to these parts, being quite distinct from the two-ranked chocolate Barley (H. coeleste), which is cultivated in parts of the Himalaya. Ordinary Barley (H. vulgare) is cultivated in smaller quantities than the preceding kinds by Chinese and Thibetans. In Hupeh and in the river-valleys of western Szechuan I met with occasional patches of H. hexastichon trifurcatum. This variety is the Mi-me (Rice-wheat) of the Chinese.

On the mountains Rye (Secale fragile) is very sparingly grown and the grain eaten.

Oats are not much grown by the Chinese in the parts through which I travelled, but they are cultivated to a considerable extent by the Thibetan and other tribesmen in the highlands. The Chinese prefer Avena nuda, which they designate Yen-me; the Thibetans and tribesfolk favor Avena fatua. The grain of both these kinds is roasted and ground into oatmeal, or cooked and eaten whole.

Next to rice and wheat, Maize, or Pao-k'o (Zea Mays), is the most important cereal. This plant is of American origin, but it has been so long cultivated in China that the date of introduction is not ascertainable. In the rice-belt it is relegated to such land that is for one reason or another not suitable for rice. It is in the more mountainous parts that maize is the staple crop. It occupies the gullies and slopes of the mountains, and commonly so steep are these that one wonders how the people manage to sow and reap the crop. Wild pigs rob the maize fields, and when the crop is in ear the farmers beat gongs and make as much noise as possible during the night to scare these animals away. In open country tall thatched look-outs are erected, where the juvenile and female members of the family sit and watch for thieves during the daylight.

In the Yangtze valley maize is always a summer crop, and two crops are frequently harvested. In the mountains its cultivation extends up to 8000 feet, and in exception-ally favorable districts even higher. Green corn is a delicious vegetable, but the Chinese do not use it extensively in this form. When ripe the sheaths of the cobs are folded back, exposing the grain; they are then tied in bunches and suspended from the roofs of houses, where they can be kept dry. The grain is ground up and made into meal-cakes; it is also used for making spirit. From the culms sugar is some-times extracted, but their chief use is for fuel.

False Millet (Sorghum vulgare), the Kao-liang or Hsu-tzu of the Chinese, is largely used for making wine. It is cultivated generally throughout central and western China, but not so extensively as in the northern parts of China, and notably in Manchuria. The largest areas I noted were on the fluviatile areas of the Min and Fou rivers. Its altitudinal limit is about the same as that of maize, and, like the latter, it is always a summer crop. Two distinct varieties are grown, one with purple, the other with yellowish heads. It is occasionally employed as food, more particularly in the mountainous districts, but 90 per cent. of it is used for making wine.

Other Millets met with in cultivation are Panicum miliaceum, Chan-tzu; Setaria italica, Hsiu-ku; and Panicum crus-galli frumentaceum, Lungtsao-ku, but not in large quantities. The grain is used in making cakes and for feeding bird-pets. The cereal commonly known as Job's Tears, Ta-wan-tzu (Coix lachryma), is cultivated in small patches throughout central and western China. Though occasionally used as food in the form of gruel. Job's Tears are chiefly valued as medicine. They are supposed to possess tonic and diuretic properties, and are administered in cases of phthisis and dropsy.

Of Buckwheat two species are commonly cultivated, namely, Fagopyrum esculentum and F. tataricum, the T'ien-ch'iao-me and K'u-ch'iao-me respectively of the Chinese. These constitute a most important crop, especially in the highlands, and under favorable climatic conditions two crops are harvested in one season. A field of pink Buckwheat (F. esculentum) in flower is one of the prettiest sights imaginable. It is most commonly grown on terraced mountain-sides. The other species grows twice the height of the above, and bears greenish white flowers. The altitudinal limit of buckwheat equals and possibly exceeds that of barley. After the seeds are threshed out they are ground up in water, and the husks are removed by a fine sieve. The flour is then made into dough with a little salt, to which lime is added. This dough is made into vermicelli, when it is ready for cooking and eating. Buckwheat constitutes a most important article of food amongst the Chinese who live in the mountainous districts, and also with the tribesfolk of the borderland. It is a very accommodating crop, for it thrives on the poorest of soils, requires little attention beyond sowing and harvesting, and matures very quickly.

Since the Chinese are to such a large extent a vegetarian people, the various members of the pea and bean family are necessarily most important crops. The Common Pea, Me-wan-tzu (Pisum sativum), and Broad Bean (Vicia faba), with the Soy Bean (Glycine hispida), are the most important. The two former are winter crops in the valleys and summer crops in the highlands. The soy bean is everywhere a summer crop. Peas and broad beans are eaten both fresh and dried. They are also ground into flour and made into vermicelli. The young shoots of the pea are eaten as a vegetable. The soy bean, Huang-tou, is of even greater value than the preceding; it is planted everywhere—in fields by itself, around rice and other fields, and as an undercrop to maize and sorghum. It yields seeds of three colors, namely, yellow, green, and black. The Chinese distinguish three kinds of the yellow and two kinds each of the green and black. These varieties yield a succession of beans, the black being fully a month later than the other. The Huang-tou is cooked and eaten as a vegetable, or ground into flour and made into vermicelli; preserved in salt it makes an excellent pickle. It is also extensively used in the manufacture of soy sauce and soy vinegar. A variety with small yellow seeds is largely employed for making bean-curd. While in central and western China the soy bean is cultivated exclusively as a foodstuff, in Manchuria it is grown almost solely for the oil which is obtained from the seeds by pressure, and for the residual cakes that remain after the oil has been expressed. From Newchwang, the port of Manchuria, there is an enormous export trade done in bean-cake, which is in great demand as an agricultural fertilizer in all parts of

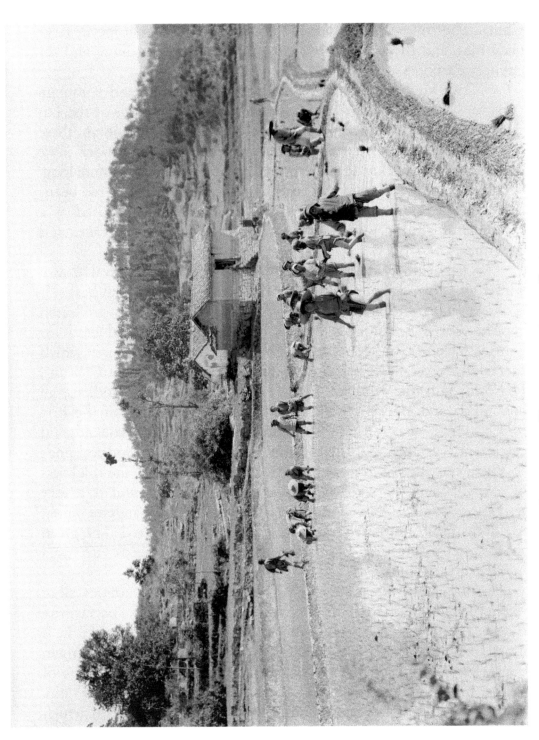

PEASANTS TRANSPLANTING RICE

CHINA — MOTHER OF GARDENS

China. The soy bean has recently been exported to Europe in large quantities, and the soy bean oil is employed in soap-making and for culinary purposes.

Two kinds of Gram, Phaseolus mungo, Lu-tou, and P. mungo radiates, Hung-tou, are grown as summer crops. The seeds of the Lu-tou (green bean) are especially valued for their sprouts. To obtain these the beans are put in jars with water and covered over. Under these conditions they quickly develop shoots a couple of inches or more long, which are highly esteemed as a vegetable. Of the Hung-tou (red bean) there are two or three varieties. The seeds of these are used as a vegetable or ground into flour and employed for stuffing cakes and sweetmeats.

The Lentil (Ervum lens), Chin-me-wan-tzu, is cultivated as a winter crop, being commonly associated with peas and broad beans. It is, however, by no means extensively grown. The seeds are eaten cooked. Oil is occasionally expressed from the seeds and used for lighting purposes. Other pulses are Dolichos lablab, Pien-tou, of which there are several varieties, Canavalia ensiformis (Sword Bean), Phaseolus vulgaris, Yun-tou, Vigna catiang, and Cajanus indicus, all commonly and extensively cultivated. Though the seeds of the first four are eaten, it is more for the pods, which are sliced, cooked, and eaten as a vegetable, that these plants are valued. The cylindrical pods of Vigna Catiang are from 1 ½ to 2 feet long, and about the thickness of a lead-pencil. Though the Chinese esteem it, I found it a very tasteless vegetable. As a winter crop in parts of the Yangtsze valley, Melilotus macrorhiza, Yeh-hua-tsen, is sparingly cultivated. The green shoots are sometimes eaten as a vegetable; the seeds are used medicinally for colds.

Of cabbages the Chinese have their own peculiar varieties, all of them very different from those grown in this country. The favorite variety, Peh-ts'ai, or Shantung cabbage, as foreigners have styled it, is more like a huge cos lettuce than a cabbage. This kind is grown everywhere, but attains its greatest perfection in the colder parts of China. In the Yangtsze valley it is best when grown as a winter crop. Another striking variety is the white-ribbed cabbage. Kin-ta-ts'ai, which is said to be peculiar to Szechuan. In addition to these some half-dozen other varieties are cultivated. Cabbages are eaten fresh or are preserved by salting and drying in the sun. From an American standpoint none is worth growing, being so very inferior in flavor to our own. The Roman Catholic priests have introduced the common European cabbage, but though its culture has spread widely the Chinese much prefer their own varieties. While the Chinese cabbages are all really referable to Brassica campestris, it is convenient to group them under B. chinensis. As a winter crop green kale, Kan-kan ts ai, and dark-red kale, Ts'ai-tai are cultivated through the Yangtsze valley. The young shoots of Brassica juncea and B. campestris oleifera, are also used in the same way as kale.

The Chinese cultivate a great many gourds for food, the whole cucurbitaceous family being known under the general name of Kua. Some are eaten raw, and others cooked. The male flowers, too, are eaten by the peasantry. The seeds of the water-melon are esteemed a great delicacy. They are slightly roasted, and are consumed in enormous quantities; no banquet is complete without them, and over their gossip in tea-shops or restaurants, scholars and coolies alike regale themselves with these delicious morsels. Preserved in sugar, melon-seeds form a favorite sweetmeat. As a summer crop throughout the Yangtsze valley the following cucurbitaceous plants are commonly cultivated: Cucurbita citrullus, Hsi-kua; C. pepo, Hsi-hu-lu; C. moschata, Huo-kua; C. maxima, Nan-kua; C. ovifera, Sunkua; Cucumis melo, Tien-kua; C. sativa, Huang-kua; Benincasa cerifera, Tung-kua; Lagenaria vulgaris clavata, Hu-tzu-kua; L. leucantha longis, Ts'ai-kua. When very young the fruit of Momordica charantia, Ku-kua, is eaten, and when old is used as medicine. Luffa cylindrica, Ssu-kua, is cooked and eaten when young; when old the fibre is esteemed as medicine. Lagenaria vulgaris, Hu-lu, is cultivated for its hard shells, which are converted into receptacles for holding water, oil, or wine. In addition to the above, several gourds are cultivated for their ornamental fruits, which are used for decorative purposes.

In the valleys and plains, and on the low hills bordering them throughout the Yangtsze valley and Yunnan, the Sweet Potato (Ipomoea batatas) is the most important root crop. The crop is always cultivated on ridges and is grown from both old tubers and cuttings. Tubers are planted out in May, and cuttings from the shoots of these are inserted in July and early August, and produce a fine crop in October and November. The crop from the old roots is ready in August. Sweet potatoes are eaten after being boiled, baked, and dried in chips, and constitute a truly delicious dish. As they deteriorate by keeping, they are cut into slices, scalded, and then dried in the sun. The tubers are also macerated in cold water, and the resultant starch dried and made into vermicelli. In Hupeh the sweet potato is known as the Hung-shao, in Szechuan as the Pen-shao.

In the mountainous districts the sweet potato is displaced by the Irish potato, or Yang-yu (Solanum tuberosum), which, like maize, is another plant of American origin that has become a most important crop. It was introduced by the Roman Catholic priests at the time of a great famine some sixty years ago. Its culture has spread enormously, and though it is despised by the rice-eating Chinese of the plains it has become a staple article of food with the highland peasantry. In the valleys it is cultivated as a late winter crop, in the mountains as a summer crop. Its culture is unfortunately but little understood; it is always grown too thickly, and seldom if ever properly earthed up. Both red and white-skinned varieties are grown, but the flavor is usually very poor. The potatoes cultivated by the Buddhist priests on Mount Omei are justly celebrated, but the best I ever ate in China were grown by Sifan tribesfolk around Sungpan.

Two kinds of Yam are commonly cultivated, namely, Dioscorea alata, the Chieh-pan-shao, which has enormously large, flat, branching tubers, and D. batatas, Pai-shao; both are cooked and eaten. Around Ichang the tubers of a third species are eaten. This species is known as D. zingiberensis, the Huang-chiang, or Yellow Ginger. The tuber is bitter, and is valued chiefly as a medicine. Chinese yams do not equal the sweet potato in flavor, and are not so extensively grown. Around Chengtu, Pachyrhizus angulatus, the Ti-kua, is commonly grown. The white, firm-fleshed, turnip-like tubers are eaten either raw or cooked.

White turnips, Lo-po, both the long and round kinds, are cultivated everywhere, but the flavor is very poor. Also the so-called red turnip, which really is a Radish (Raphanus sativus). All three are cooked and eaten when fresh, or preserved by being sliced and dried in the sun. Brassica napus esculenta, the Ta-t'ou-ts'ai, is very generally cultivated, but I met with it most frequently on the Chengtu plain. The whole plant is pickled and eaten with rice. The Szechuanese also cultivate most excellent Kohl-rabi (Brassica oleracea caulo-rapa).

Two aroids, Colocasia antiquorum and its variety Fon-tanesii, Kiang-tou, are very extensively cultivated for their tubers, which are cooked and eaten in various ways. Both are grown on ridges in flooded ground. The purple-colored petioles of the Kiang-tou are sliced, pickled, and eaten. The flavor of the tubers of these plants is similar to that of the Jerusalem artichoke, but inferior. Sagittaria sagittifolia, T'zu-ku, is cultivated in Szechuan and Yunnan, and the tubers are cooked and eaten in the same way as those of the Colocasia. The tubers of Scirpus tuberosus, P'ei-chi, and the fruits of the Water Chestnut (Trapa natans), Ling-chio, two very common aquatics, are esteemed as valuable articles of food.

The Lotus-lily (Nelumbium speciosum), Lien hwa, is cultivated both for its seed and its rhizome. These are used as food, but being expensive are luxuries enjoyed only by the wealthy. The fibres of the rhizome are used medicinally. Ginger (Zingiber officinale), Seng-chiang, is very extensively grown. It is prepared for the table in various ways. From Canton, ginger preserved in sugar is exported in quantity to this country. Amorphophallus konjac, Mo-yu, is sparingly cultivated throughout the Yangtsze valley. The tubers are ground up with water and made into a curd-like compound. On Mount Omei and in northwest Szechuan this plant is more generally cultivated. The bulbs of Lilium tigrinum, the Chia-peh-ho, are highly esteemed, and occur both cultivated and wild. The white bulbs of this Lily are more expensive in China than they are in this country. When properly cooked these bulbs are not at all bad eating. They somewhat resemble the parsnip in flavor.

Of the Onion family, Garlic, or Ta-suan (Allium sativum), and the common Onion, or Ts'ong (A. cepa), are cultivated extensively. Garlic is highly esteemed. Onions are eaten as "spring onions," large bulbs being absolutely unknown. A. fistulosum, the Chinese Leek, Chiu-ts'ai, is very widely grown. The leaves are bent down and covered with earth to ensure blanching. The blanched leaves, Chin-huang, are considered a delicacy. In the mountains A. odorum, A. chinense, and other species are common. These are culled and eaten by the peasantry. Szechuan, especially the more alluvial areas, produces remarkably fine Carrots (Daucus carota), Hung Lo-po. They are grown in large quantities and eaten with great relish. The Parsnip (Peucedanum sativum), Uen-shui is cultivated, but the roots are seldom thicker than a pencil. The whole plant is cooked and eaten.

Although in central and western China quite a number of plants are grown for their oil, fully 75 per cent. of the oil commonly used is the product of two members of the cabbage family. After a careful investigation of the subject I have satisfied myself that the two plants in question are Brassica juncea oleifera, and B. campestris oleifera. The latter is the Ta-yu-ts'ai of the Chinese, the former the Hsao-yu-ts'ai, or Ch'ing-yu. Both kinds are loosely designated rape by the foreigners resident in China; but in my wanderings there I never met with the true rape plant. Throughout the entire Yangtsze valley, during the winter months, enormous areas are given over to the cultivation of these two plants. Though the Hsao-yu-ts'ai is the earlier of the two, the other is the most extensively grown. These plants are in flower in February and March, and the crop is harvested in April. The seeds are crushed and steamed, and the oil obtained by expression. In Szechuan the use of the oil as an illuminant equals its culinary value. It also enters very largely into the composition of Chinese candles.

Oil is also expressed from the seeds of the Ground-nut (Arachis hypogaea), the Opium Poppy (Papaver somniferum), the Sunflower (Helianthus annuus), Cotton seed (Gossypium herbaceum), the Soy Bean (Glycine hispida), and members of the cabbage family, other than those already mentioned, notably the kales, and on the highlands from Flax seed, Shan-chih-ma (Linum usitatissimum). These oils are all used for cooking and lighting purposes and for adulterating the more valuable Ts'ai-yu. With the exception, however, of the ground-nut, they are not extensively employed. In Hupeh and Szechuan, Sesamum

VIEW NEAR HSINGSHAN HSIEN WITH TERRACED FIELDS

indicum is cultivated sparingly as a summer crop. In Yunnan its cultivation is more general. The oil from its seeds is very highly esteemed, and commands a high price in the market. It is known as the Hsiang-yu, or fragrant oil, and is eaten raw, mixed with cooked vegetables, From the seeds of Perilla ocymoides an oil, known as Su-ma, and similar to sesamum oil, is expressed; it is used in salads. This plant is, however, but very sparingly cultivated.

A large number of miscellaneous vegetables are used as food in various ways. Some are wild, but most are cultivated, and many of them are strange and novel to Americans. A handsome if tasteless fruit, the Brinjal, Chuei-tzu (Solanum melongena), is largely cultivated as a vegetable. The Chinese distinguish at least 5 varieties that differ from each other in color, shape, and time of maturing. Some of them are truly enormous, often weighing 2 ½ pounds, and measuring 1 foot in length. They are in the markets from June till October. The Tomato (S. lycopersicum) has been introduced by foreigners, and in Yunnan is frequently met with semi-wild as an escape from cultivation. The Chinese, as far as my observations go, do not eat it themselves.

A small-fruited variety of the Chilli-pepper, Ai-chiao (Capsicum frutescens), is commonly cultivated, and is particularly happy in the dry, hot valleys of the Tung and Min rivers, where it is grown as an article of export for other parts of China. Both long and round (heart-shaped) forms of Capsicum (C. annuum) are cultivated in the plains, and especially that of Chengtu. These chillies and capsicums constitute the most important relish used by the Chinese. In a green state the latter are fried and eaten with rice and cabbage. When ripe they are pounded up in a mortar, and with water added form a sauce. Roasted and ground into meal they are used for seasoning purposes. The ripe chillies and capsicums are also boiled in oil, and impart to it their pungent flavor. Oil so treated will keep for an indefinite period. The true Chinese pepper, known as Hua-chiao, is the ground-up fruit of Zanthoxylum bungei. This is a thorny shrub cultivated everywhere in small quantities, but it is only in the Min valley that I have noted it extensively grown for export.

As previously mentioned, Bamboo shoots are eaten both fresh,

AGRICULTURE

dried, and salted. When cooked as a vegetable or made into a salad, these shoots are very fair eating, but it is ridiculous to compare them with asparagus, as some writers have done. In the warmer parts of China it is the young shoots of Bambusa arundinacea and B. vulgaris that are employed. They are also an article of export to other parts of China, and can usually be bought in a dried state in most of the large cities. In mountainous districts the young succulent shoots of other species of Bamboo are eaten. In the west, one of the commonest of these is the lovely Arundinaria nitida.

Celery (Apium graveolens), Ch'ing-ts'ai, and Lettuce (Lactuca scariola), U'sen, are commonly cultivated. The celery is never bleached, and it is the stem of the lettuce rather than the leaves that it is in request. The leaves and young shoots of the following plants are used as vegetables: Cedrela sinensis, Ch'un-tien shu; Pistacia chinensis, Huang-nien-ya; Chrysanthemum segetum, Tung-hao; Malva parviflora, Mao-tung-han-ts'ai; M. verticillata, Tung-han-ts'ai; Chenopodium album, Hui-t'ien-han; Triglochin chenopodioides, Yeh-han-ts'ai; Ipomoea aquatica, Weng-ts'ai; Anaphalis contorta, Tak'ing-ming-ts'ai; Coriandrum sativum, Yen-ts'ai; Taraxacum officinale, Ku-ts'ai; Beta vulgaris, T'ien-ts'ai; Lactuca denticulata, Wo-sheng-ts'ai; Spinacia oleracea, Po-ts'ai; Crepis japonica, Huang-hua-ts'ai; Basella rubra, Juan-chiang-tzu; Celosia argentea, Chi-kung-hua; and Amaranthus paniculatus, Ya-ku.

The Kao-sen (Zizania latifolia) is very generally cultivated. Its succulent stem and very young inflorescence are cooked and eaten as a vegetable. From a European stand-point it is really very good eating. From the rhizome of the common Bracken (Pteridium aquilinum) an arrowroot-like substance called Chueh-fen is prepared. In the mountains the young fronds of this fern are eaten by the peasantry. From the thick woody root of Pueraria thunbergiana an arrowroot similar to the above is prepared. It is, however, in very little request, save in times of scarcity. The starchy roots of Potentilla discolor and P. multifida are also occasionally used for preparing a foodstuff.

The flowers of Lilium sargentiae, Yeh-peh-ho, and of Hemerocallis flava, Huang-hua-ts'ai, are eaten, as also are the yellow

355

pea-like flowers of Caragana chamlagu. The mucilaginous seeds of Plantago major, Ch'e-ch'ian-tsao, enter into the composition of a jelly, Liang-fen, which is used in summer. The Chinese are very fond of several species of fungi, and distinguish quite a number of edible kinds. Amongst their favorites are Hirneola polytricha, Cantharellus cibarius, Tricholoma gambosa, Lactarius deliciosus, and Agaricus campestris, the common Mushroom. Seaweed is imported in quantity from Japan, and is on sale in the shops of all the larger towns and villages. From this seaweed (Porphyra vulgaris) the Chinese prepare a very nutritious jelly.

The difficulty of tracing the original types of plants that have long been in cultivation and of affixing the correct scientific names to them is a very real one, and one that can be appreciated by all who have studied the history of our common garden plants. Whilst in the foregoing pages I cannot hope to have altogether escaped error in this matter, I have used every means at my command to ensure accuracy.

WAX-GOURD (BENINCASA CERIFERA)

CHAPTER XXVII

THE MORE IMPORTANT PLANT PRODUCTS

WILD AND CULTIVATED TREES OF ECONOMIC IMPORTANCE

HINA is remarkably rich in raw economic products of vegetable origin, especially in oil, fat, and saponin-yielding fruits and seeds, lacquer-varnish, tannin, and dye-products, fibres and paper-making material. Some of these products are in increasing demand for export trade with the outside world, and will undoubtedly develop into great industries of the future. In this and the succeeding chapter is given an account of the more important of the products derived from central and western China. This region is the source whence the majority of the raw articles are obtained that are exported from Hankow, the great trade entrepot of the Yang-tsze valley.

One of the most important of all Chinese products is wood oil. This is obtained from the seeds of two species of Aleurites, a small genus of low-growing trees belonging to the Spurge family. The two species for the most part occupy distinct geographical areas, but both have been recorded as growing close together in the province of Fokien. In the south of China wood oil is the product of A. montana, which bears its flowers on the current season's shoots at the time when the leaves are expanded, and has an egg-shaped fruit, sharply pointed, and unevenly ridged on the outside. This is the Mu-yu shu—literally Wood Oil tree of the Chinese. In central and western China it is A. fordii, known as the T'ung-yu shu—literally T'ung Oil tree, which produces this valuable oil. This latter species bears its flowers at the ends of the previous year's shoots before the leaves unfold, and has a flattened-round, apple-like fruit, only slightly pointed, and perfectly smooth on the outside. These two trees have been very much confused by botanists, and it is well to emphasize their distinctive characters. The T'ung-yu is the more hardy tree of the two, and is much more widely distributed, furnishing fully nine-tenths of the so-called wood oil used in China and exported from thence. Within the last two decades wood oil has attracted considerable attention in the United States and in Europe as a possible substitute for linseed oil, and it is annually imported into these countries in vastly increasing quantities. Chemists have investigated the products of the two trees named above, and find no appreciable difference in the oils.

The Mu-yu (A. montana) is common in the regions around Wuchou to the west of Canton, where it is chiefly used, and from whence it is exported to Hongkong and else-where. The trade is not large; in 1910 it was estimated at 52,106 piculs.[1]

The T'ung-yu (A. fordii) is abundant throughout the Yangtsze valley from Ichang westward to Chungking; more especially it luxuriates in the region of the gorges and the contiguous hill country up to 2500 feet altitude. It is essentially a hillside plant, thriving in the most rocky situations, and on the poorest of soils, where there is a minimum rainfall of 29 inches; it will also withstand drought and a few degrees of frost. It is a quick-growing tree, seldom exceeding 25 feet in height and averaging less, with a much-branched, flat-topped head, 15 to 30 feet or more through, and is highly ornamental in flower and foliage. The flowers, produced in great profusion during April, are white, stained with pink, and have yellow markings, especially near the corolla base. These are followed by green, apple-like fruits, which ripen in September and are hidden amongst the large, glossy-green, heart-shaped leaves. Each fruit contains three to five seeds, which somewhat resemble shelled Brazil-nuts, but are much smaller.

The fruits break naturally in three parts when dead ripe, but they are invariably gathered before this period, and collected into heaps which are covered with straw or grass. Fermentation sets in and quickly disposes of the thin fleshy part of the fruit, after which the seeds are easily removed. The process of extracting the oil is very simple. The seeds are first crushed in a circular trough beneath a heavy stone wheel revolved by horse or ox-power. The comminuted mass is then partially

[1] One picul equals 133⅓ pounds.

roasted in shallow pans, after which it is placed in wooden vats, fitted with wicker bottoms, and thoroughly steamed over boiling water. Next, with the aid of an iron ring and straw, it is made into circular cakes about 18 inches in diameter. These cakes are arranged edge-ways in a large press and, when full, pressure is exerted by driving in one wedge after another, thereby crushing out the brown, somewhat watery and heavy-smelling oil, which falls into a vat below. This T'ung oil is packed in tubs and bamboo baskets, and is ready for export. The yield is about 40 per cent. by weight of the seeds. The refuse cakes are used on the fields as fertilizers.

T'ung-yu is the chief paint oil throughout the Chinese Empire, being used for all outside woodwork; as a drier it excels linseed oil. The Chinese do not paint their boats, they oil them, and the myriads of such craft which ply on the Yangtsze and other rivers of China are all coated and the upper works kept waterproof with this oil. The crude oil boiled for an hour becomes a syrupy oil or P'ei-yu, which is used as a varnish for boats and furniture. Boiled for two hours with the addition of certain mineral substances (T'u-tzu and T'o-she), a varnish called Kuang-yu is produced which, when applied to silk gauze and pongees, renders them waterproof. T'ung-yu is also used as an illuminant and as an ingredient in concrete; mixed with lime and bamboo shavings it is used for caulking boats. Besides these, and dozens of other legitimate uses, wood oil is also employed as an adulterant in lacquer-varnish. Lamp-black produced by burning this oil or the fruit-husks is a most important ingredient in the manufacture of Chinese ink. The trade in T'ung oil is very large. From Hankow in 1900 the quantity exported was 330,238 piculs, valued at Tls. 2,559,-344. In 1910 the trade had risen to 756,958 piculs, valued at Tls 6,449,421.

I have given rather full details of this subject on account of its great importance, and because its value is only beginning to be realized by the Western manufacturer. The U. S. Department of Agriculture has introduced Aleurites fordii into its experimental stations, and expects to establish an industry in the production of T'ung oil some-where in the United States. It is worthy of the serious attention of countries other than the United States. In South Africa, Australia, Algeria,

THE MORE IMPORTANT PLANT PRODUCTS

Morocco, and other places, for instance, this tree would probably thrive, and its experimental culture might with advantage be undertaken by the various Departments of Agriculture in those British Colonies and French Protectorates. Of all the varied economic vegetable products of China, the wood oils are preeminently of a kind to receive attention, with a view of establishing the industry in Colonial possessions.

Another member of the Spurge family yields the valuable Chinese vegetable tallow of commerce. This tree, Sapium sebiferum, occurs in all the warmer parts of China, and is remarkable for the beautiful autumnal tints of its foliage. This tree is known by several colloquial names in southern China it is the Chiu-tzu shu; in central parts the Mou-tzu shu; in the west the Ch'uan-tzu shu. It is a long-lived tree, growing 40 to 50 feet tall, and having a girth of 5 to 6 feet at maturity. In Hupeh, where the industry is well looked after, the larger branches are kept pruned to facilitate the gathering of the fruits. The fruits are three-celled, flattened-ovoid, about 15 mm. in diameter. When ripe they are blackish brown and woody in appearance, and are either gathered from the trees by hand or knocked off by the aid of bamboo poles. After being collected, the fruits are spread in the sun, where they open, and each liberates three elliptical seeds, which are covered with a white substance. This covering is the fat or tallow, and is removed by steaming and rubbing through a bamboo sieve having meshes sufficiently small to retain the black seeds. The fat is collected and melted; afterward it is moulded into cakes, in which state it is known as the Pi-yu of commerce. After the fatty covering has been removed the seeds are crushed, and the powdered mass undergoes the same processes as are described for extracting wood oil. The oil expressed from the seeds is the Ting-yu of commerce. Very often no attempt is made to separate the fat and the oil. The seeds with their white fatty covering are crushed and steamed together and submitted to pressure, the mixed product so obtained being known as Mou-yu. The yield of fat and oil is about 30 per cent. by weight of the seeds. In China all three products are largely employed in the manufacture of candles. The pure Pi-yu has a higher melting point than the Ting-yu or the mixture Mou-yu. All Chinese candles have an exterior coating of insect white wax, but when made from Pi-yu only the thinnest covering of wax is necessary (one-tenth of an ounce to a pound). All three products of the vegetable tallow tree are exported in quantity to America and Europe, where they are used in the manufacture of soap, being essential constituents of particular forms of this article. Chinese vegetable tallow is an increasingly important article of trade. In 1910 some 178,204 piculs, valued at Tls. 1,878,418, were exported from Hankow.

Every one is familiar with some form or other of the lacquer-work of China and Japan, but the varnish employed for lacquering has not yet found a market in Western countries, owing to certain poisonous properties it possesses, and to the want of knowledge as to the correct way of applying it. Lacquer is prepared from a varnish obtained in its crude state from Rhus verniciflua, the Che shu of the Chinese. This tree grows 25 to 60 feet tall, producing hand-some pinnate leaves, from 1 to 2 ½ feet long, and large panicles of small greenish flowers, which are followed by fruits rich in fatty oil. It is wild in the woods and abun-dantly cultivated along the margins of fields throughout central China, especially in the mountainous areas of west-ern Hupeh and eastern Szechuan, but is much less common west of these regions. Its altitudinal range is from 3000 to 7500 feet, the optimum being 4000 to 5000 feet above sea level. This tree, like the art of lacquering, was introduced from China into Japan in very early times, and is cultivated there to-day. It is one of the many plants which first reached Europe from Japan, of which country it was erroneously considered native.

In China, varnish trees are the property of the ground landlord and not of the tenant who holds the land; the varnish is also claimed by the former. When the tree has attained a diameter of about 6 inches, tapping for varnish commences, and this operation is continued at intervals until the tree is 50 to 60 years of age. If the tapping is too severe, or the trees too young, injury or death ensues. The tapping operation is begun in late June or early July at a time corresponding with the opening of the flowers, and is continued throughout the

WOOD OIL TREE (ALEURITES FORDII); OPIUM POPPY IN FOREGROUND

summer. Oblique incisions from 4 to 12 inches in length, and about 1 inch in width, are made in the bark of the tree down to the wood, and the sap which exudes is collected in shells, bamboo tubes, and similar receptacles. Wooden pegs are driven into the trunk to facilitate climbing, in order to reach the main branches. The tapping is done early in the morning and the sap gathered from the receptacles into which it has flowed from the incisions each evening. In showery weather it dries rapidly, and often has to be scraped away. The sap continues to exude from the wound for about seven days, and then a fresh, thin slice of bark is removed, which causes another exudation. This is repeated seven times with an interval of about seven days between each operation, so that the work on each tree occupies about fifty days. After being tapped, the tree is allowed a period of from five to seven years to recover; the old wounds are then reopened and fresh ones made. A large tree yields from 5 to 7 pounds of varnish. This, as it exudes, is pure white in appearance, but quickly oxidizes to grayish white, changing to black. To prevent contact with the air the crude varnish is covered as soon as possible with layers of oil-paper.

Crude varnish furnishes only one color, namely, black, and when applied to wood floors, or pillars, is the most indestructible varnish known. To obtain brown varnish P'ei yu (ante, p. 360) is added, in the proportion of 25 to 50 per cent., to the crude varnish, according to the shade of brown required. The more P'ei yu added, the quicker the varnish will dry. Red varnish is produced by added cinnabar (mercuric sulphide) to brown varnish in about equal parts. Yellow varnish is obtained by adding to the brown varnish orpiment (arsenic sulphide) in slightly less than equal quantity.

Enormous quantities of raw varnish are exported from central China to other parts of the country and to Japan. In 1910 the exports of varnish from Hankow totalled 15,424 piculs, valued at Tls. 1,043,434. This commercial product is frequently adulterated with wood oil. Three tests for adulteration are commonly employed—(1) smell; (2) the varnish is held up and allowed to drop, the strand of varnish will remain unbroken if it is pure, but will break if adulterated; (3) placed on a sheet of soft Chinese paper, the varnish runs, if it is adulterated, owing to the paper absorbing the oil adulterant. Everywhere in China this varnish is known to resident foreigners as Ningpo varnish. The genesis of the name is interesting, since the substance itself is not produced in the neighborhood of Ningpo, but is imported from Hankow and elsewhere. In the early days, when foreigners first settled at Shanghai, most of the carpenters employed to build houses for them were Ningpo men. For all indoor work—floors, pillars, and furniture they employed this varnish, and foreigners promptly dubbed it Ningpo varnish.

A peculiarity of Ningpo varnish, or Chinese lacquer, to use its correct name, is that it hardens only in a moist atmosphere and remains in a tacky condition if exposed to sun-light and heat, the essentials in hardening copal varnish. In China it is applied only during cloudy weather when the atmosphere is surcharged with moisture or when drizzle is falling. For indoor work its drying is facilitated by hang-ing about the rooms cloths saturated with water. The kind used on ships contains P'ei-yu in almost equal parts, and this mixture dries rapidly even in moderately dry, hot weather. How important the knowledge of this peculiarity is may be gathered from the following fact. Many years ago an experimental consignment of Ningpo varnish was received in London. It was applied in the same way as ordinary copal varnish, in full sunlight and heat, with the result that it refused to harden, and remained tacky, and the failure resulted in its being condemned as valueless!

The only change which takes place in the composition of the lacquer in drying at ordinary temperature is the slow absorption of oxygen, finally amounting to 5.75 per cent. by weight of the original substance. Complete oxidation is found to be due to the action of a ferment, to which the name laccase has been applied, which is only active in a certain humidity of the atmosphere. Quite recently, however, the presence of a special ferment has been questioned, and the absorption of oxygen attributed to an obscure chemical reaction depending on the presence of a compound of manganese with a proteid-like substance. Chinese lacquer, in a raw state, unfortunately possesses properties which are poisonous to many people, producing swellings and eruptions of the skin in the same way as does its close ally, the Poison Ivy (Rhus Toxicodendron). Certain people are immune, but this feature will probably always militate against its use in Western lands. Perhaps the chemists will one day discover a means whereby this poisonous property can be neutralized or eliminated.

The fruit of R. verniciflua is shining, grayish yellow, roundish and flattened on two sides, 6 to 10 mm. long. These when crushed and treated in a wedge-press in the same way as wood oil seeds, yield a fatty oil known as Che-yu, which is used for making candles.

Trees belonging to three different families produce fruits rich in saponin which are in common use for laundry-work and other purposes. The most generally distributed of these Soap trees is Gleditsia sinensis, a handsome tree known colloquially Tsao-k'o shu, abundant throughout the Yangtsze valley up to 3500 feet altitude. It grows 60 to 100 feet tall, and has a thick trunk, smooth gray bark, a spreading head with massive branches furnished with small, pinnate leaves and inconspicuous greenish flowers, unisexual or hermaphrodite in character. The latter are followed by pods or beans which, when ripe, are black, 6 to 14 inches long and ¾ to 1 ½ inch wide. These pods are broken up and are in general use for ordinary laundry-work, producing a good lather in either cold or hot water. They are also used in the process of tanning hides. The saponaceous fat is contained in the pod itself, which is the only part utilized, the hard, flattened, brown seeds being discarded. It is probable that more than one species is included under the above name, for the Gleditsia family is in need of revision. In Yunnan another species which has much longer (20 inches) and wider pods is employed for the same purposes. It is known as G. delavayi. Around Peking a third species, designated G. macrantha, occurs. A much rarer Soap tree, except in the vicinity of Kiukiang, is Gymnocladus chinensis, the Yu-tsao-chio of the Chinese, which is the Asiatic representative of the Kentucky Coffee-tree of North America. This tree grows 50 to 60 feet tall, and though occasionally seen with a flat, fairly widespreading head, has usually only short branches; the bark is smooth and light-gray, the leaves much divided, often 2 feet across, pea-green in color, and very handsome. The flowers, clustered, grayish without, purple within, are followed by flattened, brown pods, 3 to 4 inches long, and 1 ½ inch broad. These pods or beans are immersed for a time in hot water, which causes them to swell and become rounded in outline. Afterwards they are strung on short strips of bamboo and are then marketed. These swollen pods, colloquially Fei-tsao-tou, are broken up and used in laundry-work, more especially for cleansing choice fabrics. They are also cut up into fine shreds and ground to a paste with sandalwood, cloves, putchuck, musk, and camphor, and thoroughly mixed with honey to form a perfumed soap called P'ing-she Fei-tsao (camphor-musk soap). This is a dark-colored substance of the consistency of soft soap. It is used by women for cleansing their hair, and as a cosmetic for their hands and face; also by barbers as a salve on the heads of their customers after shaving.

Yet another Soap tree is Sapindus mukorossi, colloquially known as the Hou-erh-tsao. This occurs throughout the Yangtsze valley up to 3000 feet altitude, growing 60 to 80 feet tall, with a thick trunk, smooth gray bark, and widespreading umbrageous head; the pinnate leaves are 8 to 12 inches long. The flowers are small, greenish white. produced in large terminal panicles, and are followed by shining brown, globose fruits about the size of a large marble. The fruits are used for washing white clothes, being considered for this purpose superior to the pods of Gleditsia. Each fruit contains a large, round black seed. These are strung into rosaries and necklaces, which are much worn during hot weather.

During recent years the demand for vegetable products useful for tanning purposes has become unlimited. For certain purposes Chinese nut-galls furnish the finest tanning material in the world. These nut-galls (Wu-pei-tzu) develop on the leaves of Rhus javanica, Peh-fu-yang shu, as an excrescent growth due to protoplasmic irritation, occasioned by an insect (Chermes) which punctures the leaf to deposit its eggs. The tree is of small size, and very abundant in the Yangtsze valley up to 3500 feet, more especially in rocky places, producing panicles of white flowers in late August and September. The galls are hollow and brittle, and vary considerably in shape and size, being more or less irregular, and 1 to 4 inches long. In China they are used for dyeing blue silk and blue cotton cloth black. The Occidental demand for nut-galls is greater than the supply, and the exports increase annually. In 1900, 24,800 piculs, valued at Tls. 454,584, were exported from Hankow; in 1910 the exports from this port had increased to 53,784 piculs, valued at Tls. 936,234.

Another less common species is R. potaninii, colloquially known as the Ch'ing-fu-yang, which produces galls known as Ch'i-pei-tzu. These are used in Chinese medicine. The world is sadly in need of an indelible black ink, and chemists might well turn their attention to Chinese nut-galls in their quest for this treasure, since they possess possibilities worthy of investigation.

In the chapter on fruits reference is made to the cultivated Persimmon (Diospyros kaki), but it is necessary here to mention the feral form, known as Yu-shih-tzu (literally Oil Persimmon). This wilding is abundant in the mountains of central and western China up to 4000 feet altitude, where it forms a large tree 50 to 60 feet tall. The fruit varies from flattened-round to ovoid, and from ¾ to 2½ inches in diameter. It is always rich golden yellow in color when ripe, and this color best distinguishes the smallest fruited forms from its near relative D. Lotus, Kou-shih-tzu, which has flattened-round fruit, dark purplish colored when dead ripe. To obtain the varnish oil for which this tree is esteemed, the fruit is plucked in July when about the size of a crap-apple, and still green. By means of a wooden mallet the fruits are reduced to pulp, which is placed with cold water in large earthenware jars fitted with covers, and allowed to decompose. The contents of these jars are stirred occasionally, and at the end of thirty days the residue of the pulp is removed and the resultant liquid, now a nearly colorless varnish, is poured into other jars. To give the varnish a warm brown tint, the leaves of Ligustrum lucidum, La shu, sometimes erroneously called the Tung-thing shu, are steeped in the jars for ten days or so, according to depth of tint desired. This varnish is used for waterproofing purposes generally, its principal use being in the manufacture of umbrellas. For this purpose it is applied as a gum varnish between the several layers of paper forming the screen of the umbrella, and serves to make them adherent as well as waterproof.

THE MORE IMPORTANT PLANT PRODUCTS

When completed, the umbrella receives a thin outside coating of Kuang-yu, or lustrous oil (see p. 360). Persimmon varnish is widely used, and is in great demand for the above purposes. It is produced in most parts of China, but scarcely figures as an article of export.

The art of making paper in China dates back to about the commencement of the Christian era. Previous to this, silk and cloth were employed for writing upon, but the early annals of the race were recorded on tablets of bamboo, and this latter method obtained in the days of Confucius (552-478 B.C.). What materials were first employed by the Chinese in paper-making are not known with certainty, but were probably bamboo or the Paper-mulberry, Kou shu (Broussonetia papyrifera). A good case in favor of the latter could be made out, since the inner bark of this tree requires less preparation than bamboo culms. True paper money first originated in the province of Szechuan during the reign of the first Emperor of the Sung Dynasty (A.D. 960). A certain Chang-yung introduced it to take the place of the iron money then in use, which was inconveniently heavy and troublesome. These notes were called Chih-tsi or Evidences, and were apparently made from the inner bark of the Paper-mulberry. Marco Polo, speaking of Kub-lai Khan's mint at Peking, says, "He makes them take the bark of a certain tree, in fact, of the Mulberry tree, the leaves of which are the food of the silkworm—these trees being so numerous that whole districts are full of them. What they take is a certain fine white bast or skin which lies between the wood of the tree and the thick outer bark, and this they make into something resembling sheets of paper, but black." The famous Venetian's error in calling this the silk-worm Mulberry is pardonable enough, since the trees are very closely allied, and somewhat similar in appearance. Paper money is still made from the paper prepared from the bark of the Kou shu, and the same paper, P'i-chih, owing to its toughness, is used for wrapping up silver, for tags on silk goods, and as a lining between the fur or cotton and the outer fabric in fur-lined or wadded garments. The B. papyrifera occurs all over China up to 4000 feet altitude, and if left alone forms a much-branched tree 35 to 45 feet tall with a smooth dark gray bark. In a bush form it is abundant by the wayside and on cliffs. Most of the paper

369

(which is called Kou-pl-chih—literally bark paper) made from this tree and used in western China comes from the province of Kweichou. In Hupeh the slender branches from young trees and bushes are cut into lengths, steamed in vats to facilitate the removal of the bark, which is converted into string and cordage.

The material from which the original India paper (a Chinese not an Indian product), which came from Canton, was made is unknown. Possibly it was prepared from Ramie fibre (Boehmeria nivea), but I venture the suggestion that it may have been obtained from the bark of Broussonetia papyrifera.

Bamboo supplies the material for the manufacture of all the better class papers used for printing and writing upon, papering windows, and a hundred and one other purposes. Several species are employed for this purpose, one of the commonest being Phyllostachys heteroclada. This bamboo is abundant in central and western China, especially in alluvial areas near streams up to 4000 feet altitude. It grows 12 to 18 feet tall, with fairly slender dark green culms; commonly it forms extensive groves. The stems are cut into lengths, made into bundles, and immersed in concrete pits, being weighted down and kept under water by heavy stones. After three months they are removed, opened up, and thoroughly washed. Next they are restacked in layers, each layer being well sprinkled with lime and water, holding potash salts in solution. After two months they are well retted. The fibrous mass is then washed to remove the lime, steamed for fifteen days, when it is removed, thoroughly washed, and again placed in concrete tanks. The mass is next reduced to a fine pulp with wooden rakes, and is then ready for conversion into paper. A quantity of the pulp is put into troughs with cold water and mucilage prepared from the roots of Hibiscus Abelmoschus. An oblong bamboo frame, the size of the desired sheet of paper, having a fine mesh, is held at the two ends by a workman and drawn down endways and diagonally into the liquid contents, which are kept constantly stirred in the trough. It is then gently raised to the surface, and the film which has collected on the top is deposited as a sheet of moist paper when the frame is turned over. After the surplus water has drained away from the mass of moist sheets of paper the whole is submitted to pressure. It is then dried either in kilns or in the sun, according to quality, the sun-dried being the inferior. Since much water is necessary in the process of paper-making the mills are always erected beside streams.

The more common paper in daily use is made from rice-straw by a similar but less intricate and quicker process. The stems of a reed (Imperata arundinacea Koenigii), known as Mao-ts'ao, and common in many parts of western China, are also used locally in the manufacture of paper, being frequently mixed with rice-straw.

Chinese rice-paper, so called by foreigners, is prepared from the pith of Tetrapanax papyrifera, a shrub closely allied to the common Ivy of Europe, and colloquially known as T'ung-ts'ao. This plant has handsome palmate leaves, and stems filled with a pure white pith. This pith is cut, using a rolling, circular motion, by means of a sharp, heavy knife, into thin sheets. Formerly much of this cutting was done in Chungking, the raw material being imported from the province of Kweichou. Rice-paper is used by Chinese artists for painting upon, and also in the manufacture of artificial flowers.

Sericulture and silk-weaving are among the most important industries of Szechuan. Nearly every part of the province produces silk, but there are certain well-defined areas in which the industry is famous—for example, Kiating Fu, Chengtu Fu, and Paoning Fu. Hosier [1] estimates the annual production of raw silk at 5,439,500 pounds, valued at Tls. 15,025,230. This industry has been exhaustively dealt with by Hosie and others, and I propose here only to briefly mention certain trees, the leaves of which the silkworm are fed upon. The overwhelming proportion of Szechuan silk is produced by the worm of Bombyx mori, the common domesticated species, which is fed principally on the leaves of the White Mulberry (Morus alba), known as the Sang shu. This Mulberry tree is abundantly cultivated up to 3000 feet altitude, and in the more populous parts of the province a traveller is seldom out of sight of groves of this tree. The trees are kept low by pollarding to admit of the leaves being easily gathered, but little attention is otherwise accorded them. Since the suppression of opium cultivation the officials have turned their attention to improving and

[1] Report on Province of Ssuch'uan, p. 67.

extending the sericulture industry. The finest Chinese silk is produced in the neighborhood of Hanchou in the Chekiang province, where a broad-leaved and particularly fine Mulberry is cultivated (M. alba latifolia), for the purpose of feeding the silkworms. The recently established Bureau of Agriculture at Chengtu Fu, and magistrates in charge of certain districts, have introduced the Hanchou Mulberry in the hope of improving the local product. During the last two or three years there has been a considerable increase in the area devoted to sericulture, and there is a possible danger of over-production. More attention might well be paid to the spinning of the yarn in order to produce a more even thread, which would result in a smoother and finer woven fabric.

Around Kiating Fu the infant silkworms are fed for the first 22 days of their lives on the finely chopped leaves of Cudrania tricuspidata, the Tsa or Cha shu, a low-growing tree (very often only a bush), closely allied to the Mulberry, with thorny branches and dark-green, tough leaves. For the succeeding and final 26 days they are fed on the Mulberry. By feeding first on the Cudrania leaves, it is claimed that the worms produce more silk of a tougher and more durable quality. Hosier was the first to discover and make known this interesting fact to the outside world, and subsequent observers have confirmed his statements.

Around Paoning Fu in the north, and Kikiang Hsien in the south, a certain amount of silk is obtained from the worm of Antheraea pernyi. This species feeds on the leaves of various scrub oaks, and being bivoltine, produces two crops a year. Several species of Oak are concerned, including Quercus variabilis, Q. serrata, Q. fabri, and Q. aliena, all of which, though they attain to the dimensions of trees, are commonly met with from 2000 to 4000 feet in the form of bushes covering the hillsides. This Oak-feeding silkworm was introduced from the province of Shantung many years ago and the industry is much more important in Kweichou province than it is in Szechuan. This wild-silk, as it is called, differs from ordinary silk in its harder texture and is spun from dry cocoons, whereas ordinary silk is spun from cocoons lying immersed in boiling water. In 1907, near the hamlet of

1   Three Years in Western China, p. 22.

THE MORE IMPORTANT PLANT PRODUCTS

Luyang-ho, alt. 2500 feet, in the northwest corner of Fang Hsien, I chanced upon several plantations of Ailanthus vilmoriniana, grown for feeding the worm of Attacus cynthia. The trees were all young saplings. This was the only place in my travels where I saw this particular kind of sericulture practiced. In parts of northeastern China I understand it is more general, the species there employed being the ordinary Ailanthus glandulosa, the Ch'ou-ch'un shu of the Chinese, and Tree of Heaven of foreigners.

CHAPTER XXVIII

THE MORE IMPORTANT PLANT PRODUCTS

CULTIVATED SHRUBS AND HERBS OF ECONOMIC VALUE

HINESE agriculture is mainly devoted to the production of foodstuffs for local consumption, the surplus being disposed of by sale and the proceeds invested in the necessities or luxuries of life which cannot be produced locally. Nevertheless, in the more fertile parts of the Empire, certain economic crops other than those for culinary purposes are grown expressly for sale or exchange. This is particularly true of the rich province of Szechuan, where a number of such products are produced, as will be seen from the brief account of the more important which follows.

Had this been written twenty years previously it would have been necessary to give considerable space to the Opium Poppy, but so vigorously has the edict for the suppression of this crop been promulgated that only a brief notice of it is necessary. When the Imperial Decree, prohibiting the cultivation and consumption of opium throughout the Chinese Empire within a period of ten years, was published on September 20th, 1906, I confess to being one of those who considered it a fatuous effort calculated to accomplish nothing, though well-meaning enough. It seemed impossible that such a gigantic task could be accomplished in such a brief period of time. Public sentiment was obviously in favor of the decree, but to certain provinces, for example Szechuan and Yunnan, the export of opium represented their principal source of income. That Indian opium could be dispensed with and none be inconvenienced save the wealthy and opium-smoking connoisseurs living in the prosperous coast ports was perfectly clear to anyone who had travelled in western China. In 1908

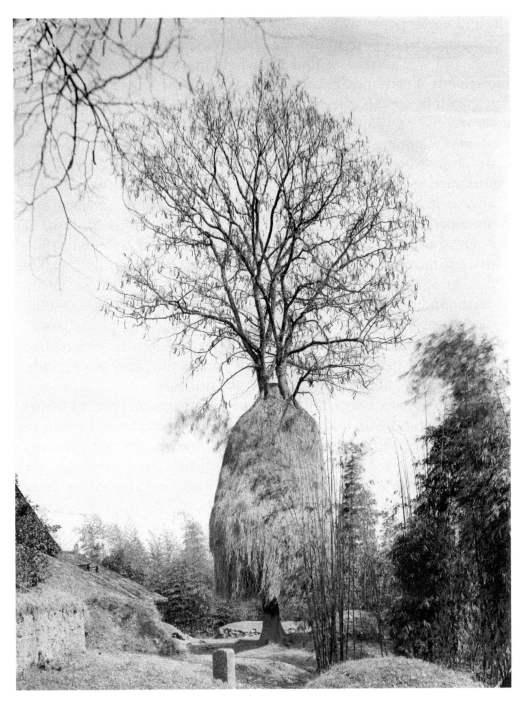

SOAP-TREE (GLEDITSIA SINENSIS) USED AS A STACK FOR RICE STRAW the area under poppy in Szechuan was far greater than it had ever been before. In 1910 I traversed this province from east to west and north to south, and was amazed to find the whole industry of poppy-growing blotted out of existence. Except in a few out-of-the-way places, where it was grown by stealth, the cultivation had ceased. What has happened since the end of 1910 I do not know, but from what I saw brought to pass in a couple of seasons, together with the undoubted general disfavor in which opium-smoking was viewed by the people, I am constrained to think that the poppy and opium will disappear from China as it has done from Japan. The problem before officials, and more especially those of the western provinces, is to find a source of revenue to take the place of that formerly derived from opium. In 1904 Hosie estimated the production of opium in Szechuan at 250,000 piculs. In 1910 some 28,530 piculs of opium (produced in Szechuan, Yunnan, and Kweichou provinces), valued at about Tls. 29,000,000, passed through the port of Ichang. In 1909, 51,817 piculs passed through this port. Formerly the exports of opium alone from Szechuan nearly sufficed to cover the imports of cotton-yarn and piece-goods, commodities essential to the people of that province.

The literature on Chinese opium and opium-smoking in China is enormous, and with exception of what is written above, I desire to add only three significant facts, which, if known, are not generally appreciated. For the benefit of those who believe, and those who do not believe, that India, abetted by the British Government in times past, is responsible for the opium vice in China, I would mention that (a) opium has been known in China since the Tang Dynasty (A.D. 618), and was cultivated in Szechuan for medicinal purposes during the closing years of that dynasty (circa A.D. 900); (b) the pipe used for smoking opium in China is of a design peculiar to the country itself; (c) the races of Poppy cultivated in western China are allied to the races grown in Persia and quite distinct from those grown in India.

It is known that in early times the peach, orange, and silk travelled from China by the ancient trade route across central Asia to Persia, from whence they reached Europe. Is it not, therefore, reasonable enough to suppose that Opium Poppy may have travelled

376

THE MORE IMPORTANT PLANT PRODUCTS

from Persia to China by this same overland route?

The poppy is (or was) a winter crop in Szechuan, being garnered in April and May in ample time to prepare for the rice-crop. No other crop even remotely approximating the pecuniary value of opium can take its place.

Several plants yielding fibres valued for textile and cordage purposes are grown in China. In Szechuan the most important of these is the true Hemp (Cannabis sativa), colloquially known as Hou-ma. This crop is abundantly cultivated around Wen-chiang Hsien and P'i Hsien. It is a spring crop, the seeds being sown in February and the plants harvested the end of May and beginning of June, just as they commence to flower. The stems are allowed to grow thickly together and reach 8 feet in height. The culms are reaped, stripped of their leaves, and often the fibre is removed there and then. More commonly, however, the stems are placed in pits filled with water and allowed to ret for a few days; they are then removed, sun-dried, stacked in hollow cones, surrounded by mats, and bleached by burning sulphur beneath the heaps. After these processes the fibrous bark is stripped off by hand. The woody stems that remain after the bark has been removed are burned, and the ashes resulting, mixed with gunpowder, enter into the manufacture of fire-crackers. Hemp, or Hou-ma, is the best of the fibres produced in western China for rope-making and cordage purposes generally. It is also used locally for making grain-sacks and coarse wearing apparel for the poorer classes. Quantities are used in the city of Paoning Fu for these latter purposes. It is in great demand on native river-craft and is largely exported down river to other parts of China. It is this hemp that is principally exported from Szechuan. Hemp is an annual and is grown as a summer crop in the mountains for the sake of its oil-containing seeds. Hemp oil is expressed and used as an illuminant and is said not to congeal in the coldest weather. In Hupeh it is known as T'ang-ma.

Another annual plant cultivated for its fibre is Abutilon avicennae, the T'ung or T'uen-ma of Szechuan and Hupeh. This plant is widely cultivated as a summer crop in western China up to 3000 feet altitude. The fibre is of inferior quality and is used locally for making cordage and in caulking boats, but is less valuable than that of the true Hemp and less important as an article of export from Szechuan. Jute (Corchorus capsularis), colloquially known in Szechuan as Huang-ma, is very sparingly cultivated on the Chengtu plain and elsewhere. It is not exported from the province.

The brown fibre from the leaf-bases of a palm (Trachycarpus excelsus), known in Hupeh as Chung-ma, is the coir-fibre of the Yangtsze valley. This coir is made into bales and exported down river from Szechuan in quantity. It is used for rope-making, mats and mattresses, brushes, is converted into rude raincapes, and is an all-round useful fibre.

The most important textile plant in China is the much-discussed China-grass, Ramie, or Rhea (Boehmeria nivea). This member of the nettle family is both wild and cultivated in all the warmer parts of the Middle Kingdom up to 4000 feet above sea-level. It is a herbaceous perennial and grows 3 to 6 feet tall; the leaves, broadly ovate, abruptly cuneate, or truncated at base, have dentate margins and are silvery on the underside. In Hupeh the wild plant is called Ch'u-ma, the cultivated plant Hsien-ma. In Szechuan the cultivated plant is also known as Hsien-ma and occasionally as Yuang-ma. These various colloquial names are most perplexing and are almost hopelessly confused.

In Szechuan small patches of this China-grass are to be found around nearly every peasant's home. Southwest of Chungking and also north of Lu Chou in several districts, it is cultivated on a very extensive scale. Much of the fibre is woven into grass-cloth and used locally. A certain amount is also exported down river. Szechuan grass-cloth is rather coarse and very much inferior to that produced in parts of southern China. It is not a prominent export from the west. In 1910 the exports from Hankow amounted to 120,034 piculs, valued at Tls. 183,332. This is classified in the customs returns as Ramie fibre, and does not include that woven into grass-cloth.

Cotton-cultivation is a comparatively recent industry in China, having been introduced early in the eleventh century A.D., from Khoten. It met with strong opposition from those interested in the production of silk, China-grass, and other fibres, and was not fairly established until some time during the Yuan (Mongol) dynasty (A.D. 1206-1386), when a public-spirited woman, Lady Hwang, distributed seeds throughout Kiangan, now the great cotton region of China. Chinese cotton has a notoriously short staple, but is strong and durable. It has undoubtedly become exhausted from lack of any attempt at seed selection and from long cultivation in the same regions. Cotton cultivation should receive early attention from the new government, and seeds of standard varieties from India, Egypt, America, and elsewhere might be secured and experimentally grown. There is no question but that China could produce cotton infinitely superior to the present product if new and suitable varieties were obtained and properly cultivated.

Very little cotton, Mien-hwa, is grown in western China, and cotton-yarn and cloths are the great import into Szechuan. The value of foreign imports into Chungking is about Tls. 20,000,000, five-sixths of which is made up of cotton manufactures, the bulk of which comes from India.

Before the importation of mineral oil from foreign countries became general, the only lamps in use were vessels filled with vegetable oil and fitted with rush wicks. These rush-lights are still in common use in the west, more especially among the poorer classes. The wick consists of the pith of Juncus effusus, known as Teng-ts'ao, which is widely cultivated for this purpose. The plant grows 3 to 6 feet tall and is also largely employed in the manufacture of matting and mats, used under bed-mattresses, and on divans. It is expressly cultivated for this purpose in parts of Szechuan, the principal seat of the matting industry being Sui Fu, where both whole and split rushes are used. In Yunnan Scirpus lacustris, Pu-chih-ts'ao, which produces stems 6 to 8 feet tall, cylindrical at base, gradually tapering upwards and becoming obtusely triangular near the summit, is used for mat-making. It is also sparingly employed for the same purpose in Szechuan, where, however, it is chiefly used by the shop-keepers as string.

Rice-straw is largely used for making bed-mattresses and sandals and to a less extent for rope. Wheat straw is braided and used for making large, wide-brimmed summer hats. Certain districts like Shuangliu Hsien, near Chengtu, are famed for their straw-braid, but the industry is of local importance only.

Tobacco (Nicotiana tabacum), called Yen, was probably introduced into China from America, contemporaneously with maize—just when is a matter of dispute, but some sinologues consider it was about A.D. 1530. It is cultivated all over China, and nowhere within the Middle Kingdom are finer tobacco leaves produced than in Szechuan. Within the rice-belt tobacco is a spring-crop, the seeds being sown in late October and the crop harvested by mid-June. In the maize-belt it is grown as a summer crop but not extensively. The districts of Chint'ang and Pri Hsien, on the Chengtu plain, are noted for their tobacco. In these districts one crop only is taken from the plants, but in the warmer parts of the province contiguous to the Yangtsze River, three crops are secured before the plants are ploughed under.

Tobacco leaves are prepared in three ways: (1) the large leaves are dried on screens, kept flat, packed into bales to form Ta-yen, or large tobacco; (2) the smaller leaves are dried in the same way to form Erh-yen, or second tobacco, which, when treated with Chinese rape-oil and red-earth (Tu-hung) is pressed and shaved into fine shreds and used for smoking in water-pipes, being known as Shui-yen, or water tobacco; (3) So-yen, or cord tobacco, prepared by cutting off the leaves with a piece of the stem to form a hook, by means of which the leaves are suspended under the eaves of houses or from rafters indoors and allowed to dry, naturally shrivelling and curling in the process. This So-yen is rolled into rough cigars, which are inserted into the bowl of long-stemmed pipes and smoked. It is also exported from Szechuan. In the mountains up to 9000 feet altitude the small-leaved Nicotiana rustica, Lan-hwa-yen, is sparingly cultivated for local use. This receives no preparation beyond being dried in the sun, and naturally the quality is very inferior.

Undoubtedly the climate and soil of Szechuan are suitable for the growth of tobacco, but, unfortunately, the Chinese methods of curing the leaf are slovenly in the extreme, with the result that the prepared article is of low-grade quality. The Chinese are fast becoming a nation of inveterate cigarette-smokers. Much of the local Szechuan tobacco could be used in the manufacture of cigarettes were proper factories erected. This has been done at Hankow and elsewhere, where cigarettes are manufactured from tobacco grown in the neighborhood and nearby provinces.

Sugar is a very important crop in western China and enormous quantities are produced in certain parts of Szechuan, where it is cultivated in the drier regions of the rice-belt up to 2500 feet altitude. Two kinds of Sugar-cane (Saccharum officinarum) are grown: (1) red-cane, used for chewing; (2) white-cane, for the extraction of sugar. The Red-cane (S. officinarum rubricaule) produces culms 8 feet tall, an inch or more in diameter, and is treated as an annual. The canes are cut as they mature and sold as required; the canes that remain at the end of the season are taken up by the roots in November, cleaned and stored in earth-burrows until required for sale. About the end of March portions of these canes are laid lengthwise under the soil, and young growths that develop from each joint in due season constitute sugar-canes. These culms are dark red-purple outside, yellowish within, very firm, and rich in sugar.

The White-cane (S. officinarum sinense) is treated as a perennial, producing two or three crops before being re-newed. It grows 10 to 15 feet tall, with long-jointed stems nearly an inch in diameter. This is more extensively grown than the red variety, and supplies nearly all the sugar used locally or exported from the province. Chinese methods of crushing the cane are very imperfect, and their refining processes are most primitive. The canes contain a high percentage of saccharine, and the industry, if perfected, could become of vast importance.

Sugar has been cultivated in China from immemorial time. It is everywhere called T'ang, and generally supposed to commemorate the T'ang dynasty (A.D. 684-907), one of the most famous in Chinese history. Sugar, however, was known to the Chinese at least as early as the second century B.C., and is mentioned in a poem which was written some-time between A.D. 78 and 139.

Formerly the Chinese used only vegetable dyes for their silk and other fabrics, and it is much to be regretted that in China, as elsewhere in the world, these are being rapidly displaced by aniline dyes derived from coal-tar. The latter are more convenient to handle, but unfortunately the colors are not fast. The coal-tar product is on sale in every town and market village in western China, made up in small bottles and imported from Germany.

The only dye-plant at all extensively grown in Szechuan today is Strobilanthes flaccidifolius, T'ien-hwa, which produces an indigo. In certain parts of the Chengtu plain this is grown in quantity, and the same is true of the district of Mien Chou and elsewhere, but its cultivation is on the decline. It is planted on ridges which are kept flooded between. When the plants are about 3 feet tall they are cut down and the leafy shoots placed in concrete pits full of cold water. After steeping for about 5 days the stems are removed, leaving a green-colored water. Slaked lime is placed in the water to precipitate the indigo. The water is allowed to drain off, and the dye is found deposited at the bottom of the pit.

Around Shasi, in Hupeh, Polygonum tinctorium is cultivated as the source of an indigo which is there used for dyeing cotton cloth.

As a red dye Safflower (Carthamus tinctorius), Hung-hwa, was formerly very extensively grown, but it is only occasionally met with today, though still esteemed for dyeing the more costly silk fabrics. The flowers of the Balsam (Impatiens balsamina), colloquially Chih-chia-ts'ao, are similarly used and valued.

Yellow dyes are obtained from turmeric, the root of Curcuma longa, still extensively grown in Chienwei Hsien on the lower Min River, and from the flowers of the Huai shu (Sophora japonica), a common and widely dispersed tree. Another, but much more rare tree (Koelreuteria apiculata), is known by the same colloquial name, and the flowers are used for the same purpose as those of the Sophora. The fruit of Gardenia florida, Chih-tzu-hwa, is used for dyeing certain woods yellow, and also as a yellow color in paint.

Green dyes were formerly obtained from the leaves of Rhamnus utilis, known as the Tung-lu, a very common Chinese species of Buckthorn, extremely variable in the size and shape of its leaves and abundant as a thorny bush by the wayside everywhere up to 4000 feet

THE MORE IMPORTANT PLANT PRODUCTS

altitude. Another species (Rhamnus tinctorius), Chiao-lu-tsze, was also employed for the same purpose. These have been almost totally displaced by aniline dyes.

As mentioned on page 367, the gall-nuts (Wu-pei-tzu) produced on the leaves of Rhus javanica are extensively employed for dyeing fabrics—more especially silk black. With this dye it is essential that the material be first dyed blue. The burr-like cupules of two very common species of Oak (Quercus serrata, Q. variabilis), known as the Hwa-li and Hwa-k'o-li respectively, are also commonly employed as black dye for silk-yarn and fabrics. In this case it is immaterial what the original color may be. The curious cone-like fruits of Platycarya strobilacea, colloquially known as the Huan-hsiang shu, are in general use as a black dve for cotton-yarn and cotton goods generally. Pine soot, obtained by burning the branches of the common Pine (Pinus massoniana) is also employed as a black dye for cotton goods.

As a dark brown dye and tanning agent the tubers of a yam are commonly used in Yunnan and are exported in quantity to Tonking and elsewhere. It is probably Dioscorea rhipogonioides, a species common in Formosa, where it is called Shu-lang and much used for dyeing and tanning fish-nets. In western Hupeh the root-bark of Rosa banksiae, called Hu-p'i, is used for this purpose.

Both sesamum and soy beans are cultivated extensively in western China, but for local consumption only. The large exports of these products that pass through Hankow are brought down by the Peking-Hankow railway. Szechuan is capable of growing enormous quantities of these valuable plants, but cheaper and better facilities for transport are necessary before the products can become articles of external trade. When the much-discussed Hankow-Szechuan railway is fait accompli the raw products of the west will be available as articles of export, and a much needed stimulus given to the agricultural industries of the regions concerned.

CHAPTER XXIX

TEA AND TEA-YIELDING PLANTS

THE TEA INDUSTRY FOR THE THIBETAN MARKETS

THE most widely known product of China is, of course, Tea, Ch'a, which today is very extensively cultivated in India, Ceylon, and Java, and also experimentally in several other countries. In China the value of this plant has been appreciated from very early times. It is known to have been cultivated in Szechuan during the early Han dynasty (202 B.C.-A.D. 25). However, it was not in general use among all classes before the sixth and seventh centuries A.D. Very early in the seventeenth century tea first became known in Europe, having been brought from Japan by Dutch traders.

The Tea plant (Thea sinensis) is considered to be a native of Assam, whence it was long ago introduced and cultivated in China. Augustine Henry, in 1896, received through a Chinese collector whom he had trained specimens of undoubted Wild Tea. Henry writes:[1] "Hitherto the tea plant has been found wild only in Assam, the cases of its spontaneity recorded from China being very doubtful. In all my trips in Szechuan and Hupeh I never met with it. The present specimens are above suspicion, coming from virginal forest (in the extreme south-southeast corner of Yunnan) and at an immense distance from any tea-cultivation, the nearest being Ptuerh, 200 miles west. Bretschneider, in his Botanicon Sinicum, part II, p. 130, has some remarks on the antiquity of tea in China. It is probable that it was found wild in these southern provinces which did not form a part of the ancient Chinese Empire, and I dare say it will be found wild in these mountains from Mengtse to Szemao. It is not probable at all that tea came from so far away as Assam." I have italicized Henry's

[1] Kew Bulletin, 1897, p. 100.

384

concluding statement, with which I most emphatically agree. As recorded in Chapter IX, I discovered specimens of the tea plant in north-central Szechuan growing in situations which left no good reason for regarding them as other than spontaneous. However, in view of the long-cultivated character of this shrub I prefer to regard them as probably wild plants. It is worthy of note that growing in the same locality I found wild plants of the China Rose (Rosa chinensis) in some quantity. The tea plant is an evergreen, belonging to the rain forest area of the temperate zone in China. This represents the rice-belt throughout the Yang tsze valley, which has long since been cleared in all but the most precipitous places to make way for cultivation. This fact would account for the present absence of the tea plant in a wild state throughout these regions.

The great tea-growing districts for export trade with the Occident and for consumption within China itself are in the middle-eastern parts of the Empire. The export trade in this commodity has declined enormously during the last quarter of a century. Some 75 years ago the tea industry was introduced on business lines into India and Ceylon, with the result that today these countries supply the greater portion of the world's demand. Antiquated methods of cultivation and preparation, absence of cooperation amongst the growers, and heavy taxation, are responsible for the decline of the Chinese product. It is true that Chinese tea is in quality and delicacy of flavor far ahead of Indian and Ceylon teas, but tea-drinkers generally have acquired a taste for the rougher, dark colored teas, and China's conservative methods are killing what was once her greatest export industry. Hankow is today the great tea-mart of China, the trade being largely in the hands of Russians. Large factories have been established expressly for the purpose of preparing teas for the Russian market, Indian and Ceylon teas being imported for blending purposes. In 1910 the exports of tea from Hankow were valued at Tls. 18,423,474.

With the ordinary tea industry of eastern China we are not further concerned, but in the west a specialized form of this obtains which merits a detailed description. Tea is grown all over Szechuan for provincial consumption, but in the western parts it assumes much greater magnitude, being there grown and specially prepared for the Thibetan market. The one great export from China to Thibet is tea, either in the form of compressed bricks or bales. The subsidy given by the Chinese government to the Thibetan authorities at Lhassa and elsewhere in Thibet is also paid in tea.

To the Thibetans tea is an absolute necessity of life, and deprived of this astringent they suffer in various ways. That astringency is one of the properties most desired is evidenced by the fact that the bark of oak trees is ofttimes used when tea cannot be obtained. The ordinary everyday meal of these people consists of tea mixed with a little butter and salt. To this mixture roasted barley-meal is added, and the whole is kneaded to the consistency of dough, in which condition it is eaten. Buttered tea is also their national beverage. To the American palate this concoction as prepared by the Thibetans bears only the remotest possible resemblance to tea. I have tried it often but never succeeded in persuading myself to like it.

Much has been written on the possibility of Indian tea-planters having a share in this tea trade with Thibet. From the close proximity of Assam to Lhassa and southeastern Thibet generally, one would suppose that the difficulties would not be very great, yet the trade has made little progress. The opposition of the Lamas and the obstinate conservatism of the people are very real difficulties in the way. There is also another and equally important factor which should not be lost sight of, namely, the nature and quality of the tea that is in demand. Now it is safe to say that the veriest sweepings from the Indian tea factories would make better tea than that partaken of by the average Thibetan; but this is not the important point. To secure a share of this trade Indian planters must be prepared to supply the Thibetans with the kind of article to which they are accustomed, and not with something different, even though it be of a superior quality. The trade is very considerable and worth striving after, furthermore, there is no reason why it should not be increased. I was travelling on the Chino-Thibetan frontier during the time of the British Expedition to Lhassa, and discussed with Chinese merchants interested in the Thibetan tea trade the possibility of India taking a share in the trade. It was very evident that they greatly feared Indian competition, and were keenly alive to the possibilities of such. From Darjeeling to Lhassa is only about 30 stages (350 miles approx.), while from Tachienlu the journey occupies over three months. The physical difficulties of the route are greater on the Chinese than on the Indian side, yet the people of Lhassa still draw their tea-supply from China. And further, Chinese tea, apart from that taken in exchange for musks, skins, wool, gold, and medicines, was, until very recently, paid for by the Thibetans in Indian rupees.

The brick-tea prepared for Thibet is a totally different article from that prepared in Hankow for the Russian market. It is also so totally different from ordinary Chinese tea that some have supposed it to be the product of a distinct plant. My wanderings in western China led me through the tea-producing areas and the markets which supply the commodity to the Thibetans; my observations, therefore, may be of interest and value.

The two great trade-marts for China and Thibet are Tachienlu, in the west of Szechuan, and Sungpan, in the extreme northwest corner of that province. The official route to Lhassa passes through Tachienlu, and this town is the mart for southern and central Thibet, including Lhassa, Chamdo, and Derge. The mart for the Amdo and Kokonor regions generally is Sungpan. At this latter town the trade is purely one of barter, tea being taken in exchange for furs, wool, musk, and medicines. The tea for the two markets is prepared very differently, grown in distinct localities, and is best discussed separately.

The tea for the Tachienlu market is virtually all grown within the prefecture of Yachou Fu, more especially in the mountainous districts to the northwest and south of the town. The manufacturing business is controlled by the government and provincial authorities, who issue a definite number of licenses to establishments in the towns of Yachou, Mingshan, Yungching, and T'ienchtian — all within the Yachou prefecture. The independent department of Kiung Chou, a little to the northeast of Yachou, also has a share in this trade, but there the licenses are all issued by the Imperial Government and are not connected with the provincial authorities at Chengtu. The industry is a very ancient one, the plant itself having been grown in this vicinity since the dawn of the Christian era.

To supply the licensed establishments the peasants and farmers cultivate the tea plant. The culture extends up to 4000 feet above sea-level, the bushes being planted around the sides of the terraced fields on the mountain-sides. Very little attention is given them and they are usually allowed to grow smothered in coarse weeds to a height of from 3 to 6 feet. Less frequently are the bushes kept free from weeds. During the summer months the leaves and young twigs are plucked off and placed, handfuls at a time, in heated pans for a few minutes, and then spread out in the sun to dry. They are then collected into large sacks or into loose bales and carried down to the towns and villages, where they are purchased by agents of the tea establishments. Occasionally the bushes, when they have become old, are cut down, the branches dried in the sun, and afterward tied into bundles and carried down for sale. The very young leaves and tips of the shoots are commonly gathered by the growers and prepared into tea for home consumption and local trade, the old coarse leaves and branches being considered good enough for the Thibetans.

I visited a brick-tea factory in Yachou, where I observed the following processes of manufacture. The sacks of leaves and bundles of leafy sticks, after they had fermented for a few days, were taken in hand by women and children who picked off the leaves and shoots, sorting them into four grades, each grade being determined by the size and age of the leaves. The sticks, often 1 to 2 inches in circumference, after the leaves have been removed, were chopped small by means of a large knife fixed in a block of wood. Mixed with coarse leaves and sweepings these chopped-up sticks constitute the fourth grade. A small packet of the very worst of this grade is inserted in the ends of each bamboo-cylinder as a gratuity to the repackers and muleteers at Tachienlu.

A certain British consul has likened this brick-tea to "crows' nests pressed into cakes." This aptly describes the product so far as the fourth quality is concerned, but the first quality, prepared at Yachou, is really very good tea. I was surprised at the care and attention bestowed on its manufacture, the processes being as follows: After the leaves had been

HUMAN PACK HORSES: BRICK TEA FOR TACHIENLU MARKET

sorted and graded they were steamed in a cloth suspended over a boiler. The steamed mass was then put into collapsible moulds, together with a little of the dust from smashed sticks and leaves which had been treated with glutinous rice-water to make it cohere, and then the whole was submitted to great pressure. When the mould was removed the tea was in the form of bricks (chuan), each measuring 11 inches by 4 inches and weighing 6 English pounds. After being dried for three days, these bricks are wrapped in paper on which the maker's trade-mark is stamped, a patch of gold-leaf of minute proportions or a plain piece of red paper to denote the quality being also enclosed. Four of the bricks are then placed end to end in a plaited bamboo-cylinder, and after this has been fastened at the ends the tea is ready for transit. These bamboo-cylinders, when filled with tea, are called Pao; they weigh 25 pounds and measure about 4 feet in length. They are carried on the backs of coolies, to the town of Tachienlu, where they pass into the hands of Thibetans. The bricks of the finer quality teas and those intended for the interior of Thibet and distant Lhassa, are removed from the bamboo-cylinders and repacked, 12 together, in raw yak-hides, with the hair inside and the free edges neatly sewn together. The inferior quality teas are largely consumed in eastern Thibet and are not repacked. From Tachienlu the packages are carried on the backs of yak and mules to their destination.

The Pao packed in Yachou city always weigh 18 cattie?[1] (24 pounds English), but in other places they vary according to quality, being either 12, 13, 14, 15, or 16 catties, each town having its own particular weight for the different qualities. Tea from Yachou city and Yungching Hsien follow the main road. That from Mingshan and T'iench'uan a by-road. Both routes converge at the town of Luting chiao, and there pay toll on crossing the river. Either route is terribly difficult, and one marvels how such loads can be carried by men over such fearfully mountainous roads. The average load consists of 10 pao of 18 catties each. But loads of 12 and 13 pao are very common, and on several occasions I have seen men carrying 20 pao. These, however, only weighed 14 catties each, but even then the total weight of the load was 370 English pounds!

[1] Catty— 1 ⅓ English pounds.

TEA AND TEA-YIELDING PLANTS

The distance between Yachou and Tachienlu is about 140 miles (probably less), and the journey for coolies laden with tea occupies 20 days. Although the work is inhuman, thousands of men and boys are engaged in this traffic. With their huge loads they are forced to rest every hundred yards or so, and as it would be impossible for the carrier to raise his burden if it were once deposited on the ground he carries a short crutch, with which he supports it when resting, without releasing himself from the slings.

For each pao carried from Yachou to Tachienlu the carrier receives 400 cash (about thirty cents in American money). Out of this he has to keep himself and pay for his lodgings. Nevertheless, the pay is really good for the country, and it is this extra remuneration that tempts so many to engage in the work of transport.

It is very difficult to obtain accurate information as to the extent of this transfrontier tea-trade, but statistics culled from various, more or less reliable, sources, show that at the lowest estimate some 5400 tons of brick tea worth approximately $750,000 enter Tachienlu annually.

Tea for the Sungpan market is grown in two distinct localities, in the west and north-northwest of the Chengtu plain, respectively. Each district has its own peculiar mode of packing the product. In the west it is grown in the moun-tains bordering the banks of the Min River in the district of Kuan Hsien. A centre of the industry is the market village of Shui-mo-kou, some 90 li beyond the city of Kuan Hsien itself. This tea is not pressed into bricks after the manner of that for the Tachienlu market, but is made into rectangular bales some 2 ½ feet by 2 ½ feet by 1 foot each, weighing 120 catties (160 English pounds), and covered with bamboo-matting. A considerable quantity of this tea finds a market among the Chiarung tribes, the distributing centres being Monking Ting and Lifan Ting. The mountainous regions of An Hsien and Shihch'uan Hsien constitute the northwestern tea district, the principal centre being the market village of Lei-ku-ping within the district of An Hsien. The prepared. product, however, all passes through Shihch'uan Hsien, and is controlled by specially appointed officials. The tea prepared in this region is packed in oval bales, each weighing 65 to 70 catties (about 90 English pounds), encased in the usual bamboo-matting.

The routes by which Kuan Hsien and Shihch'uan Hsien teas travel converge at Mao Chou, an important town situated on the left bank of the upper Min River, six days' journey south of Sungpan Ting. To Mao Chou the tea is mostly carried by men, two small or one large bale being the usual load. From Mao Chou to Sungpan mules and ponies are largely employed for transporting it, their loads being twice the weight of those carried by men. Both women and men, however, are also engaged in the carriage of tea from Mao Chou northward, and the merchants constantly complain of insufficient means of transport.

The preparatory processes undergone by the tea destined for the Sungpan market are less intricate than those described for brick tea. The leaves and young branches are gathered, panned, and dried in the sun. The panning process is sometimes omitted, and very commonly the bushes and their overgrowth of coarse weeds are cut together, dried in the sun, and tied into bundles. The leaves are collected into sacks or bales, and with the bundles of leafy sticks carried down to the market villages and sold to tea establishments. The manufacturers allow the leaves to ferment in heaps for a few days, and afterward submit them to a rough sorting. The sticks are chopped up with the coarse leaves and steamed over a large pan of boiling water. The moist, heated mass is then firmly pressed into bales, covered with matting, and allowed to dry.

The tea is practically all of one quality, and very little superior to the most inferior kind entering Tachienlu. Cheapness is the main consideration, a bale of 120 catties being valued in Sungpan at Tls. 8. This trade is a monopoly in the hands of five establishments, who pay to the provincial government at Chengtu a fixed tax of about 1 cent per catty. Payment is done by purchasing permits called Yin piao, which bear the official stamp. Each permit covers a bale of 120 catties or two smaller ones, and costs Tls. 1.20.

Whereas at Tachienlu the tea passes directly into the hands of Thibetans, at Sungpan it remains in the hands of the five tea establishments. These are owned by Mohammedan Chinese, who, in addition to carrying on a considerable local trade, have trusted agents travelling all over northeastern Thibet bartering tea for furs, wool, musk, medicines, and other Thibetan commodities.

The tea trade of Sungpan is an improving one, but it is virtually impossible to obtain reliable figures as to its volume. There are, of course, Chinese official returns stating the number of Yin piao sold annually, but where official peculation is so general such returns are notoriously untrustworthy. Piecing together information gathered during my three visits to Sungpan, I suggest that the tea-trade averages about $375,000 annually.

From all sources the total annual value of the tea exported from China to Thibet is about one and a quarter of a million dollars. On paper this may not appear very great, but if the sparse population of Thibet and the difficult means of intercommunication be duly considered, it will be seen that the trade is really a very considerable one. Indian teas cannot compete with the Chinese product in central and northern Thibet, but around Lhassa and in southern Thibet generally, they ought to command a market.

In all the larger medicine shops in Szechuan and, incidentally, elsewhere in the Empire, a product known as P'uerh tea is on sale. It is packed in circular cakes, flat at top and bottom, about 8 inches across, and covered with bamboo leaves fastened by strips of palm leaves. This tea is grown in the Shan states, largely in the district of I'bang, and is the product of a variety of the true Tea-plant (Thea sinensis assamica). It takes its name from P'uerh Fu, a prefecture in southern Yunnan, and the trade entrepot of that region. The leaves, after the necessary preliminary processes, are steamed and pressed into cakes, in which form they are easily transported. P'uerh tea has a bitter flavor, and is famous as a medicine all over China, being esteemed as a digestive and nervous stimulant. It also finds its way into the wealthy lamaseries of Thibet, where its medicinal properties are highly appreciated.

Although a beverage known as tea is partaken of throughout the length and breadth of the Middle Kingdom, it is by no means all infused from the leaves of the genuine tea-plant. In the mountainous parts of central and western China many substitutes are employed by the peasants, who seldom taste the real article. In western Hupeh the leaves of Malus theifera and several other kinds of Crabapple and Wild Pear, grouped under the colloquial name of T'ang-li-tzu, are used as a source of tea and exported to Shasi for the same purpose. The infusion prepared from these leaves is of a rich brown color, very palatable and thirst-quenching. It is called Hung-ch'a (red tea), and is widely used among the poorer classes in the west.

The leaves of Pyracantha crenulata, the Chinese Buisson ardent, are also in common use as a source of tea. This evergreen is everywhere abundant up to 4500 feet altitude, and is known as the Ch'a kuo-tzu, literally, Tea shrub. Like its European relative it produces a wealth of scarlet fruit in autumn. The leaves of several species of Spiraea (S. henryi, S. blumei, S. chinensis, and S. hirsuta) are less commonly used as tea, being known as Tsui-Ian ch'a. The leaves of the Weeping Willow (Salix babylonica) are occasionally employed as tea, and in the upper Min valley chips of willow-wood are likewise used. I have drunk all these various teas, but that infused from these willow-chips was bed-rock, being decidedly weak and nasty!

In the chapter on Mount Omei mention is made of the sweet tea prepared from the leaves of Viburnum theiferum. The leaves of the common White Mulberry, steamed, mixed with cabbage-oil, and pressed into cakes constitute Ku-ting-ch'a (bitter tea). The infusion prepared from this is drunk in hot weather and esteemed as a cooling beverage.

The product known as tea-oil is not produced by the tea-plant, but is expressed from the seeds of Thea oleifera, known as the Ch'a-yu kuo-tzu, a relative of the true tea-plant, from which it may be readily distinguished by its hairy shoots. It is a shrub, common as a wild plant in the sandstone ravines of north-central Szechuan. In parts of eastern China it is abundantly cultivated for the sake of its oil, but in the west I only met with plantations in the district of An Hsien. It is, however, reported as being cultivated in the department of Kiung Chou and elsewhere. The oil is used to adulterate cabbage-oil, and by Chinese ladies as a dressing for their hair. The refuse cake is valued as a fertilizer, and when applied to rice fields is said to destroy the earth-worms which often attack the young rice plants.

CHAPTER XXX

INSECT WHITE-WAX

EXT to sericulture the most important industry in the prefecture of Kiating is that concerned with the production of insect white-wax or Peh-la. This product has attracted the attention of many travellers, and has been often discussed before. It possesses several peculiarly interesting features, and cannot be omitted from any account of the economic products of western Szechuan. It is produced by a scale-insect (Coccus pela), and is deposited on the branches of an Ash (Fraxinus chinensis) and a Privet (Ligustrum lucidum); the insects are bred in one district and transported to another for the production of the wax. All this sounds very simple, yet it has taken nearly five centuries to establish these facts. According to Chinese historians insect white-wax first became known to the Chinese about the middle of the thirteenth century. Nicolas Trigault, a Jesuit missionary, wrote some account of the industry in parts of eastern China in the year 1615. During succeeding centuries several accounts of it were published, but it was not until 1853, when Mr. William Lockhart, of Shanghai, sent specimens of crude wax to England, that the wax-producing insect became scientifically known. In the crude wax a number of dried, full-grown bodies of the female insect were discovered, and were identified by Westwood as a new species of Coccus. Robert Fortune, in his travels around Ningpo in 1853, had noted the industry, and stated that "the tree on which the wax is deposited is undoubtedly a species of Ash." In 1872 the illustrious Baron Richthofen wrote of the production of insect white-wax in western China, a fact not previously known to the people of the Occident.

In 1879 Mr. E. C. Baber made a lengthy report on the white-wax industry of western China from observations near Fulin.

CHINA — MOTHER OF GARDENS

Unfortunately, this talented observer possessed no botanical knowledge, and, being misled by vernacular names, he increased if anything the mystery which shrouded the botanical aspect of the subject.

In 1884 Mr. (later Sir Alexander) Hosie, then Consular Agent at Chungking, undertook, at the instigation of the Kew authorities, the thorough investigation of the subject. He travelled through the principal wax-producing districts of Szechuan, collected specimens of the two host plants and of the wax itself, noted the mode of culture, and the preparation of the commercial white-wax. The two host plants were identified by the Kew authorities as Ligustrum lucidum and Fraxinus chinensis, the first named being the tree on which the insects breed and the latter the tree on which the wax is deposited. There can be little doubt that the Ligustrum is the natural host of the wax-insect, and much of the difficulty in elucidating the subject was due to the fact that this tree has two or three different vernacular names. In central and western China it is usually designated the La shu (Wax tree) or Ch'ung shu (Insect tree), but it is occasionally, and particularly in the eastern provinces, called the Tung-ching shu. This last name simply means Wintergreen tree, and is usually applied to Xylosma racemosum, a tree commonly planted around shrines and tombs. Many wild guesses were made as to the identity of this Tung-ching shu, and with each hazard the subject became further involved.

The districts of Omei Hsien and Hungya Hsien, both within the prefecture of Kiating, are the headquarters of the wax-producing industry, but the insects are bred in the Chiench'ang valley, in the prefecture of Ningyuan Fu, nearly 200 miles distant. A few insects are bred around the town of Chienwei Hsien, a day's journey to the south of Kiating, but these are said not to produce so much wax or of so good a quality as those from the Chiench'ang valley.

The insects develop during the winter months, and the cone-like scale or gall is ready for removal about the end of April, being then full of the minute eggs of the insect. So far as my observations go, they indicate that it is always on the Privet that the insect breeds, but Baber asserts that either tree will serve, and this is probably true.

INSECT WHITE-WAX AND TREE (LIGUSTRUM LUCIDUM)

CHINA — MOTHER OF GARDENS

Several of these cone-like scales, full of eggs, are wrapped together in thin paper bags, which are arranged in airy crates and carried by porters with all possible speed to the city of Hungya, where they are disposed of to the farmers. During the month of May hundreds of coolies are engaged in this traffic. The larva hatch out quickly, more especially if the season is hot and early, in which case the travelling is mostly done at night by the aid of lanterns. The journey of nearly 200 miles over difficult mountain roads is accomplished in six days. Aided by relays, the porters who carry these insects cover 30 to 40 miles per day; in ordinary circumstances 20 miles a day is a high average for porters.

For the production of the wax it is immaterial whether the Ligustrum or Fraxinus is used. Some districts favor the latter, others the former; very frequently the two trees are grown side by side. The trees are planted round the edges of the fields, and are polled some 5 to 6 feet from the ground. The lateral shoots, which develop from the polled heads are always one or more years old before the insects are placed on them. The propagation of these trees is effected by taking thick branches, slicing off a portion of the bark and a little of the wood, and surrounding the incised area with a ball of mud and straw. Roots form in the ball of mud, and the branch is then severed from the parent tree, and is planted at the side of a field where it quickly develops into a tree.

In the wax-producing area of the Kiating prefecture millions of these pollarded trees are cultivated by the farmers and peasants. Previous to the arrival of the insects in May, the branches on which it is intended to place insects are denuded of their laterals along the basal half of their length. The cultivator, having purchased his insects, wraps loosely a few cones in a broad leaf and suspends these tiny bags midst the branches of either Fraxinus or Ligustrum trees, or of both. The larva quickly hatch out and crawl up into the tree and ascend to the leaves, where they remain for fourteen days until their mouths and limbs are strong. During this period they are said to moult, casting off a hairy garment which forms in the earliest larval stage. After this period the insects descend to the naked branches, on the underside of which they attach themselves and commence at once to deposit wax. During this early stage heavy rains and wind are much dreaded, since they dislodge the insects, and consequently ruin the business for the season. The deposit of wax, which at first looks very like hoar-frost on the branches, continues up to the latter end of August. (The Chinese reckon 100 days from the time of suspending the insects in the trees.) The deposit is always heaviest on the underside of the branch, and seldom extends equally all round.

About the end of August the white coating is scraped from the branches (very often the branches are cut off) and thrown into boiling water. The wax is dissolved and floats on the surface of the water. It is collected by being skimmed off, and while in a plastic state is moulded into thick saucer-shaped cakes. The insects sink to the bottom of the vessel containing the boiling water, and are collected and thoroughly crushed to express every particle of wax before being finally flung to the pigs.

The wax excretion has been attributed to disease, but in the light of present knowledge it seems feasible to regard it merely as a device on the part of Nature to protect the insect from its enemies. The Chinese idea is that the insects live on dew, and the wax perspires from their bodies.

The natural enemy of the wax-insect is a species of Lady-bird, which breeds with them and preys on the larva The Chinese designate this enemy Wax-dog (La-gho). After the larva have hatched out the farmer goes round his trees in the heat of the day, and belabors their stumps with a club for the purpose of dislodging this foe.

The cooperation which obtains in this industry between two separate and distinct districts has led to much confusion. The explanation seems to be that owing to peculiar climatic conditions the insect breeds freely in Chiench'ang valley, and for similar reasons deposits wax freely in the Kiating prefecture. At any rate, it is obvious that one cannot have wax and insects too, since to obtain the former it is necessary to kill the latter by immersion in boiling water. I am convinced that the cooperation or mutual dependency is simply one of self-interest on the part of both districts.

CHINA — MOTHER OF GARDENS

Insect white-wax bears a close resemblance to spermaceti, but is much harder. It is colorless and inodorous, or nearly so, tasteless, brittle, and readily pulverizable at 60° F. It is slightly soluble in alcohol, and dissolves with great facility in naphtha, out of which fluid it may be crystallized. It melts at about 180° F., floats in water, and is said to harden by long immersion in cold water.

The wax is largely used in the manufacture of Chinese candles, a little being mixed with the fats and oils employed in their manufacture; a thin coating is also applied to the outside of the candles. The best candles contain 2 ½ ounces to the pound, inferior ones not more than 1 ounce. Since the ordinary fats and oils melt at about 100° F., the advantage of an outer coating of white-wax with its high melting-point is obvious. In paper-shops insect white-wax is largely employed to impart a gloss to the higher grades of paper. In medicine-shops it is universally used as a coating for pills, and is itself supposed to possess medicinal properties. It is also employed as a polish in jade and soap-stone ware and in the more delicate articles of furniture, to give lustre to cloth, and is made into images of Buddha; but its primary uses are in the manufacture of candles and in paper-glazing.

The annual output varies considerably, the industry being almost entirely dependent upon suitable climatic conditions. In poor seasons 50,000 piculs is an average crop, whereas in very favorable years it is more than double this quantity. Formerly the prefecture of Paoning produced a fair amount of white-wax, but the industry has there become neglected of recent years. Today virtually the whole supply of western China is produced in the Kiating prefecture.

In spite of the increased consumption of foreign candles and kerosene oil, the demand for insect white-wax remains steady, and the industry concerned with its production shows very little sign of decadence. In western China, owing chiefly to difficulties and dangers of navigation, on the Yangtsze, and the consequent heavy freights, foreign goods are an expensive luxury enjoyed only by the wealthy. With the advent of railways changes will certainly take place, and this interesting insect-wax industry may at some future date become extinct.

INDEX

INDEX

INDEX

INDEX

INDEX

INDEX

INDEX

INDEX

INDEX

INDEX

INDEX

INDEX

INDEX

413

INDEX

INDEX

INDEX

INDEX

INDEX

Lightning Source UK Ltd.
Milton Keynes UK
UKHW031821040919

349185UK00007B/166/P

9 780995 433